A CENTURY OF WOMEN

A CENTURY

THE MOST INFLUENTIAL EVENTS IN

OF WOMEN

TWENTIETH-CENTURY WOMEN'S HISTORY

DEBORAH G. FELDER

CITADEL PRESS
Kensington Publishing Corp
www.kensingtonbooks.com

CITADEL PRESS BOOKS are published by

Kensington Publishing Corp.
850 Third Avenue
New York, NY 10022

All Kensington titles, imprints, and distributed lines are available at special quantity discounts for bulk purchases for sales promotions, premiums, fund-raising, educational, or institutional use. Special book excerpts or customized printings can also be created to fit specific needs. For details, write or phone the office of the Kensington special sales manager: Kensington Publishing Corp., 850 Third Avenue, New York, NY 10022, attn: Special Sales Department, phone 1-800-221-2647.

CITADEL PRESS and the Citadel logo are Reg. U.S. Pat. & TM Off.

First Citadel Press printing: November 2003

10 9 8 7 6 5 4 3 2 1

Printed in the United States of America

Library of Congress Cataloging-in-Publication Data:

Felder, Deborah G.
    A century of women : the most influential events in twentieth-
century women's history / Deborah Felder.
        p.   cm.
    "A Birch Lane Press book."
    Includes bibliographical references and index.
    1. Women—United States—History—20th century—Chronology.
I. Title.
HQ1410.F44   1999
305.4'0973'0904—dc21   98-37126
                                                                        CIP

ISBN 0-8065-2526-6

To the memory of my grandmother

NINA RAE HICKS FISHER

1893–1985

CONTENTS

1920–1929

1930–1939

1940–1949

1950–1959

1960–1969

1970–1979

PREFACE

Nina Fisher, to whom this book is dedicated, was a child of six when the nineteenth century gave way to the twentieth. Nina, like her sisters and her mother, Anna Hicks, an Iowa farm wife and a Quaker who raised nine children, was born into a society in which women were legally barred from voting in national elections and were not enfranchised in most states. Contraception and abortion were illegal. At the turn of the century there were few women doctors and even fewer lawyers. Most women gave birth at home. Infant mortality was about 122 per 1,000 live births, and many new mothers continued to die from childbed (puerperal) fever. Housework was labor-intensive; indoor plumbing was very rare, and electricity and the telephone were newfangled concepts. Forty-one percent of African American women worked outside the home for wages, most of them in agriculture or as domestic servants, as compared with 17 percent of white women workers, most of whom were immigrants. Child labor was common. The women's labor movement was just beginning to take shape.

Anna Hicks would survive the average female life expectancy of forty-eight years by nearly a decade, dying of gallbladder disease at the age of fifty-seven. Nina, her youngest daughter, was ambitious, adventurous, and individualistic—traits she shared in common with many other young women who came of age during the Progressive Era. She taught in a one-room schoolhouse, then worked her way through Northwestern University. By the time she met my grandfather, a successful and urbane Chicago sportswriter nineteen years her senior, my grandmother had shortened her skirts, discarded her corset, and bobbed her hair and was looking forward to voting for the president in the next election. Reduced to near poverty at the start of the Great Depression and with a daughter to support, she disdained public relief and became a social worker, eventually earning a master's degree in the field. She was gratified by my mother's attainment of a law degree but was disappointed that she did not practice her profession, preferring instead to conform to the standard of womanhood in the 1950s and 1960s by being a stay-at-home suburban mother who was supported financially by her husband and defined by her role as homemaker.

By the last decades of the century, the women of my generation, the post–World War II baby boomers, and women in their twenties and thirties, were vigorously pursuing a variety of chosen careers; many were struggling to combine successfully the needs of work and family, and still others had become grandmothers. On average, they could look forward to a life span of between seventy-five and eighty years. They could legally choose to use contraception and obtain abortions. They were allowed by law to sue for discrimination and sexual harassment. In ever-increasing numbers they entered professions once open only to men and obtained a legal right to further their careers by networking with male colleagues in private clubs that were previously the exclusive preserves of men. The lives of women at the close of the twentieth century were significantly different from the lives of their mothers, grandmothers, and great-grandmothers.

This book chronicles and attempts to delineate the influential events that have shaped the destiny of women during each decade of the twentieth century. For purposes of historical cohesion, I have chosen to concentrate on the experience of women in the United States. The destiny of American women has been affected not only by war, economic depression, technological advances, and social imperatives, but also by the efforts of women who organized as never before in such groups as the Women's Trade Union League, the National American Woman Suffrage Association, and the National Organization for Women to effect social and political changes intended to bring about improvements in the quality of life and to raise the status of women. Throughout the decades women frequently found themselves forced to take two steps backward for every social, economic, and political step forward, but, unlike their foremothers, they chose not to suffer in silence, knowing that the price paid for silence is often too high. For nearly one hundred years women's voices were collectively and individually raised for the greater good, resulting in positive change and an increased awareness of the issues facing women in every circumstance and at every stage of life. It will be interesting to see how women in the twenty-first century work to resolve these issues and how they will build on the progress made on their behalf throughout the decades of the twentieth century.

ACKNOWLEDGMENTS

The preparation of this book owes much to the many excellent works on women's history published during the 1970s, 1980s, and 1990s, as well as the biographies of women involved with the events chronicled here. I urge readers to seek out the books contained in the bibliography as well as other works in order to round out their knowledge and understanding of women's history in every century and in every country of the world.

Further acknowledgment is due first to my editor, Jim Ellison, whose support and patience were invaluable assets throughout the writing of *A Century of Women*, and last, but certainly not least, to my husband, Daniel Burt, who helped with the project in many measurable and immeasurable ways.

1900–1909

The ideal American woman, circa 1900: The Gibson Girl, drawn by magazine
illustrator Charles Dana Gibson   *Library of Congress*

1900

Prohibitionist Carry Nation Hatchets Saloons

> I stand for prohibition,
> The utter demolition
> Of all this curse of misery and woe;
> Complete extermination,
> Entire annihilation—
> The saloon must go!
>
> Temperance workers' rhyme,
> often quoted by Carry Nation

Although she is regarded today as a cartoon character of massive proportions, with a face that resembled the hatchet she used to smash up saloons, temperance crusader Carry Nation's fierce rampage against what she called "bastions of male arrogance" is nevertheless an influential event in the history of the American temperance movement. Nation and her hatchet focused national attention on the cause of Prohibition and helped to create a public mood favorable to the passage of the Volstead Act, which became the Eighteenth Amendment, banning the manufacture and sale of alcoholic beverages. The ratification of the amendment was the culmination of a half-century crusade undertaken by the women who believed that Prohibition was the only solution to the widespread problem of male alcohol abuse.

The hard-drinking men and the well-filled saloons of the Old West are well-known aspects of American historical lore, but overindulgence in liquor was considered a problem in other parts of the country as well. Temperance societies began to form in the early decades of the nineteenth century, and while the majority of "drys," as antidrinking and antisaloon advocates were known, were men, many women joined the cause in their concern over drunkenness and its effects on families and the workplace. Drinkers frequently neglected their jobs and families;

Carry Nation in a characteristic pose with hatchet and
Bible   *Brown Brothers*

wages were spent on beer and whiskey instead of rent and food, and
drunken men were often violent toward their wives and children. The
cause of temperance was embraced by women reformers such as Susan
B. Anthony, although it remained a minor issue in relation to other
causes like abolition and woman suffrage.

A number of states passed temperance laws early in the century, but
most of them were soon repealed. After Maine became the first state to
legislate Prohibition (1851), other states began to call for similar legislation, and emphasis shifted from advocacy of temperance to the demand
for government prohibition. In 1869 the Prohibition Party was formed to
seek national legislation against the manufacture, transportation, and sale
of alcoholic beverages. In its early years, however, the Prohibition Party
had little political influence.

During the early 1870s a series of antidrinking "crusades," led by
women, swept through hundreds of small towns in the Midwest. The
women, praying and singing, invaded and managed to temporarily close
many saloons and exhorted liquor dealers to stop selling their "demon"
wares. The "Singing Sisters," as the public called the crusaders, were

viewed with both admiration and derision, but their small, eccentric efforts contributed to the formation of a national organization that combined evangelism with political awareness: the Women's Christian Temperance Union (WCTU). Founded in 1874 in Cleveland, Ohio, the WCTU was the first truly national women's organization, with a large membership representing all parts of the country and all ranks of life, although its greatest strength was in the Midwest. The union became a particularly effective agent of social change during the presidency of reformer Frances Willard, a former dean of women at Northwestern University. Under Willard, whose motto was "Do Everything," the WCTU became a small government with numerous departments working on behalf of such issues as suffrage, temperance, health, and hygiene, classes in school, and age-of-consent marriage laws. However, the WCTU has always been associated with the temperance movement, which, along with the Anti-Saloon League (founded 1893), it helped to popularize.

Next to Frances Willard, Carry Nation can certainly be considered the WCTU's most famous temperance worker. She was born in 1846 in Garrard County, Kentucky, the eldest child of trader and planter George Moore. Her mother was a mentally unbalanced woman who was descended from Scottish royalty and insisted that she be called "Queen Victoria." In 1867 twenty-year-old Carry married physician and scholar George Gloyd, whom she soon discovered was an alcoholic. After divorcing Gloyd in 1877, Carry married itinerant lawyer and minister David Nation. Nation was an indifferent provider, who did not earn enough to support his wife and her daughter by Gloyd. The family moved about a good deal, and Carry took in boarders to supplement their income. A nonsectarian religionist, Carry engaged in temperance work that included antisaloon crusades and reading the Bible to prison inmates and lecturing them on the evils of alcohol. The Nations were living in Kansas, a legally "dry" state in theory but not in practice, when Carry, then president of the Barber County chapter of the Women's Christian Temperance Union, became convinced of her divine appointment to destroy saloons. Heeding the "call," she began to supplement public prayers and denunciation with the destruction of saloon liquor and property. Wielding a pewter hatchet and accompanied infrequently by likeminded women, Carry swept into saloons with the cry, "Smash, smash! For the love of Jesus, smash!" Despite her formidable appearance, she was often attacked and beaten badly and was arrested some thirty times. From Kansas, Nation traveled to New York and soon became a national figure in the temperance movement. Her celebrity status was solidified by the many newspaper articles written about her and by publicity on the part of her victims, the saloonkeepers, who hung out signs reading "All Nations Welcome But Carry" and devised foul-tasting cocktails called Carry Nations. She lectured on temperance, started a temperance magazine, was exhibited much like a sideshow attraction at Steeplechase Park in Coney Island, and marketed souvenir hatchets. When she died, in 1911, she was buried in a grave that remained unmarked until 1923, when friends raised funds to erect a stone that read "Carry A. Nation. Faithful to the Cause of Prohibition. 'She Hath Done What She Could.'"

Although Carry Nation received little support from suffrage organizations, the attention she garnered for the Prohibition effort, together with the influence of the WCTU, gave suffragists another issue to cite during the last two decades of their campaign to obtain the vote for women, since the attainment of woman suffrage meant that women would be able to vote for Prohibition. Many suffragists became so angered at brewers for coming out publicly against suffrage, they turned their attention to the Prohibition fight instead. The Prohibitionists supported woman suffrage in the belief that women would overwhelmingly vote dry. However, by the time the Nineteenth Amendment guaranteeing women the right to vote was ratified in 1920, legalized Prohibition was in full force, and the decade of the speakeasy and the flapper, who enjoyed drinking cocktails along with men, was about to begin. The excesses of the Roaring Twenties, the violence of the bootleggers, and the privations caused by the Great Depression resulted in a backlash against Prohibition, even among members of the WCTU. Many women, including the thirty-thousand-member Women's Organization for National Prohibition, worked to repeal the Eighteenth Amendment, and in 1933, at the urging of President Franklin D. Roosevelt, the Twenty-first Amendment ending Prohibition was ratified by Congress. The nation was again "wet," a state of affairs that surely would have prompted Carry Nation, had she been alive, to take up her hatchet once more for the cause.

The International Ladies Garment Workers Union Is Formed

In the black of the winter of nineteen nine,
When we froze and bled on the picket line,
We showed the world that women could fight
And we rose and won with women's might.

Chorus:
Hail! the waistmakers of nineteen nine,
Making their stand on the picket line,
Breaking the power of those who reign,
Pointing the Way, smashing the chain.

And we gave new courage to the men
Who carried on in nineteen ten,
And shoulder to shoulder we'll win through,
Led by the ILGWU.

"The Uprising of the Twenty Thousand,"
in Philip S. Foner, *Women and the American Labor Movement*

Women had been considered cheap labor since their entrance into the factory workplace in the newly industrialized America of the early nineteenth century. They were poorly paid, especially in comparison with male workers, and the factories in which they worked were uniformly dirty, noisy, smelly, and dangerous. Women garment workers in New York City, most of them Jewish and Italian immigrants, might spend up to eighteen hours a day, night shifts included, sewing garments in dimly lit rooms that were stiflingly hot in summer and drafty in winter. The materials they used were flammable, sweatshops were firetraps, and machines were often cleaned and adjusted while still in use, which resulted in frequent injuries. Employers sometimes "accidentally" short-changed women workers or agreed to salary advances in return for the bestowing of sexual favors. Immigrant women who did piecework at home fared little better, since they lived in poorly constructed tenements that possessed many of the same hazards as sweatshops and worked for the same unsavory employers.

During the late nineteenth and early twentieth centuries working women were paid one-half to one-third the wages of men, a discrepancy that was not corrected even when men and women did the same job. To justify this inequality of income, employers claimed that women were working only for "pin money" to buy luxuries. In truth, most women worked solely to keep themselves and their families fed, clothed, and sheltered. Some immigrant women tried to save part of their wages to bring their families to America. One such woman was Elizabeth Hasanovitz, an unmarried garment worker. In her autobiography, *One of Them*, Hasanovitz described how she budgeted her $2.55 weekly wage: $1 for rent, $.60 for carfare, and $.06 for newspapers. After she had spent a variable amount on a diet of bread, butter, milk, beans, and sugar, little if any of her wages was left over. Hasanovitz attempted suicide after

A New York City sweatshop, circa 1910 *Brown Brothers*

living for nine weeks on this budget and later wrote: "Does it pay to
live after all? Work, work, and never earning enough for a living, eternal
worry how to make ends meet."

In 1910 a government industrial commission studied the conditions
of women working in trades and industry at the turn of the century and
the hostility of many male unionists toward their employment. In its
report, one member of the commission, a veteran labor leader and American Federated Labor spokesman, concluded that women were "not
qualified for the condition of wage labor" and that "wherever a large
number of women are employed in any occupation there the point will
be reached where woman gets as much as man by making man's wages
as low as woman's." It would be better, many members of the commission argued, if instead of competing with their men for jobs and wages,
women stayed at home, the "queen of a little house—no matter how
humble—where there are children rolling on the floor." Such senti-
ments, as the commission in fact had discovered from their study, did
not reflect reality. Many families, both white and African American,
immigrant and native born, counted on the extra income from wives and
daughters in order to survive. The earnings of women were also needed
to supplement male income during periods of unemployment, sickness,
or injury. "So essential was it for women to work," writes historian Philip
Foner in *Women and the American Labor Movement,* "that immigrant communities would take root and persist only in areas where sources of

female employment were available." Women industrial workers often began to work at age sixteen or seventeen and remained in the workforce for an average of six or seven years. "Marriage always ended their labor outside the home," writes Foner, "at least for awhile; not a few of them found it necessary to return to the factory or shop in order to keep the family alive."

In 1890 3.7 million American women had jobs; by 1900 that figure had jumped to over 5 million. In New York City, which employed more women industrial workers than any other American city, more than 350,000 women were gainfully employed, most in service occupations. Of these, approximately 65,000 women worked in the garment industry. Some women garment workers belonged to local unions; those who did received higher wages and enjoyed more sanitary working conditions than nonunionized women. However, in an age of monopolies and trusts, factories producing women's garments operated in small, isolated, competitive units, unlike large factories, which mass-produced goods. In addition, union activity was marked by ideological disputes between Socialists and anarchists. Despite sporadic strike activity, it was easy in such an unstable union atmosphere for sweatshop employers to continue to exploit their workers. By the turn of the century the need for a stable national union representing garment workers had become evident.

On June 3, 1900, delegates from the United Brotherhood of Cloak Makers' Union No. 1 of New York and Vicinity and other interested garment workers met at New York's Labor Lyceum to form a new national union, the International Ladies' Garment Workers' Union (ILGWU). The amalgamation of seven local unions, the ILGWU represented 2,310 garment workers in New York, Newark, Philadelphia, and Baltimore. On June 23 the American Federation of Labor (AFL), the most powerful labor organization in the United States, issued a charter to the ILGWU. By 1904 the union had 5,400 members in sixty-six locals in twenty-seven cities, and by 1913 it was the AFL's third largest affiliate.

In its early years the majority of ILGWU members were men, and although the union's male founders and leaders could not ignore the presence of women workers, who dominated the ladies' garment industry, especially in shirtwaist manufacture, they agreed that women should be discouraged from union leadership. Women, they believed, made poor union organizers and even poorer union leaders, since (according to them) women were preoccupied only with marriage. In a 1902 speech to ILGWU delegates, suffragist Carrie Chapman Catt linked the poor labor status of women with their lack of political power. As Foner observes: "Not one delegate reminded Catt that the unionization of women was an important factor in the achievement of higher wages for them." In 1903 there were only two women delegates to the ILGWU convention. The United Garment Workers brought women into positions of responsibility, but UGW locals were company unions, manipulated by employers. In addition, an open-shop campaign engineered by the National Association of Manufacturers threatened to wipe out many ILGWU gains. By 1908 it appeared as if the ILGWU might be merged with the UGW. It would take the efforts of women labor organizers plus a series of spectacular strikes to convince female workers that their best hope for a better life lay in unionism and to transform the ILGWU into a national union in which women were truly represented.

In November 1909 garment workers assembled at New York City's Cooper Union to hear speeches by Samuel Gompers of the AFL, Mary Dreier of the Women's Trade Union League (WTUL), and others concerning a proposed general strike of shirtwaist makers. The meeting had been called by Local 25 of the ILGWU and the United Hebrew Trades, a coalition of Jewish unions, in response to the behavior of the Triangle Shirtwaist Company, whose workers had gone on strike two months earlier to protest the firing of workers suspected of supporting unionization. Striking Triangle workers were joined by workers from the Leiserson Company; both companies used abusive and violent strike-breaking tactics. At the meeting, sixteen-year-old Clara Leimlich, a Leiserson employee recovering from a beating on the picket line, made her way to the platform and said in Yiddish: "I am a working girl and one of those who are on strike against intolerable conditions. I am tired of listening to speakers who talk in general terms. What we are here for is to decide whether or not we shall strike. I offer a resolution that a general strike be declared—now!" Leimlich's speech galvanized her audience, and her resolution was adopted. It was thought that no more than five thousand workers would strike; instead, between twenty and thirty thousand workers participated in the Great Uprising, as the strike came to be called. Supported morally and financially by the WTUL and joined for a time by well-to-do suffragists, the strikers braved an unusually cold and snowy winter on the picket lines, endured beatings and clubbings by police and company-hired thugs, and risked fines and jailings until the beginning of February 1910, when the Triangle Shirtwaist Company finally settled the strike. Although the Great Uprising resulted in only modest concessions for the garment workers and no formal recognition for the shirtwaist makers' union, it focused attention on the great possibilities of unionization within the ILGWU, created solidarity among women workers, and fostered a new awareness of what unity could

This poster, a 1907 lithograph by *Chicago Tribune* artist Luther Bradley, hung in Margaret Dreier Robins's office and was used as a postcard by the Women's Trade Union League to solicit milk money for the babies of striking workers during the 1910–1911 Chicago garment strike. *The Schlesinger Library, Radcliffe College*

achieve economically. "The impact of the women's strike in the waistmaking industry was an inspiration to the workers in the other branches of the industry," writes Foner, "and paved the way for the major advances in unionizing other garment workers."

The shirtwaist makers' uprising was repeated in such cities as Philadelphia, Baltimore, and Chicago, where garment workers who made men's clothing went on strike. In 1913 the ILGWU signed the "Protocol of Peace," a contract between labor and management arbitrated by outside negotiators. The protocol provided for the resolution of disputes and the protection of workers' health. During the 1920s an attempted Communist takeover led to intense conflict among members, and a disastrous strike nearly destroyed the union. However, the ILGWU rallied in the 1930s under the union presidency of David Dubinsky and the labor policies of the Roosevelt administration. By the mid-1960s the ILGWU was considered one of the nation's most powerful and progressive labor unions, with a membership of 450,000. From the late 1960s membership declined as the garment industry was driven overseas, manufacturers found new ethnic groups such as African Americans, Hispanics, and Asians to exploit as cheap labor, and the practice of industrial home work returned. By 1993 ILGWU membership was less than 150,000, and in 1995 the union merged with Amalgamated Cloth-

ing and Textile Workers to form Needletraders, Industrial, and Textile
Employees.

Throughout the history of the ILGWU and of American labor in general, women have fought for recognition and power within the unions
and have made limited gains. In the 1970s, during the height of the
women's liberation movement, women with jobs in a variety of professions, most notably office workers, formed worker advocacy organizations. The 1970s also saw the formation of the Coalition of Labor Union
Women. But in recent years a severely eroding manufacturing base cou-
pled with the often collusive and concessionary relationship between
labor and management has weakened the resolve of the rank and file,
men and women alike, to demand that they be treated as more than
simply income generators for stockholders. It can only be hoped that the
labor upheavals in the garment industry of the early twentieth century
will serve to inspire women workers in the twenty-first century to take
a stand once again.

1901

The Electric Washing Machine Is Invented

Electric servants can be depended on—to do the muscle part of the washing, cleaning and sewing. They will cool the house in summer and help heat the cold corners in winter. There are electrical servants to percolate your coffee, toast your bread and fry your eggs. There's a big clean electrical servant that will do all your cooking— without matches, without soot, without coal, without argument—in a cool kitchen.

General Electric advertisement, *McClure's* magazine, 1917

Before the invention, modification, and improvement of electric appliances, housework, the traditional occupation of middle- and working-class women, was labor-intensive and harsh. At the beginning of the twentieth century, when large families were the norm, most women prepared meals on cast-iron stoves that demanded a steady supply of firewood or coal. Homes that depended upon coal for heat needed to be cleaned more often because of the soot. The vacuum cleaners of the era were at first too large for domestic use and then too expensive for most families. Ironing was not a particularly pleasant task: some women used gas or oil to heat their irons, but the fumes from both were unpleasant and unhealthy, and these irons had no thermostatic controls. Most women continued to use flat irons, which had to be periodically heated directly on the stove and which transferred any sooty residue from the stovetop onto the clean clothes. Even the early electric irons were heavy; one model weighed in at fifteen pounds.

The most arduous household task of housewives and domestic servants employed by middle- and upper-class families was laundry. Women might spend up to one-third of their time washing load after load in washtubs or in machines with drums that had to be agitated by hand and in which water was heated by steam, coal, or gas. Each load was

then cranked through a wringer and hung up to dry. To sell families on
the merits of its washing machines, one company advertising in the 1902
edition of the Sears, Roebuck catalog promised, "Absolutely no danger
of rust spots on clothes," while another claimed its machines were "warranted not to leak." But, although a step up from the washtub, these
machines still had to be continually filled and emptied, as well as operated, by hand. In 1901 inventor A. J. Fisher incorporated an electric
motor into his model; another machine, the Thor, also boasted a power
wringer. One ad for the Thor referred to the "bugbear of washing-day"
and touted its machine as "the solution." However, electricity was not
yet a safe and reliable power source, and most American homes did not
use it. One solution was to make use of commercial laundries, a popular
option for many urban housewives until the 1920s.

Around the time of World War I, as more and more American homes
became wired for electricity, improved household technology and a shift
in the composition of households altered the nature and organization of
housework. Young women began to spurn domestic jobs in favor of jobs
in sales, clerical, or war work, except in the South, where African American women had few other job options. By 1917 there were also fewer
new immigrants available to do domestic work. Since the expanding
middle class could no longer find servants for housework, electric com-

pany ads such as the one quoted
earlier suggested that housewives
consider "electric appliances as
their servants." During the 1920s
the use of lighter metals and
longer production runs, together
with the electricity and indoor
plumbing now present in the
majority of American homes,
enabled the market for appliances, especially washing
machines, to boom. The aggressive marketing of washing

This advertisement from the 1930s
stressed the leisure time enjoyed by
the woman who was wise enough to
purchase an electric washing machine
and the unpleasantness suffered by
the woman who continued to launder
clothes the old-fashioned way.
Library of Congress

machines also had the effect of returning to the home a household chore many women had formerly paid to have done by commercial laundries.

The 1920s, popularly known as a socially liberated, roughhouse decade of bootleggers, speakeasies, flappers, hot jazz, and economic prosperity, was also a time when the role of the housewife became socially institutionalized. Domestic science, practiced by professional home economists, mandated the improvement of the status and condition of housework. More efficient time management, one function of the work of domestic scientists, was made possible by technological advance, as were rising standards of cleanliness. The most famous domestic scientists of the era were Frank and Lillian Gilbreth, whose time and motion studies were practiced on their own household, one that included twelve children.

The purchase and use of the new household technologies gave the modern housewife a sense of personal expression and helped her to feel secure in the knowledge that she was guarding the health and welfare of her family. As Sara M. Evans observes in *Born for Liberty: A History of Women in America:* "Vigilantly she attended to family nutrition with new canned and packaged products, cleaned the new bathroom to guard against germs, and decorated to enhance the cheer of her home. If she followed the advice of home economists she could become an expert at

her main job, consumption, and ensure that her family had the best possible within her budget." In the 1930s a cookbook published by "Your Gas Company" in an attempt to sell housewives on the advantages of using gas stoves and written by the "Mystery Chef" combined recipes, new technology, and domestic science in one slim volume. Among the Mystery Chef's helpful hints was one for the gad-about housewife who enjoyed attending "matinees or afternoon bridge parties" entitled "How to be able to serve a delicious hot dinner within 10 minutes of the time you arrive at home." In truth, most housewives who efficiently time-managed their housework did not run off to the theater, to bridge afternoons, or to luncheons but instead reallocated their free hours to child care, marketing, or other tasks related to the household. Household management remained particularly challenging for women who pursued jobs outside the home. For these women, housework represented the "second shift," in Betty Friedan's words, in the workday.

Supported by home economics experts and sustained by advertisers, the image of the happy housewife, who "sings at her work and never thinks of household tasks as drudgery," as a 1928 *Ladies' Home Journal* described her, reached its apotheosis in the conservative 1950s. But there were rumblings of discontent, as Friedan discovered when she began her interviews for what would later become *The Feminine Mystique*. By the 1960s and especially the 1970s, when the second wave of the women's movement hit its stride, housewives had begun to understand that despite the presence of all their shining, purring, and perfectly calibrated labor-saving appliances, there were in fact no "servants" in the vast majority of American homes except for the women who lived and worked there.

1902

The Twilight Sleep Technique
for Painless Childbirth Is Introduced

In childbirth, as in other human endeavors, fashions start with the rich, are then adopted by the aspirant middle class with an assist from the ever-watchful media, and may or may not eventually filter down to the poor.

Jessica Mitford, *The American Way of Birth*

The history of childbirth in twentieth-century America can be primarily characterized by four developments: the shift from home deliveries to hospital births, the gradual decline in the status of midwives and midwifery as a profession, the increasing use of some form of anesthesia to control labor and birth pain, and the movement toward natural childbirth. At the turn of the century less than 5 percent of women gave birth in maternity hospitals, but whereas the hospital had been an urban asylum for poor, homeless, or working-class women in the previous century, by 1900 its image had improved, thanks to the containment of puerperal, or childbed, fever and increased obstetrical skill. Early in the new century women of all social classes selected the hospital for difficult births and gradually came to regard it as a safer, more comfortable, and cleaner environment than the home for deliveries. The number of hospital births increased dramatically during the 1920s; by 1939 50 percent of all American women and 75 percent of urban women chose to give birth in hospitals; by 1970 the figure had jumped to nearly 100 percent.

In 1901 half of all home deliveries in the United States were still attended by midwives, who had represented female control over the birth process for centuries and were relied upon by working-class and poor urban, rural, and especially African American women as a more cost-effective alternative to doctors. Midwives' fees were usually half (or less) that of doctors and frequently included such services as house-

17

cleaning, laundry, and postnatal care of mother and child for several days, while the most expensive physicians attended only the birth. If a woman chose to consult an obstetrical specialist, which entailed delivery in a hospital, she could expect to pay even more. As late as 1930, women in rural Texas reported that they could hire a midwife for $.75, while a doctor cost $15.

By 1900 members of the medical and public health communities began to focus on what they viewed as a midwife "problem." Much of the focus centered on immigrant midwives, who, as Dorothy and Richard Wertz observe in *Lying-In: A History of Childbirth in America*, "were not native-born, middle-class women; had they been, they might have been encouraged toward professionalism. The urban midwives were alien, not only in citizenship, but to American custom." Early in the century, physician and public health administrator Sara Josephine Baker, whose work greatly reduced the death rate in New York City slums, supported the idea of trained, educated midwives but characterized most urban immigrant midwives as clumsy amateurs, ignorant, dirty, and superstitious. "Even the public health doctors who sought to train and license them regarded them as a temporary, though necessary, phenomenon," write the Wertzes, "to be replaced eventually by better-trained doctors who would be willing to attend the poor. The question was not whether midwives should disappear but how rapidly." Midwifery as a profession began to decline as obstetrics became a more widely practical specialty, and even general practitioners started sending their patients to hospitals. The increasing availability of the automobile also meant that rural women no longer needed to rely on midwives, although many women continued to use them. Midwifery declined, but it did not die out completely. In an attempt to regulate the profession, hospitals in New York, New Jersey, and Pennsylvania began schools for midwives in 1911. From 1921 to 1929 the Sheppard-Towner Act, which provided federal funding for prenatal and postnatal education and care offered in health centers set up across the country, included training for midwives. In the 1930s, as the northern urban midwife began to disappear, "the daughters of immigrants and even some first-generation women sought delivery by doctors because it was the American custom," write the Wertzes. "Doctors were gratified at how quickly these women abandoned old-country midwives, overcame their reluctance about male doctors, and flocked to the maternity clinics of city hospitals. Southern blacks migrating to Northern cities did the same."

During the same decade the nurse-midwife appeared, a product of the Maternity Center Association of New York and the Frontier Nursing Service, which had been founded in 1925 by nurse Mary Breckinridge to minister to families in remote areas of Appalachia. Certified nurse-midwives became important practitioners in rural areas after the Sheppard-Towner Act was repealed and, throughout the century, have continued to serve economically disadvantaged women. In 1990 nurse-midwives attended the deliveries of nearly 142,000 infants in U.S. hospitals, up from fewer than 20,000 in 1975. This represented only 3–4 percent of hospital births, but nurse-midwives attended approximately one-third of deliveries in free-standing birth centers.

By the 1950s and 1960s, write the Wertzes, "what had begun in the 1920s as a pursuit of safety, comfort and efficiency, a shared effort by doctors and patients to have the 'best' for birth, had become . . . an unpleasant and alienating experience for many women. Technological routines to control natural processes compounded with social procedures to process the patient no longer seemed warranted by the danger of birth but seemed instead to stand in the way of a human and meaningful delivery. . . . A woman was powerless in the experience of birth. . . . She played a social role of passive dependence and obedience."

During the years of the women's liberation movement, home births and midwives became more popular with some middle-class women who did not wish to view childbirth as a medical procedure controlled by male obstetricians and technology in an antiseptic, alienating hospital environment. By the 1980s physicians and hospitals alike had become somewhat more sensitive to the aesthetic and emotional needs of parents and to the preference for natural childbirth. In addition, the age at which many women were first giving birth had risen from the early twenties to the late twenties and into the thirties and beyond, a fact that made hospital deliveries desirable, especially since by 1988 one out of four babies in the United States was born by cesarean section. Although hospital delivery remained essentially an assembly-line process, governed by technology, it had become a more humane experience, especially when fathers were admitted into the birth process beginning in the 1970s.

Early in the century, one factor that helped to popularize hospital births was the promise of pain-free deliveries. In 1902 a German physician named Von Steinbuchel introduced an anesthetic procedure called "Twilight Sleep," based on the principle that it is the knowledge of pain rather than the pain itself that damages laboring women. Von Steinbuchel's technique was refined by two other German physicians and used most notably at the Frauenklinik in Freiburg. During the Twilight Sleep technique, a woman experiencing well-advanced labor contractions was injected with morphine and then given a dose of scopolamine, an amnesiac and hallucinogenic, which caused her to forget what was happening. When the fetus entered the birth canal, the doctor gave the

WOMEN COMBINE TO SPREAD
GOSPEL OF "TWILIGHT SLEEP

MRS. JOHN JACOB ASTOR.

New York, Dec. 31.—Because they believe the "twilight sleep" child-bir
method, originated in Frieberg, Germany, will insure painless birth.
a group of far-sighted women, among them Mrs. John Jacob Ast
widow of the multi-millionaire who perished in the Titanic disaste

By giving her celebrity endorsement to Twilight Sleep, Mrs. John Jacob Astor helped to popularize the use of this birthing method. *The Schlesinger Library, Radcliffe College*

mother ether or chloroform to relieve the pain caused by the birth of the head. American doctors had tried the technique and deemed it unreliable and unsafe, but several wealthy American women, such as Mrs. John Jacob Astor, became so excited by the prospect of painless birth that they traveled to Freiburg shortly before World War I to have their babies born at the Frauenklinik. Upon returning to the United States, these women, joined by women with feminist and suffragist sympathies, initiated a newspaper and magazine campaign touting the delights of delivering babies during Twilight Sleep.

In 1914 Dr. Eliza Taylor Ransom, a homeopathic physician, founded the Twilight Sleep Maternity Hospital in Boston's wealthy Back Bay area. She then began the New England Twilight Sleep Association to force hospitals to offer the procedure. The association produced films showing the technique and featuring healthy babies and circulated the movies to women's groups across the country. Brochures advertised the advantages of the method, which included not only painless deliveries, but also the abolishment of forceps, a shortened first stage of labor, less postnatal convalescent time, less danger of hemorrhage, and greater production of breast milk. The newborns of women who had undergone the Twilight Sleep procedure were said to be healthier, more beautiful, and smarter than their older siblings who had not been delivered that way. By the 1930s Twilight Sleep was used routinely by American doctors, who preferred the method, which, as the Wertzes observe, "not only attracted women to the hospital, it made them more manageable during labor and delivery." By the mid-1940s new technology, anesthetics, and analgesics had made childbirth safer and less painful even while it reduced the laboring mother to the status of laboratory rat strapped to an operating table. Various anesthesia techniques were used or counteracted depending on whether a women was undergoing an episiotomy (the cutting of the skin and muscles of the area between the vagina and anus to facilitate the birth of the baby), whether forceps were used, during cesarean births, or for pain or behavior control.

Hints of rebellion among women regarding the medical dominance of birth and the increasingly heavy anesthetization that went with it began in the late 1930s. In 1933 British obstetrician Grantley Dick-Read had published *Natural Childbirth Primer* (later retitled *Childbirth Without Fear*), which expressed the view that modern woman had been subjected since childhood to social conditioning that exaggerated her fears of childbirth. This fear caused muscular tensions in labor, which exacerbated the pain. Dick-Read argued that birth was a natural, joyous process that was never meant to be painful, and he advocated the reeducation of women about their bodies and childbirth along with relaxation and breathing exercises during labor. Thus, he argued, 95 percent of laboring women would be able to deliver with little or no anesthesia and without forceps and episiotomy, which would result in a more pleasurable or, as he put it, "ecstatic" experience for mothers and greater safety for their babies. Dick-Read's book, which, observes the Wertzes, "glorified motherhood as woman's true fulfillment in panegyrics that mixed Victorianism, sentimentality, mysticism, nature philosophy, and religion," became enormously popular in the United States, where medicine had all but eradicated the dangers of childbirth and women were free to look upon the event of birth as a joyous natural experience. This new attitude dovetailed nicely with post–World War II social and domestic sensibilities, which propagandized as well as sanctified motherhood as a woman's greatest achievement.

During the 1960s and 1970s Dick-Read's method was superseded by that of French obstetricians Fernand Lamaze and Pierre Vellay, who had studied the Russian Pavlovian theory of conditioned reflexes, what the Russian physicians referred to as "psychoprophylaxis," and had adapted it to childbirth in the West. In 1951 Fernand Lamaze published *Painless Childbirth*, which included the rapid, shallow breathing, or "panting," technique associated with the "Lamaze method." A 1959 book that helped popularize the Lamaze technique was *Thank You, Dr. Lamaze: A Mother's Experience in Painless Childbirth*, written by Marjorie Karmel, an American who had given birth in Paris using the method. Apart from the physical application of the technique, Lamaze's philosophy held that birth was a performance for which a woman rehearsed, a series of challenges to be met with courage and skill. The woman and not her obstetrician was to control the birth process. As Betty Friedan observed in *The Feminine Mystique*, natural childbirth "appealed to the independent, educated, spirited American woman . . . because it enabled her to experience childbirth not as a mindless female animal, an object manipulated by the obstetrician, but as a whole person, able to control her own body with her aware mind." In the 1970s Dr. Frederick Leboyer's "birth without violence" method featured natural childbirth conducted in a quiet, semidarkened delivery room, where the newborn was gently immersed in a tub of lukewarm water directly after birth. For a short time this technique was reputed to be the ultimate in humane delivery. However, Leboyer's view of the mother as "the enemy" in the birth process and his insistence on retaining control over the event, together with some serious questions concerning the safety of the method, caused his technique to fall out of fashion, although his practice of eventually placing the newborn on the mother's stomach to promote bonding has become standard practice.

By the end of the twentieth century Lamaze had become the birthing method of choice for the vast majority of expectant American mothers. In the 1970s and during the mini–baby boom, which began in the 1980s, it nearly became a birthing religion, as fashionable as Twilight Sleep had been years earlier. The natural childbirth movement, the Lamaze method, the sense of self generated by the women's movement of the 1970s, and the inclusion of fathers in the delivery room resulted in more positive relationships between physician and patient and, more important, greater control by both parents over the birth process. It remains to be seen whether or not twenty-first century doctors and expectant parents will improve upon what seems to have finally become a successful melding of technology and nature.

1903

The National Women's Trade Union League
Is Formed

I go to work at eight o'clock.
I work until six o'clock.
I have only one-half hour for lunch.
I work overtime in the busy season.
I do not get extra pay for overtime work.
I earn eight dollars a week in the busy seasons.
I earn three or four dollars a week in the slow season.
I have no work at all for three months.
I pay for my needles and thread.
I pay for my electric power.
My trade is a bad trade.

   "Lesson Four: A Trade Without a Union"

I met a friend yesterday.
She works at a good trade.
She goes home at five o'clock.
She goes home at twelve o'clock on Saturday.
She has one hour for lunch every day.
She earns twelve dollars a week.
Sometimes she works overtime in the busy season.
She gets extra pay for overtime.
She belongs to the Union in her trade.

   "Lesson Five: A Trade With a Union," from *New World
Lessons for Old World People*, by Violet Pike, in Philip S.
Foner, *Women and the American Labor Movement*

The lessons quoted above are from a reading primer used in English-language classes offered by the New York branch of the National Women's Trade Union League (WTUL) to teach foreign-born working women the principles of trade unionism. The WTUL, the most influential women's labor organization during the first half of the twentieth century, used such educational programs as part of their tireless effort to help women workers to organize unions.

Founded in part to bridge the gap between working-class women in the labor movement and women in middle-class reform groups, the Women's Trade Union League had its beginnings in the reform and settlement house movements of the late nineteenth century. The 1890s had seen an increase in the number of middle-class American women, some college educated, who were dedicated to the cause of helping working women overcome the miserable conditions under which they worked, although the reformers disagreed as to the most effective way to achieve this goal. Some favored better education and harder work for women laborers in the hope that they would win an employer's appreciation and, with it, higher wages; other reformers took the view that appeals to employers' wives, who would then approach their husbands, might result in better working conditions. Still others lobbied for remedial legislation or set up programs that encouraged self-sufficiency and independence.

One of the most influential reform groups of this period was the National Consumers' League (NCL). Founded in 1892, the NCL investigated a variety of industries, promoted the boycotting of goods manufactured by companies that refused to provide minimum standards of decency for their workers, and issued "white lists," which alerted consumers to recommended products and stores. The league also reached agreements with large department stores concerning late working hours at Christmas and lobbied for state laws prohibiting the work of girls under the age of sixteen after nine o'clock at night. By 1903 the National Consumers' League had set up fifty-three branches and three college societies in eighteen states. In eleven states, forty-seven factories displayed the NCL label, which, on the surface, at least, showed that those employers met the labor standards stipulated by the league.

However, the National Consumers' League did not enjoy a friendly relationship with the trade unions and especially with the powerful American Federation of Labor, which criticized the NCL for focusing on sanitary working conditions at the expense of wages and hours. In addition, the unions felt that the awarding of the league label to nonunion companies made organizing more difficult. Florence Kelley, a former Hull House resident and factory inspector who had become director of the NCL in 1899, came to realize the limitations of the NCL and understood that new means for aiding women workers would be necessary. The league eventually began to take up such causes as securing minimum-wage laws and worked with such organizations as the U.S. Department of Labor, the Women's Bureau (founded in 1919), and the

Women's Trade Union League to achieve protective labor legislation. A landmark of such labor legislation occurred in 1908 when Josephine Goldmark of the NCL and her brother-in-law, Supreme Court justice Louis Brandeis, managed to convince the Court to limit the workday of women in the case of *Muller* v. *Oregon.*

The strongest support for unionism came from middle-class settlement house workers who had witnessed firsthand the need for labor organization and from unionized women workers also active in the settlements. Although many settlement houses were hostile to trade unions, the large social settlements fostered support for the women's labor movement. Unions held regular meetings at Chicago's Hull House, at Boston's Denison House and South End House, and at the Henry Street Settlement in New York City. In addition, many union locals were founded at Hull House, Denison House, and the Henry Street Settlement. "While settlement house workers generally tended to favor the peaceful resolution of labor disputes," writes historian Philip Foner in *Women and the American Labor Movement,* "all three settlement houses supported the strikes of the women workers they had helped to organize and, in general, endorsed strikes they felt were justified. . . . In fact, most of the women's unions that existed at the beginning of the twentieth century had been organized by . . . militant women workers, often with the help of a social settlement."

The greatest obstacle to the unionization of working women was in fact the American Federation of Labor, the umbrella organization under which the unions were united. The AFL and most unions viewed working-class women as too passive, inarticulate (a conclusion that possibly showed a bias against immigrants for whom English was a second language), and preoccupied with marriage to display the commitment necessary for unionization and union leadership. The AFL in particular, while "adopting convention resolutions sympathetic to women," writes Foner, ". . . practically ignored the needs of five million female workers."

By 1902, however, the militancy and resolve displayed by striking women garment workers had given the lie to the notion of female passivity and lack of commitment. In May a group of Jewish housewives and women garment workers from New York's working-class Lower East Side formed the "Ladies Anti-Beef Trust Association" to protest the rapidly rising cost of kosher meat and the betrayal of a boycott of wholesale distributors by retail butchers. The women boycotted butchers, battered butcher shops that remained open, and set fire to meat in the streets. A Yiddish circular decorated with a skull and crossbones advised, "Eat no meat while the Trust is taking meat from the bones of your women and children." When hauled up before a magistrate and reminded that citi-

The emblem of the National Women's Trade Union
League, which dramatized the message that the league
would fight to preserve the "glory and strength of
motherhood" that was being sapped by commercial
values and industrial exploitation   *Library of Congress*

zens were not allowed to riot in the street, boycotter Rebecca Ablowitz
responded, "We don't riot. But if all we did was to weep at home, nobody
would notice it; so we have to do something to help ourselves."

The commitment of the striking garment workers and the activities of
the beef boycotters impressed workers at the Henry Street and University Settlements, who felt, writes Foner, that "these women were
upholding the best in the American tradition of protest against greed,
and had demonstrated by their militancy that lower-class women were
neither passive nor inarticulate."

A University Settlement worker, William English Walling, who was
interested in trade unionism and had observed the angry demonstrations
of the boycotters, became more convinced than ever that women workers could become effective union organizers. In 1903 Walling traveled
to England to study the work of the British Women's Trade Union
League with the intention of forming a similar organization in the
United States. At the annual AFL convention in Boston, Walling and
Mary Kenney (later Mary Kenney O'Sullivan), a book binder and an

organizer of the Chicago Bookbinders' Union as well as the Chicago Ladies' Federal Labor Union, met with settlement house workers and union leaders to form the Women's National Trade Union League (changed in 1907 to the National Women's Trade Union League). The WTUL's constitution stated that its object "shall be to assist in the organization of women workers into trade unions and thereby to help secure conditions necessary for healthful and efficient work and to obtain a just return for such work." Mary Morton Kehen, a wealthy Boston reformer and former president of the General Federation of Women's Clubs, was selected as president; Jane Addams of Hull House agreed to serve as vice president; and Mary Kenney O'Sullivan was appointed secretary.

For twelve years the WTUL concentrated its energies on union organizing. Led by the AFL and supported by local leagues in cities like New York, Boston, Chicago, and St. Louis, the group provided money and publicity, as well as tactical and political support for women attempting to unionize. League members put up bail bonds for arrested strikers, marched with them on picket lines, most notably during the garment workers' Great Uprising of 1909–10, played important roles in strikes in Philadelphia, Chicago, and among Kalamazoo corset workers and labored on behalf of Southern women textile workers. The league also published *Life and Labor*, a monthly newspaper. However, the WTUL made little effort to organize African American women workers or to lower the barriers against them in both industry and the trade unions. "The League's affiliation with and financial dependence on a blatantly racist AFL," writes Foner, "made such efforts practically impossible." An important aspect of the WTUL's programs and its training school were its health and physical culture classes, introduced by league president Margaret Dreier Robins as a way of building female workers' morale and physical well-being. Robins's concern for the health of women workers, who often labored for sixteen or seventeen hours a day while pregnant, led to the organization in 1910 of a health committee within the Chicago WTUL that resulted in the first comprehensive health plan sponsored by a labor organization in the United States.

Numerous disputes with the conservative, male-dominated AFL over control of union activities, particularly strikes, resulted in a change of direction for the WTUL. In 1915 the league turned away from direct union organizing and began to focus its activities on securing protective labor legislation at the state and federal level as a means toward solving the problems of women workers. During the 1930s and 1940s the league crusaded for minimum wage laws and an equal pay act and defended the right of women to work (an issue that caused controversy during the Great Depression, World War II, and the postwar era, since it conflicted with popular notions of gender roles). Many of the WTUL's aims were supported by First Lady Eleanor Roosevelt, who as a young woman had been a settlement worker and was well versed in the history of the women's labor movement.

By the late 1940s the influence of the WTUL had waned. Many of the league's legislative aims had been accomplished, female union membership numbered about three million, and the function of union organization and negotiation had been taken over by the AFL and the Congress of Industrial Organizations (CIO). The WTUL was also suffering financially. In 1950 the WTUL closed its national office in Washington, and its local chapters quickly followed suit. In 1955 about seventy members of the last remaining local branch in New York City met to determine the fate of the organization. Seventy-three-year-old president Rose Schneiderman, a veteran and hero of the women's labor movement, observed that "they don't need us anymore" and advised, "Let's step out gracefully."

The meeting marked the end for an organization that had played such an influential role in some of the greatest historic women's labor struggles and had given many women workers their first encouragement and training. In 1950, after the disbanding of the national league, Elizabeth Christman of the Women's Bureau called for a continuation of the ideals that had motivated the founders of the Women's Trade Union League, saying, "The organization of women in the early years was a crusade— and that is what it should continue to be in order to bring those women still unorganized an understanding of the inherent value to be gained from union membership."

1904

Mary McLeod Bethune Founds
the Daytona Normal and Industrial
Institute for Negro Girls

We burned logs and used the charred splinters as pencils, and mashed elderberries for ink. . . . I haunted the city dump and the trash piles behind hotels, retrieving discarded linen and kitchenware, cracked dishes, broken chairs, pieces of old lumber. Everything was scoured and mended. This was part of the training to salvage, to reconstruct, to make bricks without straw. As parents began gradually to leave their children overnight, I had to provide sleeping accommodations. I took corn sacks for mattresses. Then I picked Spanish moss from trees, dried and cured it, and used it as a substitute for mattress hair.

The school expanded fast. In less than two years I had 250 pupils. . . . I concentrated more and more on girls, as I felt that they especially were hampered by lack of educational opportunities. . . .

Mary McLeod Bethune, "Faith That Moved a Dump Heap,"
Who, The Magazine About People, June 1941, in Gerda Lerner,
Black Women in White America

Education for African Americans, especially after emancipation, was always a primary goal. Education represented a means toward advancement and acceptance in general society and was used as a tool to improve and uplift life in the black community. During the Reconstruction period, freedmen's schools flourished in the South because of government support, but the defeat of the Reconstruction governments and the reestablishment of white supremacy in the decades that followed brought an end to desegregated schools as well as any pretense of educating African American children on the same level as white children. Schooling for southern black children, whose parents were primarily poor sharecroppers and tenant farmers, was viewed by the white power struc-

Twenty-year-old Mary McLeod
Bethune, around the time she
finished her studies at the Moody
Bible Institute *Mary McLeod*
Bethune Council House NHS,
Washington, D.C.

ture in the same way it had
been during slavery: unnecessary and dangerous. African
American girls in particular
suffered from institutionalized racism: they were
discriminated against and
denied educational opportunities both because they
were black and because they
were female.

Out of this climate of
poverty, racism, and federal
abandonment came a num-
ber of heroic women equipped with exceptional leadership skills and missionary fervor who founded schools in an effort to better the education of
African American children. Educated at black seminaries, colleges such as
Tuskegee Institute, and normal schools, women like Emma J. Wilson,
Cornelia Bower, and Lucy Laney started schools in the late nineteenth
century with few amenities and little if any funding and, through appeals
to philanthropists, local governments, the community, and sheer force of
character, made them thrive and grow. The school founders never lost
sight of their goal, even though they were often forced to pocket their
pride and forge uneasy alliances with the white community. This tradition of dedication was carried on in the first decade of the twentieth
century by three outstanding African American women educators: Mary
McLeod Bethune (1875–1955), Charlotte Hawkins Brown (1882–1961),
and Nannie Helen Burroughs (1883–1961).

The last of seventeen children and the first free child of former slaves,
Mary McLeod Bethune was born in Maysville, South Carolina. After
attending Emma Wilson's school in Maysville, she graduated from the
Scotia Seminary in North Carolina and spent two years at the Moody
Bible Institute in Chicago. Twice rejected for missionary work in Africa,
Bethune worked as a teacher at the Haines Institute in Georgia, a school
run by Lucy Laney, at the Kindell Institute in North Carolina, and at the
Palatka Mission School in Florida. In 1904 she moved to Daytona Beach,

Florida, where she started a school for the children of African American laborers working on Henry Flagler's statewide railroad. Bethune's Daytona Normal and Industrial Training Institute, which trained students in both academic subjects and industrial skills, began in a shabby four-room cottage with five girls from eight to twelve years old whose parents paid a weekly tuition of fifty cents. A few packing cases served as desks. The indefatigable Bethune raised money for her school by baking pies, selling ice cream to railroad construction workers, and going door to door to ask for donations. As the school began to grow, Bethune solicited and cajoled funds from leading philanthropists, industrialists, and African American organizations. Her shrewd business acumen plus support from both the local black community and the area's wealthy white residents enabled the school to expand from a small cottage to a large campus, which housed Daytona Beach's first black hospital. In 1922 the school, which now focused on providing training for high school– and junior college–age students and had been renamed the Daytona Educational Industrial Training School, merged with Cookman College, a men's school, to become Bethune-Cookman College. Bethune remained president of the college until 1942 and is buried on its grounds. Fully accredited in 1929, Bethune-Cookman College today has an enrollment of over 2,500 students.

Charlotte Hawkins Brown was born in North Carolina and raised in Boston by her mother. Her education was furthered and partially supported by Alice Freeman Palmer, president of Wellesley College. She attended Salem State Teachers College and taught briefly in a church-supported school in Seladia, North Carolina, before opening her own school there in 1902. Brown raised the initial funds for her school by singing and speaking in Massachusetts resort hotels during the summer, earning $15–$20 for three programs a night. Built with the help of northern and southern whites, supported by black and white sponsors, and given a large donation by the Rosenwald Funds, the school was conceived of by Brown as a finishing school for African American girls. She named it the Palmer Memorial Institute and served as its president from 1904 to 1952. For Brown, the education of African American girls was partly a means toward educating white society, who, as she once wrote, "looked upon every Negro, regardless of his appearance, modulated tones that reflected some culture and training, as a servant."

Nannie Helen Burroughs, founder of the National Training School for Girls, was educated by her widowed mother in Washington, D.C., and was an honor student in high school. After failing to secure a teaching position in Washington because she was black, she organized a women's industrial club, which gave industrial training to working girls. Burroughs opened her school in 1909 with funds she raised herself, and she later received financial support from the Women's Auxiliary of the National Colored Baptist Convention, which she had transformed into a dynamic fund-raising organization. Burroughs, whose school motto was "We Specialize in the Wholly Impossible," began with 8 students; the school eventually trained over 2,500 girls in such practical subjects as sewing, shoe repair, home economics, laundering, interior decorating, gardening, bookkeeping, shorthand, typing, printing, nursing, and barbering. Burroughs also emphasized academic subjects and insisted that each student take at least one course in black history. Financed entirely by contributions from the black community—a source of pride for Burroughs—the National Training School for Girls was renamed the Nannie Burroughs School in 1964.

Bethune, Brown, and Burroughs lived to witness the U.S. Supreme Court's unanimous ruling in the case of *Brown* v. *Board of Education of Topeka,* which declared that segregation in public schools was unconstitutional. The court's ruling was the first historical event in the civil rights movement of the 1950s and 1960s. But the struggle of African Americans to achieve equality had begun in an earlier era with the school founders, who with equal measures of tenacity, faith, and talent endeavored to provide better education for black children. Their work stands as a testament to the tremendous influence of African American women during the twentieth century.

1910–1919

During a suffrage parade, Mrs. James Lees Laidlaw, Mrs. Norman de R. Whitehouse, and Mrs. John Blair showed what the well-dressed suffragist wore circa 1915.
The Schlesinger Library, Radcliffe College

1910

The Mann Act Outlaws Interstate Transportation of Women for Immoral Purposes

> Why, then, did white slavery figure so largely in explanations and descriptions of prostitution during the Progressive Era? One obvious reason for its popularity was its lurid and melodramatic appeal. . . . The idea of white slavery also served, however, to deflect attention away from the very real social and economic factors that led women into prostitution. The class guilt of middle-class Americans for conditions that gave rise to prostitution was projected onto a few villainous white slavers, typically represented as foreigners. Furthermore, the white slavery explanation, more than any other, emphasized women's passivity. With their own class presumption of women's supposed sexual purity, many middle-class Americans could not imagine a woman voluntarily entering prostitution. As one writer explained, "We know that no innocent young girl ever would or ever could go there of her own free will—those who are there are enticed—those who employ these artifices are men—devils in the guise of men."
>
> Ruth Rosen, *The Lost Sisterhood: Prostitution in America, 1900–1918*

Attitudes toward prostitution during the opening decades of the twentieth century provide an informative vantage point for measuring changing notions of morality and cultural values, as well as the role and the image of women. The passage of the Mann Act, which aimed at stopping the perceived threat of what was then called "white slavery"—the forcing of women into prostitution—was only one legislative victory for Progressive Era antivice reformers to enforce a changed attitude to prostitution and legalize morality. It points out as well the attempt early in the century to deal with the unsettling image of the fallen woman as well as the trafficking in sexual favors that ran counter to prevailing notions of female purity and decency.

As practitioners of the "world's oldest profession," prostitutes have always constituted one influential image of women, particularly in the dichotomy during the Victorian era that regarded women either as angels or whores, madonnas or magdalens. In this construct, respectable woman were seen as essentially asexual, pure and protected by traditional values of home and family in the role of daughter, wife, and mother. The fallen woman, outside the standards of accepted decency, gratified men's more powerful and potentially destructive sexual nature in the commercial trading of sexual favors in prostitution, regarded as a "necessary evil" by many nineteenth-century social observers. As one writer asserted, the prostitute was "ultimately the most efficient guardian of virtue. But for her, the unchallenged purity of countless happy homes would be polluted. . . . On that one degraded and ignoble form are concentrated the passions that might have filled the world with shame."

Yet such a convenient rationalization for the institution of prostitution did not survive the explosive growth of the profession in the closing decades of the nineteenth and the beginning of the twentieth century. As large, anonymous urban populations grew, prostitution flourished as it never had in rural, tradition-bound communities. Industrialization offered job opportunities for women outside the protection of home and family, but work options for women were limited, particularly in the exclusion of most woman workers from heavy industry and before the growth of clerical and service sector jobs. Between 1850 and 1900, therefore, prostitution increased in alarming numbers as working-class women, second-generation immigrants, and women who gravitated from farms to cities chose life as prostitutes, driven by economic need toward a trade in which earnings could be twice or three times greater than that of a domestic or sales clerk.

In the first two decades of the twentieth century, during the Progressive Era, reformers mounted a zealous public campaign against prostitution. Fueled by medical warnings of a potential epidemic of venereal disease and opposed to the political corruption that sustained the trade, antivice reformers changed attitudes about prostitution from its tolerance as a necessary evil to a social evil that needed to be eradicated. The causes for this crusade are complex. If prostitution challenged traditional notions of female purity and propriety, it also seemed for many a symptom of the new feminist undermining of traditional values associated with conservative American rural life. With women entering the labor force in larger numbers and asserting more independence, the Victorian notion of a woman's place was breaking down, and prostitution was a highly visible and emotionally charged symptom of this breakdown. Eliminating prostitution could, therefore, be seen as a way of restoring traditional values that repressed issues of sexual freedom and avoided larger questions of female exploitation in the workforce.

Prior to the Progressive Era, prostitution was condemned but was never classified as a criminal offense. Instead prostitution was allowed in various limited red-light districts away from direct middle-class notice. In 1890, when the reformers' call for Congress to form a national commission to investigate the causes and extent of prostitution was ignored, local groups formed municipal vice commissions to deal with the problem. Between 1910 and 1917 forty-three cities conducted formal investigations of prostitution and the political connection that was suspected in its maintenance. Driving most of these investigations was the question of why women would become prostitutes in the first place, and though many answers, such as poverty and personal inclination, were suggested, it was the specter of the white slave trade that captured the public's imagination and helped fuel a growing hysteria that culminated in the passing of the Mann Act in 1910. Designed to break up the organized trafficking in women for immoral purposes, the Mann Act was the legislative result of Congress's two-year investigation in the sale and transporting of women for immoral purposes that had begun in 1907.

Investigators interviewing thousands of prostitutes did find confirmation of rings that bought and sold women for the purpose of forcing them into prostitution, importing women from Asia and Europe to become prostitutes, as well as the more sensational evidence that some American women were being drugged and seduced and then coerced into prostitution. However, statistics suggest that white slavery was far from the principal cause for prostitution. It is likely that less than 10 percent of prostitutes were in fact coerced, far fewer than was suggested in the sensationalized posters that appeared, warning "Danger! Mothers beware! Sixty thousand innocent girls wanted to take the place of sixty thousand white slaves who will die this year in the United States." The white slavery hysteria offers less an answer to the cause of prostitution than a gauge of attitudes toward the perceived problem. By suggesting that white slavery had a foreign source, reformers could avoid the implication of prostitution as a domestic and American problem in which one solution would be to simply restrict immigration as a means of restoring America's moral purity. The facts reveal that the majority of international procurers were not "foreigners" suspected in recruiting young girls into prostitution: of the men convicted under the Mann Act, 72.5 percent were native-born Americans.

In a larger sense, the suggestion that white slavery was the cause of prostitution reinforced the mistaken notion that women would not voluntarily choose such a life, that only through drugs and other forms of coercion was such depravity possible. Such a view ignores considerable evidence that the vast majority of prostitutes entered their profession willingly, though certainly in most cases out of dire economic necessity. Others, even more disturbingly to the reformers, preferred prostitution to other options and enjoyed the sexual experience and freedom prostitution offered. Such evidence of deeper economic causes for prostitution and evidence of sexual freedom on the part of women were simply too controversial to be faced directly. Even such a practical reformer as Jane Addams could not admit that women might willingly become promiscuous, declaring that only by "horrible devices" were chaste women defiled and then "degraded morally" so they would willingly become prostitutes. White slavery, therefore, provided a reassuring, though inadequate, answer to the vexing problem prostitution posed to moral standards and traditional conceptions of womanhood. By eliminating the white slave traffic, reformers hoped that prostitution could thereby be eliminated.

Once the Mann Act was passed and cases of white slavery were prosecuted between 1910 and 1913, 337 convictions were obtained, but prostitution was far from eliminated, either through the Mann Act or other local laws prohibiting the trade. Instead prostitution was forced underground. Prostitutes were compelled to turn from brothels to the street and to rely on the greater control and protection of pimps and organized crime. Prostitutes were now part of a criminal underclass with the causes for and consequences of prostitution still neglected. As Ruth Rosen summarizes:

> Despite the Progressive reformers' relentless moral efforts to eliminate prostitution from American life, the closing of the red-light districts scarcely banished commercialized sex from the urban landscape. On the contrary, prostitution has remained an ineradicable and seemingly permanent fixture of the commercialized sex marketplace.
>
> It is one of the ironies of history that much of the Progressive legislation—aimed at creating a more rational, efficient, and orderly society—backfired in ways never imagined by Progressive reformers. The effort to create a properly sober and "Americanized" society, for example, resulted in the criminal chaos and social disorder associated with Prohibition. Similarly, the attempt to eliminate prostitution from American society drove the Social Evil underground, where it became more closely yoked to liquor, drugs, theft, and increased violence.

Prostitution remains a vexing social problem because of the victimization and violence that such a trade produces, especially when the prostitutes are teenage or pre-teenage girls. Equally troubling is the persistent image of the prostitute, in books and films, as a projection of unresolved social issues concerning female independence, self-definition, and sexual identity. In recent decades, despite the acceptance of the less repressive, more sexually liberated woman, the image of the prostitute as sexual and social deviant continues to assert a significant power. The profession also presents a challenge to feminists to reconcile whether or not prostitutes are victims or women responding to a hypocritical standard of morality and their sexual and economic place in society.

⁂

The New Medium of Film Creates the First Women Movie Stars

I am all too painfully aware that so, so much is illusion, that much of my adult life has been spent in vain attempts to emulate Gina or Brigitte or Sophie or Ali. I wonder how many others, perhaps less involved with film but just as impressionable, have also been victims of the Hollywood whitewash? . . .

Because of the magnetism of movies—because their glamour and intensity and "entertainment" are so distracting and seemingly innocuous—women accept their morality or values. Sometimes too often. Too blindly. And tragically. For the Cinema Woman is a Popcorn Venus, a delectable but insubstantial hybrid of cultural distortions.

Marjorie Rosen, *Popcorn Venus: Women, Movies & the American Dream*

"Get More Out of Life. Go to a Movie!" a Hollywood advertisement once urged Americans. Over the course of the twentieth century, women moviegoers received more than they bargained for from the larger-than-life images projected on the movie screen. Film, as a new medium for storytelling, captivated the public almost from the very start. But it was the movie star, carefully glamorized and continually publicized by the Hollywood star system and the fan magazines, who would have the most profound influence on women audiences. Incessantly confronted through the decades by a dazzling succession of what Marjorie Rosen called "Popcorn Venuses" and privy to the most intimate details of their lives, loves, and fashion choices, the women sitting in darkened theaters could not help but begin to compare themselves with the women they saw on the screen. The ambiguous relationship between stargazer and

Florence Lawrence and Arthur Johnson in the 1909 Biograph motion picture
Resurrection   *Library of Congress*

star began when the first studios began to produce movies with greater story content and compelling lead actors; the system that exploited that relationship arrived soon after.

Moviegoers in the star-drenched culture of today might find it difficult to imagine a time when American film actors were not known to audiences by their names. Yet during the early years of filmmaking, when the new medium was becoming increasingly popular, studio policy discouraged the promotion of actors by name. The reason for this policy was simple economics: studios such as Biograph and Vitagraph, tightly controlled by the distribution trust, the Motion Picture Patents Company, rightly worried that their actors would demand more money if audiences knew who they were. Actors, for the most part, were happy to remain anonymous, since many felt ashamed at participating in such a low art form, ground out as entertainment for the urban working class and often referred to derisively as "galloping tintypes." Movie actors, as one trade journal of the day put it, "have the impression that the step from regular stage productions to the scenes before the camera is a backward one."

Audiences, however, liked to identify individual "players," as movie actors were called, and invented names for their favorites, such as "the Biograph Girl," "the Vitagraph Girl," or in the case of Mary Pickford, "the Girl with the Golden Hair" and, ironically, "Little Mary," after a character Pickford frequently played. Fans wrote countless letters asking studios to provide them with information about their screen idols, but the studios, unable to grasp what singularly exploitable properties were performing before their cameras, continued to resist naming their actors.

The most popular anonymous American silent-screen star of the era was former child actor and stage ingenue Florence Lawrence, who began her film career in 1907 with the Edison Company, after the disbanding of the touring stage company with which she was performing. After a stint with Vitagraph, she was lured to Biograph Studios by producer-director D. W. Griffith. By 1909 she was famous as "the Biograph Girl" and was making two movies a week. Lawrence's popularity and money-making potential were not lost on distributor-turned-independent producer Carl Laemmle, who had recently founded his own movie studio, the Independent Motion Picture Company of America, known in the business as Imp. In 1910 he lured Lawrence away from Biograph; shortly thereafter she vanished. Laemmle planted a report in the St. Louis newspapers indicating that "the Biograph Girl" had been run over by a streetcar and killed. The next day he placed a newspaper ad denouncing the report as a lie invented by "enemies" of Imp. The ad went on to assure the public that Florence Lawrence, now "the Imp Girl," was alive and well and would be starring in Imp's next picture, *The Broken Oath*. Florence Lawrence thus became the first film star to be known to the public by her name.

To further squelch rumors of her death and to gain even greater publicity for Imp and its new star, Lawrence made a public appearance in St. Louis, where, writes film historian Daniel Blum, "more people met her train to welcome her than appeared the week before to welcome visiting President Taft." The throngs of excited fans mobbed Lawrence and tore off pieces of her clothing for souvenirs. By engineering such a clever, if unprincipled, publicity stunt, Laemmle, who would go on to found the highly successful Universal Studios, proved the vast popularity of movie actors, underlined their value as commercial properties, and set in motion what would later become the corporate glorification and marketing of top-billed screen actors known as the Hollywood star system.

On the subject of rising to movie stardom, actress Gloria Swanson is reputed to have said: "I have decided that when I am a star I will be every inch and moment the star. Everyone from the studio gateman to the highest executive will know it." As movies became more and more popular, it was not enough for studios to acknowledge the star power of actresses like Swanson: the public had to realize it, too. There were in effect two industries in Hollywood: the making of movies and the marketing of movie stars. One method used by the studios to ensure that fans would continue to yearn for the screen presence of favorite actors was to cast their stars according to type. As a result, stock characters, once the staple of stage melodrama and vaudeville, became an integral part of moviemaking, and the images and personalities of the stars became etched in the public's mind as inseparable from the types of women they played. Mary Pickford, publicized as "America's Sweetheart," was typed as the spirited, but always virginal, child-woman; Lillian Gish was sweet young womanhood personified; Theda Bara embodied the predatory vamp from whom no man was safe; Clara Bow, the "It" girl, typified 1920s sex appeal. In the 1930s, when the Hollywood star system came of age, Jean Harlow in her slinky "drop dead" gowns, was *the* sexy "platinum blond dame," while languorous Greta Garbo and glamorous Marlene Dietrich projected not only sophisticated sexuality, but the essence of female mystery. Jean Arthur and Barbara Stanwyck epitomized the tough and sassy career-minded woman. Marie Dressler and Shirley Temple, the two biggest box office female stars of the Depression, were symbols in their own right: Dressler, a large, homely woman and an excellent comic actress, portrayed women who were tough yet vulnerable; Temple, projecting innocence and hope, was every parent's dream daughter. The films of the 1940s, reflecting World War II, turned such screen dream women as Betty Grable and Rita Hayworth into cheesecake pinup girls. Joan Crawford, shoulder pads squarely centered, was the image of the vamp (*Humoresque*) or the personification of suffering womanhood (*A Woman's Face, Mildred Pierce*).

Casting women according to type did not end with the demise of the studio system: in the 1950s and 1960s models of screen allure included Marilyn Monroe, the century's ultimate pinup; Audrey Hepburn, the essence of girlish gamine charm; Grace Kelly, the cool blond beauty; and Doris Day, who played comically vigorous, career-minded virgins or habitually frenetic housewives and mothers. Each decade has brought forth female movie stars (and, latterly, television stars) who have not only represented women of the prevailing culture in the roles they have played, but who have also helped to determine, for better or worse, how each culture has imagined its women.

Fan magazines such as *Photoplay* (first published in 1911) further exploited and confused the relationship between star and fan. As Martin Levin, editor of *Hollywood and the Great Fan Magazines*, has observed, the fan magazines were "a cooperative venture between the myth makers and an army of readers willing to be mythified." This was especially true from the start of the Great Depression in 1929 to the onset of World War II, when most people were poor or struggling financially and, as Levin writes, "hardly anything changed except the double bill at the Bijou." The stars were the privileged elite, but through the agency of the fan magazines, they also attempted to convince the moviegoing public that in spite of their wealth and celebrity, they had "heart" and in some cases actually envied their fans. It was reported that sophisticated Constance Bennett supported no fewer than "four needy families"; Myrna Loy wistfully envied the secretaries who were able to shop on their lunch hour in perfect leisure and anonymity; other women movie stars, some on their second or third spouses, outlined their heartfelt commitments to marriage and motherhood. Readers, mostly women, were beguiled by such story headlines as "In Hollywood, Health, Friends, Beauty, Even Life Itself, Are Sacrificed on the Terrible Altar of Ambition" and "So You'd Like to Be a Star?" Whether the stories were true or not was beside the point, since the creation of mythology relies upon a certain level of invention, and the public derived a vicarious thrill in believing that they really were sharing the lives of the stars. As Agnes Specht, a movie fan from Cleveland, Ohio, wrote in a 1936 letter to *Motion Picture* magazine: "Through [the magazines] we learn that all these glamorous people are just simple human beings like ourselves and that they have our ambitions, struggles, heartaches and hopes. And through this knowledge we understand them better." What women movie fans needed to understand was how deftly they were being manipulated to compare themselves with people whose careers were dedicated to self-promotion and for whom wealth and celebrity were a burden only when it suited them. In addition, the stars' confessional behavior and the fans' response to it ultimately had the effect of creating a society in which it became increasingly difficult to separate public and private life, not to mention reality and fantasy.

As for Florence Lawrence, the once adored silent-screen actress who, with Carl Laemmle, helped to invent the concept of the Hollywood movie star, fortune was not kind to her. In 1914, while performing a dangerous stunt, she was seriously injured and was forced to give up her film career. She made one screen appearance in 1916 and attempted a comeback in the early 1920s. Her comeback failed, and she was soon forgotten. MGM put her on its payroll in the 1930s, along with several other old-timers, as an act of charity, and for a time she occasionally found work as an extra. In 1938, at the age of fifty-two, she committed suicide by eating ant poison. Today her sad story would be fodder for the many magazines and tabloids devoted to intimate details of celebrity lives. She would be a star once again, guaranteed that mythical place in history reserved for those who have sacrificed everything on Hollywood's Altar of Ambition.

1911

Dr. Alice Hamilton Publishes the First Study
of Occupational Disease

It was no public crisis, open epidemic, or general plague that she
uncovered and corrected. Only the attrition of lives, so scattered
and insidious that no one gave it attention. But she solved its
causation—by the perfection of her scientific ability, and made it a
public matter—by her consummate statesmanship. Her science,
as it were, had to be sold; she sold it.

Editorial, *Industrial Medicine*, August 1935, quoted in Lloyd C. Taylor Jr.,
The Medical Profession and Social Reform, 1885–1945

Recognized as a pioneer in the fields of public health and industrial
medicine, toxicologist Alice Hamilton, through her research and public
advocacy, demonstrated the necessity of ridding factories, mines, and
mills of the industrial poisons that were the source of many illnesses of
American workers. Her promotion of the implementation of better
hygienic conditions in workplaces helped save and extend the lives of
countless workers.

The younger sister of classicist Edith Hamilton, Alice Hamilton
(1869–1970) was born in New York City and grew up in Fort Wayne,
Indiana. Her parents were proponents of social and economic reform and
championed feminism, and Hamilton and her three sisters were raised in
an atmosphere enlivened by frequent discussions of ideas and issues.
After attending Miss Porter's boarding school in Connecticut, Hamilton
decided to become a doctor. Her decision to enter medicine was initially
based on a desire for the independence and adventure she felt the profession could offer her and not because of any particular scientific interest. As she recalled in a 1947 *New York Times Magazine* interview, "I
wanted to do something that would not interfere with my freedom.
I knew nothing about science, but I realized that if I were a doctor, I

could go anywhere I wanted—to foreign lands, to city slums—and while carrying on my profession still be of some use."

While studying medicine at the University of Michigan, Hamilton developed a strong interest in both scientific research and social and economic problems, a result of her exposure to the work of economist and labor advocate Richard Ely. After obtaining her medical degree in 1893, Hamilton completed her internship and then went to Germany for further work in bacteriology and pathology. In 1897 Hamilton accepted a professorship of pathology at the Women's Medical College of Northwestern University in Chicago and went to live at Jane Addams's Hull House, where she founded one of the first child welfare and outpatient clinics in the United States. Hamilton's work with the clinic convinced her that the unwillingness of settlement houses to impose outside cultural standards upon poor, working-class, primarily immigrant families— their clients—represented a dangerous impediment to public health. "It must . . . be remembered," she wrote in an essay on social settlements and public health for *Charities and Commons*, "that the low standards of poor people are often not the result of choice but of necessity. Life in our city slums does not lend them to believe in the possibility of clean streets and wholesome water, and healthful homes, and they resign themselves to the evils which they feel powerless to combat."

In 1902 Hamilton resigned her professorship to resume her research at Chicago's McCormick Memorial Institute for Infectious Diseases. There she became profoundly influenced by Sir Thomas Oliver's *Dangerous Trades*, the most authoritative study of industrial diseases. As Hamilton searched American medical literature for studies on industrial toxicology, she discovered that such studies were either largely nonexistent or out-of-date. Her investigations into the subject also revealed a deep suspicion on the part of the medical profession regarding industrial medicine, considered by many physicians to be a product of socialism and tainted with sentimentality and ideological bias. There were industrial "surgeons" employed by large corporations that had high accident rates, but these company doctors were barely competent physicians with little knowledge of surgery. They were present in factories primarily to protect the company from possible lawsuits arising from accidents and, like both management and labor, showed little concern about the effects of industrial pollution, which rarely led to legal action.

In 1908 Hamilton was named to the Illinois Commission on Occupational Diseases and the same year began to lecture on the subject of industrial illnesses. In 1909 she was appointed to direct a commission study on the incidence of industrial poisonings, most prominently from exposure to lead, a metal used in a wide variety of industries. The final

A 1925 portrait of Alice Hamilton   *The Schlesinger
Library, Radcliffe College*

report, completed in 1911, was the first authoritative American study of
its kind. Hamilton, a member of the Women's Trade Union League,
agreed with WTUL president Margaret Dreier Robins that women
should be prohibited from working in lead industries. In *Industrial Poisons in the United States*, Hamilton wrote, "Lead is . . . a race poison. . . . In
the case of the man a poison can act only on the germ cell, but in the
case of the woman the toxic action can continue throughout nine months
of pregnancy." Lead poisoning also destroyed the body's resistance to
tuberculosis. Called by Alice Hamilton "a disease of the working
classes," tuberculosis was further aggravated by poor nutrition, inadequate housing, and fatigue caused by long work shifts and was prevalent among mill workers, the majority of whom were women and
children. When the United States entered World War I in 1917, Hamilton surveyed conditions in metal plants throughout the country. She
found that managers of munitions factories rarely screened machines,
provided safeguards against explosions, or protected workers, many of
whom were women, from poisoning by mercury, lead, and TNT. Super-
intendents, foremen, and physicians used the suggestions in Hamilton's

report on the munitions industry as guidebooks to help them implement better environmental and hygienic standards in their factories.

In 1919 a twentieth-century feminist milestone was reached when Hamilton became Harvard University's first woman professor. Hamilton was a professor of industrial medicine at Harvard Medical School until 1925, when she accepted a professorship at Harvard's School of Public Health. During the 1920s, an era of political conservatism and American nativism, Hamilton's advocacy of social medicine and increased health insurance for workers, her conspicuous leadership in reform, and her participation in the Health Committee of the League of Nations led to charges of radicalism from such reactionary groups as the American Medical Association. Undeterred by these charges, especially when voiced by the medical establishment, Hamilton continued to press for a national program of social insurance to protect citizens against sickness, disability, unemployment, and old age. Some of the reforms she advocated were realized during the Roosevelt administration of the 1930s; other reforms, such as Medicaid and Medicare, government health insurance for the elderly and disabled, would not be fully implemented until the Johnson administration of the 1960s. The national health program, a federally funded system of uniformly standard medical care available throughout the nation, was championed by Hamilton and her colleagues during the 1930s and 1940s, but such a program was continually stonewalled by the AMA and remains an elusive goal for present-day advocates.

In 1935 Alice Hamilton retired from Harvard to serve as a special adviser on industrial medicine for the U.S. Labor Department's Bureau of Labor Standards. During her government tenure, she pressed for the complete elimination of child labor, a form of child abuse that had been perpetrated by American industry since the nineteenth century. Protective labor legislation for children was finally realized when the Fair Labor Standards Act of 1938 was enacted. From 1944 to 1949 Hamilton served as president of the National Consumers' League.

Alice Hamilton's pioneering career and dedication to social reform is illustrative of the strong feminist advocacy toward female achievement that took hold during the Progressive Era in the United States and reached its culmination in 1920 with the passage of the Nineteenth Amendment, which guaranteed women the right to vote. Many women, inspired by those pioneers already at work in the professions, benefited from the atmosphere of feminist support. Alice Hamilton, writing in her autobiography, *Exploring the Dangerous Trades*, theorized that it had been easier for women to become doctors during the early years of the twentieth century when feminism was a powerful force and "a woman doctor could count on the loyalty of a group of devoted feminists who would choose a woman because she was a woman." This sensibility would fade as medical schools began to apply quotas on female admission and the number of women entering the profession declined, only to rise again during the 1970s and 1980s, when women began to find their feminist roots once again.

❧

More Than One Hundred Women Garment Workers Are Killed in the Triangle Shirtwaist Fire

At 4:40 o'clock, nearly five hours after the employees in the rest of the building had gone home, the fire broke out. The one little fire escape in the interior was never resorted to by any of the doomed victims. Some of them escaped by running down the stairs, but in a moment or two this avenue was cut off by flames. The girls rushed to the windows and looked down at Greene Street, 100 feet below. Then one poor, little creature jumped. There was a plate glass protection over part of the sidewalk, but she crashed through it, wrecking it and breaking her body into a thousand pieces.

Then they all began to drop. . . .

New York Times, front page, March 26, 1911

Although the shirtwaist makers' strike of 1909–10, also known as the Great Uprising and the "Uprising of the Thirty Thousand" (between twenty and thirty thousand women garment workers participated), established the International Ladies' Garment Workers' Union (ILGWU) as a major union and created solidarity among women workers, it resulted in only modest concessions for them. The powerful garment industry in general remained intransigent concerning worker demands for better pay, shorter hours, and improved working conditions. The Triangle Shirtwaist Company, which had precipitated the 1909 strike in the first place, refused to accept demands for more fire escapes and unlocked doors. The company's callous and criminal disregard for the safety of its workers led to the worst single disaster in twentieth-century women's history.

The event took place at a sweatshop owned by the Triangle Shirtwaist Company located on the top three floors of the ten-story Asch Building on the corner of Washington Place and Greene Street in New

York City's Greenwich Village (the building is now part of New York University). The building contained only two elevators and two narrow staircases, and the door to one of the staircases was kept locked. The exits leading to the roof were locked as a precaution against theft; the owners of the company worried that workers would take shirtwaists to the roof and drop them to accomplices on the street below. According to the report in *The New York Times*, "The building had experienced four recent fires and had been reported by the Fire Department to the Building Department as unsafe, on account of the insufficiency of its exits."

Late on Saturday afternoon, March 25, some five hundred people, the majority of them young immigrant women, most of them in their teens, were busy cutting fabric or sitting at sewing machines placed so closely together that the chairs of the seamstresses dovetailed. Finished shirtwaists hung in lines above the tiers of workers, bins overflowed with scraps of material, and more scraps, lint, and oil-soaked rags littered the floors. Suddenly, on the eighth floor, a smoldering bin of fabric waste burst into flame. Before anyone could reach the bucket and the water barrel, the blaze spread to stacks of material piled high on the cutting tables. Soon the entire floor was engulfed in flame. Survivors from the ninth floor later reported seeing flames shooting up through the windows, up the stairway, and up the elevator shaft.

As the fire began to spread, the frightened women stampeded to the elevators and found that only one was in operation. Its capacity was twelve persons. A mass of women broke down the locked doors leading to the narrow stairwells and tumbled over one another in a desperate attempt to reach the street, where the doors opened inward. As the fire worsened, terrified women began to jump into the elevator shaft. Others followed Triangle owners Max Blanck and Isaac Harris to the roof, where they escaped to another building. On the tenth floor, seamstress Clotilda Terdanova, who was planning to be married in June, broke a window and jumped to her death. Many other women followed her in quick succession, their bodies on fire as they fell. The one fire escape, built to support no more than a few people, collapsed under the weight of fleeing women. A number of women remained trapped in the sweatshops, where they succumbed to smoke inhalation or were burned to death. The 150 firefighters who arrived at the scene were hampered in their efforts by falling bodies and nets that broke under the weight of people falling from a height of eighty-five feet. Ladders reached only to the sixth floor of the building, and the trucks could pump no water to reach beyond the seventh floor. In eighteen minutes the fire had run its course and 146 people lay dead.

An artist's interpretation of the aftermath of the Triangle Shirtwaist fire.
The drawing was published in the Socialist monthly magazine *The Masses*.
Library of Congress

Over one hundred thousand mourners attended the mass funeral, and
there were mass protests and angry demonstrations, especially on New
York's Lower East Side. Further uptown, the Women's Trade Union
League (WTUL) held a memorial meeting at the Metropolitan Opera
House. Among those present were many of the women philanthropists
who had contributed money to the Great Uprising. When called upon to
speak, veteran labor leader Rose Schneiderman had this to say: "I would
be a traitor to those poor burned bodies, if I came here to talk good fellowship. We have tried you good people of the public and we have

found you wanting. . . . Every year thousands of us are maimed. The life of men and women is so cheap and property is so sacred."

An investigation into the Triangle Shirtwaist Fire exonerated company owners Blanck and Harris, the county, the state, and the insurance companies. Subsequent reforms in building safety, fire prevention, and insurance practices came too late for the twenty-three beneficiaries who received $75 each as payment for the loss of their loved ones three years after the tragedy. For an outraged Rose Schneiderman and her sisters in the labor movement, there was only one way to ensure that such a disaster would never happen again: continued strikes and stepped-up defiance toward exploitative and greedy employers. "I can't talk fellowship to you who are gathered here," Schneiderman told her audience at the WTUL meeting at the Metropolitan Opera House. "Too much blood has been spilled. I know from my experience that it is up to the working people to save themselves. The only way they can save themselves is by a strong working-class movement."

The working-class movement Schneiderman advocated in the wake of the Triangle Shirtwaist fire evolved only sporadically, despite continued strikes by workers. The most famous of these was the 1912 strike by immigrant woolen mill workers in Lawrence, Massachusetts, the majority of whom were women and children. Organized by the left-wing Industrial Workers of the World (the Wobblies), whose leaders included Elizabeth Gurley Flynn and "Big" Bill Haywood, women strikers protested the inequality in pay between the sexes and carried banners with the slogans "We want bread and roses too." The police violence that took place during the strike, some of which was directed toward children, turned public opinion against the mill owners, who met the workers' demands after two months. The settlement of the strike represented a victory for the mill workers and for the Wobblies, who moved on to organize other strikes. But conditions for women workers in Lawrence and elsewhere could not be sustained without unions supported by organized labor, and most of the men in the powerful American Federation of Labor remained convinced that women were not worth organizing. After so many years of fighting not only bosses but also male labor leaders, women became, as garment worker Elizabeth Hasanovitz put it, "too tired to rebel any more." It would take the increased presence of women workers in factories during World War I and the efforts of the Women's Bureau, established in 1920, to secure government regulations of the conditions under which women worked in order to avoid the kind of tragedy experienced by the shirtwaist makers of 1911.

❧

The First International Women's Day Is Celebrated

Some leaders are born women.

> Saying on a T-shirt worn at the 1983 UN observation of International
> Women's Day, quoted in news summaries, March 18, 1983

On March 8, 1908, New York Socialist women garment workers com-
memorated an 1857 labor rally of New York seamstresses by staging a
demonstration to call for better working conditions, voting rights, and
an end to sweatshops and child labor. In 1910 this event inspired Clara
Zetkin, feminist, German Socialist Party leader, and founder of the
Socialist women's movement, to offer a resolution at the International
Socialist Women's Congress in Copenhagen that the day of the demonstration of the American working women should become an International
Women's Day and that March 8 each year be dedicated to fighting for
equal rights for all women in all countries. On March 8, 1911, International Women's Day was observed for the first time in Austria, Denmark,
Germany, and Switzerland with parades and demonstrations to protest
the lack of representation by women in trade unions.

An event comparable to the labor rallies held each year since 1889 on
May Day, International Women's Day was observed annually in Europe
and Asia after 1911. Over the decades International Women's Day
expanded its focus on labor and equal rights to include celebrations of
women's achievements and denunciations of czarist tyranny in Russia,
warfare, and fascism. International Women's Day was not observed in
the United States until 1969, when feminist Berkeley student Laura
Rand Orthwein and her friends staged a parade to mark the event. Orthwein (who had adopted the name Laura X in protest against women's
legal position as chattel of their fathers and husbands) and her friends
also published a pamphlet entitled "Women in World History" and
started the Women's History Research Center Library, which by 1974
would have a collection of nearly one million documents concerning
women's issues from all over the world. Orthwein opened a shelter for
battered women and their children in 1969, and in 1970 she started the
National Clearinghouse on Marital and Date Rape. During the 1970s
she worked for the enactment of marital rape laws in every U.S. state.

In 1977 several women who would later found the National Women's
History Project (NWHP) began working with the Education Task Force

A round-table discussion on the topic "The Exploited Half: Women, the World's Poorest" during the 1983 United Nations observance of International Women's Day. *Left to right:* Edith Van Horn, Carolyn Reed, Robin Morgan, Theresa Funiciello, Gloria Steinem (panel moderator), Motlalepula Chabaku, and Karen Sauvigne. *UN/DPI Photo*

of the Sonoma County, California, Commission on the Status of Women (CSW) to initiate a national Women's History Week. The initiators chose the week in March that included International Women's Day. The establishment of a National Women's History Week was in great part a response to the lack of information in school texts about women in history. As Mollie MacGregor, director of the Sonoma County CSW and a founder of the National Women's History Project, has explained: "In 1977, with the exception of Betsy Ross and Queen Isabella, women were simply absent from history texts. We wanted to see more women discussed in school curricula, starting with kindergarten and going straight through grade 12." The first National Women's History Week celebration, held in 1978, was greeted with enthusiasm, and within a few years a number of California schools and community groups were participating in the event. By the 1980s thousands of schools and communities across the United States were celebrating National History Week, supported and encouraged by resolutions from state departments of education, governors, city councils, school boards, and the U.S. Congress.

In 1987, at the request of museums, libraries, and educators, the Women's History Project, founded in 1980, petitioned Congress to expand the national celebration of National Women's History Week to include the entire month of March, allowing more time for schools and communities to explore the increasingly accessible field of women's history. The same year, Congress approved a resolution designating March as National Women's History Month. Celebrated by programs in schools, museums, libraries, and as part of other community group activities,

National Women's History Month has also become a vehicle for diversity education in workplaces across the country. Materials on women's history, many developed by the NWHP, are now used for Women's Equality Day (August 26) and to incorporate women into annual observances such as Black History Month and Hispanic Heritage Month.

In the 1990s, school- and community-sponsored activities during National Women's History Month have done much to educate citizens of all ages on the importance of acknowledging the invaluable contributions of women throughout history. These annual celebrations, begun in 1911 with the first observance of International Women's Day, empower girls and women to broaden their ideas about what they can accomplish in their own lives, in the present and in the future.

1912

Juliette Gordon Low Founds the Girl Scouts of the USA

I will do my best to be
   honest and fair,
   friendly and helpful,
   considerate and caring,
   courageous and strong, and
   responsible for what I say and do,
and to
   respect myself and others,
   respect authority,
   use resources wisely,
   make the world a better place, and
   be a sister to every Girl Scout.

             The Girl Scout Law

Sports have often been cited by sociologists, psychologists, and women's studies scholars as the traditional way in which boys learn to work together in teams, thus giving them an advantage in the corporate world later on. The sports metaphor applies equally to girls, who not only play sports but also possess their own socially adaptive ability to work well together in groups when they choose to do so. Girls' clubs and organizations can be as effective as athletics in narrowing aspects of the gender gap. Since its founding by Juliette Gordon Low in 1912, the Girl Scouts have stressed the attainment of goals (another cited gender difference between boys and girls), as well as group cooperation and teamwork. The original stated mission for the new organization was that it should "train girls to take their rightful places in life, first as good women, then as good citizens, wives, and mothers." Although the Girl Scout mission statement was a clear reflection of the times in which Juliette Low lived, it nevertheless recognized what she believed to be true: that intellectual, physical, and moral strength were as important to the development of girls as the learning of skills that would make them good homemakers, wives, and mothers.

The woman who devoted most of her adult life to Girl Scouting was born into a wealthy and accomplished family in Savannah, Georgia, in 1860. Nicknamed "Daisy," Juliette Gordon was the second oldest of six children born to Nellie Gordon and William Washington Gordon II, who fought as a Confederate captain during the Civil War and after the war commanded the Georgia Hussars militia, a post previously held by his father and grandfather. He later served as a diplomat during the Spanish-American War and for three terms served in the Georgia State Legislature. Nellie Gordon was a quick-witted, unconventional woman, with artistic and musical talent and a penchant for sliding down banisters in the family home. Like her mother, Juliette Gordon was gifted in art and also wrote poetry and composed theatricals. She attended a Virginia boarding school headed by the granddaughters of Thomas Jefferson and an exclusive finishing school in New York. In 1886 she married William Low, the son of a wealthy cotton merchant. The couple moved to England, where they enjoyed a life comprising such high-society pleasures as fox hunts and balls among the British and European aristocracy. The childless marriage lasted for nineteen years, until Low's death in 1905, but during those years it had become an increasingly unhappy one. A divorce had been discussed but never settled, and when Low died, his wife was shocked to learn that he had left the bulk of his estate to his mistress. Juliette Low contested the will and regained $500,000, which she would later use to found the Girl Scouts of America.

Juliette Gordon Low spent six years after her husband's death traveling in Great Britain, India, and Egypt and studying sculpture in Paris. In 1911, while visiting England, she met Sir Robert Baden-Powell, a British military hero, and his sister Agnes, who had founded the Boy Scouts and the Girl Guides. Low was inspired by the Baden-Powells' work in scouting and formed her own troop of Girl Guides in Glen Lyon, Scotland, situated near her country home. The troop of seven girls, from impoverished families in the area, learned knot tying, camping, first aid, map reading, and signaling. Determined to find a way for the girls to avoid the fate of leaving their valley for factory jobs in the city, Low also taught them to raise chickens and spin wool and helped them find markets for their products. After starting a similar troop in London's Lambeth district, Low returned to Savannah to bring Girl Guiding to the United States. On March 12, 1912, the day of her homecoming, Low telephoned her cousin Nina Pope, the headmistress of a Savannah school, and told

Juliette Gordon Low pinning the Golden Eaglet, the highest award
in Girl Scouting, on a scout, circa 1918   *Juliette Gordon Low Girl Scout
National Center*

her, "Come right over! I've got something for the girls of Savannah, and
all America, and all the world, and we're going to start it tonight." The
same evening, Low's niece Daisy Gordon was registered as the first Girl
Guide in the United States. The first troop consisted of eighteen girls,
who formed two patrols named the Carnation and the White Rose. In
1913 the name of the organization was changed from Girl Guides to Girl
Scouts.

The early Girl Scouts first wore dark blue middy blouses, skirts, and
a light blue tie. The next year the Scouts voted to change the uniform to
khaki, deeming it a color "more practical for our hikes, our picnicking,
and our camping." A grayish green uniform was introduced in 1927, and
the lighter green uniform most associated with the Girl Scouts today
debuted in 1948, the creation of well-known fashion designer Main-
bocher. The first proficiency badge, child nurse, was earned in 1913 by
Girl Scout Elizabeth Purse. Early Scouts also pursued badges in such
diverse areas as telegraphy, farming, and electrical work. The same year,
the first Girl Scout handbook, *How Girls Can Help Their Country*,
appeared. Adopted by W. J. Hoxie from the British Girl Guide handbook by Agnes Baden-Powell and Sir Robert Baden-Powell, the handbook featured such practical advice as "How to kill and dress poultry"
and "How to secure a burglar with six inches of cord," as well as articles
on such radical subjects as ecology, organic foods, and career opportuni-

ties for women. Juliette Low rewrote the handbook in 1916. That year the first troop of girls ages seven to ten was organized in Marblehead, Massachusetts, as "Junior Scouts," later renamed Brownies.

During World War I American Girl Scouts volunteered their services, working in hospitals, staffing railroad station canteens for trains transporting soldiers, growing vegetables, selling war bonds, and collecting peach pits for use in gas mask filters. This record of service established the Girl Scouts as a national organization and resulted in a sudden expansion in membership.

By 1927, the year of Juliette Gordon Low's death, Girl Scout membership numbered 167,925, and there were troops across the country, as well as in Hawaii. Through the decades, prominent women such as First Ladies Lou Henry Hoover, Eleanor Roosevelt, and Hillary Rodham Clinton have served as presidents and honorary presidents of the organization, and many other well-known women of influence have cited their Scouting experience as one of the most positive of their lives. Since 1912 the Girl Scouts of the U.S.A. has changed and grown with the times, continually introducing programs that reflect the needs and interests of its members. In 1997 that membership numbered approximately 3.5 million Daisy Scouts (ages five to six), Brownie Scouts (ages six to eight), Junior Scouts (ages eight to eleven), Cadette Scouts (ages eleven to fourteen), and Senior Scouts (ages fourteen to seventeen), making the Girl Scouts of the U.S.A. the largest voluntary organization for girls and young women in the world. The success and influence of the Girl Scouts is a tribute to its founder, who worked so hard on her organization's behalf and who was described in 1927 by the National Board of Girl Scouts as "not only the first Girl Scout, but the best Girl Scout of them all."

1914

New York Socialite Mary Phelps Jacobs
Patents the Brassiere

Positively appalling . . . this preposterous preoccupation with
bosoms. . . . They've become the dominant theme in American
culture—in literature, advertising . . . in everything. I'll wager you
anything you like, if American women stopped wearing brassieres,
your whole national economy would collapse overnight!

Terry-Thomas to Milton Berle
in *It's A Mad, Mad, Mad, Mad World*, 1963

No part of a woman's anatomy has received as much public and private
attention as her breasts. These milk-producing glands, designed primarily as a source of infant nutrition, have always offered maternal, erotic,
and visual pleasure as well as frustration because of their size and despair
because of their susceptibility to disease. Young adolescent boys are fascinated by breasts and often find them threatening, as they do many
physical aspects of femaleness. Men, for the most part, simply find them
fascinating. Breasts seem to charm the most when clothed in bikini tops
or in strategically designed undergarments, as the popularity of Victoria's Secret catalogs clearly shows. But for most women the public exhibition of a shapely, nearly nude bosom and the attention that goes with
it rank behind the ongoing quest to find that elusive object, the attractive, well-fitting, correctly supportive bra. Plain, padded, strapless, or
sport, bras have become an indispensable part of every woman's
wardrobe, thanks to New York socialite Mary "Polly" Phelps Jacobs,
who, for fashion's sake, found a substitute for that stiff, whaleboned
obstacle to female freedom of movement: the corset.

Credit for the invention of the modern brassiere (bras had existed in
one form or another since ancient times) has been variously given to
Jacobs, a descendant of steamboat inventor Robert Fulton, and the sug-

I dreamed I danced
a ballet in my

maidenform bra
®

Stage struck, dream struck! I'm soaring,
leaping, twirling, whirling! The spotlight's on me...
kept in beautiful form in my Maidenform* bra.
Maybe you've dreamed of a dream of
a bra with figure-perfect fit like Maidenform's.

The dream of a bra: Chansonette* in white or black acetate
satin; also in broadcloth or nylon taffeta...from 2.00.
Send for free style booklet. Maidenform, New York 16, N.Y.

There is a *maidenform* for every type of figure.*

© 1954 Maiden Form Brassiere Co., Inc.   *Reg. U. S. Pat. Off.

Costume: Cavriola-Braillet

A 1954 "I Dreamed" ad from Maidenform
Reproduced by permission of Maidenform

gestively named Otto Titzling, a German immigrant. In 1910, while working for his uncle, a women's undergarment manufacturer, Titzling invented a chest halter for young aspiring opera singer Swanhilda Olafsen after hearing her complain of discomfort and the lack of support corsets gave to her large breasts. Titzling neglected to patent his invention and so never received credit for his innovation. Titzling's story, however, may be apocryphal or it may be true, depending on which historical source one chooses to believe. Most fashion historians select Mary Jacobs, also known as Caresse Crosby, as the first American inventor and popularizer of the brassiere (a word that first appeared in 1911 and may or may not have derived from Paris dress designer Philippe de Brassiere, who is also said to have invented the bra). In 1913 Mary Jacobs purchased an expensive sheer evening gown that clearly revealed her corset. With the help of her maid, Jacobs devised a brief, backless bra from two white handkerchiefs, a strand of ribbon, and cord. Female friends who admired Jacobs's lightweight, impromptu fashion received them as gifts. But when Jacobs received a letter from a stranger, containing a dollar and a request for her design, she decided that she had better try to patent her invention. In 1914 the U.S. Patent Office awarded Jacobs a patent for her Backless Brassiere, and the socialite produced several hundred handmade bras with the help of friends. She later sold her patent rights to the Warner Brothers Corset Company of Bridgeport, Connecticut, for $1,500 (some sources say $15,000), beginning what would become a highly profitable industry.

Innovations that followed Mary Phelps Jacobs's design included elastic fabric and the padded bra in the 1920s and the strapless bra and standard cup sizes in the 1930s. Sized bras were created by Russian-Jewish immigrant Ida Rosenthal, the founder, with her husband, William, of the Maidenform company. Rosenthal combined her own design experience and paper patterns to group American women into bust-size categories and produced a line of uplift bras designed for women of every age and shape. The Victoria's Secret bra ads of today might ooze sex and hint at voyeurism, but for sheer imagination, even they cannot hope to rival the Maidenform ads of the 1950s and 1960s. In them a model is pictured clothed for a variety of activities from the waist down and wearing only a well-fitting Maidenform bra on top. The caption read "I dreamed I [went horseback riding, danced a ballet, got married, etc.] in my Maidenform bra."

Bra fashion and breast-shape preferences have always fluctuated with the times. During the flapper era of the 1920s, the flat-chested, boyish look was popular; breasts stayed flat, along with rear ends, for the slinky, "drop-dead" evening gowns of the 1930s. The derriere eclipsed the bust in the 1940s, as shown in the famous wartime pinup picture of Betty Grable. But the presence of pinup Rita Hayworth's lace-clad *poitrine* and buxom Jane Russell's cantilevered bra, designed by Howard Hughes and worn by her in Hughes's 1943 film, *The Outlaw,* proved that breasts were not entirely forgotten during the era. In the 1950s and early 1960s, the years of the feminine mystique, big breasts in push-up bras were the ne plus ultra of female allure. In a feminist reaction against the bra as harness, some young women of the late 1960s and early 1970s burned their bras to symbolize female liberation, while other women elected simply to let their breasts swing unencumbered. The late 1960s also saw a trend toward less structured bras, characterized by designer Rudi Gernreich's "no-bra bra." The 1980s and 1990s saw bras suitable for every woman's shape and activity, including the highly touted "WonderBra," guaranteed to provide cleavage to the smallest bosom. Toward the end of the century, form often replaced function as women, ever dissatisfied with the shape of their bodies, took too seriously the incessant, hyped-up, Hollywoodized image of the perfect pair of breasts—big and firm. The message that bigger is better, especially when the image is marketed for maximum titillation in expensive satiny bras, has not provided the vast majority of women with what they need and should crave most—healthy breasts in a healthy body.

Mother's Day Becomes a National Holiday

By and large, mothers and housewives are the only workers who do
not have regular time off. They are the great vacationless class.
                          Anne Morrow Lindbergh, *Gift From the Sea*, 1955

The realistic depiction of the stay-at-home mother of the 1950s offered
by Anne Morrow Lindbergh contrasts sharply with the era's illusory
notion that women could ask for no greater reward than to spend every
waking hour happily engaged in the sanctified task of mothering their
children (and, in many cases, their husbands as well). The postwar doctrine of what has been called the "feminine mystique," after the title of
Betty Friedan's 1963 book, was in some measure a throwback to an era
early in the century when the image of the beatific, soothing mother in
her gently rustling skirts had mythical, not to say religious, significance.
It was during that so-called simpler time of middle-class family cohesion and virtuous womanhood that a day was officially set aside to annually honor mothers and motherhood.

Although a precedent for a mother's day existed in the medieval English observance of a Mothering Sunday, held on the fourth Sunday in
Lent, the modern evolution of the holiday began in the United States in
1890, when Mary T. Sasseen of Kentucky suggested to a gathering of
teachers that annual homage be paid to mothers every April 20, her own
mother's birthday. Her suggestion was not met with enthusiasm. Two
years later Universalist Baltimore Sunday school teacher Robert Cummins proposed an annual memorial service in honor of Emily Pullman,
the mother of the church pastor as well as the mother of the inventor of
the Pullman sleeping car. Cummins suggested that the service be held
on the Sunday closest to May 22, the date of Mrs. Pullman's death. The
service, which eventually became dedicated to all mothers worldwide,
was repeated for many years, but only at the Baltimore church. In 1902
Fred E. Hering of Indiana appealed to the Fraternal Order of Eagles to
support a national observance dedicated to mothers, but the members of
the brotherhood did not show interest in his proposal.

Credit for successfully establishing the national and international
observance of Mother's Day belongs to Anna May Jarvis (1864–1948), a
schoolteacher, a suffrage-temperance worker, and an unmarried woman
without children. After attending the Female Seminary in her home-

Anna May Jarvis, whose devotion to her own mother and belief in the "beauty, truth, and fidelity of mother love" eventually led to the establishment of Mother's Day as a national day of observance *Library of Congress*

town of Grafton, West Virginia, and Mary Baldwin College in Stanton, Virginia, Jarvis returned to Grafton to teach school. However, her real career was looking after her mother, a deeply religious woman to whom she was completely devoted. After the death of her father in 1902, Jarvis and her mother went to live with relatives in Philadelphia; three years later, on May 9, Mrs. Jarvis died, leaving her daughter grief-stricken and consumed with guilt for all the things she felt she should have done for her mother. For the next two years Jarvis brooded over her loss and at the same time reflected on the thoughtless and neglectful behavior of grown children toward their mothers. In 1907, on the anniversary of her mother's death, Jarvis invited a group of friends to her Philadelphia home to announce her idea for an annual nationwide celebration honoring mothers. This time, the proposal for a Mother's Day elicited unanimous support. One of Jarvis's friends, clothing merchant John Wanamaker, offered financial backing.

On May 10, 1908, at Anna Jarvis's instigation, simultaneous Mother's Day services were held in Philadelphia and at the Andrews Methodist Church in Grafton, where Jarvis's mother had taught Sunday school for twenty years. At the conclusion of the Grafton service, Jarvis handed each mother a white carnation, her mother's favorite flower. Jarvis promoted the white carnation as the symbol of Mother's Day because she felt the flower typified "the beauty, truth, and fidelity of mother love." Following these memorial services, Jarvis began what has been called one of the most successful one-person letter-writing campaigns in history. She sent hundreds of letters proposing an official Mother's Day observance to congressmen, governors, mayors, newspaper editors, ministers, and influential business leaders throughout the United States. By

1911 every state in the nation had proclaimed official Mother's Day holidays. In 1914 both houses of the U.S. Congress passed resolutions requesting the president to proclaim Mother's Day a national day of observance. On May 9, 1914, President Woodrow Wilson issued a proclamation directing "government officials to display the U.S. flag at their homes or other suitable places on the second Sunday in May as a public expression of our love and reverence for the mothers of our country." It is interesting to note that at the same time Wilson was publicly encouraging expressions of love and reverence for mothers, suffragists were unsuccessfully appealing to him to support their crusade to gain the vote for women. Wilson, who dismissed the question of woman suffrage as "not a problem that is dealt with by the national government at all," failed to perceive that mothers would benefit more substantially from obtaining the right to vote than from an annual gesture of recognition.

The larger historical and political picture notwithstanding, Mother's Day became a popular holiday in the United States and was soon observed in Canada, Mexico, parts of South America, and Japan as well. But what had been a triumph for Anna Jarvis became a source of bitterness and disillusionment. After a disastrous love affair, she vowed not to marry and spent her days nursing a blind sister, attending Sunday school conventions, and supervising the observance of her holiday. She lived to see what she had meant to be a religious observance slowly become a secular and commercial holiday exploited by florists, greeting card companies, candy manufacturers, and department stores, gift shops, and restaurants. Jarvis initiated lawsuits against companies seeking to profit from Mother's Day, but her suits failed, and within a short time she had exhausted her savings and lost her family home. Her sister died, and Jarvis lost her sight and her hearing. Ailing and penniless, she was placed in a private sanitarium, where she was supported by friends until her death in 1948 at the age of eighty-four.

In the decades since Anna Jarvis established Mother's Day, the observance has been both a joyous occasion during which families celebrate their maternal parent and a burden that serves to remind some offspring of conflicts with their mothers. Throughout the century, social and individual attitudes toward motherhood itself have fluctuated. The romantic image of the powerful, benign mother, popular during Anna Jarvis's time, gave way to an awareness, culled from Freud and reinforced by early feminism and the entry of greater numbers of women into the labor market, that the concept of motherly perfection was pure myth. In 1942 Philip Wylie published his sensational and notorious best-seller, *Generation of Vipers,* in which he brutally attacked what he perceived to be a pervasive cult of mother worship, or "momism." Wylie floridly observed, "Megaloid momworship has got completely out of hand. . . . The machine has deprived her of social usefulness; time has stripped away her biological possibilities and poured her hide full of liquid soap; and man has sealed his own soul beneath the clamorous cordillera by handing her the checkbook and going to work in the service of her caprices. . . . The mealy look of men today is the result of momism and so is the pinched and baffled fury in the eyes of womanhood."

During the 1950s *Generation of Vipers* often shared bookshelf space in middle-class households with Benjamin Spock's more benevolent *Common Sense Book of Baby and Child Care.* But if Dr. Spock offered positive reinforcement to mothers, self-described experts writing on family life in the 1950s often did not. These "experts" urged women to devote themselves completely to their children while at the same time agreeing with Wylie (and with his companions in misogyny, Marynia Farnham and Ferdinand Lundberg, authors of the 1947 best-seller *Modern Woman: The Lost Sex*) that mothers were the source of most of the nation's social and psychological disturbances. Sociologists and psychologists claimed that the task of preventing every social ill from juvenile delinquency to tooth decay belonged exclusively to mothers. It is no wonder that womankind was baffled and furious.

The more assertive daughters of the baby boom, many of whom are working mothers, have been confronted with their own group of "experts" offering both support and censure for the choices they have made regarding motherhood and the ways in which they are raising their children. But middle-class mothers in the last two decades of the twentieth century have also benefited by the greater presence of fathers in the parenting equation. The current emphasis on the importance of family life, together with an evolving consciousness that women are individuals and not merely gender objects, has helped to raise the status of mothering—a cause for celebration on Mother's Day as well as every day of the year.

Vogue Becomes the Leading Fashion Magazine

The best way to familiarize oneself with smart fashion is to have a speaking acquaintance with it—or at least a bowing acquaintance. If a young woman happens to have a social position that brings her naturally into touch with people of taste and places of fashion, her role is much easier. If she hasn't, she should avail herself of every opportunity to observe the current mode correctly worn. She should lunch, occasionally, at a fashionable restaurant, even if she can't order anything but a poached egg. She should go to first nights at the theater, to the opera, to the races, and study the snapshots of the mode.

Edna Woolman Chase, Always in Vogue, 1954

Edna Woolman Chase's demurely phrased advice on how to become a woman of fashion seems a quaint relic of a time when the attainment of a fashionable life meant striving for a place in the haute bourgeoisie and beyond. But Woolman Chase was to an extent only echoing the philosophy of the socialite founders of *Vogue*, Arthur B. Ternure and Harry W. McVickar, who conceived of the magazine in 1892 as the "dignified, authentic journal of society, fashion and the ceremonial side of life." A competitor for *Harper's Bazar* (changed to *Bazaar* after the magazine was purchased by William Randolph Hearst in 1913), *Vogue* has always been, as former editor Grace Mirabella asserts in her memoir, *In and Out of Vogue*, "about the best of everything—the best clothes, the best parties, the 'best people.'"

Despite early financial backing and ongoing consumer support from New York's wealthy elite, *Vogue* was an unprofitable venture until 1909, when it was bought by Condé Nast, the former advertising manager of *Collier's* magazine. The entrepreneurial Nast, who would go on to found the celebrity-focused *Vanity Fair* magazine in 1913, was determined to strengthen the status of *Vogue* as a "class publication," one that maintained a loyal following among America's upper class. Nast's publishing philosophy rested upon the now familiar but then revolutionary idea, writes Mirabella, that "the best way to attract advertising was not to push endlessly to boost circulation, which was costly, but to guarantee advertisers a readership eager for their products by narrowing the target circulation and tailoring the magazine in such a way that its readers would correspond demographically and exclusively to the profile of that advertiser's customers." As Nast wrote in a 1913 essay on class publications, "The publisher, the editor, the advertising manager and the circulation man must conspire not only to get *all* their readers from one particular class to which the magazine is dedicated, *but rigorously to exclude all others*." Nast contributed to the development of the special cachet of *Vogue* by recruiting his staff from among New York's social elite, frequently hiring editors at cocktail parties.

Suggestions for The Hostess

VOGUE

July 15th 1916
Price 25 Cents

The Vogue Company
CONDE NAST, Publisher

A 1916 cover drawn by Helen Dryden, who created many
covers and editorial illustrations for *Vogue*. The magazine's first
photographic cover appeared in 1932 and was the work of
Edward Steichen.

The magazine's often gadfly group of stylish, upper-crust editors was
presided over from 1914 to 1952 by the unflappable Edna Woolman
Chase, its first editor in chief. Chase was a New Jersey native and a
descendant of Quaker settlers, who began working in the circulation
department of *Vogue* in 1895, when she was eighteen. A small woman
who dressed conservatively and whose behavior typified the somewhat
repressive dignity and refinement peculiar to upper-class women born in
the previous century, Chase, writes Mirabella, "upheld everything about
Vogue that was exclusive, aristocratic, and grand." Chase's tenure at *Vogue*
coincided with the heyday of French couture and such fashion designers
as Paul Poiret, Coco Chanel, Jean Patou, Elsa Schiaparelli, Cristóbal
Balenciaga, and Christian Dior.

Vogue may have been the preeminent couture-focused magazine, but by the end of the 1930s it and its stylish sister, *Harper's Bazaar,* were not the only fashion magazines. *Mademoiselle* and *Glamour,* founded in the Depression years of 1934 and 1939, respectively, had arrived to reach a new demographic force: working women. Except for a few accounts of the financial woes of wealthy friends, there is remarkably little discussion of the Great Depression in Edna Woolman Chase's memoir; the magazine, like many of its readers, seems to have remained largely unaffected by the event. World War II, however, was an event even *Vogue* could not ignore, especially since it depleted the magazine's staff. Chase and Jessica Daves, who would succeed Chase as editor in 1952, soldiered on and felt, Chase writes, that "we were making a good wartime product, a class magazine keyed to the new conditions, and judging from the circulation figures, which were the highest in our history, the public thought so too."

By publishing photos of such war-related nonfashion scenes as London during the blitz and concentration camps, *Vogue* began to broaden its appeal, but it was the rise of ready-to-wear clothing and sportswear and the emergence of the American fashion designer after the war that eased the magazine toward the democratization Condé Nast had so strongly resisted. "The 1950s in American fashion," writes Mirabella, "were about breaking down barriers . . . about bridging the gap between the hundred or so women who could afford to buy at the couture and the vast numbers who had no access to high-quality design at all. Through mass production, ready-to-wear democratized access. Yet unlike Levittown, it also did so with style." The increased buying power of middle-class women in the postwar boom years was a reality that fashion magazines like *Vogue* could not ignore; fortunately, even in the dowdy 1950s, ready-to-wear was often expensive enough to stand comparison with couture clothing in the pages of *Vogue.*

Vogue during the hip 1960s operated under the flamboyant editorship of Diana Vreeland, a fashion legend and astute image maker, who raised glamour and well-groomed exotica to a high art by producing shoots that created fanciful black-and-white and four-color fashion worlds. Vreeland, whose widely reported sayings included "Never fear being vulgar, just boring" and "People who eat white bread have no dreams," disdained, writes Mirabella, "what she thought of as uninspired 'cookie cutter' clothes. Instead of trying to better them, she took them to their extreme—or ignored them. And she lived in the realm of fantasy, with no idea of—or interest in—the lives of real, earthbound women. And those women, unacknowledged by her and her colleagues in the 1960s, had turned their backs on fashion. They had also turned their backs on fashion magazines."

Chosen to succeed Vreeland in 1971, Grace Mirabella endeavored to bring *Vogue* into step with the liberated woman of the 1970s, adding text, interviews, arts coverage, and serious health pieces to the magazine's usual menu of couture and ready-to-wear fashion features. "What was once a magazine for society women had become a magazine for all women who wanted a little style in their lives," writes Mirabella. But despite a circulation that had grown during her editorship from 400,000 to 1.2 million, Mirabella was replaced as *Vogue* editor in 1988 by the younger Anna Wintour, former editor of British *Vogue*. Wintour's revamping of *Vogue* to appeal to a younger, well-heeled readership seems to have had little effect on the magazine's American circulation, which in 1996 was reported at slightly less than 1.2 million.

In the 1990s the traditional, family-centered women's magazines such as *Family Circle, Good Housekeeping, Ladies' Home Journal,* and *Redbook* edged out the fashion magazines with circulations in excess of 2.5 million. The only fashion- and issues-oriented magazine that boasted nearly as many readers was the almost thirty-five-year-old standard-bearer for single women, *Cosmopolitan*. But in adapting to changing times, the domestic and the fashion magazines had begun to blur their distinctions in several ways: both featured attractive, well-dressed (in *Cosmopolitan*'s case, half-dressed) models or celebrities on their covers as well as articles on relationships, sex, fitness, health, work issues, and the arts. The domestic women's magazines included fashion and beauty spreads; the fashion magazines have occasionally acknowledged the state of motherhood. This blending of style and substance can be seen in a positive light as a recognition of the diverse lives American women lead. However, women's magazines have also created a false sense of intimacy with their readers. The magazines send their message that readers' concerns are *their* concerns, yet articles on such topics as sex, health, and relationships are rarely researched in enough depth to provide for a complete picture and can confuse as well as enlighten. Ultimately, the majority of issues-oriented articles in women's magazines have contained about as much substance as the magazines' fashion and beauty pages. For both the domestic and fashion magazines, the "mode," as Edna Woolman Chase called fashion, has remained the message.

The Woman's Peace Party Is Founded

We revolted not only against the cruelty and barbarity of war, but even more against the reversal of human relationships which war implied. We protested against the "curbed intelligence" and the "thwarted good will," when both a free mind and unfettered kindliness are so sadly needed in human affairs. In the light of the charge made later that pacifists were indifferent to the claims of justice, it is interesting to recall that we thus early emphasized the fact that a sense of justice had become the keynote to the best political and social activity in this generation, but we also believed that justice between men or between nations can be achieved only through understanding and fellowship, and that a finely tempered sense of justice, which alone is of any service in modern civilization, cannot possibly be secured in the storm and stress of war.

Jane Addams, *Peace and Bread in Time of War*

The outbreak of World War I, in August 1914, delayed any resolution to the woman suffrage question in Britain and gave suffragists in Europe and America a new reason to challenge male-dominated public policy. During the years prior to World War I, most of the American social reformers who founded the Woman's Peace Party (WPP) saw a connection between violent imperialism abroad and social violence at home. In 1912 Woman's Peace Party member Lucia Ames Mead wrote in *Swords Into Plowshares* that it was "no mere coincidence that race hatred and civic corruption have had such a recrudescence among us since we have become imperialistic in our foreign policy." Most anti-imperialist women reformers were not active in the prewar peace movement, however. Committed to positive action, they regarded the traditional peace organizations as too stuffy and genteel to be effective.

In November 1914 English suffragist and Women's Social and Political Union (WSPU) member Emmeline Pethick-Lawrence gave a speech at a mass meeting of the Women's Political Union in New York City in which she called for a worldwide "women's war against war." Imprisoned in England's Holloway jail for her militant suffragism, she had been on a hunger strike and had been brutally force-fed. Pethick-Lawrence declared that it was time for the peace movement to learn from the suffrage movement and characterized the established peace organizations as "passive and negative." It was time, Pethick-Lawrence maintained, for women to be angry and act angry, "active and militant."

After hearing Pethick-Lawrence's speech, Crystal Eastman, a radical lawyer known for her work in fair labor practices and workmen's compensation, formed a committee called the Woman's Peace Party of New York. In December 1914, after Pethick-Lawrence spoke in Chicago, the Chicago Emergency Federation of Peace Forces was formed, with Jane Addams as chair. Also on hand in Chicago was Hungarian suffragist and pacifist Rosika Schwimmer, who, with suffrage leader Carrie Chapman Catt, had met with Secretary of State William Jennings Bryan and President Woodrow Wilson in September in an unsuccessful attempt to persuade the United States to mediate in the European conflict. Schwimmer, Catt, Addams, and other antiwar activists and pacifists called for a national conference of women's organizations to be held in Washington, D.C., in January 1915. The national Woman's Peace Party emerged out of the Washington conference, which was attended by over three thousand women. The following month Dutch suffrage leader Dr. Aletta Jacobs invited the members of the Woman's Peace Party to attend an International Conference of Women at The Hague from April 28 to May 1. The conference was attended by some 2,400 delegates and included Jane Addams; Wellesley professor, Boston city planner, and Quaker pacifist Emily Greene Balch (who would go on to win the Nobel Peace Prize in 1946); peace activist Fannie Fern Andrews; and Emmeline Pethick-Lawrence. Carrie Chapman Catt chaired the initial meeting to create a platform for the "mother half of humanity," and the conference endorsed a plan devised by Rosika Schwimmer and Canadian college English instructor Julia Grace Wales for neutral mediation in the European war. The conference led to the establishment of the International Committee of Women for Permanent Peace. The Woman's Peace Party was designated the American arm of this committee.

Until the United States entered the war in 1917, the platform of the Woman's Peace Party dovetailed neatly with the suffrage movement. Party members insisted that the equality of women was essential to peace and declared that it was time "for men to stand down and for the women whom they have belittled to take the seat of judgment." Citing the connection between male militant policies and the oppression of women, Grace Colbron wrote in *The Woman Voter* that "the military state is the state in which a woman has no place; the military mind is the mind that sees in women only a drudge or toy, and gives her the one right only to existence—the possibility of bearing sons who will in time become soldiers. . . ." It is, Colbron argued, the "spirit of militarism" that has been responsible for keeping women "in political, legal and economic bondage throughout the ages. . . ." The preamble and platform of the Woman's Peace Party, adopted on January 10, 1915, made the connection even clearer: "We demand that . . . women be given a share in deciding between war and peace in all the courts of high debate—within the home, the school, the church, the industrial order, and the state. . . ." The party platform went on to call upon "all civilized nations" to reinforce democracy by "admitting the mother half of the human race to articulate citizenship."

The Woman's Peace Party, riding the wave of antiwar sentiment that pervaded the United States directly after the outbreak of war in Europe, soon had twenty-five thousand members. By 1915 disputes between the United States and Germany and Great Britain over wartime incidents on the high seas and commerce resulted in a campaign of preparedness on the part of the American government. This campaign intensified after the sinking of the *Lusitania* in May. Alarmed by the ambitious naval building program announced by Secretary of the Navy Josephus Daniels, the Woman's Peace Party sent a letter of protest to President Wilson. While admitting the necessity of "real preparedness against real dangers," the letter took issue with what the party perceived as a "preposterous preparedness against hypothetical dangers" and went on to warn that such militaristic behavior "would tend to disqualify our National Executive from rendering the epochal service which this world crisis offers for the establishment of permanent peace." The letter, which cleverly echoed Wilson's thoughts in several earlier public messages regarding the U.S. role in the war, appealed so strongly to antiwar ex–Secretary of State William Jennings Bryan that he published it in *The Commoner* magazine. Wilson, who had seemed a champion of antipreparedness, shifted his position after receiving the letter from the Woman's Peace Party. His adoption of a preparedness program was attacked by members of the Woman's Peace Party and especially by Crystal Eastman of the New York City branch. After the party realized that attempts to mediate in the war had failed and concentrated its efforts on an antipreparedness campaign, the New York City branch became the party's most aggressive crusaders. Eastman—who was credited, as one party member put it, with having "built the peace party up from a polite society affair into an active democratic decisive organization"—and her group were criticized for inflammatory rhetoric and for such radical behavior as featuring a large dragon representing the war machine to mock munitions manufacturers in a "War against War" exhibit.

The Woman's Peace Party had an ally in government—Jeanette

Rankin, the first woman elected to the House of Representatives and a pacifist, who cast her vote against the U.S. declaration of war in 1917. But even the deeply felt pacifism of Rankin and such party leaders as Jane Addams and Florence Kelley could not sustain a large membership or claim cohesion for the organization after the entry of the United States into the war. Carrie Chapman Catt, once active in the Woman's Peace Party, decided that the suffrage movement could not politically risk a stance of opposition to the war and instructed members of the National American Woman Suffrage Association (NAWSA) to work on behalf of both the war effort and suffrage. Some of the party's founders quit in the belief that any wartime interest in peace was dangerous, not to say treasonous. Florence Kelley resigned from the party after accepting an appointment as secretary of the Board of Control of army contracts for soldiers' clothing. Jane Addams was the party leader most tarred by the brush of pacifism, despite her work with selective service registration programs (for which she received a military citation) and in Herbert Hoover's Food Administration civilian relief programs. Addams and most of the members of the party's national board were added to the U.S. Military Intelligence Service lists of "those who did not help us win the war." Addams, once dubbed by the press as "the only American saint," was particularly singled out for vilification after she pleaded for food

An anti-preparedness exhibit by the Woman's Peace Party of New York, circa 1915. Crystal Eastman is on the far right. *Papers of Lella Secor Florence, Swarthmore College Peace Collection*

The 1919 WILPF conference in Zurich. Seated in the front row are Jeanette Rankin (*fourth from left*), Jane Addams (*sixth from left*), and Emily Greene Balch (*eighth from left*). *Records of the WILPF, Swarthmore College Peace Collection*

relief for German children and defended the rights of those arrested during the postwar Red scare.

Jane Addams and other prominent pacifists and members of the Woman's Peace Party refused to allow any thinly veiled allegations of treasonous behavior to deflect them from their purpose. In 1919 a delegation of party and former party members, which included Addams, Florence Kelley, Jeanette Rankin, Lillian Wald of the Henry Street Settlement, Emily Greene Balch (who had been denied renewal of her appointment at Wellesley because of questions about her "patriotism"), and Dr. Alice Hamilton, attended the congress of the International Committee of Women for Permanent Peace (ICWPP) in Zurich, Switzerland. During the congress, the WPP and ICWPP re-formed into the Women's International League for Peace and Freedom (WILPF), with Jane Addams as president and Emily Greene Balch as secretary-treasurer. The WILPF became the first organization to protest the punitive Treaty of Versailles and introduced a resolution by Jeanette Rankin and Ethel Snowden of England, which expressed "deep regret that the terms of peace proposed at Versailles should so seriously violate the principles upon which alone a just and lasting peace can be secured," and went on to read in part: "By guaranteeing the fruits of the secret treaties to the conquerors the terms tacitly sanction secret diplomacy. They deny the principle of self-determination, recognize the right of the victors to the spoils of war, and create all over Europe discords and animosities, which can lead only to future wars." The league could not have been more correct in its assessment of what the future held in store for Europe and the United States.

After World War II the WILPF was among the first to protest the cold war policies of the Truman Doctrine, which it insisted threatened peace far more than it supported freedom. The league also opposed the establishment of NATO, worked on behalf of the civil rights movement, especially regarding passage of the Wagner-Garagan Anti-Lynching Bill, and has worked to secure civil liberties for pacifists and war protesters. In 1961, during the height of the nuclear arms race, a sister organization, the Women's Strike for Peace, was formed. The Women's Strike for Peace, which today includes some ten thousand members, was particularly demonstrative in its opposition to the U.S. war in Vietnam.

Building on the principles established by the Woman's Peace Party, the Women's International League for Peace and Freedom has remained committed, writes historian Blanche Wiesen Cook, "to its basic assumption that peace and freedom are inseparable and that permanent peace will not be achieved until economic equality, political freedom, and social justice are insured."

1916

The First Birth Control Clinic Opens
in Brooklyn, New York

Please tell me what to do to keep from having any more babies. I
am only twenty-six years old and the mother of five children. . . .
The last time I had a six months' miscarriage and I have been weak
ever since. . . . My husband is gone to try to find work and I have to
support my children myself. I have to work so hard until I feel like
it would kill me to give birth to another. . . . I am not able to give
my children the attention that I desire. I take in washing to support
my children, I suffered this last time from the time I got that way
until I lost it and am yet weak in my back. Please! for my sake tell
me what to do to keep from having another. I don't want another
child. Five is enough for me.

Letter to Margaret Sanger, quoted in Motherhood in Bondage

The desperate situation voiced by the woman quoted above and in
letters from many women like her stands in marked contrast with the
experience of women today, who take for granted their legal and
socially sanctioned right to use birth control and to obtain contraceptives and information on contraception. In the early years of the twentieth century, no such right or sanction existed in most states of the
Union.

The prohibition against birth control began in the late nineteenth
century as a campaign by social reform groups such as the Women's
Christian Temperance Union (WCTU) and the Young Women's Christian Association (YWCA) to bring "social purity" to the nation. Although
these groups encouraged public and open discussion of social problems
like prostitution and venereal disease, they remained puritanical on the
subject of birth control, which they viewed as a means of freeing men to
pursue their supposedly greater sexual urges outside marriage. The

anti–birth control forces passed the Comstock Law, named after its chief instigator, the zealous antivice crusader Anthony Comstock. The law forbade the dissemination of pornography, abortion devices, and "any drug, medicine, article, or thing designed, adapted, or intended for preventing conception." Conveniently aided by the broad description contained in the Comstock statute, most states thereafter passed their own version of the law.

The antivice social reformers viewed the Comstock Law as protective legislation for women, but the reality was quite different. Although middle-class and working-class women alike suffered from the bar on the sale or distribution of birth control information and devices, middle-class women, who were better educated in general and received more adequate health care, had some access to contraceptives. Working-class women, many of them immigrants, poorly educated, economically disadvantaged, bound to cultural and religious beliefs, and raised to believe that husbands should not be denied sex and that large families meant more wage earners, did not enjoy even limited privilege when it came to birth control and sex education. While midwives and visiting nurses sometimes assisted during births, and a physician might be called in dire cases, childbirth in the slums was a risky experience that all too often led to damage and death for both mother and baby. Denied information from the medical establishment on birth control and fearing contraception as well, many working-class women resorted to crude and often deadly methods of abortion to end their pregnancies. In her autobiography, birth control advocate Margaret Sanger illustrates the plight of poor women by citing the case of one twenty-eight-year-old woman she attended while working as a public health nurse on the Lower East Side of New York in the 1910s. The woman, who had three young children and whose husband earned a small wage as a truck driver, was seriously ill with an infection after self-inducing an abortion. During her recovery, she asked Sanger how she could prevent another pregnancy. Sanger in turn consulted the attending doctor, who suggested that the husband be told to "sleep on the roof." Three months later Sanger was called to the woman's home again, only to find her in a coma following another attempted self-induced abortion. The woman died ten minutes after Sanger's arrival.

The early decades of the century, a time of calls for social reform as well as an era in which socialism became an influential ideological force, featured several women reformers who were committed to defying the Comstock Law and to disseminating information on birth control. Antoinette Konikow, a Russian immigrant physician and founding member of the Socialist Party, was the first to focus on birth control in her articles on sex education for the Socialist daily newspaper the *New York Call.* The most outspoken and notorious proponent of birth control prior to World War I was the anarchist and free speech advocate Emma Goldman. A magnetic and domineering figure in radical social reform, Goldman was especially notorious for her belief in sexual relationships between men and women outside the bonds of marriage—what was then referred to as the practice of "free love." Goldman understood that without effective birth control, women could not gain control over their bodies and enjoy true sexual freedom. Her experiences as a midwife had also exposed her to the same desperate situations among the poor regarding pregnancy as Margaret Sanger. Goldman believed that birth control, which she defined as "largely a working-man's question, above all a working-women's question," would provide poor women with a safe alternative to abortion and free them from domination by and dependence on men. When Goldman was jailed for lecturing on birth control and for giving the first public demonstration of contraceptives, a reporter wrote that she had been arrested for "saying that women need not always keep their mouths shut and their wombs open."

Emma Goldman was an extremely influential force on other women radicals, as a role model and an explicator of the new morality. One woman who was strongly influenced by Goldman was Margaret Sanger, the reformer most strongly associated with the birth control movement in the United States. Sanger, who was involved with the Socialist Party and wrote articles on sex education for the *New York Call*, believed with Goldman that female liberation began with a woman's control of her body and that birth control was a free-speech issue. But Sanger also became convinced that limiting family size, especially among the poor, was a necessary step in social progress. In 1914 she founded the magazine the *Woman Rebel* (in which she introduced the term "birth control") to give contraceptive information to working-class women, to discuss problems of women's sexual liberation, and to catalog all the injustices created by the capitalist system. The magazine lasted for seven issues until it was declared by the post office to be obscene and therefore unmailable. Sanger's next written effort, *Family Limitation*, was a detailed birth control pamphlet that not only recommended and explained a variety of contraceptive methods, including douches, condoms, pessaries (a precursor to the diaphragm), sponges, and vaginal suppositories, but also defended a woman's right to abortion. After being arrested for violation of the Comstock Law, Sanger fled to England, where she found a new mentor (and lover) in the scientist and sexologist Havelock Ellis. Ellis trained Sanger in methods of medical research to find advanced contraceptive techniques and sent her to Holland, where the Mensinga

Margaret Sanger (*left*) and Ethel
Byrne inside the courtroom where
they were tried and convicted of
dispensing "obscene" materials at
their birth control clinic   *Used by
permission of the Planned Parenthood
Federation of America.*

diaphragm was dispensed in
state-run birth control clinics.
Sanger was impressed by the
Dutch use of the diaphragm,
which had cut the maternal
death rate in half, and realized
that the safe and effective
device could save lives in the
United States by helping
women to space out their pregnancies over a period of several
years. The diaphragm was also
viewed by Sanger as the ideal
contraceptive because, unlike
condoms, it gave women control over contraception.

When Sanger returned to
New York in 1916, she took the
next step in her campaign to
provide women with birth con-

trol information and contraceptives by opening a birth control clinic in
Brooklyn. The clinic, staffed by Sanger, her sister, Mrs. Ethel Byrne,
and a friend who spoke Yiddish, dispensed diaphragms, birth control
advice, and copies of an article titled "What Every Girl Should Know."
After ten days of operation, the clinic, already visited by five hundred
women, was shut down by the New York City Police Department, and
Sanger and Byrne were indicted for dispensing "obscene" materials.
Ethel Byrne, who was tried first, found guilty, and sentenced to thirty
days in jail, went on a hunger strike that lasted for nearly a week and,
owing to Sanger's untiring press agentry, was highly publicized in the
newspapers. Public outcry over the injustice of Ethel Byrne's treatment
and the help of the birth control movement's new socially prominent
supporters eventually resulted in a governor's pardon for Margaret
Sanger's sister. After Mrs. Byrne's release, Sanger was tried and convicted and served her thirty days without protest.

After her release from prison, Sanger campaigned for doctor-staffed birth control clinics and began publishing the *Birth Control Review*. In 1921 Sanger and Mary Ware Dennet founded the American Birth Control League, which later became the Planned Parenthood Federation of America. Two years later the league established the first doctor-staffed birth control clinic in the United States. The Clinical Research Bureau (CRB), under the direction first of Dr. Dorothy Bocker and later of Dr. Hannah Stone, benefited from a small but important legal provision of the 1918 New York obscenity law. The New York Court of Appeals had ruled that only licensed physicians, and not nurses, could prescribe or provide information on contraceptives exclusively for the purpose of curing or preventing venereal disease. Since the law did not refer specifically to condoms, the contraceptive the lawmakers had in mind, a liberal interpretation theoretically allowed for the dispensing of diaphragms in cases where a woman's health was at risk if she became pregnant. Federal law, however, banned the importation of contraceptive devices. Sanger and others in the movement were forced to smuggle diaphragms into the United States from abroad, which meant that only a relatively small number of women could take advantage of their use. In addition, many doctors continued to advocate abstinence as the only moral and reliable form of contraception.

During the 1920s Sanger and her colleagues worked to amend obscenity laws so that doctors could prescribe contraception for healthy as well as sick women. She also solicited the support of progressive reformers, such as woman suffrage campaigner Carrie Chapman Catt, feminist writer Charlotte Perkins Gilman, and Jane Addams. Ever single-minded, Sanger claimed to Catt that the legalization of birth control was the next logical campaign for suffragists, who had won the vote for women in 1920. Catt wrote to Sanger that her reform movement was "too narrow to appeal to me" and went on to describe the sexual freedom offered by birth control as a perpetuation of a society based on male superiority and standards, rather than a society in which men emulated the moral virtues of women. "A million years of male control over the sustenance of women," wrote Catt, "has made them sex slaves, which has produced two results: an oversexualizing of women and an oversexualizing of men." Catt further argued that any social gains provided by birth control would result in "some increase in immorality through safety." Charlotte Perkins Gilman, who favored the wife-as-mother model over the promising but to some feminists unrealistic model of the wife-companion, took a similar view. Jane Addams believed with Catt that the mission of women, ideally virtuous and nonsexual, was to curb and refine the unrestrained appetites of men and flatly refused to support the birth control movement. The opinions of such prominent social reformers as Carrie Chapman Catt, Charlotte Perkins Gilman, and Jane Addams regarding the birth control movement serves to remind us that feminism has never represented a single ideology or agenda that fits all women who have through the decades claimed to be feminists but is, rather, a belief system that is open to and greatly benefits by individual interpretation.

Margaret Sanger had begun her crusade to legalize birth control by arguing that working-class women could use contraception as a weapon against an oppressive system. But by the 1920s, as working-class women failed to respond to her message because of modesty or cultural and religious beliefs, she began to gravitate toward the more receptive middle class. At the same time, she allied herself with the eugenics movement and preached contraception as a means for the dominant classes to regulate society by controlling the reproduction of the "unfit." Sanger later dissociated herself from the eugenics movement, but criticism for her involvement in it nevertheless served to somewhat tarnish her image. However, it is a fact that Sanger's tireless efforts—and the efforts of like-minded reformers—on behalf of legal birth control eventually benefited women of all classes. The Comstock Law was liberalized in 1929, and in 1936 a U.S. Circuit Court of Appeals, in a case brought before it by Dr. Hannah Stone, ruled that physicians could dispense contraceptives "for the purpose of saving life or promoting the well-being of their patients." In 1965, the year before Margaret Sanger's death, the United States Supreme Court struck down the last remaining state law prohibiting the private use of contraceptives. By then the birth control pill and an IUD prototype had joined the diaphragm as viable forms of contraception for women. Over the horizon was the most intense battle for reproductive rights women would ever wage—the fight to legalize abortion.

Jeanette Rankin Becomes the First Woman Elected to the U.S. Congress

We're half the people; we should be half the Congress.

Jeanette Rankin, calling for more women in public office,
quoted in *Newsweek*, February 14, 1966

Social bias against the participation of women in politics existed for centuries before Jeanette Rankin was elected to public office and was not challenged effectively until the women's liberation movement of the 1960s and 1970s. Women were socialized to believe the Aristotelian precept that politics was a realm in which the fundamentally immoral (though powerful) man strove for higher moral purpose. Women, already moral and pure (though without power), provided a refuge in the home from public life, a world considered unnatural and degrading to the "fairer sex." As Janet A. Flammang observes in *Women's Political Voice*, "Public persons (male property owners) were responsible, rational, and capable of achieving the highest good—participation in political life. Private persons (women and slaves) were not fully rational, were confined to lesser spheres of activity necessary to the operation of public life, and were capable of achieving goodness only in their inferior spheres and associations." The suffragists, feminists, and social reformers of the nineteenth and early twentieth century did not disagree with the concept of women's moral superiority; rather, they used it to argue for the inclusion of women in public life. It was in the climate of feminism and social reform that suffused the women's portion of the Progressive Era in the early years of the twentieth century that Jeanette Rankin came of age as a suffragist, pacifist, and politician.

Born near Missoula, Montana Territory, in 1880, Rankin was the oldest of seven children. Like many frontier women, Rankin's mother had been a schoolteacher before her marriage; her father was a successful rancher and lumber merchant. Raised in a close family atmosphere that combined upper-middle-class expectations with western informality, Jeanette Rankin and her sisters were able to take advantage of the numerous career opportunities offered to women because of the loose structure of frontier society. Rankin attended public schools in Missoula and in 1902 graduated with a BS in biology from the University of Montana. She taught briefly in country schools, served a short apprenticeship as a seamstress, and took in sewing until the death of her father in 1904. For the next four years Rankin assumed full responsibility for her younger brothers and sisters.

In 1908 Rankin left home to study at the New York School of Philanthropy. After practicing as a social worker for a brief time in Montana and Washington, she enrolled at the University of Washington, where she studied economics, sociology, and public speaking. In 1910 Rankin joined the successful Washington State suffrage campaign, an experience that helped convince her that peace initiatives should be incorporated into the suffrage movement. From 1911 to 1916 Rankin urged the Montana State Legislature to grant woman suffrage, worked for suffrage groups in New York, California, and Ohio, served as field secretary for the National American Woman Suffrage Association (NAWSA), and lob-

A portrait of Jeanette Rankin taken in 1917, the year the United States entered World War I. Rankin, a pacifist who had voted against United States entry into the war was inconsistently described by one journalist as both "a dagger in the hands of the German propagandists" and "a crying schoolgirl." *Library of Congress*

bied for suffrage in fifteen states. Rankin's frequent campaign trips to Montana helped to win the vote for women there in 1914.

In 1916 Rankin was elected to Congress on a progressive Republican platform that called for woman suffrage, protective legislation for children, tariff revision, Prohibition, and "preparedness that will make for peace." Although she was the first U.S. woman representative whose election represented a milestone not only for women, but for the nation in general, the popular press was more interested in Rankin's personal characteristics than in her legislative potential or accomplishments. When she arrived in Washington to take her seat, the reporters sent to interview her were told to ask her if she could make what was then considered the nation's national dessert—pie. The magazine the *Nation* described her appearance at the opening day of the Sixty-fifth Congress, reporting, writes Flammang, that she looked like "the typical woman from top to toe and paying special attention to her hair color and style, nose, chin, cheeks, jaw, small figure, and well-fitting garments with a V-shaped opening at the neck, sporting lace where a man would use flat linen stiff with starch." Journalistic emphasis on the feminine aspects of women in public office and how they got along with the men rather than interest in their work as elected representatives dogged female legislators until the 1960s, when journalists and political scientists began to collect biographical data on them and to interview them about their jobs.

Jeanette Rankin's politics would very soon garner more public attention than her appearance, however. In April 1917, four days after she had been introduced to Congress as its first woman member, Rankin, a member of the Woman's Peace Party (WPP), voted against United States entry into World War I. Contrary to popular belief, Rankin did not cast the only dissenting vote; forty-nine members of Congress voted with her. But as Rankin later remarked to a friend, none of the forty-nine men who voted against war suffered consequences for their action as she did. Publicly identified as a pacifist for the first time, Rankin was vilified by superpatriots and the press. The Helena, Montana, *Independent* described her as "a dagger in the hands of the German propagandists, a dupe of the Kaiser, a member of the Hun army in the United States, and a crying schoolgirl." She was denounced from the pulpit as a disgrace to womanhood and an example of how unsuited women were for the demands of public office. The jingoistic public response to Rankin's vote clearly illustrates the traditional view of women in regard to politics—the notion that women were not rational enough to engage in public life and should confine themselves to supporting the male power structure.

Rankin was also denounced by many suffragists, who felt that she had betrayed them. Carrie Chapman Catt feared that Rankin had imperiled passage of the suffrage amendment and wrote to a friend, "Whatever she has done or will do is wrong to somebody, and every time she answers a roll call she loses us a million votes." One influential suffragist leader who supported Rankin was Alice Paul, a founder of the Women's Party. Paul and Women's Party member Hazel Hunkins maintained that if political power were given to women, the possibilities of war would be diminished. But as Hannah Josephson observes in *Jeanette Rankin: First Lady in Congress:* "Both suffragist leaders proved to be wrong in the long run, Mrs. Catt for saying that Jeanette's vote had put the suffrage amendment back 'for years and years,' and Alice Paul for claiming that votes for women would make wars less likely." Rankin later said of her vote that "I knew we were asked to vote for a commercial war, that none of the idealistic hopes would be carried out, and I was aware of the falseness of much of the prowar propaganda." It was, she declared, "not only the most significant thing I ever did, it was a significant thing in itself."

Jeanette Rankin spent the remainder of her first term in Congress sponsoring protective legislation for women and children (such legislation would be passed in 1921 as the Sheppard-Towner Act) and continuing to work for passage of a federal suffrage amendment. After an unsuccessful bid for the Montana Republican senate seat, she continued in the race as a candidate of the newly founded National Party, a politically eclectic group of Non-Partisan League farmers, prowar Socialists, antiwar progressives, and Prohibitionists. After losing the election, Rankin finished her term in Congress and in 1919 traveled to Zurich as a delegate to the International Congress of Women, which became the Women's International League for Peace and Freedom (WILPF). For the next twenty years Rankin took on a variety of advocacy positions. She was on the board of the WILPF and served briefly as the league's field secretary, lobbied for passage of the Sheppard-Towner Act, and worked as a lobbyist for the Women's Peace Union and the National Council for the Prevention of War (NCPW). In 1940 Rankin won reelection to Congress, running as a Republican pacifist. Remaining true to her beliefs, she argued against lend-lease, the draft, military expenditures, and the repeal of the neutrality legislation of the 1930s, and the day after the Japanese attack on Pearl Harbor she cast the single vote against U.S. entry into World War II. Her lone stance in the House effectively destroyed any chance Rankin might have had for reelection in 1942. After her second term she traveled abroad, especially in India, to study pacifist methods and ideas. During the 1950s she quietly opposed U.S. cold war policies, including the nation's involvement in the Korean conflict. In the late 1960s Rankin once again entered the limelight when the Jeanette Rankin Brigade, a group comprising feminists, pacifists, rock musicians, students, and antiwar activists, was organized in 1967 to protest the war in Vietnam. As the brigade's leader, Rankin demonstrated with the group in Washington, D.C., on January 15, 1968, the date of the opening of the last session of Congress in President Lyndon Johnson's administration. Shortly afterward, Rankin, then eighty-eight, decided to run again for Congress, but failing health prevented her from mounting a campaign. She died in 1973 after a long life in which she consistently adhered to her political convictions, which is far more than can be said of most politicians past or present.

Other "firsts" in the history of women in politics followed Jeanette Rankin's milestone election in 1916. In 1924 Miriam "Ma" Ferguson of Texas was the first woman elected governor of a U.S. state. In 1933 Hattie Wyatt Caraway of Arkansas, after finishing out her late husband's term of office, became the first woman elected to the U.S. Senate. She was also the first woman to preside over Senate sessions, to conduct Senate hearings, to chair a Senate committee, and to be Senate president pro tem. The first African American woman elected to the House of Representatives was Shirley Chisholm of Brooklyn, New York, in 1968. In 1972 Chisolm also became the first African American to run for the presidency. That same year, Barbara Jordan of Texas was elected to Congress, becoming the first African American woman representative elected from a southern state. In 1984 Democratic congresswoman Geraldine Ferraro of New York became the first woman candidate for vice president on a major party ticket.

The presence of women in federal and state legislatures has fluctuated throughout the decades. At the federal level, the proportion of women in Congress increased in the 1920s, fell during the Depression years of the 1930s, rose in the 1950s, declined in the 1960s, and rose again in the 1970s with the women's movement. A similar pattern occurred in state legislatures. But the number of women elected to public office, especially at the federal level, remained relatively small until 1992, when an unprecedented number of women gained seats in the U.S. House of Representatives. Despite gains, women remain far from constituting half the Congress, as Jeanette Rankin insisted they should. It can only be hoped that future elections will even the balance.

1917–1918

World War I

Kaiser Wilson
Have You Forgotten Your Sympathy with the Poor Germans
Because They Were Not Self-Governed?

20,000,000 American Women Are Not Self-Governed

Take the Beam Out of Your Own Eye

Suffragist banner at the picketing of the White House, 1917

World War I presented both a challenge and an opportunity for the burgeoning women's movement in maintaining the momentum for women's franchise and the continuing struggle for equality. While America's hard-fought struggle to remain neutral kept the country safe from the devastating effects of total war that decimated Europe between 1914 and 1917, its eventual late entry into the Great War helped make an Allied victory possible and would cause the United States to emerge as an economic world power, initiating the so-called American Century. For women the Great War proved an unexpected ally, accelerating their acceptance into the workforce in jobs formerly restricted to men and their eventual winning of the ideological battle that insisted that one outcome of "the war to make the world safe for democracy" would be the vote for women.

For suffragists the war represented a crisis of conscience and a challenge to long-held moral principles. Peace had been an inextricable element, along with the franchise and equal rights, of most women's organizations. War was seen as a distinctly male malady that women's full representation in national life would help to cure. As early as 1869 Elizabeth Cady Stanton declared, "The male element is a destructive force, stern, selfish, aggrandizing, loving war, conquest, acquisition, breeding ... discord, disorder, disease, and death." Seemingly on the brink of their final victory, suffragists had to decide how to deal with a popular, patriotic war as the nation's overriding priority. Opposition risked alienation and confirmation that women were in fact not ready to assume full responsibility in national life; support violated principles and sidetracked momentum for suffrage. Carrie Chapman Catt, despite her activism in the Woman's Peace Party (WPP), asserted her leadership in the National American Woman Suffrage Association (NAWSA) to urge that the group should work for *both* the war effort and suffrage, fearing that the movement had too much to lose by opposing the war. Alice Paul, the leader of the Women's Party, with a large percentage of Quakers among its membership, refused to support the war or compromise in pursuit of suffrage, and the group, along with Socialists and radicals opposed to the war, would become early victims in an unprecedented abrogation of civil liberties during wartime. The women's movement was effectively split by the war into radical and moderate factions, leaving open the question whether the eventual passage of the Nineteenth Amendment is attributable to Catt's patriotic accommodations or Paul's opposition and the ensuing controversy over the government's treatment of the dissenters.

THE SUFFRAGE WATCHFIRE BEFORE THE WHITE HOUSE.

Three members of the Women's Party picket the White House during World War I. Growing patriotic fervor resulted in increasingly hostile and violent behavior on the part of onlookers and the eventual arrest of over two hundred picketers. *Library of Congress*

A young woman assembling gas masks for the Goodrich Rubber Company. The orginal caption declared that she was "thinking of her soldier sweetheart." *National Archives*

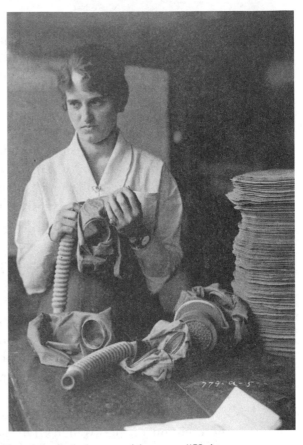

On January 10, 1917, the Women's Party began a picketing vigil outside the gates of the White House. These "silent sentinels," holding banners that asked "Mr. President, What Will You Do for Woman Suffrage?" and "How Long Must Women Wait for Liberty?" at first were ignored by the police, earned support from onlookers, and gained the attention of President Wilson, who courteously raised his hat to the picketers as he passed them. With America's entry into the war, the demonstration was increasingly seen as unpatriotic and even subversive, aggravated by banners that labeled the president as "Kaiser Wilson" and carried the slogan "Democracy Should Begin at Home." Onlookers grew increasingly hostile and violent, and on June 22 picketers began to be arrested on a charge of obstructing sidewalk traffic. Over two hundred women were arrested, with ninety-seven sent to the infamous Occaquan workhouse in Virginia, where guards cursed and beat the women prisoners at random. Alice Paul demanded to be classified as a political prisoner; when her request was refused she began a three-week hunger strike, during which she was force-fed. Unable to stop the outcry against such treatment or the cycle of picketing and additional arrests, the administration unconditionally released all the picketers in November. Several months later the U.S. Court of Appeals invalidated all the prison sentences and the original arrests.

Meanwhile, the National American Woman Suffrage Association dissociated itself from the picketers and fully and publicly entered the war effort. Members joined with other women across the country, knitting socks for the soldiers, canning food, selling Liberty Bonds, and adjusting family menus with "meatless," "wheatless," and "butterless" days. On October 27, 1917, the last great suffrage parade took place in New

York City, demonstrating the integration of the suffragists into the patriotic spirit of the day. Suffragists marched alongside women workers in industry and Red Cross nurses, symbolically asserting their responsibility in the national crisis and justifying their claims to the full rights of citizenship.

Women also earned increasing respect as they were recruited to take the place of men in the workforce who had enlisted or been drafted into the military. Though in smaller numbers than in World War II, women took jobs that had been exclusively the province of males before the war. Women worked in factories, oil refineries, and steel foundries, holding essential positions in explosive, armament, railway, automobile, and airplane production. Thousands of additional women were hired in textile mills to produce military uniforms. Female clerical workers were recruited to serve the growing government bureaucracy, particularly in the War Department. Although there was no dramatic change in the absolute numbers of women in the workforce during the war, the kinds of jobs women assumed challenged the conventional view that women were capable only of very limited kinds of work. Their efforts on behalf of a grateful nation also won warm praise and public acclaim, a debt that was an important factor in the government debate over the franchise for women.

One of the most important outcomes of women in the workforce was the creation of the Women's Division of the Ordnance Department, which regulated conditions of women workers in munitions and ordnance plants during World War I, a forerunner of the Women's Bureau of the Department of Labor, established in 1920. By the end of the war, government acknowledged that working women deserved the protection of labor laws, and the Women's Bureau has remained an essential lobbying arm for women workers in the fight for improved conditions and equality with male workers. Another important outcome of the war was the creation, in June 1917, of the American Women's Hospital Services, to offer an all-female medical force to circumvent government policy that prohibited women physicians from military service. All-female medical units of doctors, nurses, and ambulance drivers went to France to serve the civilian population, helped in the reconstruction of Europe after the armistice, and in the 1930s enhanced health care throughout Appalachia. The efforts of the American Women's Hospital Services would eventually help women doctors to be allowed in the military in 1943, although it would be another decade before women physicians were allowed to join the military with commissions and full rank.

It is clear that World War I helped redefine the role of women in

America, extending women's sphere of influence beyond the home and providing the final pressure, whether in patriotic support of the national will or in opposition to the slow pace of governmental accommodation, that finally won women the vote. Continuing opposition to suffrage would be futile in the face of women's persistent appeals and in their beneficial contribution to the war effort. In its alteration of the traditional women's role, the war would also help clarify the additional and ongoing struggle for equality that would persist after the vote had been won.

1919

The League of Women Voters Is Founded

The cultural emphasis on surface appearances, on competition, and on consumption helped to undermine the prewar reform agenda developed by a broad range of women's organizations and premised on female sensibility and the collective strength of women. . . . Suffragists seemed to recognize the changed context when they transformed the National American Woman Suffrage Association . . . into the League of Women Voters (LWV). They presumed that enfranchised women should be understood as individuals, citizens with a direct relationship to the state via the franchise. Their duty was to train women to be good citizens. . . .

Sara M. Evans, *Born for Liberty: A History of Women in America*

On March 24, 1919, the National American Woman Suffrage Association (NAWSA), founded in 1890 and presided over by Carrie Chapman Catt since 1900, convened for the last time. With passage of the Nineteenth Amendment virtually guaranteed, NAWSA had finally achieved its hard-won goal: securing the vote for women. At the meeting, Catt proposed the formation of a new organization, which she described as "a league of women voters . . . a league that shall be nonpartisan and non-sectarian in nature." Delegates at the meeting voted to name the organization the League of Women Voters (LWV). Because of her tireless efforts on behalf of the suffrage movement, Catt was elected the league's president for life, but the actual first-term president was another NAWSA leader, Maud Wood Park, who had worked for suffrage since before the turn of the century. Because the Nineteenth Amendment had not yet been ratified, Catt urged the newly formed LWV to continue to press for suffrage. She also felt the group needed to work toward eliminating any remaining legal discrimination against women. The league would also politically educate newly enfranchised women,

This poster from the League of Women Voters dramatizes the message that a woman's vote is a powerful force that can affect public policy as it moves from the ballot box directly to Capitol Hill. *Library of Congress*

study issues at all levels of government, and take positions on social issues.

During the 1920s the LWV supported voter registration drives and lobbied for a variety of protective legislation for women and children, including the Sheppard-Towner Act, which provided federal funding to help reduce maternal and infant mortality. The LWV lobbied for thirty-eight separate pieces of legislation but was successful only in aiding passage of Sheppard-Towner and the Cable Citizenship Act (1922), which guaranteed the independent citizenship of married women. Before the act was passed, women who had married noncitizens could lose their U.S. citizenship if their husbands were deported. The LWV also worked with a broad peace coalition formed in 1925 by Carrie Chapman Catt. Meeting as the first National Conference on the Cause and Cure of War, the coalition included the American Association of University Women, the General Federation of Women's Clubs, the YWCA, and the Woman's Christian Temperance Union. The LWV took on the jury system as well, lobbying on behalf of women jurors, a right denied to women since the colonial era. As late as 1961 the Supreme Court upheld the right of Alabama, Mississippi, and South Carolina to prohibit women from sitting on juries. The Court's decision was overturned in 1975.

The League of Women Voters had its roots in the social reform movements of the Progressive Era and so began as a group concerned with the rights and status of women. But as the politically conservative 1920s evolved, the LWV became more a club movement, shifting its emphasis from women's rights to a civic goals agenda, partially, writes Christine Lunardini in *What Every American Should Know About Women's History*, "because the women's movement itself was split over the issue of equal

rights and civic goals seemed more attainable." To help encourage
women to take part in the democratic process of voting, the LWV
adopted the slogan "Democracy is a bandwagon and there are too many
empty seats." By the 1940s the LWV had characterized itself as a citizen's organization dedicated, like other women's groups in the post-
suffrage era, to improving women's lives rather than advancing the cause
of women's rights. Anna Lord Strauss, president of the LWV from 1944
to 1950, went so far as to complain: "If I hear much more about women's
rights I am going to turn into a violent anti-feminist." In her view, "the
feminist approach" had "little appeal" to league members who "think of
themselves as citizens first and as women incidentally." During the
1950s the league even considered changing its name to the League of
Active Voters. The LWV, a solidly liberal organization, reflected the lib-
eralism of Eleanor Roosevelt, who, write Leila J. Rupp and Verta Taylor
in *Survival in the Doldrums,* "rejected feminist identification while serving as an example of what women could do in leadership roles." As
Rupp and Taylor observe: "Rejecting identification with feminism and
even with any characterization as a women's organization, League officers sharply distinguished themselves from the 'feminists' or 'equal
rights.' " In 1954 the league even dropped its opposition to the Equal
Rights Amendment because, write Rupp and Taylor, "it did not seem
important enough to oppose and its membership knew little about the
amendment." In 1974 the LWV trumped itself with regard to its "anti-
feminist" stance by voting to include men as full members.

    The League of Women Voters has remained an aggressively nonpar-
tisan citizens' group, which in recent years has become more interested
in supporting women candidates for public office, at least at the local
and state level. With a current national membership of over one hundred thousand, the league has continued its goal of educating the electorate by sponsoring political research and publishing its findings in the
LWV publication, the *National Voter.* The League of Women Voters has
been particularly effective in its sponsorship and organization of televised presidential debates, events that have sometimes significantly
affected the outcomes of elections and have served to provide voters
greater access to the views and public personas of political candidates.

1920–1929

The free-spirited flapper of the 1920s, complete with bobbed hair, cloche hat, short skirt, and raccoon coat. This woman is more modest in appearance than some of her sisters—who might have sported stockings rolled down below the knees (to show the world that she did not wear a corset or garters), a cigarette holder, and a flask of forbidden liquor. *Brown Brothers*

1920

Congress Ratifies the Nineteenth Amendment, Guaranteeing Women the Right to Vote

The right of citizens of the United States to vote shall not be denied or abridged by the United States or by any state on account of sex.

Congress shall have power to enforce this Article by appropriate legislation.

> Amendment XIX, giving nationwide suffrage to women

Hurrah! and vote for suffrage and don't keep them in doubt. I notice some of the speeches against. They were very bitter. I've been watching to see how you stood, but have noticed nothing yet. Don't forget to be a good boy and help Mrs. Catt put "Rat" in Ratification.

> Telegram to Tennessee senator Harry Burn
> from his suffragist mother, August 1920

In November 1920, ninety-one-year-old Charlotte Woodward, like many other newly enfranchised American women, voted for the first time in a presidential election. What was so significant about Woodward's participation in the electoral process was the fact that she was the only woman alive who had attended the 1848 Seneca Falls Women's Rights Convention, popularly considered to be the seminal event in the history of woman suffrage. For nearly a century, American women, led by suffragists such as Susan B. Anthony, Elizabeth Cady Stanton, Lucretia Mott, Anna Howard Shaw, and Carrie Chapman Catt, had fought hard and long, state by state, to gain the vote for women. On August 18, 1920, the battle for nationwide woman suffrage was finally won when Congress ratified the Nineteenth Amendment to the Constitution.

The history of the final battle for woman suffrage begins in 1890 with the formation of the National American Woman Suffrage Association (NAWSA). A merger of the New York and Boston wings of the suffrage movement, NAWSA was organized to present a stronger, more united front on behalf of the movement. NAWSA's first president was seventy-five-year-old veteran suffragist Elizabeth Cady Stanton, who had always viewed suffrage as only one of the many reform issues related to women's rights. Moreover, she had become increasingly convinced that the Bible and organized religion were to blame for women's lack of equality. After resigning the NAWSA presidency in 1892, Stanton set to work with a committee of feminists on *The Woman's Bible*, an analysis of the treatment of women in the Old and New Testaments. Stanton was succeeded as NAWSA president by seventy-two-year-old Susan B. Anthony, who dismissed *The Woman's Bible* as "flippant and superficial" but was appalled at the censure Stanton endured within NAWSA because of it. In 1894, when members of NAWSA passed a resolution maintaining the group's nonsectarianism and disavowing any connection with theological publications such as *The Woman's Bible*, Stanton resigned from the organization.

NAWSA's internal quarrels and its lack of a functioning national head-quarters weakened the organization's effectiveness. Susan B. Anthony, although an inspirational leader who shared with younger suffragists a single-minded concern with winning the vote, was unable to unite the movement. Between 1896 and 1910 no new woman suffrage states were won and only six states held referenda on suffrage, all of which were lost. The Susan B. Anthony federal woman suffrage amendment, which had been introduced into Congress in 1878 and which contained the wording that would later be used for the Nineteenth Amendment, seemed moribund. Southern attitudes also jeopardized nationwide suffrage. White southerners, historically dedicated to the concept of states rights, used the racist Jim Crow laws to prevent African Americans from voting. Southern suffragists worried that a federal suffrage movement would call attention to the South's flagrant disregard for the provisions of the Fourteenth Amendment ("Citizenship rights shall not be abridged") and the Fifteenth Amendment ("Race no bar to voting rights"). Some southern suffragists advocated voting rights for white women only; others felt threatened by the inclusion of both African Americans and northern immigrant "foreigners" in the political process. Susan B. Anthony and other NAWSA members felt that nothing could be done for African American women until all women won the vote. After the NAWSA conventions of 1899 and 1903, the woman suffrage movement separated itself from the cause of black civil rights.

After Susan B. Anthony stepped down as president of NAWSA in 1900, she was replaced by Carrie Chapman Catt. But Catt, a brilliant tactician who devised a plan to gain support at the grass-roots level, was forced to resign the presidency in 1904 to care for her ailing husband. She was replaced in turn by Anna Howard Shaw, a Methodist pastor and a physician. Shaw was a dedicated suffragist and a gifted speaker but proved to be a poor administrator. The period from 1896 to 1910, writes Eleanor Flexner in *Century of Struggle*, "came to be known among suffragists as 'the doldrums.'"

The first decade of the twentieth century was not completely devoid of activity on the part of the suffrage movement, however. Younger women, many of them college educated, founded grass-roots suffrage organizations such as the College Equal Suffrage League and the Boston Equal Suffrage League for Good Government. These grass-roots groups conducted door-to-door campaigns in working-class areas as well as in middle- and upper-class neighborhoods in an attempt to interest women in the movement. Groups of women traveled throughout Massachusetts by trolley, making speeches at every stop and holding spontaneous outdoor meetings. Wherever suffragists stopped to speak, they managed to find crowds, since, as Sara Evans observes in *Born for Liberty*, "the scandalous spectacle of a woman speaking on a street corner drew curious listeners by the score."

In 1907 Harriet Stanton Blatch, the daughter of Elizabeth Cady Stanton, organized the Equality League of Self-Supporting Women, later called the Women's Political Union, in New York City. The league was formed, Blatch later wrote, as "the best means of putting new life into the suffrage campaign" and because its founders "saw the need of drawing industrial women into the suffrage campaign and recognized that these women needed to be brought in contact, not with women of leisure, but with business and professional women who were also out in the world earning their living." Members included writer Charlotte Perkins Gilman, Florence Kelley, and Rose Schneiderman. The league formed a highly successful alliance with the Women's Trade Union League, lobbied unsuccessfully but vigorously in Albany for a woman suffrage bill, and in 1910 opened the first suffragist newsstand on East 23rd Street in New York. The stand sold suffragist pamphlets and magazines, buttons, ribbons, postcards, and copies of addresses made by Susan B. Anthony. The league, which boasted a 1908 membership of some nineteen thousand, was also responsible for initiating the suffrage parades that would become an integral part of suffragist strategy. As Eleanor Flexner observes: "The gusto with which the Equality League launched the first one of these in New York City in 1901 was such that

A suffrage kiosk in New York City   *Library of Congress*

the other suffrage groups could not afford to stay out, but the reluctance of their participation was thinly concealed. . . . Yet within a year or two parades had become so respectable that even a Mrs. O. H. P. Belmont was in line, and other cities were trying out the idea." (Mrs. Belmont was a wealthy New Yorker who had provided bail for striking workers during the garment industry's Great Uprising of 1909 and who rented an entire floor of a building on Fifth Avenue for the National Woman Suffrage Association. She later joined Alice Paul's militant Women's Party.) Harriet Stanton Blatch and her organization, as well as similar groups, had managed to broaden participation in the movement and to unite it more effectively, goals NAWSA had yet to accomplish.

In 1910 suffragists scored a victory when the state of Washington passed a woman suffrage amendment, the first state in fourteen years to do so. The movement was further stimulated by similar victories in California, Oregon, Arizona, Kansas, Montana, and Illinois. News of increasingly militant suffrage activity on the part of British suffragettes provided an added spur. Englishwomen had begun their suffrage campaign later than their American counterparts, but they made up for lost time by their unequaled militancy and the violence of their tactics. In 1903 Emmeline Pankhurst, her daughters, Christabel and Sylvia, and other suffragettes had formed the Women's Social and Political Union (WSPU), a group that did not view "gentle persuasion" as a viable method of winning the vote for women. Instead the WSPU believed that the only way to convince a recalcitrant male Parliament to grant woman suffrage was through civil disobedience and confrontation with the ruling class. WSPU members chained themselves to public buildings, mutilated art in museums, stormed the House of Commons, blew up postal boxes, and held mass marches on Parliament. Suffragettes were sent to prison, where they organized hunger strikes and were brutally force-fed by their captors. These forcible feedings had the effect of swaying public opinion in the suffragettes' favor.

American women watched the suffragettes closely. Carrie Chapman Catt, president of the International Woman Suffrage Alliance, took note of British tactics but was too consummate a politician to sanction the kind of violence and militancy endorsed by the WSPU. Harriet Stanton Blatch, who had been married to an Englishman and had lived in England before organizing the Equality League of Self-Supporting Women, applied British strategy in the form of parades and street corner speeches. The most militant of the era's suffrage leaders was Alice Paul, a Quaker and a social worker who had been a graduate student at the London School of Economics. Paul had participated in WSPU demonstrations, had been repeatedly imprisoned, and had joined the hunger strikes, during which she was force-fed through her nose. When Paul returned to the United States, she organized a demonstration of five thousand suffragists in Washington, D.C., on March 3, 1913, the day before President Woodrow Wilson's inauguration. Crowds of angry, jeering men slapped demonstrators, spat at them, and poked them with lighted cigars. A near riot broke out, which stopped the demonstrators before they could reach the White House. Forty people were hospitalized, and it took a cavalry troop to restore order. The march garnered a great deal of publicity favorable to the suffrage cause, and pilgrimages were organized to Washington from all over the country with petitions collected at the grass-roots level. On July 31, 1913, an automobile procession to the Capitol presented a group of senators with suffrage petitions carrying two hundred thousand signatures. Delegations began to visit the president, "whose early pronouncements on woman suffrage," writes Flexner, "beginning with his famous remark that the matter had never been brought to his attention, were not promising."

Alice Paul next established the Congressional Union (CU), an auxiliary organization to the NAWSA. Paul and the CU devised a simple strategy for winning nationwide suffrage, that of holding the party in power (the Democrats) responsible for denying women the vote. Paul also proposed that the some four million women who possessed the vote in suffrage states use political pressure to convince both Democrats and

Republicans to change their position on suffrage lest they lose votes. NAWSA leaders not only felt that Paul's plan was doomed to failure, they viewed it as harassment and therefore a politically unviable tactic for the essentially genteel organization. When Carrie Chapman Catt returned to the NAWSA as president in 1915, she expelled Alice Paul from the organization. Paul countered by forming the Women's Party with Crystal Eastman (the Woman's Peace Party) and Maude Wood Park (later president of the League of Women Voters), among other like-minded radical suffragists. Both Paul and Catt planned to use their organizations to press for a federal suffrage amendment. Catt would centralize all the NAWSA activities, and the organization would continue the suffrage campaign state by state, moving toward the goal of ratification of a federal amendment by 1920. Alice Paul and her Women's Party favored a more activist approach. During the 1916 presidential campaign between Woodrow Wilson and Republican Charles Evans Hughes, the Women's Party countered the Democrat's slogan, "Vote for Wilson; he kept us out of war," with "Vote against Wilson; he kept us out of suffrage." The Women's Party, with a membership of fifty thousand as compared with the NAWSA's two million, mounted a vigorous anti-Wilson campaign, which, although it ultimately failed (Wilson was reelected), nevertheless focused even more attention on the suffrage issue.

After the United States entered World War I in 1917, the Women's Party began a daily, around-the-clock picketing of the White House. Carrying banners that referred to "Kaiser Wilson" and proclaimed that "Democracy should begin at home," the Women's Party repeatedly accused the Wilson administration of hypocrisy in fighting a war to guarantee democracy abroad while at the same time denying democratic rights to women at home. Several months after the picketers started their silent White House vigil, the police began making arrests. The picketers, who had been demonstrating legally, were set free without sentence—at first. When they returned to the picket lines, they were arrested on a charge of obstructing sidewalk traffic, found guilty, and imprisoned in the Occaquan workhouse in Virginia. There Alice Paul, journalist Dorothy Day, and other picketers went on a hunger strike and were force-fed. Paul, whose hunger strike lasted for twenty-two days, was considered insane by prison officials and forced to undergo a mental examination. Pressured by the public outcry over this maltreatment of the picketers, the courts invalidated the arrests. The released picketers were hailed as heroines, and the suffrage cause generated still more favorable publicity. More significant, the House Rules Committee brought the dormant federal suffrage amendment to the floor for debate.

From left to right: Marjorie Shuler, Maud Wood Park, Senator Thomas J. Walsh, Senator James E. Watson, Senator Joseph E. Ramsdell, Helen Hamilton Gardener, and Senator Reed Smoot look on as Vice-President Thomas R. Marshall signs the bill approving passage of the Nineteenth Amendment in 1919. *The Schlesinger Library, Radcliffe College*

NAWSA completely dissociated itself from the activities of the Women's Party. The organization actively supported the war while continuing to divide, conquer, and keep what Carrie Chapman Catt called "suffrage noise" going in state suffrage referenda, whether or not the targeted states voted in favor of suffrage. "Where state referenda could be won," writes Sara Evans, "campaigns were to be waged to maintain and increase the number of congressmen dependent on female as well as male votes. In states where women could vote, NAWSA would lobby and petition their delegations to introduce and fight for the passage of the federal amendment. Where referenda were unlikely, suffragists were charged with working for presidential suffrage or the right to vote in party primaries."

By 1918 NAWSA's painstaking work and the Women's Party's dramatic demonstrations had created a public climate favorable to passage of the federal suffrage amendment. On January 10, 1918, Jeanette Rankin of Montana, the first woman elected to Congress, introduced the suffrage

Carrie Chapman Catt (*center*) and other women voting in 1920 for the first time
Brown Brothers

amendment onto the floor of the House. As Eleanor Flexner writes, "Endless lobbying and tallying by both suffrage groups had shown that the vote would be painfully close and that no one could foretell the outcome. It was with real anguish that the women keeping their tallies up in the galleries saw the hair-line finish, and their supporters rounding up every possible vote." Four congressmen with determining votes came to the House from their sickbeds; one came from the deathbed of his suffragist wife. The final tally was 274 in favor of suffrage and 136 against. The amendment had passed with exactly one vote more than the required two-thirds.

It would take another year and a half to win over the Senate, which passed the Nineteenth Amendment on June 5, 1919. During the congressional ratification process, antisuffragist factions, known as "antis," which included southern white supremacists, liquor interests, anti-Bolsheviks, northern political bosses, and the National Women's Organization to Oppose Suffrage, worked to block final passage of the amendment. But the effort of the "antis" were in vain: on August 18, 1920, Harry Burn of Tennessee cast the deciding vote in favor of ratification. The amendment carried 49–47, thus enfranchising twenty-six million women of working age after seventy-two years of struggle. As Flexner observes, any "subsequent court action by die-hard 'antis' had no effect on women voting at the polls in November 1920 or on subsequent history."

Passage of the Nineteenth Amendment can be seen as the culminating event of the Progressive Era. Although the next great battle on behalf of women's rights would be waged by Alice Paul and the Woman's Party to achieve an equal rights amendment, the four decades following enfranchisement would be a time of institutionalized reform that was not strictly gender based, but, rather, reflected individual and government initiatives and for women would come to echo the behavior of the modern era's great role model, First Lady Eleanor Roosevelt. By obtaining the most basic of individual democratic freedoms—the right to vote—women gained access to the political process that would help to shape the future. Inclusion into the world of politics would take longer. "In 1920," writes Flexner, "Mrs. Catt warned suffragists that the franchise was only an entering wedge, that they would have to force their way through the 'locked door' to the place where real political decisions are made, whether on issues or on candidates." As Carrie Chapman Catt cautioned women, "You will have a long hard fight before you get behind that door, for there is the engine that moves the wheels of your party machinery. . . . If you really want women's vote to count, make your way there."

1921

Betty Crocker, Advertising's Symbol of Female Domesticity, Makes Her First Appearance

She feeds the homeless, helps friends move, bakes cookies for the young women in her dormitory, produces videos encouraging kids to stay in school and takes care of her immediate, extended, adopted, and foster families. She's the heart of the kitchen as well as everywhere else she happens to be, which is never one place for very long. She's Betty Crocker and she represents all women of today.

> General Mills 1996 press release announcing the winners of the Betty Crocker Search for the seventy-five women who "most embody the characteristics of Betty Crocker, one of America's most trusted and familiar names"

In 1921 the Washburn Crosby Company of Minneapolis, Minnesota, a flour milling concern and forerunner of the commercial food giant General Mills, Inc., sponsored a promotion for its Gold Medal flour, offering a pincushion in the form of a flour sack if consumers could complete a jigsaw puzzle. The promotion provoked thousands of responses as well as questions about baking. James Quint, the company's advertising manager, is credited with creating a fictional woman to reply to these inquiries. A common signature was selected from among handwriting samples of women employees as the most distinctive (the basis for the signature still in use today). The surname "Crocker" was chosen to honor the recently retired director of the company, William G. Crocker, and "Betty" for its friendly-sounding name. After the formation of General Mills, Betty Crocker became the foundation of their corporate image and advertising, a personalized name and identity to promote confidence in the company's product line.

In 1924 the "Betty Crocker Cooking School of the Air" debuted on

The changing look of Betty Crocker through the years: 1936, 1955, 1965, 1968, 1972, 1980, 1986, and 1996   *Reprinted by permission of General Mills*

radio, becoming a popular program on the fledgling NBC network in 1927. In celebration of the fifteenth anniversary of the Betty Crocker name in 1936, a portrait was commissioned from Neysa McMein, a New York graphic artist, who first created the Betty Crocker likeness of motherly domesticity that served for the next twenty years. Since the 1950s, when six well-known artists, including Norman Rockwell, were invited to provide a new interpretation of Betty Crocker, there have been seven subsequent updates of Betty Crocker's image (1955, 1965, 1968, 1972, 1980, 1986, and 1996), reflecting changing hairstyles and fashion as well as the image of American women over the years. The 1972 portrait depicted, as General Mills' publicity stated, a "more businesslike Betty Crocker, symbolizing American women's newly significant role outside of the home," while the 1980 portrait "has a softened image and more casual coiffure and clothing, allowing all women to more readily identify with her." In 1986 Betty Crocker was shown as a professional woman, "approachable, friendly, competent and as comfortable in the boardroom as she is in the dining room." Through all the changes in Betty Crocker over more than half a century, "the goal has been to present an image of Betty Crocker to which modern women can relate, an image that recalls the promise of thoroughly tested products and up-to-date recipes."

The Betty Crocker name and image has proven to be the largest and most successful advertising and marketing campaign in history. During the 1940s surveys revealed that the name "Betty Crocker" was recognized by nine out of ten American homemakers. According to *Fortune* magazine in 1945, Betty Crocker was the second best-known woman in America, behind Eleanor Roosevelt. In the 1950s Betty Crocker became a television character in a variety of programs, including several appearances offering cake-baking instructions to George Burns and Gracie Allen. In 1989 a marketing survey assessing the power of product endorsements by a variety of well-known celebrities, such as Bill Cosby, Bob Hope, and James Garner, showed that Betty Crocker ranked first in the 25–49 and 50–64 age groups and second in the 65+ group (first was TV news anchorman Walter Cronkite).

The significance of Betty Crocker goes well beyond her influence in marketing products. In essential ways, the character's image reflects how women have been seen and have seen themselves in the last half of the twentieth century and reveals the interesting conjunction of advertising and consumerism in fashioning a womanly ideal. Beginning as a means of providing a giant food conglomerate with a human face and personalized identity, Betty Crocker offered a woman more than a trusted endorsement and stamp of approval when she went shopping for processed food. The character has continually been used to suggest a changing, though essentially consistent, ideal of womanhood that tries to balance womanly beauty and the traditional conception of women as homemakers. The succession of Betty Crocker portraits provides an interesting mirror for women over the years, reflecting the changing image of the American woman, who keeps her core of domestic strength intact despite increasing self-definition outside the home and family. Additionally, Betty Crocker graphically captures the unresolved tension between images of woman as traditional domestic icon and woman as stylish, independent, and modern. Moreover, the Betty Crocker advertising campaign points up the ways in which women's self-image has been manufactured and manipulated through advertising as part of American consumer and celebrity culture that has had such a marked influence on women's identity and sense of self.

From the 1920s on, concepts of female beauty and female roles became key elements in advertisers' creation of demand for products in a growing mass market. The launching of Betty Crocker in 1921 coincidentally coincided with the first Miss America Beauty Pageant, another source of tracking the feminine image through the century and a means of establishing a standard of female beauty and identity. As Lois W. Banner, author of *American Beauty*, has observed:

> By 1921 the basic institutions of the American beauty culture had taken shape. The fashion and cosmetic industries existed. So, too, did beauty contests, the modelling profession, and the movies. All continued to expand during the following decades, building on increased affluence, the growth of the pleasure ethic, and the heightened sophistication of advertising. Shifts in the internal structures and external relationships of the beauty institutions did, of course, occur. Yet after about 1920 no new institutions concerned with the creation and dissemination of beauty appeared—with the exception perhaps of television. Moreover, the themes that had dominated the development of beauty culture in the nineteenth and early twentieth centuries continued to do so. These included the conflicts between feminism and fashion and between social classes in asserting fashion leadership; the willingness of American women to identify with glamorous figures of stage, society, and especially screen; and the commercialization of the beauty culture and the concomitant emphasis on a youthful appearance as the desideratum of beauty.

The American beauty culture was largely created by advertisers who helped shape the female image to reflect the perceived needs that their products could remedy or reinforce. Advertising, which doubled in volume in the 1920s, was largely targeted at women, who spent the bulk of the family income. The development of the home appliance market and the processed food industry helped drive the depiction of women as ideal consumers whose identity was defined by their role as homemakers. The cosmetic and fashion industry crafted a competing image of women for whom fashion and beauty was the essential quality of self-definition. In her study *Beauty Bound*, Rita Freedman has described advertising as forms of "mythical discourse" that "predispose the viewer to accept the commercial message as truth rather than construct. They sell not only the product but also the prevailing social standards and thereby reinforce attitudes about feminine beauty." In this sense, Betty Crocker as icon combines the two major elements of the female ideal: domesticity and beauty.

Decoding the images of women in advertising over the twentieth century can uncover the ways in which the female ideal has changed, accommodating an expanded definition as women moved beyond home and family to pursue careers and identity beyond that of wife and mother. Yet women's sense of self continues to be defined externally, prompted by the overriding female role as consumer. Women are seen in terms of what they can have, through products, and by the products manufacturers decide they need and will buy in order to strive for an image of beauty very much controlled by fashion and cosmetic concerns. Even the notion of women's hard-won emancipation has a consumer implication. As Christopher Lasch observed in his best-selling book *The Culture of Narcissism*, "The advertising industry thus encourages the pseudo-emancipation of women, flattering them with its insinuating reminder, 'You've come a long way, baby' and disguising the freedom to consume as genuine autonomy. . . . It emancipates women and children from patriarchal authority . . . only to subject them to the new paternalism of the advertising industry, the industrial corporation, and the state."

To make such a leap from the ostensibly benign and reassuring values of domesticity and beauty represented by Betty Crocker may seem extreme. But she, like other highly publicized images of women over the century, has asserted a significant pressure on women as consumers by marketing a prevailing feminine ideal, establishing a synergistic relationship between identity and consumption. Betty Crocker, like so many other female images, possessing both standards of domestic and physical ideals, reveals the battleground of many unresolved tensions in women to join traditional roles of family and home with those of independence and self-identity, between outwardly defined concepts of beauty and acceptance of less physical manifestations of self-worth.

The First Miss America Is Crowned

> The event made a national ritual of the by then powerful notion
> that the pursuit of beauty ought to be a woman's primary goal.
>
> Lois W. Banner, *American Beauty*

By the time the Miss America pageant was inaugurated, on September 5, 1921, the ceremonial custom of deciding which women were, to quote the Brothers Grimm, the "fairest of them all" was firmly established in American culture. During the nineteenth century cities and states began to hold festivals and carnivals at which queens were chosen, and while the selection of a festival or carnival queen might rely on such attributes as outstanding civic leadership, family connections, or community popularity, the physical attractiveness of a candidate counted as well. "As early as the ante-bellum era," writes Lois Banner, "the beauty was a recognized type, and public competitions offered a way to regularize the selection procedures and more forcefully to announce the way women were supposed to look. At the same time, public festivals reinforced the centrality of physical beauty in women's lives and made of beauty a matter of competition and elitism and not of democratic cooperation among women."

The first modern beauty contest involving the display of women's faces and figures before judges was the 1854 creation of showman Phineas T. Barnum, who had already held successful dog, bird, flower, and baby contests at his New York City American Museum. Prizes for Barnum's women's beauty contest included a diamond tiara if the winner were married and a dowry if she were single. Because the initial candidates were women of dubious reputation and not the respectable beauties Barnum had hoped to attract, the promoter turned the competition into a photographic (then a daguerreotype) contest. Barnum offered to pay the postage of the photos sent to him, suggested that the women's names need not be included, and stated that he would not accept photographs from "disreputable persons." All the candidates would receive prizes and have their portraits painted from their photographs; the portraits would be displayed in a gallery called the Congress of Beauty, described in pure Barnum huckster-speak as an exhibit that would encourage "a more popular taste for the Fine Arts, stimulate to extra exertion the genius of our Painters, and laudably gratify the public curiosity."

Barnum's photographic beauty contest proved popular and by the beginning of the twentieth century had been adopted as a promotional device by newspapers all over the country. The ability to sponsor such contests was due in great part to the development of the halftone plate, which had made newspaper reproduction of photographs possible. In 1911 the *Ladies' Home Journal*, which had earlier condemned beauty contests as unwomanly, joined the bandwagon by sponsoring a competition to find the five most beautiful young women in the United States. The winners would receive a trip to New York City, where their portraits would be painted by Charles Dana Gibson, the artist who had created the Gibson Girl. From 1895 through the first two decades of the twentieth century, the Gibson Girl was the standard of beauty for American women. As Gibson drew her, she was tall and stately, with a small mouth and thick, dark hair swept up in a pompadour. Unlike an earlier beauty icon, Lillian Russell, the Gibson Girl was slender, but she nevertheless had an hourglass figure, with a large bosom and generous hips.

The early beauty contests often offered as prizes opportunities for careers in modeling, movies, or the theater. To many contestants, winning a beauty contest could mean the difference between a life spent in poverty or a chance to raise one's social status. A famous example was red-haired Clara Bow, born in extreme poverty, who catapulted to movie stardom and immortality as the flapper era's ideal "It" girl after winning a screen test through a *Photoplay* magazine photographic beauty contest. For some contestants, winning might mean the acquisition of a position in the chorus of the *Ziegfeld Follies*. When Florenz Ziegfeld, a theatrical producer whose *Follies* were advertised as "glorifying the American girl," was asked by *Vanity Fair* to describe the ideal woman in a 1926 issue of the magazine, he responded by listing the average measurements of a Ziegfeld girl and then went on to define the perfect woman as one who possessed "symmetry" and "femininity, an overworked term but indicative of loveliness, grace, and imagination." Broadway producer-manager Lee Shubert's definition in the same issue was equally ambiguous: his ideal woman was "tall but . . . not too tall," "brunette," and had "a beautiful figure." These descriptions of the physical attributes of the ideal woman were offered by well-known men of the moment who had made careers out of choosing women who would be physically attractive to audiences. Ziegfeld's and Shubert's highly publicized showgirls and female stars, agency models, and early beauty contest winners not only represented standards of beauty and fashion for American women, but also supported the notion that there actually were standards to strive for.

At the turn of the century, beauty contests began to appear regularly at beach resort areas. "These contests," writes Banner, "were casual affairs, although in 1920 an official queen of the five New York City beaches was chosen, and in 1921 the winner of this event became a contestant in the Miss America competition." As women's bathing suits became less and less voluminous, the bathing beauty became a recognized symbol of female pulchritude. Champion swimmer and movie actress Annette Kellermann pioneered the one-piece suit, and film director and producer Mack Sennett, known for his Keystone Kops slapstick comedies, became equally famous for his bevy of relatively scantily clad bathing beauties. The more revealing bathing suits were considered scandalous by well-to-do vacationers at seaside resorts, and the Atlantic City Business Men's League, the promoters of the first Miss America pageant, worried that a protest against the proceedings would mar the festivities. "On the one hand," writes Banner, "the contest, held during the first two weeks in September, seemed a way of increasing tourism by extending the summer season past September first; on the other, a conservative protest might emerge against what was in effect the first major national occasion in which young middle-class women would expose themselves in bathing suits before a panel of judges."

To deflect criticism, contest managers stressed the wholesome, unsophisticated athletic qualities of Miss America candidates and insisted that

Fifteen-year-old Margaret Gorman, the first Miss America, in her demure swimsuit and flat-heeled bathing shoes   *Library of Congress*

they neither wear makeup nor bob their hair. Atlantic City police dressed like Mack Sennett's Keystone Kops, as a way, observes Banner, "of legitimizing through laughter the force of sexuality." A distinguished panel of newspaper editors and illustrators of beautiful women served as judges. The first Miss America, chosen from among 1,500 contestants, was fifteen-year-old Margaret Gorman, Miss Washington, D.C. The smallest and youngest contestant ever to win the contest, Gorman was blond, blue eyed, and petite (five feet one inch, 108 pounds, measurements 30-25-32) and bore a striking resemblance to Mary Pickford. Like the other contestants, Gorman wore a conservative swimming costume; hers was knee length and somewhat baggy. Her prizes included a tiara replication of the Statue of Liberty's headpiece, a large American flag fashioned into a coronation robe, and a $5,000 oversize trophy that sported a silver mermaid reclining on a base of teakwood. American Federation of Labor president Samuel Gompers was quite taken with Margaret Gorman and rather pompously described her in *The New York Times* as representing "the type of womanhood America needs—strong, red-blooded, able to shoulder the responsibilities of homemaking and motherhood. It is in her type that the hope of the country resides." It is difficult to know whether the seventy-one-year-old Gompers was unaware that Margaret Gorman was a girl of fifteen and not quite ready to shoulder the responsibilities of an adult woman or whether he was holding true to his long-held conviction that a woman's place was in the home and not in the organized labor movement. The 1922 winner, Miss Ohio, was five inches taller than Margaret Gorman, had broad shoulders, and was slim and athletic, a look that was more in line with the flapper standard of beauty prevalent in the 1920s. As Banner observes, "Giving the award over the years to several types of beautiful American women appealed to the democratic instincts of Americans, if nothing else."

The Miss America pageant went through several refinements over the course of the century. In 1936 the talent competition was added to the pageant, thus affording judges and other viewers the entertaining sight of contestants vigorously twirling batons or playing "Lady of Spain" on accordions through the years. In 1945 Bess Myerson became the first Jewish Miss America and the first to win a college scholarship offered by the pageant as one of the awards. The Miss America of 1947 was the last to be crowned in her swimsuit—that year a two-piece suit was worn by every contestant. The pageant was televised for the first time in 1954, and a year later master of ceremonies Bert Parks first sang the contest's signature song, "There She Is." In 1968, during the second wave of the women's movement, protesters picketed the pageant with signs proclaiming "Let's Judge Ourselves as People," crowned a live sheep as Miss America, threw such items of female oppression as corsets, girdles, bras, curlers, high-heeled shoes, and issues of *Ladies' Home Journal* into a "freedom trashcan," and auctioned off an effigy with the pitch "Gentlemen, I offer you the 1969 model. She's better every year. She walks. She talks. She smiles on cue. *And* she does housework." African American contestants began appearing in the 1970s, but it was not until 1984 that the first African American Miss America, Vanessa Williams of New York, was crowned. However, after *Penthouse* magazine published nude pictures taken of her before her victory, Williams was forced by the Miss America Organization to relinquish her crown to the first runner-up, Miss New Jersey, Suzette Charles, who is also African American.

By the 1990s the pageant had introduced further changes, among them the "Focus on Achievement," during which contestants were expected to discuss a social issue. Contestants were required to do their own hair to avoid, as one pageant official put it, looking like "forty-year-old Stepford Wives"; the evening gown competition became the evening wear competition; the winners' "reign" was changed to "year of service"; and the first hearing-impaired Miss America, Heather Whitestone, was crowned. In 1995 television viewers were invited to call a 900 telephone number to vote on whether or not the swimsuit competition should be discontinued. Although this was called a marketing gimmick by the National Organization for Women, voters nevertheless overwhelmingly elected to keep the swimsuit competition. Two years later the Miss America Organization ruled that contestants could wear two-piece swimsuits with "full coverage" on top and "full-to-moderate coverage" on the bottom. The model shown wearing the suit reflecting the new guidelines sported ample cleavage and a high-top bottom that revealed her belly button.

Beauty contests in the twentieth century have represented what Lois Banner calls "the breakdown of Victorian prudery." This breakdown has been particularly evident in the inclusion of very young and adolescent girls in beauty pageants. Dressing potential little beauty queens to resemble Las Vegas showgirls has always seemed only a slight step removed from kiddie porn, in addition to sending the wrong message to girls about what it means to be female. However, few questions concerning the appropriateness of little-girl pageants were asked until the murder of six-year-old beauty queen Jon Benet Ramsay, in 1997. One result of the media frenzy following the murder was a slight decrease in the number of contestants entered in children's beauty pageants. Teenage beauty contestants, who are struggling with identity issues, can receive positive reinforcement for their looks, but that may not necessarily help them as adults in the long run unless they decide to strive for careers in show business. What both girls and women ultimately learned from beauty contests over the course of the twentieth century was, as Lois Banner observes, that despite "the pretensions to intellect and talent, physical beauty remained the overriding feature of the ideal American woman."

The Sheppard-Towner Act Is Passed by the U.S. Congress

> Of all the activities in which I have shared during more than fifty years of striving, none is, I am convinced, of such fundamental importance as the Sheppard-Towner Act.
>
> Florence Kelley, director, the National Consumers' League, quoted in Sheila M. Rothman, *Woman's Proper Place.*

The Sheppard-Towner Maternity and Infancy Protection Act, enacted to reduce maternal and infant mortality rates, was the first federally funded health care program, as well as the first welfare program, in the United States. Under the act, states would be provided with matching federal funds in order to establish prenatal and child health care centers, where women trained in child care would teach expectant mothers, primarily from the working class, personal hygiene and offer advice on how to maintain and improve the health of their infants and children. Passage of the act represented a victory for public health advocates such as Dr. Alice Hamilton, a proponent of social medicine, and Dr. Sara Josephine Baker, whose efforts as assistant health commissioner of New York had dramatically decreased the death rate in city slums earlier in the century. Conceived and implemented as a method for preventing the onset of disease, Sheppard-Towner also gave women an important role in community health and welfare and, as Sheila Rothman observes, "expanded the responsibility of the state; the Act assumed that it was the obligation of the state to guard the health of its citizens."

In 1926 Dr. Sara Josephine Baker, who had become famous for stating during World War I that it was "six times safer to be a soldier in the trenches than to be born a baby in the United States," reinforced this concept with regard to Sheppard-Towner-funded well-baby clinics by stating that they "should be as free as the public schools . . . public health is not a special privilege but a birthright. . . . The infant welfare station is as much a part of public function as the public baths, public playgrounds, libraries and schools." Dr. Baker's position was a worthy one, and her argument entirely well founded, but in the end neither she nor the other supporters of Sheppard-Towner were able to overcome the powerful opposition to the act that eventually resulted in its demise only eight years after it was passed.

The Sheppard-Towner Act faced opposition from the start. Largely the work of the Children's Bureau, which had been lobbying for federal legislation to fund the education of women in prenatal and postnatal care since 1912, the proposed act aroused the antipathy of the American Medical Association. Although the AMA avowed that every mother and child should receive adequate medical services, it was wary of any state expansion of health care and opposed the administration of the Sheppard-Towner program by the Children's Bureau, a lay organization. The Children's Bureau, careful to avoid encroaching on the professional territory of physicians, proposed that public health nurses provide no remedial medical services under Sheppard-Towner, only preventive health care. The AMA worked to prevent passage of Sheppard-Towner but was unsuccessful, possibly, writes Rothman, because of "Congressional fear of the new, and therefore unknown, power of female voters." The com-

A baby weigh-in, circa 1922. At Sheppard-Towner clinics, public health nurses worked with local doctors to educate women on infant nutrition as well as the rules of illness prevention. *Brown Brothers*

bination of vigorous sponsorship, public support, and political expedience resulted in the passage of Sheppard-Towner in 1921.

Pioneered and administered by women, Sheppard-Towner programs established some three thousand child-health and maternity consultation centers and "health mobiles" to educate mothers in prenatal care and provided hospital facilities for problem pregnancies and deliveries. The centers were staffed by women physicians and public health nurses, who had worked at settlement houses, with municipal departments of child hygiene, or in public schools rather than in hospitals. The implementation of Sheppard-Towner programs required the support not only of the lay community, but of local doctors as well, especially in small-town and rural areas, where clinics had to rely on physicians to conduct preventive health examinations. Local doctors, forced to take a stand on public health issues, gradually began to expand their private practices to include the preventive mother-and-child health care offered by publicly funded Sheppard-Towner clinics. This development delighted the AMA, which had remained antagonistic toward Sheppard-Towner. The association's journal published instructions on how to conduct preventive health examinations and advised physicians on the best way to "prepare forms suitable for use by private practitioners of medicine in carrying out the purposes of the periodic health examination." Additionally, there was a growing trend during the 1920s toward medical specialization, particularly in the areas of pediatrics and obstetrics.

By the late 1920s the medical establishment was ready to insist that Sheppard-Towner programs, carried out by nurses and social workers without medical degrees, were unessential and in fact dangerous to the health of pregnant women. "By emphasizing the pathology of pregnancy and the potential ability of medical oversight, research, and institutions to eliminate this pathology," writes Rothman, "the specialists made a convincing argument." The campaign to prevent the extension of the Sheppard-Towner Act was the work of medical specialists and the AMA, who endeavored to convince the government that they possessed superior skill and training and denigrated the woman-staffed clinics by characterizing them as nonprofessional and therefore illegitimate. The politically powerful AMA and other like-minded conservative organizations labeled the act as a "Bolshevik plot" and conducted a smear campaign against such Sheppard-Towner supporters as Florence Kelley, whom they referred to as "the ablest legislative general Communism had produced." The campaign was effective, and in 1929 Congress refused to allot funds for a continuation of Sheppard-Towner. Aspects of the act would be revived in the New Deal social programs of the 1930s, but by then, as Sheila Rothman observes, "a mother had to consult a pediatrician in order to raise a healthy child and concomitantly, to go to an obstetrician in order to avoid complications. The hegemony of the medical expert had begun."

1922

Women Track and Field Athletes Are Included Under the Jurisdiction of the Amateur Athletic Union

> There is no girl living who can manage to look anything but awful during the process of some strenuous game played on a hot day. . . . If there is anything more dreadful aesthetically or more depressing than the fatigue-distorted face of a girl runner at the finish line, I have never seen it. . . .
>
> Paul Gallico, *Farewell to Sport*

Women athletes of today would surely react to novelist Paul Gallico's somewhat sour observation with righteous indignation, not to say derision. However, male attitudes toward the appearance of women playing sports was one of the many obstacles encountered by women in their struggle to be accepted as athletes rather than stereotyped as ladylike females lobbing shuttlecocks over a net. Facing bans and restrictions on the kinds of sports they could play and denied venues for competition, women athletes in the twentieth century have had to overcome numerous social and cultural barriers to achieve their right to compete at the highest level. One of the watershed victories in this struggle was the admission of women sports in 1922 under the jurisdiction of the Amateur Athletic Union (AAU), the American governing body for amateur sports in America. Women were finally recognized as athletes, and the history of sports in the twentieth century was no longer male dominated.

American women in sports prior to AAU acceptance faced a long history of exclusion based on a narrow conception of women's physical capabilities and the promulgation of a womanly ideal that disallowed the rigors and strenuousness of physical competition. Certain sports were prohibited based on concerns for women's health, particularly their risk of their childbearing potential. Throughout the nineteenth century strenuous physical activity was generally viewed as inimical to women's best interests as potential mothers and contrary to acceptable standards of proper ladylike behavior. When more women entered colleges and universities in the last half of the nineteenth century, sports for women slowly entered college physical education programs, but largely with an emphasis on exercise alone in the forms of calisthenics. Barriers against competition in such sports as tennis, golf, and swimming gradually were dropped early in the twentieth century, but prohibition, particularly in track and field, remained in place until the 1920s.

The AAU, which sought to control all amateur sports in the United States, took charge of women's swimming in 1914 and finally accepted women's track and field competition under its jurisdiction in 1922. Such an admission to nationally sanctioned competition in the previously regarded male sport was a breakthrough for women athletes. No longer relegated to the so-called more genteel sports like tennis and golf, women athletes in AAU track-and-field competitions helped legitimize the presence of the woman athlete in sports previously regarded as exclusively male, as revolutionary as the inclusion in 1998 of women's ice hockey in the Olympic Games. The AAU's control of track and field for women also expanded amateur participation outside schools and colleges to include women from high schools, athletic associations, and industrial and commercial clubs, setting uniform standards for women participants and encouraging national showcasing of women's athletic prowess. The first National Track & Field Championship for women took place in Newark, New Jersey, on September 29, 1923. The level of competition afforded by AAU sanctioning offered for the first time a national stage for women athletes in track and field and pointed the way toward expanded participation by women internationally through the Olympic Games.

When Baron Pierre de Coubertin reintroduced the Olympic ideals in the 1890s and created the modern Olympic Games, he was adamantly opposed to any participation by women. Instead, his Olympic vision was restricted to young adult male athletes. Women were allowed, however, to participate in the Olympics as early as 1900 in a one-time-only women's Olympic golf tournament and in tennis, which remained on the Olympic schedule until 1924. Swimming and diving for women were added in 1912, but no Americans competed. During the first postwar Olympics in Antwerp in 1920, the U.S. team of women swimmers dominated the competition. Women fencers made their first appearance at the Paris Games of 1924. Finally, after Coubertin resigned from the International Olympic Committee (IOC), the International Olympic

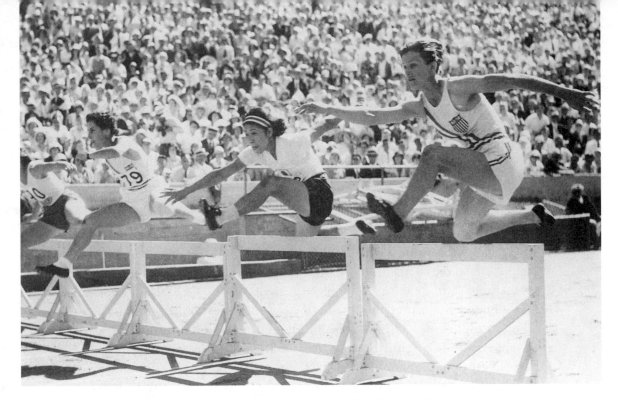

Babe Didrikson (*far right*) taking a hurdle during the 1932 Olympic Games in Los Angeles *Library of Congress*

committee agreed to stage five women's track-and-field events for the 1928 Games: the 100- and 800-meter races, 400-meter relay, high jump, and discus. The furor caused by the collapse of some women runners in the 800-meter race revived concerns over women's health and women athletes' proper place in Olympic competition, despite the fact that male runners in the 800 meters also suffered from the effects of the grueling race. There was widespread lobbying for the exclusion of women in track and field for the 1932 Games in Los Angeles. A final decision by the IOC was postponed until 1931, before which a successful women's track-and-field demonstration was staged at the 1930 Olympic Congress in Berlin. One important spectator was Avery Brundage, president of the AAU and a representative of the International Amateur Athletic Federation (IAAF). Under Brundage's leadership the IAAF strongly supported keeping women's track and field in the Games. This allowed the United States to field one of its greatest teams of women athletes, which included the sensational Babe Didrikson, who would emerge from the Los Angeles Games as the first genuine woman sports superstar of the twentieth century, whom sportswriter Grantland Rice called "the greatest athlete of all . . . for all time."

Didrikson grew up in Texas and was a star athlete in basketball in high school. Hired by the Houston Employers Casualty Company as a stenographer, she was encouraged to play sports for the company's women's basketball team before taking up track and field. In an unprecedented move, Didrikson entered the AAU women's national track and field championship in 1932, not as a member of a sponsored team, but as an individual contestant. She won six events, broke four women's world records, and also won the team championship by herself, scoring twice as many points as the second-place team. Two weeks later, as a member of the U.S. Olympic team, Didrikson won gold medals and broke world records in the javelin throw and the 80-meter hurdles. The next day she took the silver medal in the high jump. Didrikson would capitalize on her notoriety as a sports phenomenon in golf as an amateur and professional in the Ladies Professional Golf Association, which she helped to found in 1946. In 1982 a poll was taken among America's leading sports historians to name the ten most outstanding and influential athletes or administrators in American sports history. Didrikson ranked second, right below her namesake, Babe Ruth.

Didrikson, through her many achievements and celebrity status, redefined the role and stature of women athletes, opening up what had formerly been a narrow masculine world and legitimizing professional sports for women. But it was the AAU's decision in 1922 to lower the barrier to women in competition that helped pave the way for her impact on a national and world stage. After the 1920s the notion of a woman sports figure became possible, and though barriers still exist that limit the woman athlete, the leveling of the playing field for women in sports can be said to have truly begun with the AAU's 1922 decision to admit that women deserved the same rights and opportunities as male athletes in sports previously considered beyond women's abilities.

The Landmark Six-Volume *History of Woman Suffrage* Is Published

Reverend Anna Howard Shaw:
    This huge volume IV I present to you with the love that a mother beareth, and I hope you will find in it the facts about women, for you will find them nowhere else. Your part will be to see that the four volumes are duly placed in the libraries of the country, where every student of history may have access to them.
                With unbounded love and faith,
                Susan B. Anthony

        Flyleaf inscription presented to Anna Howard Shaw
        by Susan B. Anthony upon the publication of volume IV
        of *The History of Woman Suffrage*

In 1922 Ida Husted Harper completed the massive six-volume *History of Woman Suffrage* that was begun in 1876 under the supervision of Elizabeth Cady Stanton, Susan B. Anthony, and Matilda Joslyn Gage in an attempt to document the struggle to win the vote for women. The first three volumes covered the years from 1848 to 1883. After Matilda Gage died, Anthony asked her friend and biographer, Ida Husted Harper, to edit the fourth volume, and after Anthony died Harper completed the final two volumes, bringing the story of the suffrage battle to its climax with the passage of the Nineteenth Amendment in 1920. This documentary record of the suffrage movement is a remarkable achievement: the single indispensable source on the movement and the thoughts and beliefs of the participants, particularly for the insights it provides into Elizabeth Cady Stanton and Susan B. Anthony. *The History of Woman Suffrage* is also a fitting memorial to the many other suffragists who labored so tirelessly and are now obscured by the massive shadow cast by Stanton and Anthony. *The History of Woman Suffrage* in its collection of letters, speeches, convention notes, and personal recollections of its principal leaders offers a unique insight into the struggle for women's rights and equality in the nineteenth and twentieth century, and as Susan B. Anthony urged her friend Anna Howard Shaw, it deserves its place as one of the foundation texts of the women's movement.

The genesis of *The History of Woman Suffrage* began in 1876, following the notorious women's rights protest at the Centennial Celebration of the Declaration of Independence. Anthony, Gage, and three other women gained admission to the celebration carrying their own Declaration of the Rights for Women. As recorded in *The History of Woman Suffrage*, the women listened to the reading of the Declaration of Independence, which opened the ceremonies, and:

> Not quite sure how their approach might be met—not quite certain if at this final moment they would be permitted to reach the presiding officer—those ladies arose and made their way down the aisle. The bustle of preparation for the Brazilian hymn covered their advance. The foreign guests, the military and civil officers who filled the space directly in front of the speakers stand, courteously made way, while Miss Anthony in fitting words presented the declaration. Mr. Ferry's face pale, as bowing low, with no word, he received the declaration, which thus became part of the day's proceedings; the ladies turned, scattering printed copies, as they deliberately walked down the platform.

The declaration protested the denial of woman's right of trial by a jury of one's peers, taxation without representation, and the unequal legal codes for men and women.

A month after the centennial protest, Anthony and Stanton in Stanton's home in Tenafly, New Jersey, began rummaging through the accumulated letters, convention notes, and newspaper clippings they had collected over a quarter century in the women's rights movement. They had met in 1851 in Seneca Falls, New York, after a lecture given by the celebrated abolitionist William Lloyd Garrison. Anthony was thirty-one, reserved, and single; Stanton was thirty-six, outgoing, and the mother of three boys. Together they formed a perfect complementary partnership. Anthony became the women's movement's logician and organizer; Stanton, its theorist and emotional center. They formed the National Woman Suffrage Association (NWSA) in 1869 and broadcast their views in the *Revolution*, a feminist newspaper published by Anthony and coedited by Stanton. Stanton describes her partnership with Anthony in the first volume of *The History of Woman Suffrage:* "In writing we did better work together than either could do alone. While she is slow and analytical in composition, I am rapid and synthetic. I am the better writer, she the better critic. She supplied the facts and statistics, I the philosophy and rhetoric, and together we made arguments which have stood unshaken by the storms of thirty long years; arguments that no man has answered." *The History of Woman Suffrage* was seen by the pair as the collection of those arguments and a history of their efforts to forward them, a legacy similar to the one celebrated on the hundredth anniversary of the Declaration of Independence.

When they began work on their history, neither Anthony, Stanton, nor Gage expected it to expand to the proportions that it did, envisioning instead several pamphlets that could be completed over a few months. In the process of sorting their material, Anthony reported that in this "delightfully quiet & pleasant home—[we] are working for dear life— trying to gather up the threads of our Women's Rights History in this country—we propose to have a general history—and interwoven with it a brief sketch of one & another of the leaders—with their pictures—all to be condensed of course—as we propose 1 vol—octavion of 6 or 8 hundred pages." The trio eventually produced after fourteen years of labor three volumes of over three thousand pages. Anthony took the lead in arranging publication, and Stanton and Gage arranged the material and wrote the history. A fourth volume was published during Anthony's lifetime, and the final two volumes were finally completed in 1922.

In preparing their history, Anthony had trunks and boxes of old papers shipped from her home in Rochester, and the three women called for contributions and recollections from other women in the movement. Lucy Stone, the founder of the American Woman Suffrage Association

Ida Husted Harper, who reluctantly agreed to complete the task of writing the final volumes of *The History of Woman Suffrage*, a work begun in 1876 by Susan B. Anthony, Elizabeth Cady Stanton, and Matilda Joslyn Gage
Library of Congress

(AWSA), refused to contribute in the expectation that her organization would write its own version of suffrage events. Despite Stone's reluctance to participate and the trio's own internal disagreements, the project continued. Anthony in particular found the experience of rereading the old documents almost unbearable: "It makes me sad and tired to read them over, to see the terrible strain I was under every minute then, have been since, am now and shall be for the rest of my life." The emotional record of these years emerges clearly in the first three volumes of *The History of Woman Suffrage*, a quality somewhat missing from the final three volumes in Harper's less intense and immediate handling of the events and the issues.

Ida Husted Harper was in fact intimidated by Anthony into taking over the project, which she was more than a little reluctant to do. Harper later recalled her reaction to Anthony's hints that she should complete the project: "I was overwhelmed with the consciousness that within the innermost recesses of her being was the intention that I should undertake this stupendous task." When asked directly by Anthony to assume responsibility for *The History of Woman Suffrage*, Harper at first refused, prompting Anthony to issue an ultimatum: "Think this over till morning, and if you decide that you will not undertake it, I'll burn up the material and that will be the end." With such a threat Harper had to relent, and she doggedly pursued the project for sixteen years following Anthony's death in 1906. In a real sense, *The History of Woman Suffrage* had become for Susan B. Anthony her principal legacy to posterity. At the end of her life she had no savings, no heirs, only her movement to preserve and protect and the cause she hoped would continue after her death. The project had become her great memorial and testimony, a way of passing on the movement to future generations.

By 1922 Anthony's legacy and by implication that of all the other suffrage leaders and supporters was completed in a work that tracked the history of the American suffrage movement from 1848 to 1920. *The History of Woman Suffrage* can rightfully be regarded as, to quote historian Christine Lunardini, "one of the most extraordinary accounts of a political and social movement that had ever been recorded."

✤

Emily Post's *Etiquette* Is Published

> Few of the hundreds of etiquette books published in America since the time of Jackson left any more than a thumbprint on American behavior until Emily Post came along in 1922. Then, in the way that Victrola identified phonographs, Kodak cameras, Frigidaire refrigerators, and Kleenex cleansing tissues, "Emily Post" became a synonym for etiquette. Purchasers of her book rarely ask for it by title, let alone its full title, *Etiquette: The Blue Book of Social Usage.* To ask for "Emily Post" was sufficient.
>
> Esther B. Aresty, *The Best Behavior*

The genteel social behavior of women so prized among Americans during the eighteenth and nineteenth centuries was not quite as evident during the first two decades of the twentieth century. By the turn of the century, the wealthy were shocking and delighting less privileged Americans with their vulgar displays of what came to be known as "conspicuous consumption." The "new woman" of the Progressive Era, young, athletic, assertive, and businesslike, was challenging many of the behavioral conventions dictated by tradition.

The modernization of women was not lost on writers of etiquette: some seventy-one etiquette books and twice that number of magazine articles were published in the first decade of the century. As they had done during the previous century, writers of etiquette books stressed correct behavior not just for those striving for acceptance in high society, but for Americans of all classes. Magazines featured articles titled "Are We Polite?," "Has Courtesy Declined?," "The Decay of Manners," and "Modern Manners and the Unmannerly Age." Many etiquette experts focused on women as the most unmannerly segment of modern American society. As Esther Aresty observes, "As in the past, some of the most severe critics were themselves women, annoyed with the way their sex

Emily Post, socialite, novelist, magazine writer, and arbiter of correct social behavior, whose name became a "virtual synonym for etiquette"   *Library of Congress*

was invading business and athletics, and in their rush for new liberties endangering the natural rights of women to be catered to and protected." Amelia Mason, writing in *Century* magazine, chastised women for being as pushy and aggressive as men and for dressing like men, in tailored suits: "The typical girl of the day puts on mannish airs with mannish clothes and spices her talk with slang." The modern girl, wrote Mason, also "puts down her parents, her elders, and her superiors."

American women were destined to become even less Victorian in their behavior during the decade that followed. In the era of the suffragist and World War I, women began imitating ballroom dancer Irene Castle's bobbed hair and shortened skirts and dispensing with the time-honored custom of attending social functions accompanied by chaperones. "Prohibition," writes Aresty, "delivered a coup de grâce to the weakened restraints of the new generation and ushered in a period of defiant laxness." The postwar era not only signaled the rise of the

Charleston-dancing, bathtub-gin-drinking, cigarette-smoking, scantily clad, and suntanned flapper who swept aside most pretenses to convention, it also featured a new crop of war millionaires and an expanding middle class eager for instruction in the finer points of social behavior. Publishers reissued etiquette books written early in the century, but these books did not adequately reflect the changing times. The "old hat approach," writes Aresty, "brought Emily Post out of her corner, fists clenched, ready to go the full fight to a decisive victory as the new etiquette champion."

Born in Baltimore in 1873, Emily Post was the daughter of Bruce Price, a wealthy and noted architect who had designed the Château Frontenac in Quebec and was a planner of Tuxedo Park, New York, then an enclave for the rich. Shortly after her marriage to financier Edwin Post, Emily Post began her career as a novelist and magazine feature writer and in 1909 produced a prize-winning novel, *The Title Market.* She was persuaded to write a book of etiquette by her friend Frank Crowninshield, the editor of *Vanity Fair* magazine, and Richard Duffy of the publishing company Funk and Wagnalls. Post's book dealt with etiquette questions in a straightforward and sensible manner, while at the same time extolling the social virtues of Europeans. In an age when advertisements stressed the calamities that could befall women guilty of such social blunders as not using the correct deodorant, mouthwash, or fork, Post, in her *Etiquette: The Blue Book of Social Usage,* took the view that the "real outcasts" were those who "with inexcusable rudeness attract attention to the fault." Using her expertise as a novelist, Post created social scenarios complete with dramatis personae, such as Mrs. Wordly, Mrs. Newwed, Mr. Stocksan Bonds, Mrs. Cravin Praise, Mrs. Climber, and the Richan Vulgars. When Post revised *Etiquette* a few years after it had become the number one nonfiction best-seller in 1923, she showed herself to be in tune with the times by changing a chapter entitled "Chaperons and Other Conventions" to "The Vanishing Chaperon and Other New Conventions." Post explained such concessions to 1920s "flaming youth" by insisting, "The young girls of today do pretty much as they like. . . . We must realize that the modern generation will not be thwarted. It does what it wants." By middecade Emily Post had become, writes Aresty, "a virtual synonym for etiquette because she spoke in a *new* voice filled with passion and conviction that promised salvation and solution to all who were adrift in uncertainty about correct behavior—at the precise moment when Americans longed for such leadership."

Emily Post broadcast on the radio after 1931 and produced a daily column on good taste that was syndicated in more than two hundred newspapers. Her influence reached beyond her readers: during the 1920s high schools across the country, inspired by *Etiquette*, began including classes in social training for girls as part of their curricula. The book itself has been revised and updated since it first appeared, and in 1992, thirty-two years after Post's death, it went into its fifteenth printing.

Despite incursions in the genre by Amy Vanderbilt in 1952 and Vanderbilt's reviser, Letitia Baldrige, in 1978 and 1981, Emily Post's *Etiquette* remains the preeminent twentieth-century good manners manual of choice. *Etiquette*'s only serious rival during the 1990s was Judith Martin, aka Miss Manners, whose etiquette columns successfully combined wit, mordancy, and gentility as appropriate to late-twentieth-century upwardly mobile sensibilities as Emily Post's cautionary social dramas were to the flappers and parvenus of the Jazz Age.

1927

Sex Hormones Are Discovered

If Shakespeare had been a chemist, he would have loved estrogen, a hormone fit for comedy, tragedy and a sonnet or two.

Natalie Angier, "New Respect for Estrogen's Influence," *New York Times*, June 24, 1997

The discovery of female sex hormones in 1927 and the isolation and naming of their components by chemists in the years that followed set the stage for a series of medical developments that would profoundly affect the lives of women over the course of the twentieth century. By 1930 the Ascheim-Z pregnancy tests had come into wider use. This was the so-called rabbit test, in which the urine or blood from a woman suspected of being pregnant was injected into a female rabbit, which was killed a few days later; if the woman was pregnant, hormones in her urine or blood gave the rabbit's ovaries an appearance of pregnancy. By the late 1930s progesterone and estriol, a component of estrogen, had been isolated, and U.S. biochemist Edward Doisy had isolated the major estrogenic substance, estradiol, which is secreted by the ovaries and turns to estrone in the blood. Further research revealed that estrogen is also secreted by the adrenal glands atop the kidneys and is produced in the fat tissues of the breasts, buttocks, and thighs.

The discoveries of estrogen and progesterone led to greater understanding of the female reproductive system and how it functions throughout a women's life, from puberty to menopause. One significant medical result arising from increased knowledge of female sex hormones was the development of the birth control pill, researched from the late 1930s to the 1950s and given FDA approval in 1960. The "Pill," as oral contraceptives came to be known, represented even greater reproductive freedom for many women; for many others it became a reminder that contraception was, unfairly, a woman's responsibility. In addition, the birth control pill, whether used for contraception or low dose as a reproductive cycle stabilizer during the premenopause years called perimenopause, sometimes produced unpleasant side effects and posed risk factors that could endanger the health of some women. By the 1970s, although health risks associated with the use of oral contraceptives became widely known and advertised, some ten million American women were taking birth control pills. The decrease in the use of the Pill that began in the 1980s was in part the result of the AIDS epidemic, which brought back the condom as a safe and usually reliable contraceptive device.

During the last two decades of the century, the medical profession and the media tended to pay less attention to the pros and cons of oral contraceptive use to prevent pregnancy than they did to the positive and negative effects of estrogen in the body. As Natalie Angier of *The New York Times* reported: "Estrogen can be heroic, governing human fertility and nurturing the heart, bones, blood vessels and brain so pervasively that soon estrogen may be prescribed for middle-aged men as it is today for women. It can play Lady Macbeth with blood on her hands: estrogen has been implicated in cancers of the breast, ovary and uterus, autoimmune diseases, asthma, fibroids, mood disorders and migraines." In 1997 researchers discovered evidence suggesting that estrogen's influence possibly extended to the lungs, kidneys, intestines, bladder, and colon. For millions of perimenopausal, menopausal, and postmenopausal women using or considering estrogen replacement therapy, the steady volume of information in the 1990s regarding estrogen and its sister hormone, progesterone, was helpful as well as baffling and often frustrating.

Hormone replacement therapy (HRT), also known as estrogen replacement therapy (ERT), was first prescribed in the 1940s to alleviate what doctors referred to as the "symptoms" of menopause. Also known as "change of life," "the change," and the "climacteric," menopause was, and to an extent still is, considered by the medical profession to be less a normal, if admittedly physically and emotionally uncomfortable, event in a woman's life than a disease needing constant medication. By the 1970s massive advertising campaigns resulted in the rise of the principal synthetic estrogen Premarin to the fifth spot as the most popular prescription drug in the United States. By 1975 six million women were taking Premarin. By 1991 ten million women were using HRT. Articles and books, as well as physicians, praised HRT, claiming that it prevented hot flashes, loss of libido, vaginal dryness, heart disease, depression, osteoporosis, and even wrinkling. During the mid-1970s studies showed that HRT was associated with increases in endometrial cancer, especially among women who had taken estrogen for more than a year, gallbladder disease, and possibly breast cancer. In 1979 the FDA required that all estrogen products include an insert describing the risks as well as the benefits of taking estrogen. The insert stated that estrogen relieved hot flashes and vaginal dryness but was contraindicated for women with a history of cancer, breast cysts, blood clots, and arteriosclerosis and those with kidney or liver disease, seizure disorders, or heart disease. The authors of the chapter on menopause in *The New Our Bodies, Ourselves*, published by the Boston Women's Health Book Collective, asserted that "millions of women have been the unwitting subjects of a mass experiment that the passage of time revealed to be life-threatening for some." There was increased worry over the possible harmful effects of estrogen beginning in the 1980s, when studies showed a link between estrogen and breast cancer, as well as estrogen and cancer of the uterus (adding progestin to estrogen was shown to lessen the danger of uterine cancer, although later studies would suggest that progestin might also increase the risks associated with HRT).

Subsequent studies suggested that among those women with breast cancer, survival rates are higher for those who are on HRT, but such studies have provided little comfort for women, who are in the midst of what many perceive to be a breast cancer epidemic. It has also been speculated that estrogen-mimicking chemicals in the environment contribute to the development of the disease. Another synthetic estrogen, diethylstilbestrol (DES), prescribed to three to six million American women between 1941 and 1971, has had deleterious effects on the health of women. Prescribed by doctors in the mistaken belief that it would prevent miscarriages, DES was removed from the market during the 1970s after it was shown to cause clear-cell adenocarcinoma of the vagina or cervix, as well as several other reproductive abnormalities, in the daughters of women who took the drug.

During the 1990s the medical profession more readily acknowledged both the benefits and the risks associated with HRT and continued to research estrogen and estrogen receptors in the hopes of creating and perfecting so-called designer drugs, such as tamoxifen and raloxifene, which would have all the protective benefits of estrogen without the potentially injurious side effects. Despite these efforts, there was a backlash against HRT during the 1990s, led by media-savvy physicians such as Susan Love, author of *Dr. Susan Love's Hormone Book*, and Christiane Northrup, author of *Women's Bodies, Women's Wisdom* and a booklet titled *Estrogen: The True Story Every Woman Over Forty Needs to Know*. Love and Northrup questioned the wisdom of HRT, in their view a therapy overprescribed in a "one size fits all" dosage by doctors mainly concerned with retaining control over their patients and a medical establishment that has continued to insist that menopausal women are in some way diseased. As feminist writer Germaine Greer cynically observed: "Menopause is a dream specialty for the mediocre medic. It requires no surgical or diagnostic skill; it is not itself a life-threatening condition; there is no scope for malpractice action. Patients must return again and again for a battery of tests and checkups." The HRT backlash has also focused on drug companies, which have become rich by manufacturing and marketing menopause drugs like Premarin, Prem-Pro, and low-dose combination birth control pills. The anti-HRT message has gotten through to nearly 70 percent of American women, who have elected either to try homeopathic and naturopathic remedies, as well as vitamins and enhanced nutrition and exercise, in lieu of HRT, or to simply let nature take its course.

During the latter decades of the century, sex hormones also had cultural significance: estrogen and progesterone, as well as testosterone, were used by sociologists and psychologists in the debate over nature versus nurture as one way to explain so-called feminine and masculine behaviors as well as physical traits. Such explanations have been partly justified, given the powerful influence of sex hormones in the body, but they have also had the effect of reducing women and men alike to physical and emotional stereotypes. To paraphrase Simone de Beauvoir, one may be born female, but it takes a complicated set of social attitudes and imperatives, rather than simply estrogen and progesterone, to become a woman.

1928

Margaret Mead Publishes *Coming of Age in Samoa*

> At the present time we live in a period of transition. We have many standards but we still believe that only one standard can be the right one. We present to our children the picture of a battle-field where each group is fully armoured in a conviction of the righteousness of its cause. And each of these groups make forays among the next generation. But it is unthinkable that a final recognition of the great number of ways in which man, during the course of history and at the present time, is solving the problems of life, should not bring with it in turn the downfall of our belief in a single standard. . . . Samoa knows but one way of life and teaches it to her children. Will we, who have the knowledge of many ways, leave our children free to choose among them?
>
> Margaret Mead, conclusion of *Coming of Age in Samoa*

Only a handful of books published in the twentieth century have exerted a comparable impact as Margaret Mead's *Coming of Age in Samoa*, her groundbreaking work in cultural and social anthropology. This account of the twenty-three-year-old Mead's first field trip to the Pacific Islands launched her as a pioneering researcher and helped establish her as the world's most famous anthropologist. After more than seventy years, *Coming of Age in Samoa* is still the most widely read book in the field of anthropology, a fundamental text in the nature-nurture controversy and in the social and sexual revolution of the 1960s. Only Benjamin Spock's *Common Sense Book of Baby and Child Care* (1947), whose basic philosophy can be traced to Mead's work, has had a similar impact in shaping modern thinking and popular opinion on attitudes toward the family, child raising, and gender difference. In 1983 the publication of Derek Freeman's *Margaret Mead and Samoa: The Making and Unmaking of an Anthropological Myth*, a debunking of Mead's field methods and conclusions, reopened the controversy over *Coming of Age in Samoa* and reenergized the debate between biological and cultural determinism over the essential basis of human nature that all of Mead's works tried to define. That Mead's first book should continue to spark intense, partisan debate among anthropologists and captivate a mass general audience (evidenced by a *Time* magazine cover story on the Freeman controversy and a segment of *Donohue* devoted to the issues) is a testament to the massive shadow Margaret Mead has cast over some of the most important scientific and social questions in the twentieth century.

In the context of the 1920s, Mead's setting out on her own to Samoa and her experience there are remarkable for her daring and challenge of prevailing female roles. Intensely curious and unconventional, Mead attended Barnard College, where she began studying with Franz Boas, a distinguished anthropologist and a strong opponent of the theory of racial determinism. Mead was intrigued by Boas's belief that the comprehensive study of other societies could help people understand their own culture. Pursuing her graduate degree at Columbia University under Boas, Mead rejected her mentor's advice to do her fieldwork among Native Americans, his own area of interest, insisting instead on investigating the less assimilated cultures of Polynesia. Prior to Margaret Mead, anthropology had largely been a study by males of males, and her interests and perspective would open up new territory for research as well as radical new discoveries. As she argued in her grant application, she hoped to "add appreciably to our ethnological information on the subject of the culture of primitive women. Owing to the paucity of women ethnologists, practically no ethnological [work] has been done among women as such, and this investigation offers a particularly rich field for the study of feminine reactions and participation in the culture of the group." By living with and closely observing tribal life on the Samoan Islands, with a particular emphasis on adolescent girls, Mead hoped to contrast the maturation process of the Samoans with that of their Western counterparts to determine whether the angst and upheavals suffered by young people in the West had a biological or a cultural basis.

When Mead set out on her own to the South Pacific, she had never been abroad, had never been aboard a ship, and had never stayed a night in a hotel. She also had no experience in field research and no established procedures and guidelines beyond what she developed as she proceeded. Upon arriving in Pago Pago on August 31, 1925, Mead stayed in the ramshackle hotel that had served as the setting for Somerset Maugham's story and play *Rain*. During her first six weeks there she studied the Samoan geography and language. In October she proceeded to a new site on Ta'u, a small island in the Manu'a group, "the only

island where there are enough adolescents," Mead wrote to Boas, "which
are at the same time primitive enough and where I can live with Americans. I can eat native food, but I can't live on it for six months." Mead's
decision to live at the dispensary of U.S. Navy pharmacist mate Edward
Holt and his family has drawn subsequent criticism, but Mead justified
her "neutral base" from which "I could study all the individuals in the
village and at the same time remain aloof from native feuds and lines of
demarcation." To gain acceptance by the villagers, Mead learned to eat
strange foods, such as taro, land crabs, wild pigeons, and breadfruit, to sit
on her legs native style until she could hardly walk, to dance Samoan
style, and to wash in an outdoor shower in full view of the whole village.
Mead also survived a severe hurricane that hit the island and destroyed
the village, huddling in a cement water tank. For nine months she lived
the life of a Samoan girl, observing how family life was organized, cata-
loging village hierarchy, and recording courtship patterns among Samoan
adolescents through interviews. As she writes in the introduction to
Coming of Age in Samoa, "I concentrated upon the girls in the community.
I spent the greater part of my time with them. I studied most closely the

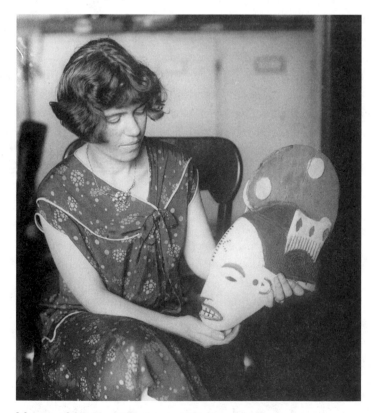

Margaret Mead in 1928, the year *Coming of Age in Samoa* was
published   *UPI/Corbis-Bettmann*

households in which adolescent girls lived. I spent more time in the games of children than in the councils of their elders. Speaking their language, eating their food, sitting barefoot and cross-legged upon the pebbly floor, I did my best to minimize the differences between us and to learn to know and understand all the girls. . . ."

What she discovered and revealed in *Coming of Age in Samoa* provided a fundamental challenge to the way the West had come to view so-called primitive peoples, undermining the basic assumptions that Western ideas and culture were inherently superior. Her observations also contradicted some of the most entrenched notions concerning child rearing, family relationships, gender assumptions, and the role of women and children in society. Among the Samoans, monogamy, sexual exclusiveness, and jealousy were unknown concepts. Birth, sex, and death were not concealed from the young but treated as natural events. Children were free to move from household to household to choose the most comfortable living arrangements, while still belonging to the larger family group of the village. Adolescent sexual freedom was essential to integrating the young into adult life of the village and was seemingly free from the trauma and neurosis that affected the maturation process in the West. All of these factors contributed to Mead's most important conclusion of *Coming of Age in Samoa* "that adolescence is not necessarily a time of stress and strain, but that cultural conditions make it so." Mead's discoveries in *Coming of Age in Samoa* challenged the notion that biological imperatives established innate conditions in human nature. As she observed in the 1972 edition, "When this book was written, the very idea of culture was new to the literate world. The idea that every thought and movement was a product not of race, not of instinct, but derived from the society within which an individual was reared, was new and unfamiliar."

Her book, capturing Samoan life with a novelist's skill in description to captivate a general readership, spread the message that another culture's values can offer important lessons for assessing our own cultural assumptions. The book's final section, relating her Samoan experiences to the problems of contemporary American society, would define the pattern for all of Mead's future work. In describing the basic differences in how the two societies raise their children, Mead argues not that the West might solve its problems by becoming Samoan-like, but that benefits are to be derived from considering alternative standards and testing previously held absolutes. The impact of Mead's book is evident in the many social programs that attempted to deal with cultural determinants in human behavior and the growing honesty in dealing with human sexuality as the century proceeded. Consequently Mead has been seen as one of the groundbreaking feminists and an early theorist in the sexual revolution and the women's rights movement of the 1960s and 1970s.

The importance and influence of *Coming of Age in Samoa* are evident in the furor that erupted in 1983 when anthropologist Derek Freeman published his attack on Mead's methods and conclusions. According to Freeman, Mead discovered what she hoped to find, a "negative instance" that contradicted the biological processes of maturation as a constant in human nature and a case for nurture over nature in the debate between cultural and biological determinants. Freeman indicts Mead's lack of sophistication in dealing with cultural difference, ignorance of the language, and sheer gullibility in recording what her young women subjects thought she wanted to hear. He also supplies data that contradict many of Mead's assertions. Mead's defenders were quick to challenge many of Freeman's own methods and conclusions, suggesting that the debate over nature versus nurture is far from resolved. Instead, moderates in the debate argue the need for a synthesis between biological and cultural conceptions of human nature, a notion with which Mead would certainly have agreed since all her subsequent anthropological research and writing worked toward defining such a synthesis. At the center of the controversy is the enormous stature of Margaret Mead. As Robert Cassidy points out, "It is no exaggeration to say that had she published only her work on Oceanic cultures, Mead would still have to be classified in the highest ranks of social science and anthropology. Add to these seminal works her writings on education, science, religion, ecology, feminism, and so on, and it is clear that Mead was a major force in the shaping of 20th-century thought on a wide variety of topics." *Coming of Age in Samoa* launched the career of one of the century's most versatile and challenging minds, and the legacy of Margaret Mead's discoveries continues to dominate scientific and cultural debate.

1930–1939

In 1936 the United States was in the midst of an economic depression, but there were women who could afford to spend $14.95 on a fashionable frock like those shown here, made of a new fabric called rayon. In addition, no stylish woman of the 1930s would venture out without a fancifully designed hat upon her head.

1930

The Great Depression Begins

The women know that life must go on and that the needs of life
must be met and it is their courage and determination which, time
and again, have pulled us through worse crises than the present one.

Eleanor Roosevelt, *It's Up to the Women*, 1933

The United States had experienced financial panics and depressions
at various times throughout its history. However, the nation had never
faced a depression as economically devastating and as long lasting as the
one that took place during the 1930s. The economic boom of the 1920s,
characterized by an inordinate expansion of credit and installment
buying, as well as overspeculation in the stock market, had led to the
uneven distribution of prosperity among various segments of American
society. The result was an economy that produced more goods than citizens could consume and that encountered a reduced foreign market for
American goods, owing to the war-debt policies of the three Republican
administrations. By 1932 the volume of U.S. industrial production had
dropped by nearly 50 percent and the gross national product by nearly
one-third. The number of unemployed Americans jumped from 4.5 million in 1930 to nearly 13 million in 1933. Although the unemployment
rate dropped slightly in 1937, in large part because of the labor policies
of Franklin Roosevelt's administration, one out of five potential workers
was without a job until the start of World War II, when production began
to revive.

The Great Depression could not help but affect both the family and
the work sectors of women's lives. Economic deprivation touched all
classes but was especially hard on the farm women whose families had
suffered through debilitating drought and the devastation brought on by
the dust storms in the prairie states and in New Mexico. Tens of thousands of farm families and sharecroppers lost their land or their leases

141

One of the most famous portraits of the Great Depression, photographed by Dorothea Lange. This photo of a migrant mother perfectly captures the worry and desperation felt by so many Americans during the Depression years. *Library of Congress*

and were forced to join workers who migrated west to seek jobs picking seasonal crops. The stoicism displayed by these migrant mothers together with the despair and exhaustion felt by them have all been perfectly captured in photographs taken by Dorothea Lange. Conditions for farm women remained difficult in the rural South, where poverty had always been present. Until a rural electrification program in 1935, only one out of ten American farms had electricity and most were typically lacking in running water. Farm women continued to have the triple responsibility of running their households, bearing and raising an average of six children, and helping to work the farm. "The Depression did not depress the conditions of the poor," writes Caroline Bird in *Invisible Scar*. "It merely publicized them."

The situation for rural African-American women was similar to that of white women, although in such a racist society African Americans were unlikely to receive the same level of publicity. Black families had always experienced hard times, so the impact of the Depression was less severe for them at first. In her autobiography, *I Know Why the Caged Bird Sings*, Maya Angelou describes her childhood in Stamps, Arkansas, during the Depression: "The country had been in the throes of the Depression for two years before the Negroes in Stamps knew it. . . . It was when the owners of cotton fields dropped the payment of ten cents for a pound of cotton to eight, seven and finally five that the Negro community realized that the Depression, at least, did not discriminate." But the discrimination that permeated American society, especially in the South, took its toll. By 1932 over 50 percent of African Americans were unemployed and were either denied relief or paid a fraction of the amount given to whites. African American women were forced to take the lowest-paying jobs available.

The majority of American women were neither poor nor rich but belonged to the middle class. The typical woman during the Depression years had a husband who was still working, although he probably had taken a pay cut in order to keep his job. These wives, always budget conscious, now struggled to make do with less. They practiced such economies as buying day-old bread, warming several dishes in the oven at the same time to save gas, buying cheaper cuts of meat, and substituting cheap ingredients for some recipes. They sewed blankets into coats and cut down adult clothes to fit children. Families moved to smaller houses or to apartments and cut out or cut down on luxuries and entertainments such as movies and Sunday drives. Instead they stayed home and listened to the radio. The Depression, as Eleanor Roosevelt observed, meant "endless little economies and constant anxiety for fear of some catastrophe such as accident or illness which may completely swamp the family budget." Since women were responsible for running households, whether or not their husbands were working, women's roles at the center of the family took on great significance during the 1930s. In *My America: 1928–1938*, Louis Adamic writes that during the Depression "thousands of families were broken up, some permanently, some temporarily, or were seriously disorganized. On the other hand, thousands of other families became more closely integrated than they had been before the Depression." The tendency of the family to gather around itself during this national crisis helps to explain the isolationism associated with the United States with regard to the events taking place in Europe in the 1930s.

Family life suffered in other ways as a result of the Depression. While divorce rates fell dramatically between 1930 and 1934, so did marriage and birth rates. It has been estimated that by 1938 1.5 million couples had decided to postpone marriage because of economic uncertainty. Not only was divorce too expensive, many couples stayed married because it was easier to get on government relief if there was a family to support. Two factors contributed to the decline in the birth rate: diminished sexual activity brought on by the stress of trying to survive in hard times and the disinclination to bear and raise children in such an unstable environment. A 1936 Gallup poll revealed that 63 percent of Americans favored the teaching and practice of birth control; contraceptive devices became increasingly available, even through the Sears, Roebuck catalog. By 1940 the dissemination of birth control information to married couples was legal in every U.S. state except Connecticut and Massachusetts.

During the Great Depression nearly 25 percent of American women worked outside the home. This was a sizable minority, which represented an increase in women's participation in the labor force from the beginning of the century. During the 1930s women worked for the same reasons they always had: out of desire or necessity. With so many men unemployed or forced to take salary cuts, married women often found themselves needing to take on the role of breadwinner or seeking jobs to supplement the family income. On the one hand, the Depression and the economic pressure it placed on families forced wives into wage work. But as Alice Kessler-Harris observes in *Out of Work*, it also "fostered a public stance that encouraged family unity and urged women, in the interest of jobs for men, to avoid paid work themselves." One prominent woman who subscribed to the popular 1930s phrase "Don't steal a job from a man" was Labor Secretary Frances Perkins. Twenty-six states enacted laws prohibiting the employment of married women, and between 1932 and 1937 the federal government forbade more than one member of a family from working in civil service.

Women as well as men suffered from layoffs, especially at the start of the decade when companies were eliminating staff and toward the end when jobs became more available to men, but U.S. Census figures from 1930 and 1940 show an increase in gainfully employed women from nearly eleven million to thirteen million. By 1940 the jobs most frequently held by women were in clerical work and sales, apparel and textile factory work, domestic service, nursing and teaching, and civil service. Despite strong public hostility toward working women, especially those who were married, employers knew the benefits in hiring them: women worked for lower wages than men. According to 1937 Social Security Administration figures, a woman's average yearly pay was $525 compared with $1,027 for men. As Susan Ware observes in *Holding Their Own: American Women in the 1930s*, "The Depression put even more pressure on women's already low pay, and women's wages dropped to the point that, even though employed, many women could not even meet basic living costs."

New Deal programs both benefited and thwarted women. The NRA codes, which were developed by the National Recovery Administration and lasted for two years, established production goals, fixed prices, and allocated resources within specific industries. Although the NRA codes raised wages, shortened work hours, and abolished sweatshop conditions, they also affected only half the women in the labor force, most notably those who worked in manufacturing and trade. The 1938 Fair Labor Standards Act (later called the Wages and Hours Act) made permanent the provisions of the NRA codes. Women benefited only marginally from such programs as the Civilian Conservation Corps and the Works Project Administration but fared better under the relief programs administered by the Women's and Profession Projects division. The Social Security Act provided maternal and pediatric programs and issued grants to mothers, but many provisions of the act discriminated against women workers, especially those who were married. The most influential legislation enacted during the New Deal was the 1935 National Labor Relations Act, also known as the Wagner Act, which affirmed the right of labor unions to organize and bargain collectively and represented a breakthrough for both men and women in the labor movement. In general, the revitalization of the labor movement and the growth of organized labor during the decade resulted in positive gains for women.

The Great Depression left its mark upon American women in a variety of ways. It propelled more women into the workforce and helped to prepare them for life during World War II. But although working women managed to take a small step forward during the Depression, they were also faced with what had become a highly romanticized concept of home and family. The return of many women to the traditional role of housewife after World War II was in part a legacy of the Great Depression. After fifteen years of dislocation and displacement, most women seemed to be ready for the enchantment of hearth and home.

1932

Amelia Earhart Flies Solo Across
the Atlantic Ocean

Amelia came into the public eye because she was an adventurer, but
she was more: she was America's sweetheart, America's shield. She
did everything better than everybody else—beckoned us on, and set
more records, and she did it seemingly effortlessly. She made us
proud to be American. Perhaps because she was cut down in her
prime—perhaps because she did not quite have time to fulfill her
potential, we can't let her go. She is thirty-nine forever. She has
become America's dream woman.

Susan Butler, *East to the Dawn*

Perhaps no other woman in the twentieth century has so defined a new
role for women as heroic adventurer as Amelia Earhart. The aviator,
whose flying records generated worldwide headlines and whose mysterious end has helped transfigure her into a woman of legendary status,
set out determinedly to win for women the possibility of a life of action
and a share in the great dramas of the century. As she recalled about her
childhood reading, "There are no heroines following the shining paths of
romantic adventure, as do the heroes of boys' books. . . . Of course girls
have been reading the so-called boys' books ever since there were such.
But consider what it means to do so. Instead of closing the covers with
shining eyes and the happy thought, 'That might happen to me someday!' the girls turning the final page can only sigh regretfully, 'Oh, dear,
that can never happen to me—because I'm not a boy!' " Amelia Earhart
altered that conclusion for countless women, creating a new breed of
heroines in fields of endeavors previously thought to be male preserves
alone. Women civilian and military pilots, astronauts like Sally Ride and
later women in the space program, as well as all women engaged in the
struggle for equality and increased job opportunites can point to Amelia

Earhart as one of the twentieth century's principal groundbreakers and mentors.

In 1932 Earhart became the first woman and only the second person after Charles Lindbergh to fly solo across the Atlantic. The event marked her as a hero of the world in one of the greatest accomplishments ever achieved by a woman. Earhart would go on to set aviation records around the world, enhancing her enormous reputation and asserting her influence on women for her daring and courage to pursue opportunities seemingly beyond the reach of women.

Born in Atchison, Kansas, Earhart was an active, outgoing child who wore bloomers instead of skirts and pursued boys' activities such as football. At first pursuing a career in medicine, she was captivated by her first airplane ride. After taking lessons from pioneer woman pilot Netta Snook, Earhart soloed for the first time in June 1921. In April 1928, one year after Charles Lindbergh's landmark solo flight across the Atlantic, Earhart was contacted by a group sponsoring a transatlantic flight that was to include "an American girl of the right image" and was chosen to be one of three crew members of the *Friendship*. Flying from Newfoundland to Wales in twenty hours and forty minutes, Earhart, whose job was to keep the plane's logbook, became the first woman transatlantic plane passenger. Called "Lady Lindy," Earhart was embarrassed by the notoriety, characterizing herself on the flight as little more than a "sack of potatoes." Yet her newfound fame as the source of inspiration for the newly emancipated women of the 1920s firmly established her aviation career. She lectured extensively on flying and was a founding member and president of the Ninety-Nines, an international organization of women pilots, and became an outspoken advocate for women. As historian Susan Ware points out in her feminist study *Still Missing*, "After the 1928 flight Amelia Earhart worked to portray her individual achievements as an example of women's capabilities in the modern world and as steps forward for all women. As Eleanor Roosevelt said of the pioneering aviator, 'She helped the cause of women, by giving them a feeling there was nothing they could not do.' In this way she made herself central to the history of feminism in the twentieth century."

Determined to prove that women could be more than window dressing in the field of aviation, Earhart set out to prove that she could match Lindbergh's achievement by her 1932 flight. As she reflected about her transatlantic experience aboard *Friendship*, "Someday I will have to do it alone, if only to vindicate myself. I'm a false heroine now, and that makes me feel very guilty. Someday I will redeem my self-respect. I can't live without it." Departing on May 20, 1932, from Teterboro Airport in New Jersey in her single-engine Lockheed Vega, Earhart flew

Amelia Earhart gained instant fame after becoming the first woman
transatlantic passenger in 1928. Her subsequent achievements in
aviation and mysterious disappearance while attempting an around-
the-world solo flight in 1937 would make her an inspiring and
legendary feminist figure in twentieth-century women's
history. *Library of Congress*

to Newfoundland and her embarcation point at Harbour Grace. With
acceptable weather reports she took off for the Atlantic crossing. One
hour into the flight, the plane's altimeter failed, and she was forced to
depend on her vision and pilot's skills to see how far above the sea she
was flying. After three hours she smelled burning oil and saw flames
coming from a broken weld in the engine's manifold ring but decided it
was safer to continue east rather than turn back heavily laden with fuel
to try to find the unlit Harbour Grace field. As she continued into the
night, the weather deteriorated, and she flew into a lightning and rain
storm. Ice formed on her windshield, and as the controls froze, the plane
went into a spin. Earhart gained control of the plane as the warmth of
the lower altitude melted the ice, but not before she had come much
"too close for comfort" to the whitecaps below. She gauged her altitude
using the sound of the engine's sputtering to indicate the lowest flying
limit. As she later recalled, "Probably if I had been able to see what was
happening on the outside during the night I would have had heart fail-

ure then and there, but, as I could not see, I carried on." When she turned on some of the reserve tanks of gasoline, she discovered that the fuel gauge was defective, and gasoline had started trickling down her neck. In danger from a potential explosion, Earhart decided to land in Ireland, short of her desired destination of Paris, in imitation of Lindbergh's flight. She set down in a pasture outside Londonderry after fifteen hours, eighteen minutes, the fastest transatlantic crossing thus far, becoming the first person to have crossed the Atlantic twice by plane.

Earhart's feat made her the most famous woman in the world, and she was feted throughout Europe and America. With characteristic modesty, Earhart confessed, "I realize this flight has meant nothing to aviation," but eventually she acknowledged, "If science advances and aviation progresses and international goodwill is promoted because of this flight, no one will be more delighted than I—or more surprised." The National Geographic Society awarded her the special gold medal they had given to Charles Lindbergh five years before. In thanking the society and President Hoover for the award, Earhart stated, "The appreciation of the deed is out of proportion to the deed itself. . . . I shall be happy if my small exploit has drawn attention to the fact that women, too, are flying." In the fall of 1932 the American Woman's Association gave its second annual award to the woman who had made the most outstanding contribution to society (the first had been given to Margaret Sanger) to Earhart.

Earhart would go on to become in 1935 the first person to fly solo from Hawaii to California, the first woman to fly solo anywhere in the Pacific, and the first to solo over both the Atlantic and the Pacific. Her final flight was to be a twenty-seven-thousand mile trip around the equator, the longest flight in aviation history. On the most dangerous leg of her journey across the Pacific, Earhart had to find the tiny island of Howland, 2,550 miles from her departure point in New Guinea. Her final diary entry before taking off on July 2, 1937, stated, "Not more than a month ago I was on the other shore of the Pacific, looking westward. This evening I look eastward over the Pacific. In those fast-moving days which have intervened, the whole width of the world has passed behind us—except this broad ocean. I shall be glad when we have the hazards of its navigation behind us." Radio contact between the plane and Coast Guard vessels was intermittent. Finally, after twenty-one hours of the expected eighteen-hour flight, the Coast Guard cutter *Itasca* received a final message from Earhart that she had approximately thirty minutes of fuel left and had not sighted land.

No trace of Earhart, her navigator, or their plane was ever found, despite the largest naval search in history. That Earhart vanished without a trace, at the height of her popularity and in her prime, has fueled many contradictory rumors and theories. In one it is suggested that Earhart was on a spying mission and was captured and executed by the Japanese; another is that she is still alive and in hiding. No conclusive proof has ever been found to disprove the most likely explanation that her plane simply ran out of fuel and crashed in the Pacific. But the aura of mystery surrounding Earhart's disappearance contributed to the legendary status she has gained as a great American hero whose stature and influence are derived from offering women an alternative role of action and adventure at the cutting edge of occupations formerly restricted by narrow gender assumptions.

The continuing fascination with Amelia Earhart in the various theories to solve the mystery of her disappearance point to her persistence as a cultural and gender hero even as conditions for women's equality and opportunity have improved. As Susan Ware has argued, "Once the women's movement offered so many choices and options to redefine what it meant to be a woman, there was less need to live vicariously . . . through figures from popular culture. Women could do it themselves. Or could they? Perhaps one key to the ongoing fascination with Amelia Earhart as a popular heroine is that her message of aspiration, individual fulfillment, and breaking down barriers still inspires today."

1935

Sulfa Drugs Are First Used Against
Puerperal (Childbed) Fever

Puerperal fever is probably the classic example of iatrogenic disease—that is, disease caused by medical treatment itself. . . . [It] is clear that doctors' need to prevent puerperal fever contributed to the dehumanization of birth. Doctors not only had to control more carefully the processes and contexts of birthcare, they also had to bring preventive treatment to each pregnant and parturient woman, however healthy, because each woman was susceptible to infection from the doctor and the medical environment. Doctors had to regard each woman as diseased, because birth provided the occasion and medicine the cause for infection. . . . More women were attracted to hospitals, however, because after 1900 hospitals offered painless birth not readily available in home deliveries. Women gain release from birthpain, at the expense of being processed as possibly diseased objects. Thus began the major transformation in birth: from home to hospital, from suffering to painlessness, from patient care to disease care.

Richard W. Wertz and Dorothy C. Wertz,
Lying-In: A History of Childbirth in America

Puerperal, or childbed, fever has been a leading cause of death among adult women since the beginning of recorded history. While the search for the prevention and eventual cure of puerperal fever with the first successful use of sulfonamide drugs in 1935 led to the virtual elimination of the disease, it also had a profound impact on childbirth in America and created an ongoing debate over the role of medicine in birth. The shift of births from home to hospital, so useful in controlling the pain and complications of births, had exposed women to a disease spread by doctors themselves; the prevention and cure of this disease would transform the birth process into a medical procedure that the subsequent

151

natural childbirth movement and the return of midwifery and home deliveries would attempt to challenge.

Puerperal fever, actually a wound infection in the genital tract, reached epidemic proportions in foreign hospitals from the seventeenth century. In America, women who almost always delivered at home were spared until the 1840s, when the fever began to appear even in some home deliveries. In hindsight, the causes for the fever are obvious. During labor the cervix, vagina, and perineum may become torn and lacerated and offer an ideal breeding ground for bacteria entering from the doctor's hand or instruments. Without sterile procedures, doctors or nurses could easily carry the deadly hemolytic streptococcus, first identified by Louis Pasteur, from other patients' wounds. The fever causes inflammation of the abdominal cavity, blood poisoning, delirium, and death within a few days. In hospitals with doctors and nurses going from infected patient to patient and from autopsies to deliveries without antiseptic prevention, the infection was spread with deadly frequency, even to homes by the visiting physician.

As early as the 1770s doctors began to identify the contagion and its mysterious spread and urged that women not be confined in beds without clean linen in unventilated, crowded wards. As Dr. Alexander Hamilton wrote in 1781, childbed fever "is remarkably infectious . . . like the plague, few escape of those affected. . . . It raged in the public hospitals of Paris, London, and Dublin, communicating from one person to another with astonishing rapidity, and its ravages were equally striking." In America, Dr. Oliver Wendell Holmes was the first physician to recognize that puerperal fever was a contagion spread by doctors. His 1843 paper delivered to the Boston Society for Medical Improvement presented his evidence that doctors were carrying the contagion from patient to patient and called for physicians to cease practicing when they or their patients became ill with the fever. Holmes's charge that doctors themselves were the agents of the disease was violently rejected, particularly his notion that the hands of doctors should be cleaned with care. It was argued that since a doctor was a gentleman, a gentleman's hands were always clean. Dr. Hugh L. Hodge in a counterattack, "On the Non-contagious Character of Puerperal Fever," urged his colleagues "to divest your minds of the overpowering dread that you can ever become, especially to women . . . the minister of evil; that you can ever convey, in any possible manner, a horrible virus so destructive in its effects . . . as that attributed to puerperal fever." Dr. Charles D. Meigs labeled Holmes's analysis "a vile, demoralizing superstition as to the nature and causes of many diseases" in which "I prefer to attribute them to accident or Providence."

Ignaz Semmelweis, the nineteenth-century Hungarian physician who identified the means of preventing the spread of puerperal (childbed) fever
Brown Brothers

It would be the Hungarian doctor Ignaz Philipp Semmelweis who first demonstrated in 1847 the contagiousness of the fever statistically and propounded the means for preventing it. Working in Vienna's largest maternity hospital, which was divided into the First Clinic, where medical students attended births, and the Second Clinic, which employed midwives, Semmelweis noticed that the death rate from the fever was more than four to one between the two clinics and that women who delivered on the hospital steps or in the corridors never contracted the disease. Since the medical personnel in the First Clinic were the only staff who proceeded from autopsies of infected women in the morgue to attend patients in the ward, Semmelweis intuited a likely source for the spreading of the fever. Some twenty years before Joseph Lister promulgated the use of antiseptics in surgery, Semmelweis ordered the medical students under his supervision to wash their hands in a chloride of lime solution after dissecting corpses and after each examination of women in the ward. The results were dramatic. Deaths in the First Clinic dropped from 12 percent to 3 percent at the end of seven months; during the next year only 1 percent of First Clinic patients died. Dr. Semmelweis's addition of the recently discovered disinfectant and his call for improved medical and hospital hygiene spelled the difference in containing the fever. Sadly, Dr. Semmelweis, whose breakthrough in childbed fever prevention saved the lives of countless women, was driven from his post by an envious superior. He returned to his native Budapest, where he eventually went mad and died in an insane asylum.

Carelessness in using antiseptics made puerperal fever a continuing problem in the twentieth century, with infection rates as high as 11 percent by 1934. The cure, however, did not come until 1935, when doctors at Queen Charlotte's Isolation Hospital in London successfully administered sulfonamides to defeat the infection caused by hemolytic streptococcus. During the 1940s penicillin became available, increasing the arsenal of antibiotics that virtually eliminated deaths from puerperal fever in American hospitals. But the tradeoff in preventing and curing puerperal fever was the transformation of childbirth from a natural female event to a medical condition and its eventual dehumanization in the sterile conditions present in hospitals. It would take the natural childbirth movement of the 1970s to create an understanding between women who believed that giving birth need not be a complicated medical event and doctors who offered women the high-tech hospital care that had served to solidify their control over the birth process.

The National Council of Negro Women Is Organized

The National Council of Negro Women was different from other black women's organizations, for although the NCNW was concerned with the phenomenon of racism, it also acknowledged the additional burden of sexism that its members had to bear.

Tracey A. Fitzgerald, *The National Council of Negro Women and the Feminist Movement, 1935–1975*

By the 1890s black women's clubs, usually centered around local welfare or education projects, had been organized in a number of American cities. These local clubs began to exchange information and delegates, which led to the formation of large federations. In 1895 African American club women were spurred to create a national organization after the antilynching efforts of journalist Ida B. Wells-Barnett prompted racist and scurrilous comments concerning the morality of black women by James Jacks, president of the Missouri Press Association. In 1896 the National League of Colored Women and the National Federation of Afro-American Women merged to form the National Association of Colored Women (NACW), under the presidency of educator Mary Church Terrell. The NACW became, writes Gerda Lerner in *Black Women in White America*, "a unifying force, an authoritative voice in defense of black womanhood. It greatly spurred local and regional organization."

In 1935, building on the success of the NACW in sustaining a national federation movement that provided African American women's clubs with encouragement, direction, expert leadership, and black pride, edu-

cator Mary McLeod Bethune, together with such prominent black
women leaders as Mary Church Terrell, Charlotte Hawkins Brown, and
Mabel Staupers, formed the National Council of Negro Women
(NCNW), in the hope of creating a superorganization that would act as
a cohesive umbrella for black women's groups already in existence.
Although Bethune had received the support of the NACW during her
struggle to establish her Daytona Normal School for Girls in Florida and
recognized the organization's considerable influence, she felt that the
NACW lacked enough of a national and structural focus on issues
directly relating to the status of African American women. In her words,
the NCNW would strive "to harness the great power of nearly a million
women into a force for constructive action."

During its early years, however, the NCNW, with Bethune as its first
president, was concerned primarily with advancing the cause of racial
equality. To that end, the NCNW lobbied for political change and served

Dorothy Boulding Ferebee (*left*) succeeded Mary McLeod Bethune as president of
the NCNW, serving from 1949–1953; her successor was Vivian Carter Mason (*right*).
In 1958 Dorothy Irene Height (*center*) became the NCNW's fourth president.
Mary McLeod Bethune Council House NHS, Washington, D.C.

as an advocate for a broad range of issues affecting African American men as well as women. After Bethune's death in 1955, the NCNW began to work more vigorously for the advancement of women and young people at a level of commitment equal to its work for equality, although the organization continued its involvement with the cause of civil rights. In the early 1960s, during the height of the civil rights movement, the NCNW worked closely with the civil rights organizations, particularly the Student Non-violent Coordinating Committee (SNCC), to achieve rights for African Americans in the South.

During the years of the women's movement in the 1960s and 1970s, under the presidency of Dorothy Irene Height, who had also served on the President's Commission on the Status of Women in 1961, the NCNW responded to the concerns of the many African American women regarding feminist issues by shifting its focus from primarily black concerns to problems encountered by women in general and by minority women in particular. In 1975 the NCNW prepared a report on the status of women in housing titled "Women and Housing: A Report on Sex Discrimination in Five American Cities" in which the authors documented "the problems women in American cities face when they try to acquire and maintain a decent place to live" and called for passage of legislation to promote female equality modeled after the civil rights statutes of the 1960s. The same year, designated "International Women's Year" by the United Nations, the NCNW received a grant from the Agency for International Development, which enabled it to invite African, Latin American, and Caribbean women attending the International Women's Year Conference in Mexico City to come to Mississippi to study the NCNW programs designed to alleviate poverty there. Through its international program, the NCNW cultivated relationships between African American women and women of color in developing countries. In the United States the NCNW worked with all segments of society to help chart and carry out community service and social programs. The efforts of older black women's organizations such as the NCNW and new member groups like the Coalition of 100 Black Women, founded in 1970 to develop programs to deal with a variety of issues facing African American women, helped to unite twentieth-century women of color in common causes. As Dorothy Height once summed up Mary McLeod Bethune's philosophy regarding the NCNW: "We are seeking to make togetherness more effective."

1936

Margaret Mitchell's *Gone With the Wind* Is Published

> If the novel *Gone With the Wind* has a theme, the theme is that of survival.
>
> Margaret Mitchell, *Wilson Quarterly*
> 11 September 1936

Except for the Bible, no book has sold more hardcover copies than *Gone With the Wind*, Margaret Mitchell's epic of the American South, Civil War, and the Reconstruction era. A publishing and cultural phenomenon, the novel sold over a million copies within the first year of its publication in 1936. It has seldom sold fewer than forty thousand hardback editions per year since then and considerably more paperback copies. Translated into twenty-seven languages in thirty-seven countries, its popularity has spread worldwide. With the 1939 release of the film version, one of the most successful films in movie history, *Gone With the Wind*'s hold on popular culture has reached an unprecedented level of saturation. It is estimated that over 90 percent of the American population has seen the film, few only once. When the film was broadcast on television for the first time, in 1976, it drew 110 million viewers, up until then the largest audience in television history. Mitchell's conception of the South during the period before, during, and immediately after the Civil War has set the southern archetype in readers' and moviegoers' imaginations, and Scarlett O'Hara, Rhett Butler, and Tara have entered the collective consciousness. Yet despite the enormous popularity and impact of *Gone With the Wind*, the novel has received scant critical attention, and Margaret Mitchell has been largely consigned to the netherworld of the popular romancer rather than considered a literary artist. As the creator of the most popular romantic novel in history, Mitchell can be viewed as one of the progenitors of the modern romance genre, but she

157

Debutante and southern belle Margaret Mitchell in her youth, looking every bit as determined as her famous anti-heroine, Scarlett O'Hara   *Library of Congress*

deserves credit as well for creating an enduring woman-centered fiction that deals in important ways with issues about the ambiguous roles of women in modern society.

Margaret Mitchell (1900–1949) was the daughter of a prominent Atlanta, Georgia, couple who were born during the devastating aftermath of the Civil War. Devoted to her native city, Mitchell was exposed to local history from both her parents. As she recalled to a reviewer when *Gone With the Wind* was first published, "The genesis of my book . . . lies years back when I was six years old." Mitchell credited her mother with fixing in her imagination the image of the South uprooted by history during tours of ruined plantations or, in her mother's phrase, "Sherman's Sentinels." Mitchell remembered, "She talked about the world those people had lived in, such a secure world, and how it had exploded beneath them. And she told me that my own world was going to explode under me, some day, and God help me if I didn't have some weapon to meet the new world." Mitchell's defense became her writing and story-telling and her theme how individuals cope in order to survive. Leaving her own secure world, first as a debutante and later as a society lady, Mitchell had until 1926 been a reporter and feature writer for the *Atlanta*

Journal. When she fell and sprained an ankle that had previously been damaged in two earlier accidents and it failed to heal properly, Mitchell convalesced at home, reading extensively in nineteenth-century Atlanta history. According to family legend, when few books remained in the library that Mitchell had not read, her husband remarked, "It looks to me, Peggy, as though you'll have to write a book yourself if you're going to have anything to read." Thus began Mitchell's ten-year labor to produce *Gone With the Wind*. Her intention was to clarify the southern experience of the Confederate defeat, particularly from the perspective of and impact on southern women. She started her story with Scarlett O'Hara's final realization on the eventual book's final pages: "She had never understood either of the men she had loved and so she had lost them both." To reach this moment of insight, Mitchell constructed her massive thousand-page epic centered on the experience of her main female character, first named Pansy, later to be christened Scarlett O'Hara.

Scarlett, one of the most intriguing and fascinating modern heroines, is a complex mixture of modern and traditional values and feminine and masculine traits. On the one hand, she can be seen as a self-centered and childish southern belle, oblivious of people who do not contribute to her sense of entitlement, all that is owed a lady in the chivalric southern tradition. On the other, she is an aggressive manipulator who rejects passive victimhood with a survivalist mentality that fuels her drive for mastery. At the center of Mitchell's novel, therefore, is a morally mixed central heroine, fascinating and admirable in her passion and resilience, deplorable in her heartlessness and self-centeredness. Ultimately Scarlett is doomed to exist between the conflicting poles of autonomy and dependence that Mitchell diagnosed as the central dilemma of southern women. In this regard, *Gone With the Wind* offers a fascinating dramatization of gender roles and expectations, relevant not just to the period in the South before and after the Civil War, but increasingly valid to the book's first readers, who were enduring the struggles of the Great Depression while absorbing the values of the new emancipated woman of the post–World War I era. As Anne Jones observes in an insightful essay on the novel, "The Bad Little Girl of the Good Old Days: Gender, Sex, and the Southern Social Order," the novel "questions not only the means but the value of sheer survival, and defines survival quite clearly as psychological and ethical as well as physical. The axes on which Mitchell imagined survival to balance are self-reliance and dependence. Carried to extreme, self-reliance becomes isolation and even solipsism; dependence, at worst, becomes the loss of selfhood and identity. Because the culture [Mitchell] lived in and the culture she imagined both placed these specific values upon one or the other sex, the novel becomes a study in gender roles, in what it means to be a man or a woman in the South."

The ambiguity of Scarlett is set from the novel's memorable opening line: "Scarlett O'Hara was not beautiful, but men seldom realized it when caught by her charm as the Tarleton twins were." Scarlett is a complex blend of her mother's feminine side and her father's masculine character, and the novel's events show how both work themselves out in Scarlett's defiance of convention and drive for independence and mastery. Yet her domination by traditional values of dependence on the old southern order and its definition of women finally dooms her. Attracted to the equally iconoclastic and masculine aggressive Rhett, she is pulled back from him by her devotion to the dutiful, chivalric Ashley Wilkes and to the old values of security and protection represented by Tara. Scarlett is, therefore, both a new woman for her readers' era and a woman incapable of articulating a meaningful role for herself beyond the traditional gender expectation of her past. Rhett, despite his outsider's stance, is no less dominated by traditional gender assumptions. In his own climactic revelation about his relationship with Scarlett and his daughter, Bonnie Blue, Rhett observes:

> I wanted to take care of you, to pet you, to give you everything you wanted. I wanted to marry you and protect you and give you free rein in anything that would make you happy—just as I did Bonnie. . . . I wanted you to stop fighting and let me fight for you. I wanted you to play, like a child—for you were a child, a brave, frightened, bull-headed child. I think you are still a child. . . . I liked to think that Bonnie was you, a little girl again, before the war and poverty had done things to you. She was so like you . . . and I could pet and spoil her—just as I wanted to pet you.

Rhett is no more able to accept the unconventional Scarlett than she is able to rest contentedly in her independence. The men as well as the women in *Gone With the Wind* must ironically be protected in their illusions as the superior guardians of women. The failure of both genders to sustain these reassuring values in the face of the changes wrought by the war and its disruptive aftermath marks the novel's tragedy, as Mitchell plays out a number of variations on conventional gender expectations.

The romance genre, reflected both in fiction and later on television through soap operas, borrows much from Margaret Mitchell, particularly her survival theme, endlessly testing characters by circumstances and tangled relationships. Yet few popular romances match Mitchell's deeply shaded complexity of her central female character, preferring instead idealization to Mitchell's richer portraiture. Most romance novels also cannot resist the pleasing resolution that *Gone With the Wind* insistently avoids. Scarlett, in perhaps one of the most daring and unsettling conclusions in fiction, is left on her own, unsupported by her love for Rhett, with only the consolation that Tara remains and that "Tomorrow is another day." The conflict that Mitchell has exhaustively dramatized between opposing gender assumptions is left unresolved, suggesting a basic tension in women and men that continues to await a satisfying synthesis.

Despite her readers' continual pleas for a sequel to resolve the suspense over Scarlett's fate, Mitchell refused to comply and struggled to cope with "the hell on earth" that her popularity brought until she was killed in an accident with an out-of-control taxicab in 1949. *Gone With the Wind* remains one of the defining literary expressions of the twentieth century, if not for its artistic qualities, then for its ability to captivate a massive popular audience with themes of history and relationships seen through a female perspective. Other great female fictional characters—Thackeray's Becky Sharpe, Flaubert's Emma Bovary, Tolstoy's Anna Karenina—were the work of male novelists. With Scarlett O'Hara, a woman writer offered her unique point of view to create a riveting central female character and a view of the past and America's central historical tragedy through the lens of a female perspective that continues to express contemporary issues and concerns.

1939

Karen Horney Challenges Freudian Conceptions of Female Psychology in *New Ways in Psychoanalysis*

Penis envy is . . . the concept of theoretical irreducibility for Freud's female psychology: that is, all female behavior can ultimately be explained by reference to it. It leads to a fatalism that characterizes his entire instinct theory.

If penis envy is inevitable, then women can only resign themselves to that which they cannot change. If it explains all female behavior, it also serves to justify that behavior. A woman's anger at her husband, for example, can be explained away by penis envy. "That such interpretations befog the real issue," argued Horney, "is my most stringent objection to them, particularly from the therapeutic angle." By mystifying what she regarded as the real cause of the woman's anger, the concept of penis envy serves to maintain the conditions that cause anger and to resign the woman to the inevitability of those conditions as well as to repress, and finally to trivialize, her rage. The therapeutic consequence is not only to teach the woman to accept the world and a self that she cannot change but also to deny her responsibility for her own actions. If the former produces an attitude of "why fight the inevitable?" the latter suggests "what can you expect from a mere woman?" Both serve to keep a woman in her place: obedient and infantilized.

Marcia Westkott, *The Feminist Legacy of Karen Horney*

In 1939 with the publication of *New Ways in Psychoanalysis*, Karen Horney mounted a determined assault on Sigmund Freud's accepted psychoanalytic explanations of female instinctual drives and neuroses. In Horney's view, Freud's analysis failed to conform with her own experience and reflected a patriarchal view that defined women by their anxiety that their gender was incomplete and inadequate. In exposing the shortcomings of Freud's notions, Horney posited an alternative view of female psychology that has formed one of the fundamental bases for feminist thought in the twentieth century. With Horney, women acquired a psychological justification to regard their gender as not inferior to men and a rationale on the deepest level of instinct and unconsciousness for equality and liberation.

In a sense, Karen Horney's entire life as a woman and a psychoanalyst is based on her central conception that

> [our] whole civilization is a masculine civilization. The State, the laws, morality, religion, and the sciences are the creation of men. . . . If we are clear about the extent to which all our being, thinking, and doing conform to these masculine standards, we can see how difficult it is for the individual man and also for the individual woman really to shake off this mode of thought.

For Horney, shaking off masculine dictates began early in her childhood. Born in Hamburg, Germany, in 1885, Horney was the younger of two children of Sonni and Berndt Danielsen. Her father, a Norwegian-born sea captain, was a strict Evangelical Lutheran who browbeat his wife and children and was subject to fits of pious rage. Although he did not approve of education for women, Horney's mother insisted upon it, and her daughter was determined to study medicine. She attended the University of Freiburg, where she met law student Oscar Horney, whom she married while Karen was a medical student at the University of Berlin. Horney's interest in psychiatry began after she sought relief for bouts of nervous exhaustion and depression in sessions with therapist Karl Abraham. She gained her medical degree in 1915 with a thesis on traumatic psychoses. Between 1911 and 1915 she gave birth to three daughters, whom she raised to be independent. During World War I Horney worked with shell-shocked soldiers at the military neuropsychiatric hospital in Berlin. After the war she was active in the Berlin Psychoanalytic Institute and opened a private practice in which most of her patients were women.

During the 1920s Horney began her work reforming the psychoanalytical view of women established by Freud, placing his central concept of penis envy as women's dominant instinct into a wider cultural context. Women, according to Horney, did not envy a man's penis so much as the superior position of men in society. The castration complex in a young girl is generated, Horney argued, when she is ultimately frustrated in her desire to emulate her father, whose gender brings with it numerous social and sexual privileges. Horney's early theories deepened Freudian thought by looking at social and environmental factors in neurosis but did not deviate too greatly from accepted Freudian doctrine.

Karen Horney's second book, *New Ways in Psychoanalysis*, created a storm of controversy by challenging the accepted Freudian concept of penis envy as a way to explain female psychology.   *Photo courtesy of Bernard J. Paris*

Horney separated from her husband in 1926, and in 1932 she emigrated to the United States. In Chicago she cofounded the Chicago Institute of Psychoanalysis and became its associate director. In 1934 she moved to New York, where she taught at the New School for Social Research and joined the New York Psychoanalytic Society and Institute. Her work during the 1930s moved further away from Freudian doctrine. Her first book, *The Neurotic Personality of Our Time* (1937), looked at the cultural effects of psychological problems, which Freud had largely ignored, but it was her second book, *New Ways in Psychoanalysis*, that signaled a radical break with Freud and the psychoanalytic community. In it Horney opposed Freud's tenet of female psychology that stated that the yearning to compensate for the lack of a penis explains women's heterosexual desire, rivalry among other women, the gratification of motherhood, female homosexuality, masochism, and jealous imitation of male behavior. According to Freud, penis envy offers all one needs to understand female behavior—from passivity to aggression and desire. In Horney's view, Freud's notion is simply an expression of masculine narcissistic self-absorption. A male, who sees the naked female body for the first time, assumes that the woman has been castrated and is inferior to him. She must, from the perspective of the male, long for what she cannot have. Men's dread of a perceived female penis envy results in compulsive masculinity or, according to Horney, "an overwhelming inner compulsion to prove their manhood again and again to themselves and others." Beneath the narcissistic glorification of the penis, however, in Horney's view, is masculine "womb envy." Horney argued that the desire for children is not, as Freud argued, a secondary manifestation of penis envy, but "primary and instinctually anchored deeply in the biological sphere." According to Marcia Westkott in *The Feminist Legacy of Karen Horney*, the "male attribution of penis envy to women is not only the consequence of their fear of women; it is also a projection of their underlying envy, the inversion of their wish for motherhood."

Horney's analysis widened the conceptions of the patriarchal determinants of human psychology that Freud uncovered to include its maternal and interpersonal determinants as well. Her reassessment liberated the notion of female psychology and sexuality from the constraints of a male standard—women defined by their lack of a penis—to assert separate, primary female instincts that validated both female sexuality and motherhood. Although Horney would in her later writing go beyond the instinctual basis of female psychology, her argument in *New Ways in Psychoanalysis* represented a powerful counterattack on Freudian doctrine that diminished the autonomy and identity of the female seen through Freud's patriarchal view.

Horney's unorthodox and revisionist analysis that defied the accepted Freudian standard met with severe criticism and censure. She was voted out of her position as a training analyst by the New York Psychoanalytic Society and Institute. Horney responded by resigning from the society and with several colleagues formed the Association for the Advancement of Psychoanalysis and its training arm, the American Institute for Psychoanalysis, which was renamed the Karen Horney Clinic after her death in 1952. Horney's later work included *Self-Analysis* (1942), *Are You Considering Psychoanalysis?* (1946), *Neurosis and Human Growth* (1950). *Feminine Psychology,* published posthumously in 1967, built on her critique of Freud to create an alternative social psychology of women that would prove to be influential in the modern conception of feminism.

Based on the psychological conflicts she witnessed in her patients and among other middle-class women, Horney identified women's basic psychological struggles in conflicting definitions of femininity. In the patriarchal ideal of womanhood, a woman's "only longing is to love a man and be loved by him, to admire and serve him." In the more independent female identity that began to emerge in the twentieth century, women have striven to become economically independent of men by developing their own abilities and skills, which conflicts with the traditional patriarchal pattern. Modern women are, therefore, caught between desires for love and work, between deference and ambition, and seductive versus aggressive behavior. Horney's analysis helps to explain various anxieties modern women contend with, as well as their guilt, self-doubt, and often depreciation of their skills and accomplishments.

Horney's work must be regarded as forming, along with Simone de Beauvoir's *The Second Sex* and Betty Friedan's *The Feminine Mystique*, one of the key foundation texts in understanding women in the twentieth century. Like de Beauvoir and Friedan, Horney challenged conventional thought and dominant intellectual models for a radical reassessment that has played an important role in reconceptualizing women's identity at the deepest social and psychological levels.

1940–1949

In advertisements during World War II, civilian women were frequently shown dressed for their work on behalf of the war effort. Knee-length skirts and dirndls, blouses, jackets, and dresses with padded shoulders, and platform shoes were popular fashion choices during the 1940s for women who did not have industrial jobs. After the war, skirts lengthened and Dior's "New Look" pared down the broad-shouldered silhouette. *Library of Congress*

1941–1945

World War II

> Instead of cutting the lines of a dress, this woman cuts the pattern
> of aircraft parts. Instead of baking a cake, this woman is cooking
> gears to reduce the tension in gears after use. . . . After a short
> apprenticeship, this woman can operate a drill press just as easily
> as a juice extractor in her own kitchen.
>
> Excerpt from the propaganda film *Glamour Girls of '43*,
> in Sara M. Evans, *Born for Liberty*

Diplomatic maneuvering, the need to solve the unemployment problem caused by the Great Depression, and a public mood of isolationism
contrived to keep the United States neutral during the armed conflicts
that raged in Asia and Europe during the late 1930s. The Depression
had forced many women to find wage work out of economic necessity,
and women were welcomed by employers who saw them as a source of
cheap labor. But women workers were generally unsupported in their
efforts to make ends meets by a society that felt more comfortable with
men and women in the traditional roles of breadwinner and homemaker.
However, when the United States entered the war after the Japanese
attack on Pearl Harbor in December 1941, women were no longer told,
"Don't steal a job from a man." Instead they were urged to help the war
effort by getting jobs as quickly as possible.

Although women, especially those who were married, entered the
labor force in unprecedented numbers between 1941 and 1945, many
initially chose to respond to the call for patriotic action by volunteering
their time to help the war effort. Some three million women worked
with the Red Cross, drove ambulances, served food and entertained soldiers at USO canteens, sold war bonds, and spotted planes for the Civil
Defense. They organized scrap metal drives in their communities and
saved bacon grease for war matériel. But by 1942, with the increasing

enlistment and drafting of men into the military, the labor force was becoming drained of male workers. Since high industrial production was imperative, the U.S. government actively prevailed upon industry to compensate for the loss of men to the military by hiring women to take their places. To entice women into factories and to allay general fears that such a gender role reversal would result in dire consequences for American society, the War Manpower Commission, with the cooperation of the media and industrial advertisers, mounted a major recruitment campaign. As Sara M. Evans notes in *Born for Liberty*, the "mobilization of women for industrial work illustrates an extraordinary degree of governmental intervention in the economy and in molding values and attitudes achieved during the war." The Office of War Information generated recruitment posters and pamphlets, and industry ads assured women that they could look glamorous even in coveralls. The War Labor Board, its feet planted squarely in both labor and management camps, announced its intention to rule that women working in previously male jobs be paid the same wage as men and agreed to intervene in labor disputes in order to prevent strikes.

The campaign proved so successful that ultimately six million women took paying jobs during the war, an increase in the female labor force from 25 percent to 36 percent. Nearly two million women went to work in heavy industry, maneuvering giant overhead cranes, cleaning out blast furnaces, handling munitions, driving tanks off production lines, operating drill presses, riveting, and welding. One million women worked for the federal government in offices, where they handled the enormous amount of paperwork created by the war. Many other women took over prewar "male" jobs such as bus and truck driver, lumberjack, train conductor, gas station operator, police officer, and lifeguard. Those women who benefited most from the wartime reallocation of labor were African Americans, older women, and married women. Before the war, 72 percent of African American women worked as domestics and 20 percent were farm hands. By the war's end, some 18 percent of African American women were working in factories. Women over thirty-five constituted 75 percent of the new female labor force; 60 percent were married, and most had school- or pre-school-age children. One of the most difficult problems facing working mothers was the lack of government-sponsored day care, an option offered to British women but unavailable to American women until 1944. Even then, day care funding represented only a fraction of what was needed, and federal and local programs served only 10 percent of the children of war workers.

Media propaganda during the war did not stop at the recruitment of women workers. Through a popular patriotic song, "Rosie the Riveter,"

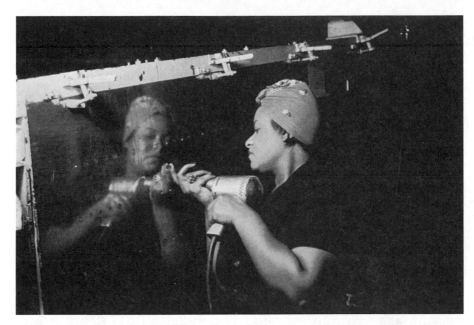

Many "Rosies" were women of color. In this 1943 Office of War Information photo, a woman is seen operating a hand drill on a Vengeance dive bomber at the Vultee plant in Nashville, Tennessee.   *Library of Congress*

the character of "Rosie" came to symbolize wartime women industrial workers. A national heroine, Rosie was visually depicted both as a strong but traditionally feminine-looking woman in form-fitting coveralls and as a burly, muscular woman in overalls. The media clearly preferred to highlight the feminine qualities of America's Rosies. In 1943 an electric company ad in the *Saturday Evening Post* read: "She's 5 feet 1 from her 4A slippers to her spun-gold hair. She loves flower-hats, veils, smooth orchestras—and being kissed by a boy who's in North Africa. *But, man, oh man, how she can handle her huge and heavy press!*" A year later the same magazine featured an ad for Eureka vacuum cleaners that extolled the virtues of the "valiant young mothers who've taken their great adventure alone. . . . We have reason to know . . . for more than 70% of Eureka's employees are women. . . . Many of them leave their work benches at night to carry on with that other vitally important job of making a home for their children, and their hard-working, war-working husbands." Equating consumerism with patriotism was too good an advertising ploy for manufacturers to pass up. Such advertisements, as well as the ubiquitous "love on the job" fiction featured in magazines, also reinforced society's view of Rosie the Riveter: that she was a housewife and mother at heart, who would (and should) gladly return to her rightful place in the home at the first opportunity.

The entry of women into the formerly all-male preserve of heavy

industry raised issues of courtesy and morality. Most men did not welcome the prospect of working side by side with women and often joked
about them, subjected them to constant wolf whistling and ogling, or
treated them with open hostility. Women workers banded together and
gave the men as good as they got by whistling back at them and shout-
ing derisive comments in kind. However, the presence of women in
some plants produced positive results: mixing men and women workers
stepped up morale, and competition between the sexes led to greater
output. In some cases, the mix of men and women in the workplace also
led to love affairs between both married and unmarried workers, a situation no doubt due to the dislocation felt by many as well as to the pro-
longed absence of husbands and sweethearts, and which was partly
responsible for the increase in the divorce rate during the war years.

Women served their country in the military as well as in civilian life.
From the beginning of the war, women's organizations insisted that
women be allowed to enlist in the services. In addition to the army and
navy nursing corps, women's branches in the army (WACs), the navy
(WAVES), the Coast Guard (SPARS), and the marines (MCWR) were
created in 1942 and 1943. Nearly 350,000 women served in the military,
mostly in clerical and supply areas, or as nurses. However, some 1,000
women served in the Women's Air Force Service Pilots corps (WASP),
flying commercial and air force transport planes. Women also served as
test pilots for the United States Air Force. The experiences of these
daring and capable women pilots was relatively unknown until the 1980s
and 1990s, when the media began to pay more attention to the exploits
of unsung women in history. The real or potential exploits of service-
women was not a focus during wartime, however. The media made sure
to glamorize women in the military as they had done women in industry.
In one example, writes Evans, " 'girls' or 'gals' peeked prettily out from
under their sailor hats, looking too cute to be threatening." The military accepted only young, unmarried women, placed them in positions
where they would not have to give orders to men, and avoided sending
them overseas as long as possible. Women with children were prohibited from enlisting; lesbians, once discovered, were persecuted, and
African American servicewomen, like black soldiers, were kept segregated. However, any reluctance on the part of the army toward the inclusion of women gave way at the end of the war: in 1946, after enlistments
went down, the U.S. War Department asked WAC nurses to reenlist to
meet labor shortages in army hospitals.

American women had been altered irrevocably by their experiences
during World War II. They had helped to make victory possible, and
they knew it. Neither they nor their daughters would forget the histori-

cal moment when millions of women began to see the promise of equality in the workplace. The *Minneapolis Tribune* had editorialized in August 1942, "WACs and WAVES and women welders . . . Where is it all going to end? . . . Is it hard to foresee, after the boys come marching home and they marry these emancipated young women, who is going to tend the babies in the next generation?" Although many women continued in paid work after the war, the values of postwar America, the disruptions of wartime, and the beginning of the baby boom would lead more women back to the home and to idealized suburban lives in the nation's burgeoning Levittowns.

1944

Seventeen, a Magazine for Teenage Girls, Is First Published

Never think for a moment: I'm only a girl in my teens. What can I do? You can do plenty.... We expect you to run the world more sensibly than we have.

Helen Valentine, the founding editor of *Seventeen*

When *Seventeen*, the first style and fashion magazine for teenage girls, appeared in 1944, thirty thousand bobbysoxers had swarmed outside Manhattan's Paramount Theater to see Frank Sinatra. When they learned that his show was sold out, the girls mobbed the street, broke shop windows, destroyed the Paramount ticket booth, and required hundreds of police to control their frenzy. The event, which captured nationwide newspaper headlines, announced the new presence and power of teenage girls and the emerging youth culture that *Seventeen* was designed to celebrate and chronicle. Over more than fifty years of publication, with a current circulation of 2.5 million, the magazine has persisted as a cultural mirror of the changes in attitude, style, and identity of teenage girls and adolescence in America. *Seventeen* documents the cultural shifts in expectations of girls undergoing a maturation process into adult values that speak both to our culture's understanding of adolescence and to its adult goals. Few publications offer a better index to the way things have changed and the way things have remained the same at this important developmental stage.

The editors of *Seventeen* did not view adolescents as merely unformed adults. Instead, the magazine focused on the relatively new phenomenon of teenagers as a distinct group with their own sense of style, fashion, and preoccupations. Childhood and adolescence are cultural ideas that have altered over the centuries. In the Middle Ages, for example, childhood was considered ended at the age of seven. Modern notions of childhood and adolescence as a distinct and important phase of emotional and psychological development begin with the concepts of Jean-Jacques Rousseau in the eighteenth century in his calling attention to the human plight that arises when a child assumes the sexual and moral responsibilities of adulthood. Yet the concept of the teenage years as separate and distinct from either childhood or adulthood is largely a twentieth-century construct. As late as the 1890s, for example, American high schools enrolled only 7 percent of the fourteen- to seventeen-year-old population; the other 93 percent, along with even younger children, worked at adult labor and were, therefore, assimilated into adult life and responsibilities. Social legislation protecting children workers and changes in cultural ideas that such legislation reflected in the twentieth century helped to establish adolescence as a distinct, protected period of maturation and development needed to acquire the social, moral, and educational skills necessary to progress from the family to autonomy and wider cultural responsibility. The teenage years of adolescence were, therefore, increasingly seen as a testing ground between childhood and adulthood with their own unique concerns, habits, and styles.

By the 1940s adolescence was a decidedly narrow band of developmental time that would both expand and contract in future decades as the youth culture took hold and adolescents' physical maturation and level of sophistication accelerated. Demure in white gloves and dressed to imitate their mothers, teenage girls in the 1940s and early 1950s were expected to enter adulthood almost immediately after high school through marriage and motherhood and were seen as junior versions of their mothers. However, the 1940s' bobbysoxer, named for an article of clothing distinctly worn by girls, called increased attention to the teenage years with their own cultural imperatives and enormous economic potential for consumption. *Seventeen* offered them their own fashion magazine, like *Vogue* and *Glamour*, but aimed at the teenage culture that the magazine helped to define. In the magazine's initial issue, a teen model, Patty Townsend, graced the cover in a smart outfit with an expression of modest vitality. Articles included a film review of Pearl Buck's *Dragon Seed* and a profile of Katharine Hepburn. There were two pages on Frank Sinatra and an article entitled "What Are You Doing About the War?" Other topics included "Why Finish High School?" and "How to Study." There was a first-date quiz and an article called "Why Don't Parents Grow Up?" Despite the hardships of the war, there were pages on shopping and fashions that the magazine assured its readers could be found "in teen departments of the best stores in the country." From its initial issue, *Seventeen* established a successful formula that it has retained ever

The first cover of *Seventeen* magazine, September 1944
Reprinted with permission of Seventeen

since by tapping into the perceived needs of adolescent girls that advertisers were also quick to exploit in offering products to help teenagers fit
in and conform to prevailing notions of teen fashion and self-definition.

In succeeding decades, *Seventeen* charted both the continuity and the
changes in adolescent values and concerns. As the jitterbug made way
for the jive, the twist, the hustle, break dancing, and the electric slide,
and love tokens changed from his military jacket to his letter sweater, his
fraternity pin, mood rings, his and hers earrings, and his private beeper
number, *Seventeen* documented each shift of style and attitude. In the
1940s dating do's and don'ts included "Do point out Johnny's best feature. Say something like: 'You have hands like a doctor's, strong and efficient.'" And "Don't ever let your irritation show on your face. When
you're angry, sit still, be quiet, smile if you possibly can, and start the
conversation moving in the right direction with 'I'm sorry'" (1946). In
the 1950s a dating dilemma included "One of my girlfriends insists that
you should not let a boy kiss you good-night unless you love him. . . .
What should I do?" (1954). In the 1960s readers on dates were advised

to "make suggestions when he asks what movie to see. Otherwise he'll think all you want to do is neck" (1968). In the 1970s girls were advised, "When a guy offers you a joint and suggests that now you can 'talk' to him, he's giving you two messages: 'Let's get high together' and 'I'm going to make out with you' " (1970). By the 1980s girls were told to "stop looking to guys as your only source of excitement and self-esteem. Then you will graduate from flings to more lasting love" (1982). Dating dilemmas of the 1990s included "My boyfriend and I made love for the first time without planning to. Now I'm afraid he won't want to use a condom when we have sex again. How can I tell him to use protection?" (1994). Throughout the decades *Seventeen* has reflected changing values toward sex and girls' identity while offering variations on the consistent essential questions of adolescent angst: "Who am I?" and "What should I do with my life?" The magazine's answers have attempted to balance an emphasis on looks and fashion with a message that a teenager's self-esteem can be enhanced through service and inner resources. In the 1940s, for example, each March issue was dedicated not to spring proms, but to the Red Cross. In the 1990s girls were urged to "consider volunteer work. It will give you a few things to start off a conversation with your crush object." The magazine's messages of the multidimensional possibilities for teenage girls and alternatives to narcissism, however, are often blurred amid the pages and pages of glossy advertisements for fashions and beauty products that drum home the unilateral point that physicality and consumption are paramount.

Despite the attempt by *Seventeen* to moderate the notion that teenage girls are defined exclusively by their looks and as consumers of fashion and beauty products to enhance them, as well as the magazine's concerted attempt to slow the momentum toward blurring the distinction between adolescence and adulthood in matters of sex and style, the magazine shares some responsibility for disturbing trends in adolescence over the last fifty years. The work of Harvard psychologist Carol Gilligan has documented that increasingly adolescence is a time of crisis for contemporary girls centered on an obsessive physicality and the pressure to mature sexually more quickly. Studies have shown that by age thirteen, 53 percent of girls are unhappy with their bodies; by age seventeen, the number has increased to 78 percent. Talk about the body and ways to improve it, a central motif in magazines like *Seventeen*, contributes to dissatisfaction, distress, and increasingly to disorders like anorexia nervosa and bulimia.

According to Joan Jacobs Brumberg's analysis in *The Body Project: An Intimate History of American Girls*, although today's sexually liberated girls should feel better about themselves than their corseted sisters of a century ago, the opposite is the case. Brumberg has shown how "the mother-daughter connection has loosened, especially with regard to the experience of menstruation and sexuality; how doctors and marketeers took over important educational functions that were once the special domain of female relatives and mentors; how scientific medicine, movies, and advertising created a new, more exacting ideal of physical perfection; and how changing standards of intimacy turned virginity into an outmoded ideal. The fact that American girls now make the body their central project is not an accident or a curiosity: it is a symptom of historical changes that are only beginning to be understood." In this regard, *Seventeen* can be criticized for enforcing a physical ideal for American girls that has serious detrimental consequences.

At ultimate risk, according to media scholar Neil Postman, is the rapid disappearance of adolescence and childhood in our culture. With twelve- and thirteen-year-old girls the highest-paid models in America, presented as knowing and sexually enticing adults, with the difference between children's and adolescents' clothing and that of adults fast disappearing, the incidence of teen pregnancy rising, and even the distinction between adult and children's crimes narrowing, Postman suggests that we are in the midst of a paradigm shift once again in the redefinition of childhood and adulthood, with the teenage years in particular threatened by extinction as a protected process of maturation and development. To maintain its relevance to contemporary teenagers, *Seventeen* has both reflected and contributed to the trend of the disappearing adolescence in America, a central irony for a magazine that helped define teenage life in the second half of the twentieth century.

1946

The First Baby Boomers Are Born

> From adolescence, the baby boomers have insisted on the
> uniqueness of each individual. They have enshrined the legitimacy
> of each person's expression of his or her own particular
> consciousness. "Do your own thing" is a clear statement of the
> freedom accorded each person. It has often been said that free
> expression has been given too loose rein by this generation, but it
> cannot be denied that the generation has also insisted on and
> acquired greater freedom in thought and behavior than its
> predecessors.
>
> D. Quinn Mills, *Not Like Our Parents*

In 1946 U.S. birthrates soared as servicemen, returning home from
World War II, began families and added to existing ones. There were
some 3,411,000 births that year as compared with 2,858,000 the previous
year. In 1957 a record 4.3 million babies were born. The baby boom
lasted until about 1965, when the birthrate began to decline. By the
middle of the 1960s there were over 70 million baby boomers out of a
total U.S. population of 197,000,000, and some 40 million of them were
females. Like the boys, middle-class baby boom girls had parents who
had experienced the Great Depression, World War II, and the Korean
conflict, events that helped to solidify a sense of patriotism and domestic values. Fathers went to work; mothers generally stayed home. Most
children were raised in a booming if inflationary consumer-conscious
postwar economy with the help of Dr. Spock, the dubious influence of
television, and the culture of rock and roll, in suburban developments
with nearby shopping centers. Until the more liberal, recessionary 1970s,
they attended well-funded, educationally sound public schools, where
secondary school curricula hinted at subversion with the teaching of J. D.
Salinger's *Catcher in the Rye* and Mark Twain's *Huckleberry Finn*. By the

A second-grade classroom of baby boomers in Middle Village, Queens, 1955. The first mass immunization program of schoolchildren with the Salk polio vaccine took place the same year.

time they entered college, their lives had been marked by social dissonance: the cold war, the potential threat of nuclear annihilation, the assassinations of John F. Kennedy, Martin Luther King Jr., and Robert Kennedy, the Vietnam War, and the draft had shaped them negatively; at the other end of the spectrum was an idealism that evolved from the Peace Corps, the civil rights movement, the peace movement, social welfare, and environmentalism. They blamed their parents' generation for war and pollution and for living unhip lives of capitalist conformity. The younger baby boomers were inculcated in their elders' choice of clothing, hairstyles, music, and drug use, if not always in their sometimes radical politics and cynicism.

Women baby boomers, especially those born between 1946 and 1960, grew up in an era that was both constrictive and progressive. In 1947 the best-selling book *Modern Women: The Lost Sex*, by Marynia Farnham and Ferdinand Lundberg, set the tone for the time by putting forth the case that a woman's true vocation should be as mother and homemaker and that women who strayed from their reproductive function and role as nurturer were seriously disturbed. Two years later the Pillsbury Bake-Off was inaugurated in tandem with the introduction by General Mills and Pillsbury of prepared cake mixes; that same year Harvard Law School announced its intention to admit women students for the first time. In 1950 *Educating Our Daughters: A Challenge to the Colleges,* by Lynn White Jr., argued that college-educated women had a special duty to ensure a stable population by counteracting the "sterility" overtaking better-educated and more affluent women and thus threatening democracy. White claimed that higher education must instill the idea that it is both an "incentive" and a "duty" for women to bear at least three children so that the United States might avoid a "drift toward totalitarianism." It was a time when colleges featured a required course called "Marriage and Family Life" and women were marrying soon after high school or college, dropping out of college to marry, and giving up their careers (usually as teachers) once espoused. In a later episode of the 1954–1960 television situation comedy *Father Knows Best,* Betty, the oldest daughter, better known as "Princess" and played by Elinor Donahue, drops out of college early on to marry the man of her dreams. She, like Elizabeth Taylor's bride character in the 1950 film *Father of the Bride,* is maddeningly calm regarding her decision to marry and so sure of herself in the face of true love that she seems almost more adult than her parents.

Baby boom girls, while struggling to excel in a public education system that demanded physical fitness, academic focus, and school spirit, also took part in carefully choreographed courtship rituals beginning as early as junior high school. To become "popular," a teenage achievement devoutly to be wished, and to attract the boy of her choice (which might lead to "going steady," a coupling state that was usually like a sexless marriage and more often than not resulted in "divorce" and recoupling with another boy), or to simply secure a date for the dance, girls needed to know the correct way to look and behave. One issue of the young-teen magazine *Calling All Girls* featured a short story in which a pretty blond teenage girl who also happens to be an excellent tennis player cannot capture her boy because she insists on beating him during every set they play. She eventually learns her lesson, lets him beat her, and goes with him to the club dance outfitted in a yellow dress that beguilingly "showed off her tennis tan." In an issue of the teen magazine *Ingenue,* popular model Colleen Corby was pictured in a soigné outfit complete with little white gloves, to all intents and purposes looking perfect. The caption asked what was wrong with the picture and on the next page reprinted the Corby shot with the answer—she had not used deodorant, her stockings were torn, her underwear had not been washed, her hair was dirty, and so on. While no one would argue the merits of cleanliness and a certain degree of tidiness, the underlying message in the *Ingenue* article was that such hidden flaws would be discovered eventually, resulting in lost dates and summer jobs, as well as social censure from other girls. The only teen girls' magazine of the era to successfully feature both fashion and issues facing teenage girls was *Seventeen*, which, for example, included an article on Alateen in 1966, even while it continued to promote the marriage track by publishing ads for Lane hope chests with the caption "Love Leads to Lane."

By the time the first baby boom women entered college, in 1964, certain liberalizing forces had crept into American culture and were coexisting with social upheaval. The birth control pill was four years old; the bikini had become the swimsuit to wear, thanks to its promotion via the surfeit of beach and surfing movies starting to attract teen audiences; and the miniskirt had been invented. In 1962 advertising agency executive and later *Cosmopolitan* editor in chief Helen Gurley Brown published *Sex and the Single Girl*, a lively, flirtatious little book extolling the sexual pleasures and social promise of the unmarried state. In it, Gurley Brown in her inimitable style interestingly anticipates aspects of Friedan's *The Feminine Mystique* when she observes that women "may marry or may not. In today's world that is no longer the big question for women. Those who glom on to men so that they can collapse with relief, spend the rest of their days shining up their status symbol and figure they never have to reach, stretch, learn, grow, face dragons or make a living again are the ones to be pitied. They, in my opinion, are the unfulfilled ones." Its career-oriented messages notwithstanding, *Sex and the Single Girl* would prove to be the explicator of what would be termed the "sexual revolution," a cultural event first experienced by baby boom women during the late 1960s and that reached its peak during the disco decade of the 1970s. Once in college and away from the stultifying sameness of the suburbs, the claustrophobic small towns, and the leftover fifties conservatism of their parents and the public schools, large numbers of young women were technically free to enjoy the ethic of sex, drugs, and rock and roll and to raise their collective consciousness concerning social issues, not the least of which was protest over the ill-conceived war in Vietnam.

Few college women during the late 1960s were ready to admit the possibility that they were being exploited as sex objects by men and that women, even those engaged in radical, leftist politics, were not entirely taken seriously as intellects or as individuals by men. Outside of academia, however, the women's movement, fired by *The Feminine Mystique* and Simone de Beauvoir's *The Second Sex*, was gaining momentum. By the end of the 1960s colleges were offering courses in women's studies, and a concept called "sexism" was being explored. By the 1970s there was an ever-growing menu of feminist literature for baby boom women to ponder. The first influential feminist polemic of the 1970s was Kate Millett's *Sexual Politics* (1970), which articulated a philosophy for what would soon be termed "women's liberation" or, more popularly, "women's lib." In the book Millett observes, "Our society, like all other historical societies, is a patriarchy. The fact is evident at once if one recalls that the military, industry, technology, universities, science, political office, and finance—in short, every avenue of power within the society, including the coercive force of the police—is entirely in male hands." That same year Germaine Greer wrote in *The Female Eunuch*, "I'm sick of pretending that some fatuous male's self-important pronouncements are the objects of my undivided attention." The feminist theme was carried on in such 1970s books as *The Young Woman's Guide to Liberation* (1971), by Karen DeCrow, who would go on to become president of NOW; *Born Female: The High Cost of Keeping Women Down* (1972), by Caroline Bird; and the first edition of *Our Bodies, Ourselves* (1973), by the Boston Women's Health Collective.

Armed with feminist political awareness and a parallel crop of books featuring advice on how to succeed in the business world, such as *The Managerial Women* (1977), by Margaret Hennig and Anne Jardin, college-educated baby boom women surged into graduate school and into the workplace, expecting to achieve at the highest level. Surveys conducted in 1977 revealed that the number of U.S. adults under thirty-five living alone had doubled since 1970. Social analysts ascribed the growing trend toward leaving home earlier and marrying later to such factors as easier credit, an increased wariness concerning marriage, and greater career opportunities for young women. Women were not only pursuing careers and advanced degrees, they were also looking for love in discos and bars, sometimes with disastrous results, as Judith Rossner's 1975 best-seller, *Looking for Mr. Goodbar,* illustrates. Based on the true story of Roseann Quinn, a twenty-seven-year-old teacher who was murdered by a man she picked up at a singles bar, Rossner's novel is a frightening chronicle of depression, sexual desperation, and female degradation. Women were similarly warned about the dangers of drug overindulgence by the highly publicized fate of twenty-one-year-old Karen Ann Quinlan, who slipped into a coma in 1975 after drinking alcohol mixed with small doses of Librium and Valium. Quinlan, who was removed from artificial life support in 1976 on the insistence of her Catholic parents, lingered in a coma for nearly ten years before dying of pneumonia.

By 1978 23.7 percent of U.S. medical students were women, an increase of 87 percent over 1973, and more women than men were entering college, for the first time in U.S. history. But despite the expectations of achieving well-paid, meaningful careers, only 140,000 women in the private sector were earning $25,000 per year or more, compared with 4,173,000 men. By 1986 U.S. women professionals outnumbered men for the first time but continued to receive on average substantially less pay than their male counterparts. In the 1980s women in business began to express dissatisfaction with what was termed the "glass ceiling," a point on the corporate ladder at which women stopped advancing. By the "yuppie" years of the 1980s, baby boom women were having children in greater numbers and trying to blend marriage, motherhood, and careers in an attempt to "have it all" and to avoid the "mommy track," a corporate attitude that held that mothers were too distracted by domestic issues to be worthy of upper-management-level positions in the companies for which they worked. After taking maternity leaves guaranteed by federal law, women often found themselves relegated to lower positions in the corporation or not hired back at all. The same was true of teaching positions. In 1988 a *New York Times* poll of 1,025 women reported that 83 percent of working mothers were torn by the conflicting demands of job and family; 48 percent of women interviewed claimed that they had sacrificed too much for career gains; 27 percent felt that the goal of the women's movement should be to help women balance work and family, including child care. The concept of career "gains" can be considered relative, since two years later women were earning on average sixty-seven cents for every dollar earned by a man doing comparable work.

The backlash against feminism that began in the 1980s, when more and more baby boom women started families, continued into the 1990s. Fueled by a new political and social conservatism, by dissension over abortion rights, by public concern over children ostensibly raised in less-than-adequate day care centers or by baby-sitters, by the reactionary notions of deep-seated hormonally driven gender differences, and by a new romanticization of motherhood, this backlash, together with an economy of questionable solidity and the demands of family life, forced baby boom women to reevaluate their priorities. They had come of age believing that they were entitled to unlimited self-expression and achievement as individuals; as adults they found it necessary to arrange their lives according to the needs of their families, as women had always done throughout the century.

⋙

French Fashion Designer Louis Réard
Invents the Bikini

> Three-year-olds veiled behind bikini tops learn a small lesson
> in body awareness, one that often leads to heightened self-
> consciousness and sometimes to tormenting obsessions.
>
> Rita Freedman, *Beauty Bound*

When spring arrives, with it come the many articles in women's magazines suggesting ways in which women can "shape up" their bodies for
summer, better known among magazine headline writers as "swimsuit
season" or even "bikini season." The assumption many women readers
carry away from these articles is that their too thin, too fleshy, or too
flabby bodies are not ready for exposure on the beaches of the world. To
redress the balance, magazines as well as catalogs such as Lands' End
also feature swimsuits strategically designed to minimize figure flaws
and maximize figure attractions. Whether slim, "pear-shaped," or "apple-
shaped" (advertised in the media of the 1990s as an unhealthy figure
type, thus guaranteeing even more body guilt on the part of those
women unlucky or undisciplined enough to possess such a shape), no
figure is ostensibly left uncorrected by swimwear designers. The ongoing quest to find the most flattering swimsuit, and the need to correct
one's figure in order to enjoy the pleasures offered by sun, sand, and
surf while minimally clad, is the result of the direction toward freedom
of movement and exposure of the female body typified by the evolution
of swimwear during the twentieth century.

At the turn of the century, swimming for the majority of women was
actually "bathing," and the garments used for this demure toe-dipping
activity were knee-length dresses, often with a sailor-blouse bodice, worn
over bloomers. On the bather's feet were lace-up slippers or cloth boots;
on her head was a hat that featured a wide ribbon with a big bow in
front and tied under the chin or a large beret-type cloth hat from which
her curls peeped coquettishly. Around the same time, however, a new
style of swimsuit, the one-piece bathing suit, was designed by aquatic
star Annette Kellermann. As a child, Kellermann had been stricken with
polio and had taken up swimming for exercise. She later became a champion swimmer, a successful vaudeville and movie star, and the author of
a popular beauty manual that stressed the importance of physical cul-

A bevy of bathing beauties circa 1906   *Library of Congress*

ture for women as a means toward staying young, lovely, and forever attractive to their husbands. Kellermann was, observes Lois Banner in *American Beauty*, "the Esther Williams of her day, and her saga of triumph over tragedy through personal endeavor was bound to appeal to upward-striving Americans." Kellermann's bathing suit was worn with tights rather than bloomers and was only marginally sleeker and more revealing than the soggy bathing dresses currently in vogue. Kellermann insisted that her design would allow women to swim more effectively, but athletic considerations regarding the swimsuit did not interest the local authorities, who in 1907 arrested her for indecent exposure when she wore the suit on a Massachusetts beach during a campaign promotion to boost its sales.

By the middle of the century's second decade, the Mack Sennett bathing beauty, athletic looking as well as attractive, was a ubiquitous presence in movies and could be found posing in magazines and ads. The bathing beauty's swimsuit was generally sleeveless, slightly form-fitting, skirted, and worn over tights. The sleeveless, baggy shape tended to prevail with more conservative types: in 1921 Margaret Gorman, the first Miss America, wore a loose-fitting suit that resembled

Nineteen-year-old dancer Micheline Bernardini in the world's first bikini. "It can be packed into a matchbox or drawn through a wedding ring and caused a sensation even in the French capital where extreme displays of epidermis are not uncommon," read the original caption. *UPI/Corbis-Bettmann*

a knee-length tunic. As skirt hems began to rise in the 1920s, swimsuits began to shrink. A 1928 *Vanity Fair* full-page photo of Clara Bow featured filmdom's "It" girl in a one-piece suit with a tank top, a close-fitting skirt that barely brushed the tops of her thighs, a pantylike undergarment, bare legs, and beach slippers. She was posed on top of a beach piling, legs crossed, one hand on her hip and the other raised high. The whole effect bespoke the self-styled freedom and audacity of the 1920s woman and coincided not only with enhanced female freedom of movement, but also with a greater shift in erotic emphasis from the female trunk to the legs. Hemlines would fall and rise throughout the century, rising most notably in 1963 when British fashion designer Mary Quant introduced the miniskirt, and shorts and pants would further accentuate the legs, but it was the bathing suit that first focused attention on this feature of female anatomy, from calf to thigh. During the 1930s the slender, shapely legs of movie star Marlene Dietrich were highly praised, and in the 1940s Betty Grable's famous swimsuited pinup pose made her an erotic object to thousands of servicemen by showing her well-proportioned limbs supporting an equally attractive derriere.

By the 1940s the two-piece bathing suit, with a halter top and waist-high bottom, was seen on beaches and among Miss America beauty pageant contestants. Then, at a July 5, 1946, Paris fashion show, designer Louis Réard unveiled a two-piece bathing suit creation that revealed more female flesh, including the belly button, than ever before. Since the fashion show occurred four days after the American atomic detonation on Bikini Atoll, Réard called his creation "the bikini," explaining that for him the name symbolized "the ultimate." The first bikini was cotton, printed with a newspaper design, and worn by nineteen-year old Micheline Bernardini, a nude dancer at the Casino de Paris. Her photo was printed around the world, and she received some fifty thousand fan letters. Americans, for the most part, were bemused by the bikini and considered it an erotic, not to say prurient, joke, an example of which was the popular 1960 song hit "Yellow Polka Dot Bikini," sung by Brian Hyland. The bikini did not begin to coopt the one-piece suit on American beaches until the mid-1960s, when the youth culture was firmly in place and the first crop of baby boomers, born the same year the bikini was introduced, was entering college. The "beach movies" of the era, which often starred twentysomething teen idols Frankie Avalon and Annette Funicello (who usually sported a one-piece suit) and always featured a bevy of bikini-clad bathing beauties, further helped to popularize the suit. In 1964 California fashion designer Rudi Gernreich designed a topless swimsuit, which he characterized as a "whimsical idea." People gawked at pictures of Gernreich's creation; few women dared to wear it, and it had a short life as a fashion statement.

The modestly revealing bra-and-low-slung-panty bikini of the 1960s and early 1970s became briefer during the sexually overheated disco decade, evolving into the string bikini and, later, the thong. By then it was considered "cute" by many parents to clothe their toddlers and preschooler girls in bikinis; young girls, in imitation of their more fully developed elders, were wearing them, too. "In this way," observes Rita Freedman, "young bodies are draped in gender, poured into the female mold, to be shaped, reshaped, and misshapen by it." In a body-conscious and youth-fixated culture obsessed with weight, dieting, and fitness, in which eating disorders have reached almost epidemic proportions among adolescent girls, the bikini and even the one-piece tank suit have seemed over the past few decades to be less symbols of female freedom, audacity, and athleticism than constant reminders that women are merely shapes forever in need of correction.

1947

Modern Woman: The Lost Sex, a Postwar Treatise on the Status of Women, Is Published

Contemporary women in very large numbers are psychologically disturbed . . . and their disorder is having terrible social and personal effects involving men in all departments of their lives as well as women.

Ferdinand Lundberg, Foreword to *Modern Woman: The Lost Sex*

The large influx of immigrants to the United States, the emergence of the feminist "new woman," World War I, the Great Depression, and the loss of men to the military during World War II all resulted in growing numbers of women in the workforce in the first five decades of the twentieth century. The percentage of women workers gradually rose from 21.2 in 1900 to 36.1 in 1945. These percentages are significant because they show that despite the traditional values that permeated American society during these decades—the concept that a woman's proper place was in the home—nearly one-quarter to over one-third of American women were in the workplace, either through desire or from necessity.

The approximately six million women who took paying jobs in heavy industry and in other so-called male jobs during World War II had been urged to do so as an act of wartime patriotism, but it was largely understood that these women workers would quit when their men came home. At the start of the war, in 1941, 95 percent of women war workers intended to quit; by the war's end some 80 percent had changed their minds. Women had become accustomed to the independence, personal fulfillment, and economic benefits of working outside the home and had begun to realize that they needed extra income in a postwar climate of rising inflation and increased consumerism. By the time male veterans had returned to reclaim their old jobs or to take up new ones, three million women had left their wartime work, some voluntarily, others because of cutbacks and layoffs. However, many women, responding to serious labor shortages in such traditionally female and low-paying occupations as teaching, nursing, and clerical work, continued to work.

By 1947, women, it seemed, were making choices and living their lives according to their needs and the needs of their families in concordance with the values and possibilities of the prevailing culture, as they in fact had done throughout the century. They might have been supported in their choices or urged by writers exploring the status of women to seek more opportunity and greater equality in the workplace, since so many of them were already present there. Instead American women were offered a treatise in which they were told in no uncertain terms that the vast majority of them, paid worker and homemaker alike, were profoundly emotionally disturbed and that their deep-seated neuroses were having a deleterious effect on all of American society.

The book that outlined this thesis in heavy detail was titled *Modern Woman: The Lost Sex*. Written by Marynia Farnham, a psychiatrist whose specialty was the treatment of children and adolescents, and Ferdinand Lundberg, a journalist and social critic, the book uses Freudian psychology to contend that in a disorganized American society, neuroses abounded in both men and women, but more dangerously in women, who were more likely to pass on their neuroses to the next generation. Relying on the work of Sigmund Freud to describe the psyches of women was not new: Freudian psychology had been a therapeutic treatment of choice among psychiatrists and had passed into the general culture in popularized and frequently misinformed versions in books, magazines, plays, and movies since it had first become fashionable in the 1920s. In 1944 psychiatrist Helene Deutsch published *The Psychology of Women*, an influential treatise that made use of Freudian theory to claim that the center of a woman's emotional life lay in her reproductive system and that women who viewed themselves as active rather than passive were suffering from "masculinity complexes." Deutsch's book provided physicians with a theoretical base for treating as neurosis any one of a number of ailments suffered by their women patients. In 1944 women in general were too busy with war work and the task of running their families and making ends meet to give much thought to whether or not they were active or passive or behaving in an "inappropriately" masculine manner. By 1947, however, the issue was well placed to capture their attention. America, feeling a sense of displacement caused by the upheavals of the war and grappling with the new and frightening phenomenon called the "cold war," was seeking cultural stability. Given the

In their bestselling postwar treatise, *Modern Woman: The Lost Sex*, authors Ferdinand Lundberg and Marynia Farnham described the "female organism" as incapable of attaining "feelings of well-being by the route of male achievement" and called for the return of women to "their maternal role in home and society."

best-seller status of *Modern Woman: The Lost Sex*, many Americans were apparently willing to consider the opinions, however narrow, of any self-described experts in order to achieve that stability.

The Farnham and Lundberg book provides readers with a social history of women and men and views America's ills as the result of the "displacement of women from their maternal role in home and society." The authors portray women who pursue careers as sick souls suffering from penis envy—the desire of neurotic women trying to imitate men. On the one hand, twentieth-century women are viewed as victims of a modern industrial society that expects them to behave like feminists and enter the professions in competition with men, exploits them as cheap labor, or forces them to live empty, narcissistic lives of fashion and chronic ennui. But women are also excoriated, as Margaret Mead wrote in her *New York Times* review of the book, as "false prophets and criminals." They are first and foremost bad mothers, incapable of nurturing their sons and husbands. Thus the sons grow up with their own set of neuroses and become too emotionally disturbed to function well within society. The authors write: "Men, standing before the bar of historical judgment, might well begin their defense with the words: 'I had a mother. . . .'"

Feminism and feminists provoke some particularly heavy criticism on the part of Farnham and Lundberg. In a chapter titled "The Feminist Complex," they acknowledge that the feminist "program . . . amounted objectively to the successful attempt to restore earlier rights and privileges" but describe feminism as an ideology that failed because "it is not in the capacity of the female organism to attain feelings of well-being by the route of male achievement" and because it was an "ideology of hatred directed against men." The preeminent villain in the annals of feminism is Mary Wollstonecraft (1759–1797), author of the cornerstone feminist document *A Vindication of the Rights of Women*. She is psychoanalyzed by the authors as a deeply disturbed, poorly educated woman whose tragic childhood with a violent father and a victimized mother left her "an extreme neurotic of a compulsive type," a man hater at her core who "had a real grievance, but it was against her parents." *A Vindication* is categorized as a work in which "some personal misfortune seemed to drive the author's pen beyond all reason." The sensitive Wollstonecraft did indeed have a difficult childhood that left her emotionally scarred, but she was also a highly intelligent, thoughtful woman who was capable of critical detachment. Farnham and Lundberg insist, however, that only "deeply disturbed women—disturbed by the nature of their childhood upbringing in the shattered home and the constricted circumstances they encountered in adult life—could have drawn what they supposed was pure wisdom from *A Vindication*." Not only do the authors fail to give Wollstonecraft credit for her heroic attempt to articulate the problems and needs of the girls and women of her time, they place little faith in the ability of feminists to interpret her work in the light of their own experiences in their own time.

The legacy of the feminists, claim the authors, is that modern women are confused about their value in society and have been unable to express their true femininity. Both women and men would benefit, they assert, if women would return to, as they put it, the "soul-vaulting" work "they did in the home of bygone days." To cure men and women of their neuroses and thus create their version of an ideal society, Farnham and Lundberg advocate such solutions as widespread psychoanalysis, public education to revalue women's traditional work in the home, government subsidies to mothers, taxes on bachelors, the replacement of "spinster" schoolteachers with married mothers (unmarried women and women without children are labeled the most severely disturbed women of all), and the education of girls in "feminine" rather than "masculine" subjects.

When *Modern Woman: The Lost Sex* appeared, it caused a great deal of controversy among its many reviewers. Philip Wylie, writing in the prestigious and literary *Saturday Review*, found it "the best book yet to be written about women," while Frederic Wertham of the *New Republic* castigated the authors for expounding "the old prejudices about women with glib assurance" and described the book as striking in its cruelty. *Kirkus*'s reviewer counseled, "Physician, heal thyself." A broader view suggests that the book's publication occurred at an opportune moment in women's history. The postwar baby boom was in its second year, and the birthrate would continue to grow into the 1950s. By then American society seemed on the surface to have attained at least some of the gender-role expectations of Farnham and Lundberg: men were at work, while the majority of women, after having married right out of high school or college, put all their energies into rearing their children, keeping their husbands happy, and making their homes tidy and attractive. But home-making and child rearing did not prove to be as "soul-vaulting" as Farnham and Lundberg claimed it should be. Women living in the silken prison formed from the so-called stability of family life in the 1950s were suffering from a discontent so profound, it could not be articulated. In 1963 Betty Friedan, a journalist-turned-freelance writer, defined this discontent as "the problem that has no name" and wrote about it in her influential book, *The Feminine Mystique*. Friedan's book overturned the thesis expounded by Farnham and Lundberg and sounded a clarion call for change that would reverberate throughout American society and lead to the women's liberation movement of the late 1960s and 1970s. *The Feminine Mystique* relieved women of the burden of trying to deny the source of their dissatisfaction and started them on a journey of exploration to discover what they could truly be when, in Friedan's words, they were "finally free to become themselves."

1950–1959

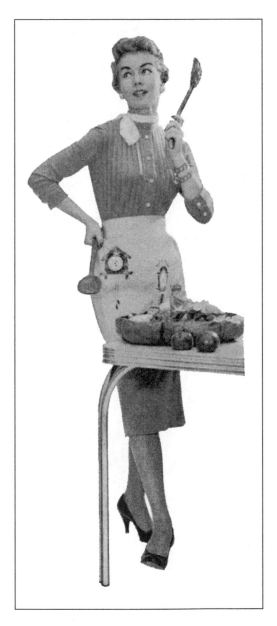

The idealized happy housewife of the 1950s: slim, trim, and always well-groomed, even while preparing dinner for her husband and children. This model bears a marked resemblance to June Cleaver, the lovely and glamorous mother of television's *Leave It to Beaver.*

1952

The Adventures of Ozzie and Harriet Premieres

> One reason that Americans became nostalgic about the fifties . . .
> was not so much that life was better in the fifties (though in some
> ways it was), but because at the time it had been portrayed so
> idyllically on television. It was the television images of the era that
> remained so remarkably sharp in people's memories, often fresher
> than memories of real life. . . . If Ozzie spawned imitators with the
> success of his rather bland family, then eventually the different
> families all seemed interchangeable, as if one could pluck a dad or a
> mom or even a child from one show and transplant him or her to
> another.
>
> David Halberstam, *The Fifties*

In the early 1990s verbally challenged Vice President Dan Quayle, apparently confusing real life with fiction, took to task the feisty, feminist television character Murphy Brown (played by Candice Bergen) for deciding to bear and raise a child out of wedlock. Quayle's denunciation of what he and other conservatives viewed as an example of ongoing moral decay and a breakdown in traditional "family values," by which was meant the two-parent home with father at the head and mother at the stove, was made much of by the media, and there followed a collective orgy of nostalgia for the family-friendly sitcoms of the 1950s. The television series most cited as exemplifying positive family values was *The Adventures of Ozzie and Harriet*, not least because of Harriet's role as a contented wife, mother, and homemaker.

Ozzie and Harriet, one of television's longest-running family comedies, was in a way the perfect show to refer to in the wake of the Murphy Brown storm in a teacup because its premise—a normal, happy fifties family playing a normal, happy fifties family—was, like the Murphy Brown scenario, perceived to be reality when it was in fact a myth. Created and written by former bandleader Ozzie Nelson, whose wife, Harriet, had been a movie actress and the vocalist in her husband's band, the show featured all the little adventures an average middle-class American family might have and two sons growing up before their parents'—and the television audience's—eyes. Even the Nelsons' television home was modeled on their real-life home in Hollywood. But there was a darker side to the genial family American viewers came to accept as representing the ideal. As David Halberstam observes:

> The low-key Ozzie Nelson of the sitcoms had little in common with the real-life Ozzie, who was a workaholic. He wrote, produced, and directed the shows and was an authoritarian, almost dictatorial presence on the set who monitored every aspect of his children's lives. . . . Ozzie Nelson was not merely a man who put great pressure on his children, but in contrast to the readily available Ozzie of the show, who always seemed to be around, he was gone much of the time—albeit at home, but gone. He would retire after dinner to his office and work all night writing the scripts and the directorial notes, sleeping late and coming downstairs around noon. The Nelsons were, therefore, for all their professional success, very different from the family depicted on the show, they lived with an immense amount of pressure and unreconciled issues. Chief among these issues was the fact that Ozzie Nelson had in effect stolen the childhood of both his sons and used it for commercial purposes; he had taken what was most private and made it terribly public.

Harriet Nelson's character in what was a show at first dominated by a benevolently (at least on television) authoritarian Ozzie as the head of the household and later by their younger son, Ricky, as a teenage rock and roll heartthrob, was that of the wonderful, all-purpose homemaker who cooked and cleaned and never complained about being seen but rarely heard, even when Ozzie dampened her attempt to join the local volunteer fire department so that she could see more of him with the sexist observation, "You gals take too long to dress. . . . By the time you got your makeup on, the fire would be out." Any personality Harriet Nelson or the character might have had was never revealed; she existed primarily to be Ozzie's wife and David and Ricky's mother. The best one can say about Harriet Nelson's television status and persona as the family's live-in maid, housekeeper, and cook is that she appeared to be so relaxed and even detached from any deep thoughts or feelings she might have possessed that it is difficult to feel pity or outrage on her behalf. Harriet Nelson, "both on television and in real life," writes Halberstam,

The television (and real-life) family
that appeared to personify the
positive moral values of 1950s
America: Ozzie and Harriet Nelson
with sons David (*right*), and Ricky
(*left*) *Wisconsin Center for Film and
Theater Research*

"accepted her life, for it was a
good one, far better than what
anyone who had grown up in
the Depression had any right to
expect." The newly middle-
class housewife of the 1950s,
who had probably grown up
during the Depression, too, might well have felt that she could do worse
than aspire to the kind of bland, seemingly secure life that Harriet was
living on television.

Like Harriet, Margaret Anderson, the sensible housedress-clad wife
and mother played by Jane Wyatt on *Father Knows Best*, also knew her
place in the background as a woman of the 1950s, but her status in the
family was a bit more evolved because, although it was her husband,
Jim (Robert Young), who ultimately solved the many problems concerning the couple's three children, there was greater respect for a mother's
point of view. The tight, loving unit represented by Jim, Margaret, Betty,
Bud, and Kathy made the Andersons truly an idealized suburban family
of the sort that viewers could relate to and wish to emulate. Unlike the
majority of two-parent video families of the 1980s and 1990s, the families of early television featured children who might have cracked jokes
and questioned authority, but they did not crack wise; the kids understood that both their mother and their father were the adults in the
family, and the parents knew it, too. But parenting in the fifties, at least
as it was portrayed on television, was not always as effortless as the Nelsons and the Andersons made it seem. Ward Cleaver (Hugh Beaumont),
the father of *Leave It to Beaver,* often appeared overly authoritarian and
frequently lost his temper with his two sons, Wally and Theodore ("the
Beaver"). These negative, "masculine" character traits were countered
by the soothing, "feminine" presence of his wife, June (Barbara Billings-
ley). June not only gentled Ward into calmness and more appropriate
courses of action, she looked lovely doing it. Instead of dowdy house-
dresses, June favored full-skirted dresses, frilly aprons, and pearls; her
hair was attractively styled, and she wore makeup even while baking

cookies and cakes for her men. June Cleaver perfectly embodied the idealized women of the feminine mystique era: she kept her house clean and inviting, sewed, baked, and cooked two hot meals a day, was a supportive, loving mother and glamorous wife-companion, and did not venture far from her household domain, either in thought or deed.

The homemaker-wife-mother icon of television reached its pinnacle in 1958 with the debut of *The Donna Reed Show*. Like June Cleaver, Donna Stone was beautiful and glamorous (vacuuming the house in a pretty dress and high heels); like all the sitcom moms before her, she was supportive and sensible. But because this was Donna Reed's show, her character had to reflect Reed's star status. Donna Stone was shown looking glamorous outside the home, she was involved in neighborhood and community activities, and usually it was she, rather than her pediatrician husband, Alex (Carl Betz), who was the family problem solver. In fact, *The Donna Reed Show* could easily have been titled *Mother Knows Best*. Donna did not need to consider the possibility of pursuing a career outside the home; for her, homemaking and motherhood were careers, ones that, in her view, demanded the same kinds of skills as those practiced by professionals. In one episode she asserts to a group of friends in her soft-spoken manner and without appearing self-aggrandizing that women aren't "just housewives" but are in reality nurses, psychologists, educators, chefs, accountants, and politicians all rolled into one. Husband Alex stands next to her, looking proud and gratified, as well he should: he had gotten an entire community of professionals working for him for free in one enticing female package.

Women viewers in the prefeminist years before Betty Friedan's *The Feminine Mystique* began to make an impact must have appreciated the Donna Stone character for her cheerleading on behalf of homemakers and mothers and applauded her premier status in the household. But during the early and mid-1960s *The Donna Reed Show* consistently received lower ratings than the family-oriented sitcoms *The Danny Thomas Show* and *The Dick Van Dyke Show*. Both series were funnier and more sophisticated than *Donna Reed* in large part because each featured a supporting cast of characters full of wit and humor. However, the Danny Williams character was clearly the lord of his household; his wife, Kathy, although feisty at times, was a housewife in the June Cleaver tradition. Laura Petrie, the beautiful, Jacqueline Kennedy lookalike and suburban housewife, played by Mary Tyler Moore on *The Dick Van Dyke Show*, was sexier and dressed more casually than her predecessors, although the series received letters from women viewers complaining that Moore too often wore tight-fitting capri pants instead of traditionally demure dresses. Laura had a more fully developed personality than previous sitcom wives (she had been a dancer before her marriage and showed some professional ego during the series) but was frequently portrayed as childish and scatterbrained. In retrospect, the tone of the series seems more blatantly sexist than other domestic sitcoms because many of the situations focused on the relationship between Laura and her television-writer husband, Rob, and *The Dick Van Dyke Show* was very much a series that reflected its time. One episode had Laura flattening a masher with a perfectly executed judo flip, whereupon the event is derisively covered in a newspaper gossip column and Rob is teased about his "adorable Amazon" of a wife. Rob then becomes ridiculously obsessed with proving that men are the stronger sex. Still, situations such as these illustrated that the husband character could behave just as childishly as the wife and had the effect of equalizing the relationship, which was essentially a loving and stable one.

Laura Petrie, like the television sitcom wives who preceded her, and Carol Brady, *The Brady Bunch* mother who came after her, was shown to be happiest and most competent in the realm of *Kinder und Küshe*. The only sitcom housewife who assertively challenged the gender status quo during the years before the revived women's movement was the inimitable Lucy Ricardo, "but by doing so," writes Halberstam, "only served to prove that men were right and that women had no place in the serious world of business and commerce. . . . Indeed, it was the very manic, incompetent quality of her rebellion that showed she should be at home burning the dinner and that women were somehow different than men, less steady, and less capable."

That video view of women would undergo a metamorphosis during the last three decades of the century when television sitcoms endeavored to reflect the changing status of women and families in American society. Examples included single, working mothers (*Julia*, 1968–1971, also notable for being the first comedy series to star a woman of color), single working women (*The Mary Tyler Moore Show*, 1970–1977), happily married women (*Family Ties*, 1982–1989), and a company run by unmarried, divorced, and widowed women (*Designing Women*, 1986–1993). Complaints against liberal media bias notwithstanding, it was clear by the end of the century that television would not portray women as it had done in the days of *Ozzie and Harriet* or *Leave It to Beaver*, at least for the foreseeable future. Only viewers deeply nostalgic for their own real or perceived happy childhoods during that era could possibly wish for the return of such a repressive and mythical kingdom.

1953

The Second Half of the Kinsey Report, *Sexual Behavior in the Human Female,* Is Published

There is no ocean of greater magnitude than the sexual function, and there are those who believe that we would do better if we ignored its existence, that we should not try to understand its material origins, and that if we sufficiently ignore it and mop at the flood of sexual activity with new laws, heavier penalties, more pronouncements, and greater intolerances, we may ultimately eliminate the reality. The scientist who observes and describes the reality is attacked as an enemy of the faith, and his acceptance of human limitations in modifying that reality is condemned as scientific materialism. But we believe that an increased understanding of the biologic and psychologic and social factors which account for each type of sexual activity may contribute to an ultimate adjustment between man's sexual nature and the needs of the total social organization.

Alfred C. Kinsey et al., *Sexual Behavior in the Human Female*

Published in 1953, *Sexual Behavior in the Human Female*—complementing the earlier 1948 survey, *Sexual Behavior in the Human Male,* and collectively forming the Kinsey Report—signaled the beginning of a sexual revolution, a period of increasing openness and frankness in dealing with human sexuality. Alfred C. Kinsey (1894–1956), a professor of zoology at the University of Indiana since 1920, and his research associates— Wardell Pomeroy, Clyde Martin, and Paul Gebhart—interviewed eighteen thousand individuals between 1938 and 1956, collecting the data that were classified statistically to form the two volumes of the report. Different from earlier sexual theorists such as Havelock Ellis and Sigmund Freud, Kinsey avoided moralizing or placing value judgments on neurotic or deviant behavior; instead he set out to uncover and quantify what people actually did sexually. The result was one of the most influential works on human sexuality in the twentieth century and one that served to establish a new empirical basis for understanding sexual practices, particularly in women. The Kinsey Report revolutionized previous understanding and remains, over fifty years after its data were first collected, the most reliable and extensive source of information about American sexual behavior. As one of the pioneers in sexual research, Kinsey rivals Freud in his impact on sexual awareness. By debunking antiquated notions and demystifying sex, Kinsey helped launch a shift in attitude to one that regarded sex as a commonplace and natural experience rather than something that is mysterious and prohibited.

Previous studies of female sexuality had never documented the variety and degree of women's sexuality that *Sexual Behavior in the Human Female* showed. Katherine B. Davis in *Factors in the Sex Life of Twenty-two Hundred Women* (1929) had demonstrated that the sexual attitudes of women were changing in the twentieth century and that married women were increasingly regarding sex not as a duty to be endured, as Victorian mores insisted, but as a pleasure to be enjoyed. The Kinsey Report, with its much wider sample and detailed information derived from personal interviews, considerably expanded this view and classified the various aspects of female sexuality from preadolescent sexual development, premarital, marital, and extramarital sex, to masturbation and homosexuality. Such topics had seldom been treated beyond the practices of prostitutes or other denizens of the demimonde, certainly not as elements of "normal" sexual practice of ordinary individuals and rarely without moral censure.

Before examining human sexuality, Alfred Kinsey had devoted twenty years to the life cycle, evolution, geographical distribution, and specification of the tiny insect the gall wasp. Kinsey had undertaken his research on sexuality to answer his students' questions on matters of sex. Finding "that scientific understanding of human sexual behavior was more poorly established than the understanding of almost any other function of the human body," Kinsey launched a massive research project to gather data. His academic specialty was taxonomy, the science of classification and identification of significant subgroups in a particular population, and Kinsey would apply his taxonomic skills to the study of sexuality. Kinsey believed that the absence of taxonomic thoroughness had marred other studies of human sexuality and had resulted in biased generalizations based on a narrow range of samples. The fundamental tenet of Kinsey's approach was tolerance or as he put it, the "sympathetic acceptance of people as they are." Kinsey explained in *Sexual Behavior in the Human Male*, "This is first of all a report on what people

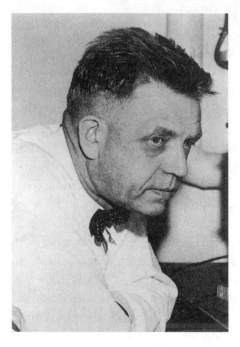

Biologist and sexual theorist Alfred Kinsey, who established a new empirical basis for understanding sexual practices in American women *Library of Congress*

do, which raises no question of what they should do."

What Kinsey and his researchers discovered in their exhaustive interviews of what they hoped would prove to be a representative sample of white males and females in America—the case histories of 5,940 white females provided the data for *Sexual Behavior in the Human Female*—was the extreme range of sexual behavior. The data suggested that any attempt to prescribe uniform standards of sexual practices was unrealistic, and efforts to legislate sexual behavior was doomed to failure. As Paul Robinson observes in *The Modernization of Sex*, Kinsey "established beyond all doubt that sexual differences were matters of degree rather than kind. Almost any sexual style, he showed, could be placed alongside another that differed from it but slightly. In this manner all forms of sexual behavior, from celibacy to promiscuity, or from extreme homosexuality to extreme heterosexuality, could be charted along a single curve. . . . Abnormality thus became a taxonomically meaningless notion." Kinsey's tolerance and the report's willingness to consider all forms of sexual behavior as acceptable was both liberating and explosive in exposing as narrow and shortsighted moral views that refused to acknowledge the wide range of sexual practices that the Kinsey Report uncovered.

Sexual Behavior in the Human Female revealed that sexual behavior that had been considered rare among women, such as homosexuality, masturbation, and premarital intercourse, was in fact quite prevalent. The cumulative effect of its findings serves to suggest the much wider nature of female sexuality and that attempts to morally confine sex to marriage for procreation were inadequate and misleading. The Kinsey Report documented how the female is very much a sexual being and that sexual expression takes many forms throughout an individual's lifetime. Kinsey's research also showed that there was a demonstrable new libidinous attitude among women who came of age during the 1930s and 1940s, which he traced to a variety of causes, including the general liberalizing effects of the war. Kinsey's data also made a case for gender equality in the enjoyment of sex, asserting that sexual arousal and climax were physically identical in men and women. Although Kinsey granted women considerably more sexual awareness and sensitivity than in previous studies, he still concluded that "the female is generally less responsive than the male." Whereas women wished for and enjoyed orgasm as intensely as men, the report's data indicated that frequency was considerably less among women. Kinsey showed that the average male had over 1,500 orgasms before marriage, while the average female had fewer than 250. Since the female's less frequent incidence of orgasms stemmed not from any physical distinction between the sexes, or as the result of any inherent modesty, Kinsey concluded that the difference was explained because of fundamental neurological differences between men and women. The male's greater sensitivity to psychological stimuli, according to Kinsey, explained the discrepancy and led to the controversial conclusion that male sexuality was predominantly mental, while female sexuality was predominantly physical, reversing the popular belief that sex for women was more an emotional rather than a physical stimulation. Kinsey's conclusion remains controversial and formed the basis for an ongoing debate over gender and sexual response.

The most famous later study of sexuality that built upon the data of the Kinsey Report was the research of William Masters, a gynecologist, and psychologist Virginia Johnson. To the data already gathered by questionnaires and interviews, Masters and Johnson added clinical tests to measure directly sexual responses. Their findings, published in *Human Sexual Response* (1966), *Human Sexual Inadequacy* (1970), and *Homosexuality in Perspective* (1979), added greatly to research in sexuality, while convincingly disproving the conventional notion of female passivity and unresponsiveness that Kinsey had, at least partially, seemed to support. With women having a demonstrable greater sexual capacity, expressed in many different forms, as well as the ability to achieve multiple orgasms, Masters and Johnson celebrated women's sexual response and concluded that women were in fact the superior sexual animal, and portrayed male sexuality in comparison as limited and one-dimensional. Their findings, though extremely controversial as science, were taken up by the feminist movement in support of a desired sexual democracy.

The importance of *Sexual Behavior in the Human Female* rests in its initiating a demystification of sexual practices among men and women. The Kinsey Report would help to justify the breakdown of more restrictive morality under the pressure of a new permissiveness of the sexual revolution that was decidedly declared with the development of the birth control pill in 1960. The Kinsey Report announced that female sexuality is a far more complex and widespread human function incorporated in a much wider definition of women's nature beyond marriage and motherhood. Prior to Kinsey, sexuality was to a great degree seen as essentially a male attribute and preoccupation, and as his data showed clearly for the first time, there exists, as in so many other areas of human experience, an equality in sexual matters among women and men.

The First *Playboy* Magazine Hits Newsstands

By the turbulent and affluent sixties, *Playboy* had become an American institution, as typical for its times and place as the *Saturday Evening Post*. Bunnies with their bulging bosoms and pleasantly empty faces reflected a new ritual as accurately as Norman Rockwell's covers did the reality of small-town America. . . . The *Playboy* life-style, which Hefner sold with the unrelenting vigor of the Music Man hitting River City, had become a serious social force and an important factor in commerce. Madison Avenue spotted the magazine's pulling power and became its evangelizer among the shakers and shapers of the consumer society. Hefner's "philosophy" triggered a national debate on the relevance of traditional sexual morality. And in that debate Hefner became, if not the American sexual revolution's Jesus Christ . . . then surely its St. Paul, the didactic popularizer of a tempered hedonism-as-religion.

Thomas Weyr, *Reaching for Paradise: The Playboy Vision of America*

It may seem out of place in a book on twentieth-century women's history to include an event such as the publication of *Playboy*, an "Entertainment for Men," which has significantly contributed to the definition of women exclusively by their physicality and to the objectification of women as "bunnies" and "playmates." Yet *Playboy* symbolically reflected its era while playing an important role in helping to launch the sexual revolution that has had a profound impact on traditional morality and the freedom with which men and women have expressed their sexuality. *Playboy* also raises important issues concerning the ways in which women have been seen through the second half of the twentieth century and helps define the battleground that feminists in the 1960s and 1970s attacked, as they challenged the various tenets of the "*Playboy* philosophy."

In retrospect, *Playboy*'s creator, Hugh Hefner, has repeatedly interpreted the launching of his magazine as an ideological assault on America's Puritan ethic of repressed sexuality and hypocritical morality, concepts that had been recently exposed by the revelations in Alfred Kinsey's *Sexual Behavior in the Human Male* (1948) and *Sexual Behavior in the Human Female* (1953). As Hefner explains, "I was trying to put out a magazine for myself, one that I would enjoy reading. It described an urban world and the play and pleasure parts of life. If you had to sum up the idea of *Playboy*, it is anti-Puritanism. Not just in regard to sex, but the whole range of play and pleasure." With the loosening of sexual mores and the increasing affluence of postwar American life, Hefner conceived of a magazine to celebrate both. As Hefner says, "*Playboy* came along and offered a new set of ethical values for the urban society. The editorial message in *Playboy* came through loud and clear: Enjoy yourself. Paul Gebhard, director of the Institute for Sex Research, once said that the genius of *Playboy* was that it linked sex with upward mobility, and that's a sociological way of expressing what I'm talking about."

The facts surrounding the creation of *Playboy* both support Hefner's contentions and qualify them with more practical, commercial considerations. Hefner, born in 1926, raised by strict Methodist parents, was a shy introvert desperate to enjoy the good life he felt excluded from in a series of low-level editorial jobs in Chicago following his discharge from the army and graduation from the University of Illinois in Urbana. A less than accomplished cartoonist and occasional satirist of the Chicago scene, with almost no money or experience, Hefner set out to launch his own men's magazine to achieve success and the liberation he had longed for at home, in the army, at school, and in his faltering marriage. As he remembers, "The most popular men's magazines of the time were the outdoor-adventure books—*True, Argosy,* and the like. They had a hairy-chested editorial emphasis with articles on hunting, fishing, chasing the Abominable Snowman over Tibetan mountaintops. . . . *Esquire* had changed its editorial emphasis after the war, eliminating most of the lighter material—the girls, cartoons, and humor. So the field was wide open for the sort of magazine I had in mind." To fill the void left by *Esquire* in the area of sophisticated male entertainment, Hefner planned his magazine, originally called *Stag Party*, with a philosophy that he announced in the first issue, published in December 1953:

> If you are a man between 18 and 80, *Playboy* is meant for you. . . . We want to make clear from the very start, we aren't a "family magazine." If you're somebody's sister, wife, or mother-in-law and picked us up by mistake, please pass us along to the man in your life and get back to *Ladies' Home Companion*. Within the pages of *Playboy* you will find arti-

cles, fiction, picture stories, cartoons, humor and special features culled from many sources, past and present, to form a pleasure-primer styled to the masculine taste.

Most of today's "magazines for men" spend all their time out-of-doors—thrashing through thorny thickets or splashing about in fast flowing streams. We'll be out there too, occasionally, but we don't mind telling you in advance—we plan spending most of our time inside.

We like our apartment. We enjoy mixing up cocktails and an *hors d'oeuvre* or two, putting a little mood music on the phonograph and inviting in a female acquaintance for a quiet discussion of Picasso, Nietzsche, jazz, sex. . . .

Affairs of the state will be out of our province. We don't expect to solve any world problems or prove any great moral truths. If we are able to give the American male a few extra laughs and a little diversion from the anxieties of the Atomic Age, we'll feel we've justified our existence.

To create a sensation for his new magazine, Hefner fortuitously acquired the rights from a Chicago-based calendar printer of nude photographs of a young Marilyn Monroe taken in 1949 to help her pay the rent before she became a star. For the first time in American publishing, a mainstream magazine published full-color nude photographs, and the conjunction of the *Playboy* philosophy and the sensation of seeing a nude Hollywood goddess brought Hefner immediate and overwhelming success. Instantly profitable, *Playboy*'s circulation grew from 53,991 for the first issue to 2 million copies a month in 1964 to its height in 1972 of 7 million copies, earning profits of $12 million for the year.

Although *Playboy* eventually published first-rate fiction and articles by important writers and journalists and featured a series of interviews with important figures, its depiction of sex continued to define the magazine and ensure its phenomenal success. Prior to *Playboy*, nudity in magazines was occasional, confined to such publications as *Modern Sunbathing* and cheap girlie magazines. Hefner's Playmates, selected because they were not professional models but "girls next door," posed in recognizable settings, the opposite of the studio shots and the "rather self-conscious fallen look . . . like the girls in other girlie magazines." *Playboy*'s first new-style Playmate was Charlaine Karalus, who worked for the magazine. She appeared in 1955, named "Janet Pilgrim," along with this editorial comment: "We suppose that it's natural to think of the pulchritudinous Playmates as existing in a world apart. Actually, potential Playmates are all around you: the new secretary at your office, the doe-eyed beauty who sat opposite you at lunch yesterday, the girl who sells your shirts and ties in your favorite store. We found Miss July in our own circulation department, processing subscriptions. . . ." Hefner had freed nudity from its former shadowy world of the professional and cultist to feature ordinary women willing to appear *déshabillé* in a national magazine. But the "average-looking," wholesome Playmates were enhanced to airbrushed perfection, with every blemish or flaw carefully removed by body makeup or retouches. Pubic hair was banned until 1971. The overall effect achieved a perfectibility of a woman's body in the terms that defined the magazine's notion of sensuality: statuesque, perfectly proportioned, and slightly vapid, a kind of human Barbie doll. In fact, *Playboy* blurred the distinction between the various sleek and sophisticated items of affluence that the magazine celebrated—cars, fashion, food, and drink—and the women it displayed.

This objectification of women would raise the ire of feminists and the women's movement in the 1960s and 1970s. Targeting *Playboy* for its role in the degradation of women, feminists attacked the magazine for displaying "their girls as if they were a commodity," as Germaine Greer observed. Gloria Steinem, who had gone undercover for an exposé as Bunny Marie in the early 1960s, called the *Playboy* philosophy "boyish, undeveloped, anti-sensual, vicarious and sad." Susan Brownmiller, in her important study, *Against Our Will: Men, Women and Rape*, described the culture of pornography and rape that *Playboy*, in her view, helped to shape, by analyzing why women's response is so different from men's to the pictorials: It comes "from the gut knowledge that we and our bodies are being stripped, exposed, and contorted for the purpose of ridicule to bolster that 'masculine esteem' which gets its kick and sense of power from viewing females as anonymous, panting playthings, adult toys, dehumanized objects to be used, abused, broken, and discarded." In *Playboy*'s defense, Hefner has explained, "We've played a decontaminating role in changing attitudes toward nudity. The feminists who criticize us don't realize how *Playboy*, far more than the women's magazines, is responsible for the nongirdle look, the bikini, the miniskirt, the openness to nudity. . . . We've helped their movement in several ways."

In a sense, Hefner is both right and wrong. *Playboy* has certainly played a significant role in documenting and celebrating a new sexual freedom against past hypocritical and repressive customs and conventions. Yet the image of women that *Playboy* has made part of mainstream culture—prompting a host of imitators, like *Penthouse* and *Hustler,* that push even further to distort the distinction between the erotic and the pornographic—is an ambivalent legacy that enforces notions of women's submissiveness, the primacy of physicality, and gender inequality. To a question on *The Dick Cavett Show* in the early 1970s about her definition of sexual equality, Susan Brownmiller responded: "When Hugh Hefner comes out here with a cottontail attached to his rear end, then we'll have equality."

Playboy has over the years altered somewhat with the times, supporting the Equal Rights Amendment, abortion rights, and rape counseling. It has also been hurt by women's criticism, bad management decisions to expand beyond magazine publishing, and changing times. In the 1970s circulation fell to 2.5 million, and as Hefner later admitted, "We went through a period when we lost our bearings and started imitating the imitators." More suggestive poses, and implications of lesbianism and masturbation, caused conservative advertisers to withdraw their accounts. A management shake-up trimmed jobs and returned the focus of Playboy Enterprises to the magazine with less lurid sexual pictorials and a renewed emphasis on high-quality written content. The enterprise is now under the direct supervision of Hefner's daughter, Christie Hefner, who has stated that *Playboy* "has to deal with more ways of intercourse between the sexes than sexual." It is unclear, however, whether *Playboy* will be able to maintain its place in America's sexual psyche or whether its philosophy is now little more than a quaint reminder of an earlier, far less enlightened sexist time. Nevertheless, the appearance in 1953 of *Playboy* marked a major shift in raising the topic of sexuality to the center of the debate over cultural and social values and women's place in men's imagination.

Simone de Beauvoir's *The Second Sex* Is Published in English

> One is not born, but rather becomes, a woman. No biological, psychological, or economic fate determines the figure that the human female presents to society; it is civilization as a whole that produces this creature, intermediate between male and eunuch, which is described as feminine.
>
> Simone de Beauvoir, *The Second Sex*

Simone de Beauvoir's controversial polemic on the subordinated status of women, first published in France in 1949 and partially translated into English in 1953, remains one of the most influential works of the twentieth century and a foundation text for the revived women's movement

Simone de Beauvoir, author of the
indispensable existentialist polemic on
the status of women, *The Second Sex*
Agence France Presse/Corbis-Bettmann

of the 1960s and 1970s. *The Second
Sex* was both praised and excoriated, provoking reaction that
ranged from the horrified gasps
by traditionalists to the impas-
sioned gratitude of women who
had finally found in de Beauvoir
the first true explicator of their
condition. As Jean Leighton
observes in *Simone de Beauvoir on
Women*, de Beauvoir's "analysis of
the subtle and insinuating way
women are molded by society to
accept their inferior role is masterful and devastating. Her perception of
how the male-dominated culture tries to transform women into an
'object' [what de Beauvoir also termed the "other"] who exists primarily
to please men had had profound reverberations." *The Second Sex* ranks
with Mary Wollstonecraft's *A Vindication of the Rights of Women* (1792) and
John Stuart Mill's *Subjection of Women* (1869) as one of the crucial documents on women's emancipation. Betty Friedan has called de Beauvoir
"an authentic heroine in the history of womanhood," and her own
groundbreaking book, *The Feminine Mystique*, which can be said to have
launched the modern women's movement in America, is inconceivable
without the conceptualization that *The Second Sex* provided.

Simone de Beauvoir was born in 1908 in Paris, the elder daughter of
Françoise and Georges de Beauvoir. Early on she rebelled against her
middle-class Catholic upbringing and education and the social restrictions imposed upon her by her gender, proclaiming at the age of nineteen, "I don't want my life to obey any other will but my own." Freed
from the prospect of a stultifying bourgeois marriage by her father's
inability to provide dowries for either of his daughters, de Beauvoir continued her studies, with the intention of pursuing a career. A brilliant
student, she earned her degree at the Sorbonne in 1929. While there
she met fellow student Jean-Paul Sartre, whom she later described in
the first volume of her autobiography, *Memoirs of a Dutiful Daughter,* as
"a soulmate in whom I found, heated to the point of incandescence, all
of my passions. With him, I could always share everything." The couple

shared their lives together for fifty-one years, until Sartre's death in 1980. Except for a brief period during World War II and during an annual six-week vacation in Rome, de Beauvoir and Sartre lived in separate apartments, coming together in the evenings to discuss their ideas and to read and criticize each other's work. Their liaison, which both viewed as essential and indestructible, precluded traditional notions of marriage and children and included a mutually agreed upon concession for "contingent loves" of lesser importance. "We have," de Beauvoir once said, "pioneered our own relationship—its freedom, intimacy, and frankness."

De Beauvoir taught philosophy at several colleges until 1943, after which she devoted herself to writing full-time. Before *The Second Sex*, none of her books looked explicitly at the condition of women, though the three novels she had published—*She Came to Stay*, *The Blood of Others*, and *All Men Are Mortal*—all featured strong female central protagonists. In one sense de Beauvoir was an unlikely spokesperson for the woman's perspective; in another she was ideal. Prior to writing *The Second Sex*, de Beauvoir could recall no disadvantages or difficulties in her own life that she could relate to her gender. "Far from suffering from my femininity," she recalled, "I have, on the contrary, from the age of twenty on, accumulated the advantages of both sexes; after *She Came to Stay* those around me treated me both as a writer, their peer in the masculine world, and a woman; this was particularly noticeable in America: at the parties I went to, the wives all got together and talked to each other while I talked to the men, who nevertheless behaved toward me with greater courtesy than they did toward the members of their own sex."

Although she had gained her independence and autonomy outside the conventional roles expected from women—childless, unmarried, and free from domestic concerns and commitments—de Beauvoir had little firsthand experience of the condition of women that she revealed in *The Second Sex*. Indeed, as she recalled, "I knew very few women of my own age and none who had led normal married lives." The idea for a study of women did not originate as a compellingly felt need but was suggested by Sartre. However, de Beauvoir's status as an outsider and exception, assessing the relationships of the sexes from her anomalous position, provides much of the book's originality and genius. De Beauvoir began her study looking at the lives of women, living normal married lives, who "in differing circumstances and with various degrees of success, had all undergone one identical experience: they had lived as 'dependent persons.' . . . I began to take stock of the difficulties, deceptive advantages, traps, and manifold obstacles that most women encounter on their path. I also felt how much they were both diminished and enriched by this experience. The problem did not concern me directly, and as yet I attributed little importance to it; but my interest had been aroused."

As de Beauvoir proceeded in her study, placing women's lives in the context of the existential and Socialist philosophy she was committed to and her biological and historical research, she arrived at her central thesis:

> Women lack concrete means for organizing themselves into a unit which can stand face to face with the correlative unit. They have no past, no history, no religion of their own; and they have no solidarity of work and interest as that of the proletariat. . . . The bond that unites her to her oppressors is not comparable to any other. The division of the sexes is a biological fact, not an event of human history. Male and female stand oppressed within a primordial *Mitsein*, and woman has not broken it. The couple is a fundamental unity with its two halves riveted together, and the cleavage of society along the line of sex is impossible. Here is to be found the basic trait of woman: she is the Other in a totality of which the two components are necessary to one another.

In de Beauvoir's analysis, women accept their subordination and objectification for certain privileges and advantages bestowed on the female but which are an evasion of full, adult, moral responsibility. For de Beauvoir, the way out of the trap is for women to reject the feminine, the various modes that dictate dependence and subservience, and to choose an autonomous and independent life as a free and active person. "The emancipated woman wants to be active," she argues, "and refuses the passivity man means to impose on her. The 'modern' woman accepts masculine values: she prides herself on thinking, taking action, working, creating on the same terms as man."

The solution to women's objectification and subordination in *The Second Sex* is more problematic than programmatic. De Beauvoir's liberated woman who has left behind any traces of the feminine resembles no one more than the free and independent male oppressor. In the keys de Beauvoir identifies to safeguard women's freedom—paid work and contraception—*The Second Sex* rejects any positives contained in the experience of motherhood and marriage and other forms of the female expression. However, the significance of *The Second Sex* rests more in its diagnosis of the problem than in its solutions. As Mary Evans observes in her study of the author's works, "*The Second Sex* has been a major landmark in discussions of relations between the sexes. Whether we agree or disagree with the conclusions of the book its significance lies in de Beauvoir's success in placing on the intellectual agenda three crucial questions about the nature of relations between the sexes, namely, the problem of the origin of sexual

difference, the nature and the elaboration of sexual inequality and difference, and the issue of how men and women should live. These issues
still dominate feminist discussion, and form an important part of debates
in a number of academic disciplines and in psychoanalysis."

The Second Sex produced a storm of controversy when it was published
in France in 1949. De Beauvoir recalled that "some professors threw the
book across their offices because they couldn't bear to read it." Albert
Camus complained that she had "made a laughing-stock of the French
male." By the time the book was published in its English translation,
opinion was more temperate. As Philip Wylie wrote in appreciation in
the *Saturday Review of Literature*, "No one can leave her book unread
and still be considered intellectually up-to-date. It makes a fresh contribution to awareness that cannot be missed any more than the contribution of Freud, say, or Einstein or Darwin—without the onset of a private
cultural lag." De Beauvoir, who was confident that existentialism and
socialism would eventually cure the imbalance between the sexes, was a
late convert to women's liberation and the women's movement in the
1970s. *The Second Sex* helped to launch both through the daringness of de
Beauvoir's analysis of the role of women and the relationship of the
sexes. Few other books have so sharply and honestly looked at such
fundamental questions while establishing the essential issues for an
ongoing debate.

1955–1956

Twin Sisters Esther Pauline and Pauline Esther Friedman Become "Ann Landers" and "Dear Abby"

> Ann Landers and Dear Abby are American institutions. As Popo points out after more than thirty years of advice giving, "Eppie and I must be doing something right. There must be some reason we're still here." Syndication ensures their daily exposure to a vast reading public that can be counted on to catapult Ann and Abby onto any list of the most influential Americans, male or female.
>
> Jan Pottker and Bob Speziale, *Dear Ann, Dear Abby*

Few other individuals have asserted an influence in reflecting and shaping American moral and cultural attitudes comparable to that of the syndicated columnists Ann Landers and Abigail Van Buren. For over four decades their columns, printed in more than two thousand newspapers all over the world with an estimated reading audience of nearly two hundred million people, have dispensed advice and commonsensical observations on the great and small problems of contemporary life. Their popularity has made the pair among the most admired women in the United States, and they have transformed the discredited newspaper feature of advice to the lovelorn into a sounding board for daily confrontations on issues of consequence to a vast popular audience. There are few better sources for gauging American attitudes and preoccupations during the last half of the twentieth century than the columns of Ann Landers and Dear Abby.

The story of how the Friedman sisters from Sioux City, Iowa, achieved their preeminence in helping to form American opinion is one of the most remarkable in journalism. In less than a year between 1955 and 1956, they were launched on independent and nearly simultaneous careers as celebrated dispensers of advice. Both were traditional homemakers of the period, volunteers and dabblers in the world outside their homes and families. Neither had graduated from college, had any particular experience or professional expertise to mark them as authorities on anything, or in fact had ever held jobs before they were hired as syndicated columnists. Both traded instead on common sense, family background, irrepressible, gutsy, and trenchant opinions, and down-home advice to captivate and persuade their audience. As Eppie Friedman, writing as Ann Landers, once insisted, "I'm the original square Jewish lady from Sioux City, Iowa." Her sister was no less modest about her background, nor less confident that despite their admitted limitations, as sympathetic listeners to America's problems, both women have made an important contribution in raising awareness about social ills and in helping to form moral opinion.

In 1955, while living in Chicago, Eppie, who had had a taste of larger

Born on July 4, 1918, the identical twins were inseparable throughout their childhood. Dressed alike in the custom of the day, they shared the same hobbies and interests, double-dated, and attended the same college, Morningside College in Sioux City. At college the Friedman twins wrote a campus gossip column, "Campus Rats," and, as one of the twins later recalled, "majored in boys." Marriage interrupted a halfhearted pursuit of degrees. Popo married a wealthy heir to a family fortune, and Eppie wed a hat salesman who determinedly rose to become a company president. Neither sought a career outside their homes, but neither their husbands, children, nor domestic life would prove to be sufficient outlets for their continual restless energy and interests.

In 1955, while living in Chicago, Eppie, who had had a taste of larger public life in Democratic Party politics, read an advice column in the *Sun-Times*. On a whim, she called a family friend at the paper to inquire whether the columnist needed any help with her mail. The column was the creation of veteran journalist Ruth Crowley, who had been dispensing advice as "Ann Landers" since 1942. The paper was in the process of looking for a replacement for Crowley, who had recently died, and despite Eppie's lack of previous work experience, including the fact that she had never written a line for publication, she was allowed to compete in the contest the *Sun-Times* was conducting for the new Ann Landers. Using a rented typewriter, Eppie produced forty sample columns in three weeks. She was the only applicant among the twenty-eight in the competition who consulted outside experts to bolster her advice, including that of Supreme Court justice William O. Douglas to settle the question of who owned the fruit that fell from a tree into a neighbor's yard. It also helped that she closely resembled the picture of Ann Landers that accompanied the column, and she won the position. As she later recalled, "The manner in which the column fell into my lap is enough to make a person believe in Santa Claus." Her first columns, which began on October 16, 1955, imitated the slightly irreverent, snappy style of her predecessor. Different from other advice to the lovelorn by such popular columnists as Dorothy Dix, the Ann Landers columns eschewed sappy sentimentality for honest and straightforward advice, grounded by kindness and compassion. As Eppie stated, "The true measure of a human is how he or she treats his fellow man. Integrity and compassion cannot be learned in college, nor are these qualities inherited in the genes." Eppie as Ann Landers drew on her "loving, happy family memories" as an antidote to the pain and desperation of the appeals she received from the individuals who wrote for advice. Hired for $87 a week, with no staff, Eppie faced the daunting task of responding to a backlog of some five thousand letters. As she had done throughout her life, Eppie turned to her twin for support, sending letters and responses to Popo in California for assistance.

After the *Sun-Times* put a stop to the unofficial collaboration between the sisters, Popo, having acquired a taste for dispensing advice through her work with Eppie, volunteered her services for free to California's *San Mateo Times*. The paper flatly refused her offer. Next she contacted the *San Francisco Chronicle*, criticizing its recently established Molly Mayfield lovelorn column as lacking imagination and sensitivity and contending that she could do better. The paper allowed her to tackle some of the Molly Mayfield letters, which she answered, as she later put it, in a "humorous but sensible" manner, with "tongue-in-cheek one-liners" that were similar in style to the columns for which Ann Landers was becoming famous. An often repeated example is her response to Blondie, who wrote, "My boyfriend took me out on my twenty-first birthday and wanted to show me a special time. I usually don't go in much for drinking, but I had three martinis. During dinner we split a bottle of wine. After dinner we had two brandies. Did I do wrong?" Her reply: "Dear Blondie: Probably." Hired by the *Chronicle* for $20 per column, she created the pseudonym Abigail Van Buren: "I chose Abigail from the Old Testament. Abigail was a prophetess in the Book of Samuel, and it was said of her, 'Blessed are thou, and blessed is thy advice, O Abigail.'" Van Buren came "from our eighth president, Martin Van Buren, because I liked the aristocratic old-family ring." Together, Abigail Van Buren "sort of sings. And I could shorten it to Dear Abby; it sounded like someone somebody would write to."

The first Dear Abby column appeared on January 9, 1956. Her sister was at first delighted, but Dear Abby's rapid success in syndication put the twins in direct competition throughout the country. Because the Dear Abby column combined humor as well as helpful advice, it rapidly became more popular faster than her sister's Ann Landers column. Both

Twin advisors Pauline Phillips (*left*) and Esther Lederer (*right*), a.k.a. Abigail Van Buren and Ann Landers, together again at their fiftieth high school reunion in 1986. Until 1975, rivalry between the sisters produced a long period of separation and silence.   *UPI/Corbis-Bettmann*

writers, however, pushed the boundary of what was considered acceptable in public discourse up to that time. As Popo recalled, "The *San Diego Union* refused to print the word 'homosexual,' and I was told the first time they ever printed it was in my column in 1957. It was quite a breakthrough." The boldness of Dear Abby encouraged Eppie in her Ann Landers columns to follow suit. According to one newspaper editor, "Those columns were on the cutting edge of the change in the capacity of Americans to talk about sex and to talk about social relations. The point is that the columns were with the mood of the country and not behind it. Before Ann and Abby, the columns had been behind it." Columns dared to take up such subjects as French kissing, venereal disease, and what were then referred to as "unwed mothers." Women and teenage girls who felt frightened or uncomfortable approaching doctors or parents with questions pertaining to sex and relationships could appeal anonymously to the sisters for help and were sure to receive sensible, solid advice, given in the columnists' inimitable style. To a question about female frigidity, Ann Landers observed, "Many are cold, but few are frozen." Such risky topics and risqué responses caused some newspapers to drop the column and prompted advertisers' protests, but the overall popularity of both columns was undiminished, and circulation grew steadily. Both women became national and later worldwide celebrities with enormous power to influence public opinion. Columns became topics for Sunday sermons and water-cooler debates. Calls for reader protest over some social policy issue could prompt thousands of letters to policy makers.

Throughout their careers both twins kept remarkably current with contemporary issues and changing attitudes on important questions, at times very much ahead of the curve on such issues as abortion rights, opposition to the Vietnam War, the destruction of social programs under the Reagan administration, and AIDS. As Eppie once observed, "The world has gotten racier, and I feel I must respond to what is going on out there. If I'm going to be useful, I'm going to have to deal with all kinds of human problems." Over the years, both columnists moved steadily from their conservative, midwestern, small-town perspectives to embrace a more flexible view of moral questions, informed both by a broadened experience of the world and the rock-solid commonsensical approach rooted in their core values. The formula sustained their popularity for almost half a century, reflecting as well as shaping American popular opinion.

The rivalry between the two sisters split the pair and produced a long period of separation and silence as well as an undercurrent of antagonism and pettiness as each reflected upon her own past and her sister's role in it. The media assisted in the breach between the two sisters, exploiting an irresistible lead: "Advice Mavens Feud Among Themselves." Reconciled in 1975 at the time of Eppie's divorce, the pair managed an uneasy truce of sorts, expressed most publicly in their joint attendance at their fifty-year reunion of Sioux City's Central High class of 1936. As biographers Jan Pottker and Bob Speziale have observed, "For the most part, the lives of both twins have been a series of small epiphanies, the kind that make life worth living. Elevating themselves beyond the traditional role granted housewives, and then, advice columnists, the Friedman twins are perceived as fallible, yet possessing innate wisdom, insight, and virtue." It is certainly these qualities that have upheld the popularity of Ann Landers and Dear Abby over the years as influential sustainers and transformers of America's opinions about itself.

1956

The La Leche League Is Founded

Once upon a time all babies in Western societies were breastfed.
They were not, as every reader of eighteenth- and nineteenth-
century literature knows, necessarily fed by their mothers, but the
human breast was the sole source of infant feeding. Today . . . what
is now taken for granted is that mothers should choose how to feed
their babies rather than simply accepting what is naturally given,
and possible.

Mary Evans, in Pam Carter, *Feminism and Breastfeeding*

In 1921 SMA, the first commercial infant formula, was put on the
market in the United States. Competing brands of formula such as Sim-
ilac, Enfamil, and Isomil would follow. The marketing of baby formula
reflected a shift in cultural emphasis during the 1920s from nursing, the
age-old method of feeding infants, to bottle-feeding, a method once used
by mothers who could not produce enough breast milk. The new popularity of the bottle over the breast was due to several factors. Advances in
sterilization and refrigeration around the turn of the century had made
possible the preparation and safe preservation of formula based on cow's
milk. Doctors, who had encouraged women to give birth in hospitals
rather than at home so that they could experience safe, pain-free deliveries with the help of medical technology, now convinced them that
bottle-feeding was the modern, scientific way to nourish their infants.
Public health nurses and social workers taught working-class women correct bottle procedure and feeding regimens. The concept of feeding
according to rigid schedules was embraced by middle-class women, who,
after having recently won the right to vote and enduring a world war and
a devastating influenza epidemic, had gained a new sense of freedom
and modernity in dress and behavior. They were not about to emulate
their corseted mothers and give in to the inconvenience of breast-

feeding, which included the tyranny of infant meals on demand or spending time mastering the art of nursing. In the 1920s, when advertisers first began aggressively to peddle such modern and improved conveniences and luxuries as automobiles, electric stoves, indoor plumbing, and the radio, the use of infant formula seemed as necessary for the well-being of the American mother as the installment of an electric icebox.

By 1946, the first year of the postwar baby boom, approximately 62 percent of U.S. mothers were bottle-feeding their babies; ten years later that figure had jumped to about 78 percent, in part because more mothers were in the workforce and found it difficult to accommodate the demands of breast-feeding in their schedules. But as Christine Lunardini observes in *What Every American Should Know About Women's History,* "Like any liberation, bottlefeeding had its costs, and by the 1950s women were beginning to feel it. Practically, they had been liberated from nursing to be enslaved by formula mixing, bottle sterilization, and, in many cases, the screams of their children waiting for the appointed times on the clock. Moreover, some realized that an important psychological bond was being lost, and medical research began to reveal that breast milk has important advantages as well." One important fact discovered about breast milk in the 1950s was that it contained six times less strontium 90, a product of the radioactive fallout caused by atmospheric testing of nuclear weapons, which had fallen on the grass and been consumed by cows.

In 1956 Marian Tompson and Mary White of Franklin Park, Illinois,

The founders and early members of the La Leche League and their children at a group meeting (*left to right*): Mary Ann Cahill, Betty Wagner Spandikow, Mary Ann Kerwin, Mary White, Marian Tompson, and Edwina Froehlich   *Courtesy of La Leche League International*

began the La Leche League, an activist organization devoted to the promotion of breast-feeding through information and instruction. Tompson, the wife of a research engineer, had encountered difficulty trying to breast-feed her first three children and was encouraged each time by her doctor to put the infant on the bottle. White's husband was a physician who had been taught nothing about breast-feeding in medical school. Both mothers learned everything they could about breast-feeding and eventually mastered the technique, and when they nursed their babies in public at a fashionable picnic on Chicago's North Side, other women gathered around them in admiration. Soon afterward, Tompson and White organized a meeting to discuss ways in which they might encourage other women to breast-feed and enlisted the support of pediatricians, obstetricians, allergists, and other medical specialists who shared their belief in the value of nursing. The name of their organization came from the Virgin Mary's Spanish title, *Nuestra Señora de la Leche y Buen Parto* ("Our Lady of the Milk and Good Delivery"), and from the fact that Spanish wet nurses were called *madres de la leche*. By 1976 the organization was known as La Leche League International, Inc., and had 2,868 groups in forty-two countries. The influence of the La Leche League was not lost on the large companies that sold infant formula. They began aggressively marketing formula in third world countries in response to lost revenue but have had to contend with La Leche League campaigns to promote nursing there as well.

By the 1980s large numbers of U.S. mothers were convinced of the benefits of breast milk, even if they were not always able to continually breast-feed for the recommended first year of a baby's life. One popular option has been to pump, or "express," breast milk and feed it to babies in a bottle. The many advocates of breast milk have cited its positive influence on a baby's brain development and a lowered risk of allergies, infections, diarrhea, eczema, diabetes, and pneumonia. Nursing is also said to speed postpartum weight loss in mothers and to lower their risk of ovarian and premenopausal breast cancer. However, breast-feeding is not an option for adoptive mothers, and other mothers simply may not wish to use the method or find it too uncomfortable or difficult. Working women in particular face considerable obstacles to breast-feeding, and the issue has added to the guilt mothers experience when they return to work soon after giving birth. The debate over breast versus bottle, like so many other issues relating to the social welfare and status of women in the twentieth century, will be resolved only by individual women making the choice according to desire and necessity, without guilt and with the expectation that they will be treated with respect however they choose to nurture their babies.

1959

Barbie Makes Her Debut

Intense feelings about Barbie do not run exclusively toward love.
For every mother who embraces Barbie as a traditional toy and
eagerly introduces her daughter to the doll, there is another mother
who tries to banish Barbie from the house. For every fluffy blond
cheerleader who leaps breast-forward into an exaggerated gender
role, there is a recovering bulimic who refuses to wear dresses and
blames Barbie for her ordeal. For every collector to whom the
amassing of Barbie objects is a language more exquisite than words,
there is a fiction writer or poet or visual artist for whom Barbie is
muse and metaphor—and whose message concerns class inequities
or the dark evanescence of childhood sexuality.

M. G. Lord, *Forever Barbie: The Unauthorized Biography of a Real Doll*

According to Mattel, the maker of the most popular doll in history,
every second, somewhere in the world two Barbies are sold. More than
a billion Barbies have been purchased since the doll was first introduced
in 1959, which means that there are more Barbies in America than there
are humans. As M. G. Lord, author of the definitive study of the doll's
origin, marketing, and cultural significance, observes, "Barbie may be
the most potent icon of American popular culture in the late twentieth
century."

But an icon of what? To feminists Barbie is a sinister symbol of
oppression, whom protesters in 1972 alleged encouraged girls "to see
themselves solely as mannequins, sex objects, or housekeepers." To
others Barbie is a feminist pioneer who, unlike other dolls like Betsy
Wetsy and Tiny Tears, taught independence and career possibilities
rather than nurturing. As Lord argues, "She could invent herself with a
costume change: sing a solo in the spotlight one minute, pilot a starship
the next. She was Grace Slick and Sally Ride, Marie Osmond and Marie

Curie. She was all we could be and—if you calculate what at human scale would translate to a thirty-nine-inch bust—more than we could be. And certainly more than we were . . . at six and seven and eight when she appeared and sank her jungle-red talons into our inner lives." Barbie remains a powerful mirror of cultural assumptions and values as well as a screen to project contradictory fantasies of female ideals.

Barbie, the apotheosis of all-American feminine virtues, traces her origins from the German demimonde. Her progenitor was a 1950s cartoon character in the West German tabloid *Bild Zeitung* named Lilli, an alluringly dressed gold digger who traded her good looks for material comforts from her string of sugar daddies. She became a 11.5-inch doll with a blond ponytail, pouty lips, and a provocative come-hither glance who was intended not for children, but as a gag gift for men or as a present for girlfriends in lieu of flowers. As a brochure promoting her sexy wardrobe claimed, "Gentlemen prefer Lilli. Whether more or less naked, Lilli is always discreet."

In 1956 Ruth Handler, one of the founders of the Mattel toy company, discovered Lilli while vacationing in Switzerland with her family. As she recalls, "We were walking down the street in Lucerne and there was a doll—an adult doll with a woman's body—sitting on a rope swing. . . . I didn't then know who Lilli was or even that its name was Lilli. I only saw an adult-shape body that I had been trying to describe for years, and our guys said couldn't be done." Handler had wanted to create an adult doll ever since she had watched her daughter, Barbara, and her friends playing with adult paper dolls. As Handler observed, they "were imagining their lives as adults. They were using the dolls to reflect the adult world around them. They would sit and carry on conversations, making the dolls real people. I used to watch that over and over and think: If only we could take this play pattern and three-dimensionalize it, we would have something special."

Handler brought the Lilli doll home to California and initiated a process of transforming her into Barbie, although her colleagues at Mattel were "all horrified by the thought of wanting to make a doll with breasts." Handler's daughter provided the doll's name (as Handler's son, Ken, would be the source for the name of Barbie's boyfriend). Charlotte Johnson, a veteran clothing designer, was hired to design Barbie's many outfits, and the doll and her clothing were manufactured in Japan. Barbie's dimensions, the bane of most Barbie's critics, with her real-scale 39-inch breasts, 18-inch waist, 34-inch hips, elongated neck, and extra-long legs, were less a matter of adult fantasy than a prerequisite to make Barbie's outfits fit and look their best. Barbie's initial success—351,000 sold in the first year—came despite considerable opposition from par-

Few Barbie aficionados own just one Barbie doll. Here, a ten-year-old poses with her Barbies, members of the Barbie family, and Barbie accessories. The bag features a picture of the original Barbie, which appeared in 1959.

ents about the sexy, adult doll. Mattel had hired motivational psychologist Ernst Dichter, the target of criticism by Betty Friedan in *The Feminine Mystique* as the arch manipulator of women as consumers, to study how parents and children responded to the teenage doll. Although girls between the ages of eight and twelve were fascinated by Barbie's outfits and enjoyed inventing fantasy situations that required constant wardrobe changes, mothers were appalled. One called them " 'daddy dolls'—they are so sexy. They could be a cute decoration for a man's bar." However, when one woman changed her mind after her eight-year-old daughter commented that Barbie was "so well groomed," Dichter evolved Mattel's marketing strategy. Barbie could be marketed to parents as a teaching tool to turn a girl into a desirable lady by awakening a girl's concern with proper appearance and the methods of sexual allure. As Lord summarizes, Dichter devised a campaign to "remind Mom what she believes deep down but dares not express: Better her daughter should appeal in a sleazy way to a man than be unable to attract one at all." Mattel also innovatively advertised Barbie directly to children. In 1955 Mattel had become the first toy company to sponsor a television series, Disney's *The Mickey Mouse Club,* and the company had pioneered television marketing upon which Barbie's success would depend. A major part of Barbie's allure was Mattel's insistence never to refer to Barbie as a doll. She was instead presented as a real entity: a teenage fashion model with unlimited means to reign triumphantly in her fantasy version of the real world.

The doll proved to be unstoppable and a money machine. At $3 Barbie was priced to sell, and with her seemingly endless supply of outfits and accessories all "sold separately," each doll virtually guaranteed a host of subsequent purchases. Barbie became the ultimate materialist consuming machine, a fantasy toy based on what she has and an acquisition that endlessly required newer and improved features, outfits, and accoutrements. Barbie has been transformed into a doctor, scientist, movie star, Olympic athlete, and scuba diver with her own sports car and dream house. She acquired a boyfriend in 1961, a number of sidekicks like Midge and Francie, a younger sister named Skipper, and African American friends Christie and Julia in 1969 (black Barbie and Latina Barbie appeared in 1980).

During her career Barbie has undergone numerous makeovers, mostly adding movable parts and speech, reflecting the planned obsolescence of the auto industry transferred to a beloved doll in which girls were encouraged to "trade in" their older versions for newer models. The most radical makeover came in 1971 as a direct reflection of the sexual revolution and the feminist movement. Barbie's eyes, which had been cast down and averted to one side in a submissive gaze, were allowed to look assertively straight ahead. But Barbie has mostly resisted the changes that have surrounded her. She ignored the anticonsumption sentiment of the 1960s, waiting for the pendulum swing to the me generation of the 1970s and the instant gratification era of the 1980s and 1990s. Through the decades Barbie has never abandoned her hold on the imagination of young girls with her mixed messages of ideal beauty and consumerism representing a challenge for parents in deciding whether to resist or give in to their children's fascination with the doll.

At her core, Barbie as a doll codifies certain standards of female physical perfection that are impossible to emulate by her possessors. Barbie resembles nothing so much as Hugh Hefner's Playmates in *Playboy*: wholesome girls next door depicted in airbrushed perfection. Barbie may have over the years been promoted from secretary to the boardroom, from nurse to doctor, and from stewardess to pilot, in response to Mattel's new Barbie slogan for the 1990s—"We girls can do anything"— but glamour and looks are always a central ingredient of her various careers, suggesting that women's achievements must always go back to physicality for ultimate validation. Barbie also teaches young girls lessons in consumption—that new possibilities are always defined by different outfits and hairstyles. Barbie ultimately depends on what she has, a lesson that externals matter most in the real world and that young girls' fantasy play allows them to explore through the doll. Barbie, therefore, is a complex vehicle for a girl's imagination: she takes girls outside the home to explore a world beyond that of caregiver and nurturer encouraged by other baby dolls; at the same time she reinforces ideals of physicality, values of beauty, and self-definition as a consumer that dominate over other ideals of women's attributes and accomplishments. It is not surprising that with Barbie as so many girls' fantasy model, adolescents have been increasingly obsessed and dissatisfied with their own bodies, with rises in anorexia nervosa and bulimia as an outcome. Despite Mattel's recent introduction of a new version of Barbie that is slightly hippier, less busty, with flat feet instead of pointed for her high heels, Barbie remains a powerful fantasy image in which the real and the desired are mixed and harmless play conspires with more pointed messages of girls' identity and sense of self-worth.

1960–1969

Seventeen-year-old British model Twiggy (Leslie Hornby), with her ultra-slim body, miniskirt, Mary Jane shoes, and boyishly cropped hair, perfectly captured the youthful, unisex style of the 1960s. Miniskirts and bell-bottoms were the two major articles of '60s fashion that would endure throughout the decade and beyond. *UPI/Corbis-Bettmann*

1960

The FDA Approves the Birth Control Pill

It's easy to forget how truly liberating the Pill seemed to be in 1960. Nothing else in this century—perhaps not even winning the right to vote—made such an immediate difference in women's lives. . . . It spurred sexual frankness and experimentation. It allowed women to think seriously about careers because they could postpone childbirth. And it sparked the feminist and pro-choice movements. Once women felt they were in charge of their own bodies, they began to question the authority of their husbands, their fathers, their bosses, their doctors and their churches. As Founding Feminist Betty Friedan has said: "In the mysterious way of history, there was this convergence of technology that occurred just as women were ready to explode into personhood."

Ladies' Home Journal, in a June 1990 article celebrating the Pill's thirtieth anniversary

Since 1960 the Pill has been part of the daily routine for more humans than any other prescribed medication in the world. It has been called "the first medicine ever destined for a purely social, rather than a therapeutic, purpose," and the impact of oral birth control has reached into nearly every aspect of women's lives in the second half of the twentieth century. According to *Newsweek* in 1967, the Western world's morals and manners had "changed more dramatically in the past year than in the preceding fifty," and the Pill was at the center of that acceleration as both the cause and the effect of a radical transformation of science, society, and culture, expressed in a variety of forms in modern women's lives. The Pill finally offered women sexual equality with men, allowed women control over childbearing, and initiated a fundamental change in sexuality from the primacy of procreation to that of pleasure—reflected in the sexual revolution, begun in the 1960s with its new sexual openness and expression. Women with the Pill no longer were prisoners of reproduction and were allowed to expand their possibilities and opportunities beyond that of motherhood. The Pill also presented serious social and cultural challenges to traditional morality and religion, to an altered definition of love and commitment, as well as unexpected health threats from unprotected sex and the consequences of delaying too long the decision to give birth while balancing the increasingly more complex matters of career, marriage, and motherhood.

Despite its enormous impact, the genesis of the Pill was tentative and guarded, with many in the science and pharmaceutical communities during the 1950s considering oral contraception "unthinkable" and predicting certain economic disaster for any drug company that dared to market it. Although there are many claimants to the title "Father of the Pill," the initiation of the Pill can be credited to the determination of two women: Margaret Sanger and Katharine McCormick. Sanger, the tireless crusader and leader of the birth control movement in America, had long dreamed of the ultimate birth control device—some form of oral contraceptive—but did not have the means to sponsor the necessary scientific research until she renewed an old friendship with Katharine McCormick. As the wife of Stanley McCormick, son of the founder of International Harvester, Katharine McCormick had control of a vast fortune, about which it was said that she could not spend even the interest on her interest. Committed to the birth control cause, McCormick was willing to bankroll the needed research on a birth control pill that got under way when Sanger in 1950 brought McCormick together with Dr. Gregory Pincus, a renowned geneticist and cofounder of the Worcester Foundation for Experimental Biology. Sanger asked him if some sort of drug was possible to stop contraception, and Pincus optimistically said it was. Pincus envisioned a pill that would probably use progesterone in some manner to block ovulation. Progesterone was then available largely owing to the work of a maverick scientist named Russell Marker, who in 1940 had discovered a cheap and plentiful source in the root of a wild yam that grew in the Mexican desert. This allowed Pincus and his team of researchers to begin tests in 1951 on the effects of progesterone on rabbit ovulation.

As the Pill was ready to be tried on human subjects, Pincus recruited the distinguished gynecologist Dr. John Rock to join his team to study the use of progesterone as a contraceptive. Rock, a Catholic, made Sanger wary, but Pincus and McCormick convinced her that "if the Church does not interfere with him, he will not interfere with it." In 1954 Rock began experiments using the new drug on three women and later fifty childless women at his clinic. Among those tested, there was almost a 100 percent postponement of ovulation, and when the women came off the drug, which Pincus began to refer to as "the Pill," seven of the fifty, or 14 percent, were able to get pregnant. The next step was field testing with more patients, including poorer, less well-educated women, to see whether they would be disciplined about taking the Pill according to the somewhat complicated reproductive cycle. Puerto Rico and Haiti were selected as the locales for mass testing beginning in 1956. In the first eight months, 221 patients took the Pill without a single pregnancy, and the side effect of nausea was reduced by adding an antacid.

In 1957 the U.S. Food and Drug Administration authorized marketing the Pill for treatment of miscarriages and menstrual disorders, with the caution that the medication could interfere with ovulation. Women and their doctors did not miss the significance of the caution, and a significant increase in prescriptions for menstrual problems resulted. The drug company, G. D. Searle, approached the release of the Pill as an explicit contraceptive with caution, despite the potential gold mine of a medication that women would be taking daily for years. By late 1959 half a million women in America were taking the Pill, most for contraception. Searle, however, feared that marketing the Pill as a contraceptive might be ruinous. "We were going into absolutely unexplored ground in terms of public opinion," James W. Irwin, the company's corporate policy counselor, later recalled. "We were overly cautious. All my experience told me that you could not do this without getting your teeth knocked out— or some of them. And we didn't lose any teeth. We had underestimated the receptivity for the product. We got quite a surprise."

In May 1960 the FDA approved the Pill as a contraceptive device. By the end of 1961 408,000 American women were taking it; by the end of 1962 the number had risen to 1,187,000; and by the end of 1963 it was 2.3 million and still rising. It was estimated that in 1965 one of every four married American women under the age of forty-five had used or was using an oral contraceptive and that actual users at that time numbered some 3.8 million. By 1967 more than 12 million women around the world were taking the Pill, and by 1984 estimates ranged from 50 million to 80 million women worldwide.

Reception to the availability of an effective oral contraceptive was immediate and explosive. "Modern woman is at last free as a man is free," playwright Clare Boothe Luce declared, "to dispose of her own body, to earn a living, to pursue the improvement or her mind, to try a successful career." A Chicago mother in her late twenties told a reporter in 1965, "Oh, I know I've put on a little weight since I started on the Pill, but I think it's just from contentment. I used to worry a lot about having another baby, and that kept me thinner, but I never have to worry

This satirical poster from the 1960s suggested that even
Uncle Sam approved the use of the birth control pill.
Library of Congress

anymore. . . . I'd prefer to wait for the next until the youngest is at least
two years old. And now I know I *can* wait." Despite disapproval by the
Catholic Church, many Catholic priests advised their parishioners to
follow their own conscience regarding Pill use, and a survey found that
21 percent of Catholic wives under forty-five were Pill users, compared
with 29 percent of non-Catholic wives. Another study concluded in 1965
that married women who used the Pill had sex up to 39 percent more
often than users of other means of contraception. Even businesses saw
profits from the perceived changes wrought by the Pill. As Harold L.
Graham, vice president of Pan American World Airways, observed in
1968, "By delaying the family during the early marriage years when both
husband and wife are working, we have a combination of disposable
income and the desire to travel. It is not that we advertise birth control.
It just happens that it helps business."

    The downside of the Pill was also emerging. A Stanford University
study revealed in 1978 that during the first five years of marriage, child-

free couples had twice the likelihood of divorce as those with young children. "Thus it stands likely," the study concluded, "that the availability of the Pill and the IUD would be a major cause of divorce." Rumors of serious side effects of the Pill began to spread almost immediately. Nausea, water retention, weight gain, and breast tenderness, as well as more serious complaints of blood clots, heart disease, elevated blood pressure, strokes, gallbladder disease, tumors of the liver, and depression were reported. In a 1969 book *The Doctors' Case Against the Pill*, the Pill's leading critic Barbara Seaman castigated the medical and drug community for ignoring women's complaints about oral contraceptives and refusing to educate about the downside of the Pill's usage. Efforts by Seaman and other women and consumer activists in the late 1960s led to modifications of the Pill as well as to special patient package inserts. Since 1978 the FDA has required physicians and pharmacists to supply comprehensive information on the Pill's possible negative effects and complications.

Some women, and increasingly feminists, have complained that the Pill is simply another example of women being forced to take sole responsibility for reproduction by ingesting a powerful and potentially harmful drug, amid their call for the development of a male birth control pill. Other feminists have complained that the Pill, in giving women their freedom in having sex, has also freed men from any responsibility in their sexual relations. Some have complained that the sexual permissiveness that the Pill made possible has gone too far and cite the instances of early adolescent sexuality as a serious concern. At the center of the continuing controversy over the Pill and birth control are a number of much larger social questions of the role of sexuality in society and the ultimate responsibility in the control of a women's body. The Pill has also helped to force a redefinition of women's biological role. Women are free now to choose, but those choices have become far more complex.

1963

The Feminine Mystique by Betty Friedan
Is Published

It was a strange stirring, a sense of dissatisfaction, a yearning that
women suffered in the middle of the twentieth century in the
United States. Each suburban wife struggled with it alone. As she
made the beds, shopped for groceries, matched slipcover material,
ate peanut butter sandwiches with her children, chauffeured Cub
Scouts and Brownies, lay beside her husband at night, she was
afraid to ask even of herself the silent question—"Is this all?"

Betty Friedan, *The Feminine Mystique*

Although a revitalized women's movement in the 1960s and 1970s
stemmed from a variety of sources, no other work in the history of feminist thought sounded the clarion call for change in the status of women
with as much reverberating success as Betty Friedan's 1963 book, *The
Feminine Mystique*. Despite unprecedented economic progress in
post–World War II America, which purchased the American dream in
suburban households with two-car garages, Friedan explored her own
and her female generation's anxiety and dissatisfaction with the expected
role of happy housewife, diagnosing a vague feeling of discontent and
aimlessness, a "problem that had no name," which she identified as the
feminine mystique. "If I am right," she observed, "the problem that has
no name stirring in the minds of so many American women today is not
a matter of loss of femininity or too much education, or the demands of
domesticity. It is far more important than anyone recognizes. It is the
key to these other new and old problems which have been torturing
women and their husbands and children, and puzzling their doctors and
educators for years. It may well be the key to our future as a nation and
a culture. We can no longer ignore that voice within women that says 'I
want something more than my husband and my children and my

home.'" Friedan's analysis of the forces that subordinated and repressed women's opportunities and desires for fulfillment beyond the role of wife, mother, and homemaker and her call for change in *The Feminine Mystique* struck a nerve among American women, and she would go on to become one of the most influential leaders of the modern women's movement that she helped to set in motion.

Born in Peoria, Illinois, in 1921, Betty Goldstein Friedan was the oldest child in a family of two daughters and one son. Her father was a jeweler; her mother, a writer and editor, had given up her career for marriage and motherhood. Her discontent with domestic life, like Friedan's own, would become an important source for her daughter's book. An academically gifted child, Betty founded a literary magazine in high school and graduated as class valedictorian. At Smith College she studied psychology and, after graduating summa cum laude in 1942, won two research fellowships to the University of California at Berkeley. Unwilling to commit to a doctorate and a career as a psychologist, Friedan left Berkeley to work as a journalist in New York. In 1947 she married Carl Friedan and a year later gave birth to the first of the couple's three children. The Friedans divorced in 1969.

In the 1950s Betty Friedan lost her job as a newspaper reporter after requesting her second maternity leave. She continued to write, however, contributing articles to women's magazines, whose messages of domestic fulfillment for women would become another important source for Friedan's assessment of the feminine mystique. Deeply dissatisfied with her own primary role as wife and mother, Friedan began to explore the causes of her discontent. Women's magazines, television, movies, and advertising, along with sociologists and psychologists, supported and reinforced a traditional image of women that centered on the home and family in the roles of wife and mother. Magazine articles in *Good Housekeeping* and *Ladies' Home Journal,* such as "I'd Hate to Be a Man" and "I'm Lucky! Lucky!" urged deference to men, repression of ambition outside the home, and concealment of intellectual ability, while glorifying traditional domesticity, for a woman to become "the fragile, feminine, dependent, but priceless creature every man wants his wife to be," as the *Ladies' Home Journal* preached. The postwar baby boom resulted from women marrying younger and bearing more children, with only 6.8 percent of women in the 1950s remaining childless, compared with 14 percent in 1900. Accompanying the baby boom was a renewed emphasis on family life, with women encouraged to devote their full attention to their husbands, children, and home. Despite expanded opportunity for women created by World War II and an increase of women in the labor pool, public disapproval of employment for married women was

Betty Friedan, seen here in the 1970s. On the table is a copy of Friedan's second book, *It Changed My Life*, in which she assesses the progress of the women's movement she helped initiate with the publication of *The Feminine Mystique* in 1963. *The Schlesinger Library, Radcliffe College*

high. In 1945 only 18 percent approved of a married woman's working if she had a husband capable of supporting her.

Friedan, stifled in her own role as homemaker and disturbed by the overriding message that women's contentment rested in domestic accomplishments alone, began to wonder if other women shared her dissatisfaction. In 1957 she sent an intensive questionnaire to two hundred of her college classmates. The answers she received of shared discontent convinced her that her ailment was widespread. She began several years of research into the origins of, as she later wrote, "the strange discrepancy between the reality of our lives as women and the image to which we were trying to conform."

At the core of modern women's dilemma, Friedan announced, was a fantasy of post–World War II happy suburban female domesticity, the feminine mystique, which was created and reinforced by educators, sociologists, psychologists, and the media. Advertisers required a large class of consumers, and women were encouraged in their role as domestic guardians whose longings could be fulfilled by buying the products companies sold. Women, according to Friedan, accept their subordination by femininity for the material and psychological pleasures their passive and protective role as wife and mother provide at a cost of feeling a prisoner in a gilded suburban palace. *The Feminine Mystique* both diagnosed the dilemma of women and called for a reassertion of female identity beyond that of domestic icon, consumer, helpmate, and caregiver. As Friedan concludes: "Who knows what women can be when they are finally free to become themselves? Who knows what women's intelligence will contribute when it can be nourished without denying love? Who knows of the possibilities of love when men and women share not only their children, home, and garden, not only the fulfillment of their biological roles, but the responsibilities and passions of the work that creates the human future and the full human knowledge of who they are? It has barely begun, the search of women for themselves. But the time is at hand when the voices of the feminine mystique can no longer drown out the inner voice that is driving women on to become complete." The book, therefore, served to heighten awareness about a woman's powerlessness in both the family and society, her limited opportunities for self-expression and fulfillment, and the negative stereotyping and discrimination women faced who sought careers, as well as the unequal salaries earned by women who worked outside the home. Finally, *The Feminine Mystique* announced a call to activism that rejected the characterization of women as helpless victims and asserted the need for increased education and opportunities that would allow women to grow into their full potential.

Friedan completed her book five years after signing the contract with her publisher. "Neither my husband nor my publisher nor anyone else who knew about it thought I would ever finish it," Friedan recalled. "I wrote every day on the dining room table, while the children were at school, and after they went to bed at night. (It didn't do any good to have a desk of my own, they used it for their homework anyhow.)" W. W. Norton, who published the book in February 1963, brought out *The Feminine Mystique* in a modest first printing of two thousand copies. Over the next ten years it sold three million hardcover copies and many more in paperback. Friedan received hundreds of letters from women who said that they had no idea, until they read her book, that anyone else shared their feelings. The book was greeted positively as well by older members of the women's movement like Women's Party activist

Alma Lutz, who declared that the book offered "a glimmer of hope that some of the younger generation are waking up."

The Feminine Mystique became a unifying force in the second wave of twentieth-century feminism, and Friedan emerged as a leading figure in the women's liberation movement that she helped initiate. In 1966 Friedan cofounded the National Organization for Women and served as its president until 1970. During the 1970s Friedan continued her activism while lecturing at various universities and writing articles for a wide range of magazines. In 1976 she published *It Changed My Life*, in which she assessed the progress of the women's movement and her relationship with it. With *The Second Stage*, published in 1981, Friedan offered a reformist view of feminism based on the acceptance of men and the family in women's quest for equality. Influenced partly by the emergence of the superwoman myth—the image of the woman who copes effortlessly with both a career and a family—Friedan suggested that this "feminist mystique" was as much a fantasy as the feminine mystique was in an earlier era. Friedan's revisionism caused a backlash from more militant feminist critics, who felt that the author had strayed from the basic goals of the movement she had helped to establish. Others applauded her call for an end to polarization and her new thesis, seeing in it a new, more humanistic and balanced direction for feminism.

Although the issues of the women's movement Friedan helped to create have shifted over the years, *The Feminine Mystique* remains one of the seminal texts of feminism, along with de Beauvoir's earlier *The Second Sex* and such later feminist works as Germaine Greer's *The Female Eunuch* and Kate Millett's *Sexual Politics*. Few other writers on the issue of women's emancipation have so effectively uncovered the causes and effects of women's subordination or better articulated a call for reform as Betty Friedan in *The Feminine Mystique*, a landmark book in women's history in the twentieth century.

✌

The President's Commission on the Status of Women Issues Its "American Women" Report

Equality of rights under the law for all persons, male or female, is so basic to democracy . . . that it must be reflected in the fundamental law of the land.

> "American Women," report of the President's Commission on the Status of Women

Unlike his predecessors Harry S. Truman and Dwight D. Eisenhower, President John F. Kennedy did not refuse an appeal to name a special commission to investigate women's concerns but responded positively, establishing the Commission on the Status of Women (PCSW) in 1961, chaired by Eleanor Roosevelt. Dependent on women voters to get elected, Kennedy had been criticized for his poor response in hiring women in his administration, lagging behind his predecessors in this regard, and he regarded the PCSW as a way of repairing the damage among his female constituency. Esther Peterson—the director of the Women's Bureau, an assistant secretary of labor, and the highest-ranking woman in his administration—approached Kennedy to establish the commission. Her motives, like Kennedy's, were political. Peterson wanted to deflect any pro-ERA activity since the unions, strong Democratic Party supporters, opposed the amendment as injurious to protective legislation for women workers. She also wished to use the commission to help push equal-pay-for-equal-work legislation favored by the unions, since lower-paid women workers threatened male jobs. For whatever self-serving reasons the PCSW was formed, its importance rested in its symbolism; the final report asserted to the public that women's concerns mattered to the government and deserved its attention. The commission's final report, appearing in 1963—the same year as the publication of Betty Friedan's groundbreaking *The Feminine Mystique*—called attention to a long list of women's problems in need of amelioration and helped initiate the modern women's movement and the radical changes in women's identity and opportunity that quickly followed.

The president's commission consisted of thirteen women and eleven men, who divided their work into seven investigatory committees comprising additional prominent women leaders from various fields. The commission received reports on such topics as "Images of Women in the Media," in which writers such as Lorraine Hansberry, Marya Mannes, and Betty Friedan testified that the media's objectification of women rarely portrayed them in any roles other than housewives and mothers. A special consultation entitled "The Problem of Negro Women," chaired by Dorothy Height, president of the National Council of Negro Women, argued that too little attention had been paid to the special burden of African American families and their lack of opportunities. In November 1962 Eleanor Roosevelt died, and as a tribute to her memory, the commission issued its sixty-page report on October 11, 1963, the anniversary of her birth. As expected, almost the entire commission opposed the Equal Rights Amendment, arguing that since the Supreme Court

Esther Peterson, director of the Women's Bureau, presenting President Kennedy with the "American Women" report detailing the findings of the President's Commission on the Status of Women, October 11, 1963 *The Schlesinger Library, Radcliffe College*

recognized gender equality as part of the Fifth and Fourteenth Amendments to the Constitution, additional constitutional safeguards were not needed "now." The only member of the commission who supported the ERA, feminist lawyer Marguerite Rawalt, fought for the insertion of the word "now," to allow room for a change in policy should the High Court alter their interpretation regarding constitutional gender safeguards.

The main achievement of the commission's report was its documentation of problems in employment discrimination, unequal pay, lack of social services for working mothers, and continuing legal inequality. The commission called for the end of prohibitions against women jurors and restrictions on married women's rights. It favored federally and privately supported child care, continuing education and increased vocational training for women, joint guardianship of children, paid maternity leave, and equal employment opportunity and urged that more women be promoted to high-level government and policy-making jobs. By calling attention to the number of disadvantages faced by women both at home and at work, the commission helped raise consciousness among union women, lawyers, academics, and organization leaders about the depth and pervasiveness of discrimination and the "double burden" women faced in the home and in the labor force, and accelerated momentum for change.

Although the commission's report received relatively little media attention, its work did prompt the creation of a permanent Citizen's Advisory Council on the Status of Women as a watchdog agency. Individual states also appointed their own commissions to make similar inquiries on the status of women, and the third annual National Conference of State Commissions on the Status of Women, in 1966, provided the occasion for the creation of the National Organization for Women. The first governmental response to the commission's report was a presidential order requiring the civil service to hire "solely on the basis of ability to meet the requirements of the position, and without regard to sex." The most important legislation, however, that was passed as a direct result of the recommendations of the commission was the first federal law prohibiting sex discrimination, the Equal Pay Act of 1963. The act sought to redress the traditional concept that men, as heads of households and principle breadwinners, were entitled to earn more than women, even when men and women did the same jobs. Many women headed households and shared equally in financial responsibilities for their families, but during the 1940s they were still paid about half of what male workers earned for the same job. State legislation that tried to redress this imbalance by establishing minimum wage laws for women was struck down by the Supreme Court as unconstitutional in the *Atkins v. Children's Hospital* case in 1923. Until the Equal Pay Act of 1963, only the state of Wyoming had passed an equal pay law for employees of the state government. The federal act provided equal pay for men and women in jobs requiring equal skill, responsibility, and effort. Although to help insure passage it excluded business and professional women, as well as almost two-thirds of working women, especially low-paid women in agriculture and domestic service from its provisions, the Equal Pay Act represented the first significant step toward ending wage discrimination for women workers. In 1963 full-time, year-round female workers were earning an average 63 percent less than male workers; by 1971 the disparity had dropped to 57 percent; and by the twenty-fifth anniversary of the act in 1998, the gap had closed to under 25 percent. Because there is an imprecision in determining what constitutes equal skill, responsibility, and effort, enforcement of the Equal Pay Act has proven difficult, and the disparity of wages between men and women has not yet been corrected. However, feminists and equal rights advocates have achieved success in court cases that consider comparable worth in job descriptions and wages, and women have won numerous lawsuits in the

1980s and 1990s, particularly in city and state jobs in which qualifications and requirements are more precisely quantified. The Equal Pay Act of 1963 has, despite slow gains, helped change attitudes and employment practices that in some cases have ended and in others mitigated wage discrimination.

The momentum for change in deeply held attitudes and customs both in the labor force and in the home regarding women's rights began to accelerate in the 1960s. The President's Commission on the Status of Women can, therefore, be rightfully seen as a symbolic turning point in the formation of a new social definition of women as autonomous individuals deserving the same rights and opportunities enjoyed by men. The commission established an important principle that government must play a role in insuring that women have equal protection under the law. Finally, the presidential commission served to initiate a national debate on the status of women that continued with renewed vigor in the final quarter of the twentieth century.

1964

Title VII of the Civil Rights Act of 1964 Prohibits Sex Discrimination in Employment

> I can think of nothing more logical than this amendment at this point. Women do not need any special privileges. We outlast you— we outlive you—we nag you to death ... [but] we are entitled to this little crumb of equality. The addition of the little, terrifying word "s-e-x" will not hurt this legislation in any way.
>
> Katherine St. George, Republican congresswoman from New York, in response to Howard W. Smith's amendment to include sex as a criterion in eliminating employment discrimination

One of the most sweeping pieces of social legislation in American history, the Civil Rights Act of 1964 made racial discrimination illegal by finally enforcing, through statute, what had been guaranteed by the Constitution. It ended the Jim Crow laws that segregated the South, paved the way for the Voting Rights Act of 1965 that would enfranchise the mass of southern African Americans, and, after a decade of paralysis in school desegregation since the *Brown* v. *Board of Education* decision, transformed the South into the most desegregated region in the country. The landmark Civil Rights Act of 1964, which also benefited all women by making it illegal for employers to discriminate on the basis of sex, was passed almost by default when a strategy to wreck the bill went awry in one of the most remarkable and theatrical incidents in congressional history.

The man who shifted the focus of the Civil Rights Act to include women's rights was Howard W. Smith, nicknamed "Judge" after his brief tenure on the bench. In his eighties, Smith, a democratic congressman from Virginia, was a thirty-three-year Capitol Hill veteran who had long been feared as the most powerful man in the House. A southern conservative, Smith had imposed his will on the nation by stopping, delaying, or watering down progressive legislation in the areas of civil rights, labor, public housing, education, the minimum wage, and medical care. As the powerful chairman of the House Rules Committee, Smith was considered by the Kennedy and Johnson administrations to be their greatest obstacle in the House in passing civil rights reform legislation. Behind a veneer of elaborate southern courtesy, his self-styled ignorance as a simple country lawyer, and his ever-present cigar or pipe, Judge Smith was the quintessential crafty lawmaker, about whom *Newsweek* observed, "Every parliamentary ruse lies right at the tip of his long bony fingers." Once, to avoid consideration of President Eisenhower's civil rights proposal, Smith refused to call a committee meeting, insisting that he had to return to his Virginia farm to inspect a barn that had burned down. As House Speaker Sam Rayburn remarked upon hearing this excuse, "I knew Howard Smith would do almost anything to block a civil rights bill, but I never knew he would resort to arson."

By 1963 Judge Smith could delay no longer, and the House Rules Committee began hearings on what he called "this nefarious bill," which he described "as full of booby traps as a dog is full of fleas." After ten days of House Rules Committee hearings, the Civil Rights Act proceeded to a full House debate by a vote of 11–4 (with only southern Democrats opposed). Judge Smith had been unable to bury the bill, but he was not finished with his efforts to insure its defeat. When the House began debate on Title VII of the act, concerned with equal employment, Judge Smith offered an amendment, adding the word "sex" to the list of discriminations (race, creed, color, and national origins) prohibited in employment. The implications were breathtaking: women would be given their first equal job rights with men, affecting every employer, labor union, and employment agency in the country, turning the Civil Rights Act of 1964 into the most radical civil rights legislation in U.S. history. Smith hoped that his amendment would make the bill so controversial that it would be killed, even by the bill's supporters. Although Smith's intentions were unmistakable, his motive in supporting women's equality were not as cravenly hypocritical as it may seem. Smith had been a congressional sponsor of the Equal Rights Amendment (ERA) as early as 1945; he had maintained ties with the National Women's Party, founded by Alice Paul, who first drafted the ERA. The NWP had pressed Judge Smith to add sex discrimination to the civil rights bill. Otherwise, the NWP argued in a resolution at their December 1963 convention, the bill would not offer "to a *White Woman*, a *Woman of the Christian Religion*, or a *Woman of the United States Origin* the protection it would afford to Negroes." By raising the stakes of the bill and threatening to usher in the brave new world of equality in employment, Smith gambled that his support of women's equality would scuttle the civil rights bill.

At first his gambit achieved the effect he wanted. The bill's sponsors spoke in opposition to the amendment, fearing that passage would strike down many state laws that were enacted to protect women from hazardous work conditions and that the issue of race would be overwhelmed and diluted by the question of gender. Yet a bipartisan coalition of five congresswomen—Frances P. Bolton (R-Ohio), Martha W. Griffiths (D-Mich.), Edna F. Kelly (D-N.Y.), Catherine May (R-Wash.), and Katherine St. George (R-N.Y.)—spoke out in favor of Smith's amendment, thrusting the predominantly male House into the unexpected position of having to take a position for or against women. Support meant a radical redefinition of cultural values and a threat to protection of gender difference, while opposition undermined the principles of the civil rights bill and alienated most women in the country. Beneath the surface in the ensuing debate was the blatantly racist point that legislators could not do for African American men and women what it refused to do for white women. As Martha W. Griffiths of Michigan, the leader of the fight for the Smith amendment, declared: "A vote against this amendment today by a white man is a vote against his wife, or his widow, or his daughter, or his sister." She insisted that it "would be incredible to me that white men would be willing to place white women at such a disadvantage. . . . You are going to have white men in one bracket, you are going to try to take colored men and colored women and give them equal employment rights, and down at the bottom of the list is going to be a white woman with no rights at all." Smith's amendment passed 137–98, but as George Meader, a conservative congressman from Michigan, declared, "Smith outsmarted himself. At this point there was no way you could sink the bill."

Smith's strategy backfired. By adding "sex" to Title VII, he created a broad new constituency that successfully worked for retention of the sexual protection clause as well as House and Senate passage of the entire measure. Instead of a bill protecting the nation's black minority, the Civil Rights Act became an act equally important to the white majority whose demand for an end to discrimination provided a national consensus that insured enactment of the bill. The House finally passed the Civil Rights Act overwhelmingly on February 10, 1964, by a vote of 290–130, and thanks to Smith's maneuvering it was a stronger bill than the Kennedy administration had originally thought feasible. In the Senate, Margaret Chase Smith fought to retain the "sex" amendment as the bill underwent an eighty-three-day filibuster by southern senators. On June 10 the necessary two-thirds majority brought an end to the filibuster, and on July 2, 1964, the Civil Rights Act was passed complete with its Title VII provisions prohibiting employment discrimination on the basis of sex.

By a series of fortuitous accidents, the plight of women's discrimina-

This healthy, normal baby has a handicap. She was born female.

When she grows up, her job opportunities will be limited, and her pay low. As a sales clerk, for instance, she'll earn half of what a man does. If she goes to college, she'll still earn less than many men with a 9th grade education. Maybe you don't care—but it's a fact—job discrimination based on sex is against the law. And it's a waste. Think about your own daughter—she's handicapped too.

Womanpower. It's much too good to waste.

An advertisement focusing on job discrimination toward women and sponsored by the Legal Defense/Education Fund of NOW   *Reprinted with permission of the Legal Defense/Education Fund of NOW*

tion became associated with the civil rights movement in advance of feminists' direct demands for national legislation to combat discrimination. The needs of women had not previously been seen as identical with those of racial minorities. Civil rights leader Stokely Carmichael had in fact declared that the appropriate position for women in the civil rights movement was "on their backs." Even Betty Friedan had resisted the formation of a civil rights–type organization on behalf of women until 1966, when the possibilities of ending gender discrimination in employment became clear as a result of the Civil Rights Act of 1964. Women had quickly filed discrimination complaints with the Equal Employment Opportunity Commission (EEOC), the enforcement agency for the new Title VII regulations, but the EEOC was slow to act on cases of gender discrimination. The inclusion of sex in the Civil Rights Act was generally regarded as a joke to be snickered at and referred to by *The New York Times* as the "bunny law" in anticipation of what might happen if a man applied to a Playboy Club for a position as a bunny. An editorial in the *Times* described the potential neutering of language and suggested that Congress ought to "just abolish sex itself," intoning, "This is revolution, chaos. You can't even safely advertise for a wife anymore."

Without an organization to pressure the agency and the administration, women's employment equality was little more than an unenforceable sentiment and a target for derision. The creation of the National Organization for Women in 1966, however, which was pledged to "take action to bring women into full participation in the mainstream of American society now," helped insure that the momentum to end gender discrimination initiated in 1964 would continue.

In September 1965, two months after the Civil Rights Act went into effect, President Lyndon Johnson issued Executive Order 11246, requiring any organization that had a contract with the federal government to take affirmative action to ensure the just treatment of employees, and potential employees, of all races, colors, religion, or national origin. The category of sex was excluded, but the order was amended to prohibit sex discrimination and extend affirmative action to women in 1967 with Executive Order 11375. By the end of the 1960s women had attained legal rights and governmental sanction to win equality in the workplace. The Civil Rights Act had helped establish a new definition of women that was not limited by any special gender characteristics. The act had rendered outmoded and irrelevant the notion of special protection for women that had previously characterized much of the attention of women's activists. With the support of the U.S. Constitution, women would increasingly expect and demand equal treatment with men in every aspect of business and private life.

1966

The National Organization for Women Is Founded

You, Betty, have got to do it. *You* are independent. *You* have no job
at stake. *You* are a woman with national visibility, the only one who
can start a national civil rights organization outside the government.

Catherine East to Betty Friedan,
quoted in Marcia Cohen, *The Sisterhood*

The genesis of the National Organization for Women (NOW) originated out of frustration over the refusal by the Equal Employment
Opportunity Commission (EEOC) to deal with women's job discrimination complaints as a result of Title VII statutes of the Civil Rights Act of
1964. Newspapers still advertised male and female jobs in separate
columns, airlines fired stewardesses who married, and some states prohibited waitresses from working at night. After gender was added to the
list of discriminatory categories prohibited as a ploy by opponents of civil
rights to wreck the bill, the EEOC was slow to enforce compliance and
labeled the sex provisions of Title VII a "fluke" that was "conceived
out of wedlock."

Martha Griffiths, representative from Michigan and a staunch supporter of the sex provision, offered a stinging attack on the EEOC's lack
of effort in cases of gender discrimination on the House floor on June 20,
1966. "Since when is it permissible," she asked, "for an agency charged
with the duty of enforcing the law, to allude to the assumed motive of
the author of legislation as an excuse for not enforcing the law?" Griffiths's attack preceded by a few days the third National Conference of
State Commissions on the Status of Women, at which several attendees,
including Betty Friedan, hoped a strong resolution would be issued con-
demning the EEOC's actions. Title VII commissioner Richard Graham
had previously sought help from independent women's groups to lobby
the EEOC for compliance with the law, as other civil rights groups had

The founders of the National Organization for Women, who included Dorothy Haener of the United Auto Workers (*far left*), Sister Joelle Reed (*second from left*), Betty Friedan (*center*), and Richard Graham of the EEOC   *The Schlesinger Library, Radcliffe College*

done. As Betty Friedan recalled in her memoir, *It Changed My Life*, "He personally had gone to see the heads of the League of Women Voters, the American Association of University Women and other women's organizations with national headquarters in Washington, to get them to use pressure to have Title VII enforced on behalf of women. And they had been appalled by the very suggestion. They were not 'feminists,' they had told him."

Activists hoped that leaders of the Conference of State Commissions on the Status of Women would agree to spearhead a public protest movement among women on the issue of employment equality. However, the conservative leadership of the convention refused to act on the resolution, since its sponsors were not official delegates to the meeting. Disgruntled delegates, including women from the United Auto Workers and leaders of several state commissions, held an informal meeting in Betty Friedan's hotel room and determined that a new organization was required to move their agenda. Friedan recalled that they "cornered a large table at the luncheon, so that we could start organizing before we had to rush for planes. We all chipped in $5.00, began to discuss names. I dreamed up N.O.W. on the spur of the moment." Friedan scribbled on a paper cocktail napkin: "to take the actions needed to bring women into the mainstream of American society, now, full equality for women, in fully equal partnership with men. NOW. The National Organization for Women." NOW was launched on June 29, 1966, with an initial membership of twenty-eight and a treasury of $135.

NOW was conceived as a women's civil rights–type organization to pressure government and lobby for changes to secure equal rights for women. Betty Friedan, NOW's first president, presented a bill of rights at the second annual convention of the organization, on November 18, 1967. It demanded paid maternity leave, tax deductions for child care, educational aid, job training, right to legal abortions, and passage of the Equal Rights Amendment (ERA). NOW announced its opposition to any policy or practice that denied equal opportunities and fostered in women "self-denigration, dependence, and evasion of responsibility" and that created contempt for women. The organization also challenged traditional notions of women's roles, as defined solely by marriage and motherhood, with a difficult choice between home and career. "Above all," NOW asserted, "we reject the assumption that these problems are the unique responsibility of each individual woman, rather than a basic social dilemma which society must solve."

NOW's early years were contentious, with the organization trying to hold together a diverse membership that grew in the first five years to fifteen thousand with a conspicuous lack of organizational skills. Advocacy of such controversial issues as legalized abortion and the ERA alienated many supporters and forced some members to withdraw. Lawyers who wanted to focus not on social issues but on legal and economic ones left to found the Women's Equity Action League (WEAL). Others were dissatisfied with Betty Friedan's imperious, impatient manner. Friedan has admitted that she knew little about running a national women's movement and was temperamentally unsuited as a coalition builder. As early NOW leader Muriel Fox recalled, "Sometimes I thought that my main role was to keep Betty from killing people and people from killing her." During the eventually unsuccessful push to ratify the Equal Rights Amendment, however, NOW succeeded in becoming the nation's largest and most powerful women's organization, yet internal conflict over women's identity and the organization's agenda has persisted throughout NOW's history.

Conceived as a civil rights organization to build consensus among women and male supporters, NOW has been pushed by activists to shift its emphasis from political to identity and cultural concerns, as the political women's movement in the 1970s was reinterpreted as personal woman's liberation, and gender equality has contended with notions of gender difference. NOW increasingly came under attack for its perceived pushing of an agenda that was "antifamily" and too extreme for the majority of women. NOW's leadership has had to try to balance calls for greater militancy, particularly concerning lesbian issues, while resisting the alienation of other members for whom equal opportunity, not radical lifestyle changes, remains the organization's principal focus. Predictably, the organization has been attacked on the Right by such antifeminists as Phyllis Schlafly, who has charged that "NOW still has nothing to say to the average American woman." But even founding president Betty Friedan has broken ranks and criticized NOW's "too narrow focus" on its initial goals and its reluctance to address the problems of a new generation of women who are struggling to juggle jobs, husbands, and children. In the early 1990s Sally Quinn wrote, "Like Communism in the former Soviet empire, the movement in its present form has outlasted its usefulness." Both comments Patricia Ireland, the ninth president of NOW, rejects. "I don't think the fight is over," she asserts. "We're still in a situation where someone has to raise the issues that make people uncomfortable, the issues that other people don't want to talk about. It is my very strong belief that it's healthy to be angry at the situation women face. So, yes, we may be militant and angry, but we're also thoughtful and intelligent." As Kate Michelman, president of the National Abortion Rights Action League, has argued, "NOW is the organization that raised America's consciousness, which was an enormous contribution, but it is no longer by itself in shaping change. They must find a way to adjust to this new reality without losing their edge."

On balance, over NOW's more than thirty-year history, the organization's perceived radicalism has been largely absorbed by the mainstream. "First they're ridiculed," Heather Booth, director of the Coalition for Democratic Values, has pointed out, "then attacked, then dismissed. Then what they're pushing for occurs and becomes the accepted norm. By then they're on to the next level of debate." As one Washington lobbyist who works closely with several women's groups has observed, "NOW is about being on the outside and shaking the foundations of the ruling class." The challenge for the organization has been to maintain its self-defined permanent state of opposition to the status quo while maintaining its relevance to a broad coalition.

1968

Shirley Chisholm Becomes the First African-American Woman Member of Congress

> Well, since the big party leaders aren't supporting me—because
> they know they can't control my vote—and since everyone who
> knows me knows I always speak my own mind, how about
> "Unbought and Unbossed" for a campaign slogan?
>
> Shirley Chisholm, suggesting her 1968 campaign slogan,
> quoted in Susan Brownmiller, *Shirley Chisholm*

The campaign slogan that propelled Shirley Chisholm into the House of Representatives as the first African-American member of Congress also became the title for her 1970 autobiography and is a fitting descriptor of her political career. During her tenure in Congress from 1969 until she retired from the House in 1983, Chisholm accomplished a number of firsts and forced herself through her independence and determination to the center of the period's most contentious political and social struggles. Through her passionate advocacy she became an influential and inspirational political role model for all women as well as for women of color.

Chisholm was born Shirley Anita Saint Hill in 1924 in the Bedford-Stuyvesant section of Brooklyn, New York. Her parents, both natives of Barbados, had left the island during the famines of the 1920s for a better life in the United States, but Chisholm at the age of four and her sisters were sent to live on their grandmother's farm in Barbados. After six years on the island Chisholm returned to Brooklyn, where she was educated in public schools. An excellent student, she turned down scholarships to Vassar, Oberlin, and Barnard to remain close to home by attending Brooklyn College. Having decided upon a career as a teacher, one of the few professions open to African-American women in the 1940s, she took evening courses at Columbia University toward a master's degree in early childhood education, while working during the day as a teacher's aide at the Mt. Calvary Child Care Center in Harlem. She eventually became a teacher at the center and later its assistant director. In 1949 she married Conrad Chisholm, a New York police detective, also a native of the West Indies. The following year, after receiving her MA, she accepted a position as director of the Hamilton-Madison Child Care Center in Manhattan.

Her experiences while working as a day care specialist for the Bureau of Child Welfare in 1959, dealing with issues affecting minority women and children, caused her to become active in local Democratic Party politics. At the time, the mostly black district of Bedford-Stuyvesant was controlled by white, male Democratic Party loyalists. Chisholm began to work for better minority and female participation and control of party affairs, became an original member of the Bedford-Stuyvesant Political League, whose purpose was to work toward the election of black candidates at every level of government, and founded the Unity Democratic Club to help get African-American leaders elected to the New York State Assembly. In 1964 Chisholm ran for and won a seat in the assembly, which she retained until 1968. She was one of only six African-American assembly members and the only black woman. Although she was branded a "troublemaker" for her independence and outspoken advocacy for women and minority issues, Chisholm was successful in gaining passage for eight bills she introduced, most important the establishment of the SEEK program, which helped young men and women from disadvantaged backgrounds to go to college. She also won approval for a bill mandating that domestic workers were entitled to unemployment insurance and one overturning certain discriminatory practices against women.

When a congressional seat representing Bedford-Stuyvesant was created through redistricting, Chisholm decided to enter the race, winning a hard-fought three-way primary election by one thousand votes. She had bypassed the local Democratic Party machine for a personal campaign, attending countless house parties to meet as many voters as she could. In the general election she faced a formidable opponent in Republican African American James Farmer, a well-known civil rights leader who had been national director of the Congress of Racial Equality (CORE). Although incapacitated for almost six weeks while recovering from an operation to remove a benign tumor on her pelvis, Chisholm nevertheless mounted a spirited campaign against the Manhattanite Farmer, who criticized Chisholm's ability and intelligence, as well as her "liability" as a woman. Since women outnumbered men voters in the district, Chisholm mobilized the women of the PTAs and bridge clubs to

Shirley Chisholm was the first African-American woman elected to Congress and in 1972 became the first woman in American history to make a serious bid for the presidential nomination of a major party. *Library of Congress*

back her and appealed to her local experience and past history of service. Another advantage was Chisholm's fluency in Spanish, which allowed her to communicate directly with the district's many Latino voters. Chisholm was elected by a 2.5–1 margin. Brooklyn had its first black representative and the nation its first black woman member of Congress.

When Chisholm was sworn in, there were only eight other African-American House members and only ten women members. Traditionally, freshman representatives quietly support their party leaders and patiently await seniority before speaking up or offering any initiatives. When Chisholm first received her committee assignment, an appointment to the agriculture committee, she accepted it grudgingly but acknowledged that it would allow her to work on such programs as food stamps and surplus food distribution to the poor. But she balked when she was assigned to the forestry and rural development subcommittees. Representing the urban community of Bedford-Stuyvesant, which expected her involvement on issues related to their concerns, Chisholm protested her assignment to Speaker of the House John McCormick, who refused to intervene. She then took the issue to the floor of the House in an unprecedented move by a freshman member of Congress. After experiencing difficulty in being recognized by the Speaker, she left her seat and marched to the microphone in front of the Speaker and insisted she be allowed to make her case for reassignment. The resolution that she introduced was passed, and Chisholm was given an assignment to the veterans affairs committee. Although this was not her first choice, Chisholm joked, "There are a lot more veterans in my district than trees!"

With her outspoken and contentious style, Chisholm bucked the status quo and set the tone for her career in Congress. She became a strong opponent of the U.S. policy in Vietnam, a vocal and highly visible supporter of the Equal Rights Amendment, and a tireless campaigner for jobs, education, and enforcement for antidiscrimination laws. In a 1970 *McCall's* article, Chisholm gained national attention when she argued that having experienced both racial and gender prejudice, she believed that sexism was by far the more intractable. Seeking a wider forum for her views on women and minority issues, Chisholm became in 1972 the first woman to make a serious bid for the presidential nomination of a major political party. Despite a lack of money and organization and the challenge of being taken seriously by the press or her male Democratic opponents, Chisholm remained in the race until the convention, when she captured 150 votes on the first ballot. Although she was disappointed by the lack of support she received from minority and white female-led organizations, her campaign for the presidency was nevertheless a significant event in African American and women's political history. Chisholm emerged from the Democratic National Convention as a national spokesperson for issues and concerns that had previously lacked a forum and a perspective such as she provided. Chisholm left the House in 1983 to return to teaching, first at Mt. Holyoke and later at Spelman College. In 1985 the National Political Congress of Black Women was created, with Chisholm as its first president. She was for three years, according to a Gallup poll, one of the "Ten Most Admired Women in the World." In 1993 President Clinton appointed Chisholm ambassador to Jamaica.

Few other women or men have had such a distinguished career as a public servant in tackling some of the most difficult social and political issues. Other African-American women members of Congress would follow Chisholm's lead, most notably Barbara Jordan of Texas, the first African-American woman elected to Congress from a southern state, but few have equaled her determination or the courage of her convictions. "Unbought and Unbossed," Chisholm's feisty rallying cry, has been taken up by the various women political figures who have profited from Chisholm's trailblazing career.

1970–1979

The "Me" decade of the 1970s was also the decade of disco. Here, two models project hipness and sophisticated ennui in fashions suitable for feverish Saturday night activity on the dance floor.

1970

The First Women's Studies Program
Is Established by San Diego State College

As the hitherto "invisible" and marginal agent in culture, whose native culture has been effectively denied, women need a reorganization of knowledge, of perspectives and analytical tools that can help us know our foremothers, evaluate our present historical, political, and personal situation, and take ourselves seriously as agents in the creation of a more balanced culture.

> Adrienne Rich, "Toward a Woman-Centered University," in *On Lies, Secrets, and Silence*

The introduction of women's studies programs helped to effect one of the most successful and remarkable transformations of higher education curriculum and academic culture in the twentieth century by forcing gender to the center of the academic debate. Prior to the women's movement of the 1960s and 1970s, knowledge taught and generated in colleges and universities was almost exclusively male dominated. The contributions of women to culture and history were restricted to a few exceptional and unavoidable figures such as Elizabeth I, Queen Isabella, Martha Washington, Marie Curie, and Eleanor Roosevelt. Despite an increase in the number of women pursuing a college education throughout the century, little was done to the traditional curriculum to reflect a different gender perspective. Women's studies courses first appeared in the last half of the 1960s, when women faculty, who had entered the professorate in stronger numbers than ever before, began to create new courses to redress this imbalance. Influenced by the goals of the women's movement and the efforts of other minority groups to claim legitimacy in the academy, most notably in black studies, the earliest feminist faculty members pursued the dual goal of integrating the traditional curriculum with alternative perspectives and previously neglected women's voices and experiences and of building a body of scholarly knowledge that considered the implication of gender in academic and social discourse.

Inevitably, the women's movement's radical critique of cultural, economic, political, and social institutions and their patriarchal domination extended to a reassessment of the content and form of the academic disciplines. The essential justification for women's studies courses and programs was that knowledge in the traditional academic disciplines was incomplete and distorted because it excluded women's experiences and perspectives. Efforts to develop women's studies as an academic discipline, therefore, was both a developmental process of generating new types of scholarship and knowledge and a transformative effort to make the traditional academic curriculum and culture truly coeducational. At its core, women's studies offered a fundamental reevaluation about the way knowledge had been organized in traditional disciplines and their limitations by an exclusionary bias. Women's studies set out to correct this academic deficiency. The remarkable and rapid success of women's studies courses and programs greatly aided an enrichment of the academic curriculum and a radical disciplinary restructuring that blurred the sharp distinctions between departments and encouraged interdisciplinary approaches. Women's studies, therefore, anticipated by some years the eventual academic reorientation in the 1980s and 1990s of Humanities and Social Sciences Departments toward cultural studies and the incorporation of multicultural perspectives.

The first wave of curriculum integration of women's perspectives came from literature faculty who helped incorporate a greater number of female voices into the literary canon and from feminist historians, who reconsidered the gender implication of the ways in which women's roles and contributions had been traditionally studied and presented. San Diego State College (now University) was in the vanguard in generating women's studies courses, which led to the launching in September 1970 of the first officially established women's studies program in the United States. Other early women's studies programs were established at Portland State University, Richmond City College (New York), Sacramento State University, and the University of Washington. By 1974 nearly forty colleges and universities had instituted women's studies programs. By the end of the decade this number had grown to over four hundred programs with some thirty thousand women's studies courses offered nationwide. Scholarly journals in women's studies began appearing in 1972 with the publication of *Women's Studies—An Interdisciplinary Journal* and *Feminist Studies. Signs: Journal of Women in Culture and Society,* which became the leading journal in the field, began publication in 1975. In 1979 the National Women's Studies Association held its first meeting.

By the end of the decade women's studies had grown from a collection
of courses and revamped syllabi to an integrated academic discipline and
a legitimate field of academic study and research. Accompanying the
creation of a women's studies discipline and the redressing of the neglect
of gender-related awareness in the curriculum and the academic culture
was a widespread effort to alter the relationship between faculty and students and the ways in which education had been conducted. With such
symbolic and pedagogic innovations as the circular arrangement of chairs
in the classroom, small-group sessions, journal keeping, and an emphasis on collectivity in teaching and collaborative efforts in research,
women's studies faculty attempted to change the concept of learning

The activism of women students and faculty led to the nation's first women's studies
program at San Diego State University. During the 1970s women on campus mounted
demonstrations such as the one pictured here to develop support groups and to take
aggresssive stands on issues relevant to women.   *Photo courtesy of San Diego State
University*

from a noun to an active verb. Their innovations, which spread quickly to colleges and universities across the country, helped redefine the nature of higher education. The changes in teaching styles and methods have been called the program's most radical and vital contribution to educational innovation. The effect of women's studies curricula and concurrent pedogogic changes has trickled down to the high school and grade school level, where textbooks increasingly offer a greater emphasis on diversity of experience, both of women and of minorities.

In 1976 the National Advisory Council on Women's Educational Programs commissioned a study from the early feminist scholar Florence Howe on the status of women's studies. The report, "Seven Years Later: Women's Studies Programs in 1976," cataloged the various successes in increased student interest and enrollment growth, the breadth and depth of course offerings, and the vitality of women's studies scholarship. Left essentially unconsidered were the problems women's studies programs and faculty faced within and without the academy. Integrating women's studies into college and university governance and tenure processes that are still based along traditional departmental lines, as well as the relationship between women's studies research and scholarship and the political and social activism of the women's movement outside the academy, remain ongoing challenges. Perhaps even more explosive is the considerable attack mounted against women's studies and other ethnic and cultural studies programs by such writers as Allan Bloom. In his controversial best-seller, *The Closing of the American Mind: How Higher Education Has Failed Democracy and Impoverished the Souls of Today's Students*, Bloom charged that curricula changes, such as those pioneered by women's studies programs, represented a denigration of so-called dead white males of the literary canon, who have been replaced by less worthy female and ethnic figures. Other cultural critics such as Dinesh DeSousa have castigated the modern university for indulging in various "victim studies" programs and threatening free speech and inquiry through political correctness. Throughout this often overly strident debate, women's studies programs have achieved the initial goal of provoking a radical reassessment of the nature of knowledge and the educational process in higher education. In addition, despite the extreme positions often taken by academics and critics on either side of the debate, the moderate core of innovations produced by the undeniable academic success of women's studies has resulted in a balance between the coeducation of knowledge and the coeducation of the student body on most college campuses. Women are now represented in greater numbers on college faculties and in college courses, and previous male biases in education have been subjected to an intense and ultimately healthy challenge.

1971

Gloria Steinem Founds *Ms.* Magazine

Could there possibly be even 100,000 women in the country who
wanted this unconventional magazine?

Gloria Steinem, before the launch of *Ms.* magazine,
quoted by Carolyn G. Heilbrun in *The Education of a Woman*

When *Ms.*, the first and only feminist mass-market magazine in history, appeared in 1971, feminism, despite inroads in raising the consciousness of women and attracting media attention to women's issues, was dubbed by *The New York Times* "a passing fad," in which "in small town USA, women's liberation is either a joke or a bore." Feminism was viewed as having limited appeal, and a magazine devoted to a feminist perspective was expected to fail. When the magazine first appeared, television newsman Harry Reasoner predicted that it would be only "six months before it ran out of things to say." Gloria Steinem, who cofounded *Ms.* having determined that the "movement needed a vehicle, and I was in the position to help," planned a two-year commitment to the magazine. It stretched to nearly two decades until *Ms.* was sold to an Australian publisher in 1987. The magazine's greatest contribution has been to provide a forum for articles on women's concerns that, prior to *Ms.*, magazines had ignored or deemed too controversial or feminist to publish. *Ms.* helped raise the level and nature of the national debate on women's identity and opportunities and established itself as an essential chronicle of the history of women's issues in the last quarter of the twentieth century.

Although *Ms.* has been from its inception a collective enterprise reflecting the efforts and vision of a number of women, Gloria Steinem was from the beginning the magazine's star and dominant influence. The daughter of an itinerant antiques dealer and a newspaperwoman turned troubled housewife, Steinem grew up in a run-down, rat-infested house in Toledo, Ohio. When her parents divorced she was forced to care for her mother, who was virtually incapacitated with depression and delusions. She escaped her grim childhood by attending Smith College and was a typical coed of the era, vaguely considering a career at least until she married. "In the 1950s," Steinem has said, "once you married you became what your husband was, so it seemed like the last choice you'd ever have." But she had little desire for children. "I'd already been the very small parent of a very big child—my mother," she remembered. "I didn't want to end up taking care of someone else."

A postgraduate fellowship in India raised her social consciousness, and she returned to freelance for magazines like *Esquire* and *Vogue*, while helping to organize farmworkers and working for the civil rights movement in her spare time. Yet during most of the 1960s Steinem was far from a feminist, though her gender hindered her in being taken seriously as a journalist and in being given weighty assignments. As one editor at *Life* told her, "We don't want a pretty girl, we want a writer. Go home." In 1968 she was hired by Clay Felker to write a column on city politics for *New York* magazine. While she was covering a speak-out on abortion, her feminist instincts were awakened, and she began writing magazine articles about women's liberation and making speeches across the country in support of the women's movement. Attractive and glamorous in appearance, Steinem quickly became a celebrity and a media-proclaimed spokesperson of the movement. She was, for example, chosen to deliver the commencement address in 1971 over fellow Smith alumna Betty Friedan, and in 1972 she was named "Woman of the Year" by *McCall's*, though many feminists considered her a late convert to the cause, publicly preferred for her prettiness over more substantive contributions. Despite writing, "In bell bottoms and a jersey body shirt, tinted glasses and a lion's mane that reaches below her shoulder blades, she looks like a life-size, counterculture Barbie Doll," *McCall's* justified its selection by declaring that Steinem "had become a household word" and "is emerging as somebody to be taken very seriously indeed, the women's movement's most persuasive evangelist . . . preaching a new-found feminism."

Ms. allowed Steinem a potential pulpit and a means to make a significant contribution to the burgeoning women's movement by reaching out to a broad audience whose view of feminism was often distorted by the national media. Plans for the magazine began in early 1971 over meetings with women journalists at Steinem's apartment in New York and elsewhere. Their goal was to create a women-owned and feminist-run magazine that would feature articles on women's subjects that they had not been able to place in the general press. Clay Felker agreed to

Ms. Rates the Presidential Candidates

Susan Edmiston on How to Write Your Own Marriage Contract

Ms.™

THE NEW MAGAZINE FOR WOMEN

Gloria Steinem on Finding Out Who We Are

Nicholas von Hoffman: Son of Women's Lib

Jane O'Reilly on The Housewife's Moment of Truth

The cover of the first issue of *Ms.* The magazine debuted in a double issue of *New York* magazine in December, 1971. *Reprinted by permission of Ms. Magazine, © 1972*

include an insert of what would become a preview of the proposed *Ms.* magazine in the December 20, 1971, year-end issue of *New York.* The title of the new magazine came from the form of address for women that was beginning to be widely used, one that did not require knowledge of women's marital status. Other rejected titles were *Sojourner* (after nineteenth-century abolitionist and early women's rights activist Sojourner Truth), *Sisters*, and, in a fit of whimsy, *Bimbos.* The magazine avoided the traditional fare of women's magazines—features on fashion, food, and domestic concerns—for issues, but it also effected a stylish and glossy presentation that had never been attempted for such intellectual material. The magazine's first cover depicted a woman in tears with eight arms, holding in each hand implements associated with a housewife: a frying pan, an iron, a feather duster, a typewriter, a steering wheel, a telephone, a mirror, and a clock. Articles included pieces on welfare and abortion and others titled "Sisterhood," "Raising Kids Without Sex Roles," "The Housewife's Moment of Truth," "Why Women Fear Success," "Can Women Love Women?", "I Want a Wife," and "Sylvia Plath's Last Major Work." *Ms.* struck a powerful chord in articulating issues that many women faced but had never seen publicly discussed. Almost the entire initial issue—250,000 copies—sold out in about eight days, 20,000 enthusiastic letters came in from women all over the country, and 35,000 subscriptions were received, enough to launch *Ms.* as a monthly in 1972. The magazine would become the most popular voice of feminism in America.

The first regular issue of *Ms.* appeared in July 1972. As Steinem recalled, "Trying to start a magazine controlled by its female staff in a world accustomed to the authority of men and investment money should be the subject of a musical comedy." The magazine was edited by consensus, with the various editors listed alphabetically rather than hierarchically. Because advertising that cast women in a demeaning light was refused, advertisers were unsure about the magazine's market and were often scared off by its content. More radical feminists considered *Ms.* too soft and middlebrow, what Ellen Willis in *Feminist Revolution* described as "a mushy, sentimental idea of sisterhood designed to obscure political conflicts between women." Other writers found *Ms.* overly rigid and ideologically narrow. As Susan Brownmiller, who quit *Ms.* early on, recalled, "The problem was that there were all those women out there who had something to say and couldn't say it in other publications. And Gloria was worried about elitism, terrified of antagonizing blacks and lesbians, burdened by the worry the magazine would say something that would be misinterpreted."

Ms. tried to balance competing and differing perspectives of its readers, some of whom were offended by articles on lesbianism and others who complained that the magazine's audience was too clearly white, middle class, and heterosexual. "There was always the question of whether *Ms.* was a feminist magazine speaking to the converted," editor Mary Peacock has observed, "or a general women's magazine having a feminist base. It was never resolved. This push and pull made for a lot of editorial flattening; neither side could win, but they should have let the authentic voices come out. The problem of the magazine, in my reading, was not so much political as not wanting to show any warts on women. 'Is it good for the women's movement?' All the feminist voices had to be perfect. It was about making women look good because we were so vulnerable." Vivian Gornick, an early contributor to *Ms.* who was also critical of the magazine, concluded that the various carping about Steinem and the magazine missed the point. "Gloria Steinem and *Ms.* are not the enemy," she wrote in 1975. "The enemy is sexism."

To its credit, *Ms.* published some of the country's finest fiction writers, such as Lois Gould, Cynthia Ozick, and Mary Gordon, as well as discovering the then-unknown, future Pulitzer Prize winner Alice Walker. It also could take particular credit for giving voice to so many women— some 530 different writers in the magazine's first year alone. *Ms.* pioneered discussion of women's health care, rape, sexual abuse, and genital mutilation. As Steinem recalled, "It's been satisfying to see sexual harassment or battered women rise from the level of cover stories in a relatively small magazine to being national issues." The success of *Ms.* in finding an audience for substantive women's issues helped push other women's magazines to deepen their approach and encouraged the general press to follow the lead of *Ms.* in covering similar content. If the magazine never effectively resolved the internal tension between its mission to provide a forum for new feminist ideas and its desire to expose basic women's issues to as many readers as possible, *Ms.* still both reflected and shaped the zeitgeist of its era, speaking directly and unapologetically for a feminist point of view that was both revolutionary and revitalizing.

1972

Congress Passes the Equal Rights Amendment

Men and women shall have equal rights throughout the United
States and every place subject to its jurisdiction. Congress shall
have the power to enforce this article through appropriate
legislation.

> Alice Paul's wording of the Equal Rights Amendment,
> introduced to Congress in December 1923

The struggle to pass an Equal Rights Amendment (ERA) to the U.S.
Constitution began in 1923 when Alice Paul, the radical feminist leader
of the National Women's Party (NWP), drafted the ERA as the logical
next step for women's rights and equality after the suffrage victory.
Despite having won the vote, women faced discriminatory legislation
throughout the United States. Women in some states were denied the
right to serve on juries; husbands could control the earnings of their
wives; and women's inheritance from a husband without a will was limited to one-third of his property, while state laws granted widowers complete control over a deceased wife's estate. Husbands could determine
their wives' legal residence, and the burden of responsibility for illegitimate children rested with the mother. Women were barred from certain employment, and unequal pay for the same job was accepted as a
standard practice. As Doris Stevens, a leader of the NWP, argued,
"There is not a single state in the Union in which men and women live
under equal protection of the law. . . . Woman is still conceived to be in
subjugation to, and under the control of, the husband, if married; or the
male member of the family if unmarried."

Yet by asserting the goal of female equality through the ERA, the
NWP was forced to repudiate much protective legislation on behalf of
women that progressive reformers had struggled to enact. "The pleas of
special protection for women only," an NWP editorial stated, "is based on

the assumption that the maternal function incapacitates women from free competition in the industrial field. This takes for granted motherhood as a constant corollary for womanhood." The logic of the NWP's position caused the group to denounce such reform measures as the Sheppard-Towner Act because it singled out women as a class for special protection, as mothers, not persons. The issue split the suffrage coalition, and the ERA was opposed in the 1920s by virtually every other women's group out of fear that the amendment would nullify important protections for women that had taken years of lobbying to win. "The political rights of citizens are not properly dependent upon sex," argued Florence Kelley of the National Consumers' League, "but social and domestic relations and industrial activities are. Women cannot be made men by act of the legislature or by amendment of the federal Constitution. The inherent differences are permanent. Women will always need many laws different from those needed by men." For other women opposed to the ERA, suffrage was not a single victory in the long struggle for female equality, but the appropriate final victory to allow women a political voice to express their unique concerns. Equal rights that wiped out the distinction between genders was contrary to the premise that secured suffrage.

Without support for the Equal Rights Amendment among the majority of women, the proposal languished in Congress, stuck in the House Judiciary Committee from 1948 until the late 1960s and early 1970s, when support for the ERA gathered momentum as a result of the women's movement's considerable impact during the period. The National Organization for Women in 1966 called for an end to sexual discrimination in the workforce and began spearheading the fight for the passage of the ERA, while becoming the strongest private feminist organization in the United States during the ratification battle. By 1971, when the Ninety-second Congress began to consider passing the ERA, supporters included the League of Women Voters, Business and Professional Women, the YWCA, the American Association of University Women, Common Cause, and the United Auto Workers, who mounted a mail campaign that generated more letters to Capitol Hill than those during the Vietnam War. Congress had suddenly recognized the political power of women, and they rushed to appease a constituency that represented more than half of the voting public. The House passed the ERA by a vote of 354–23; the Senate voted 84–8 in favor; and the ERA was finally approved on March 22, 1972.

Despite the passage of the ERA, the seeds for its eventual ratification defeat were planted by adding a time limit of seven years for approval by the needed three-fourth of the states to the essentially intact language of Alice Paul's original amendment. Congress had imposed no time limit for ratification of the Nineteenth Amendment, and opposition disappeared almost instantly. With a time limit, opposition to the ERA could marshal its strength and, without the need for holding out against the amendment indefinitely, target likely states and play a delaying action until the time limit elapsed. By the end of 1972 twenty-two of the needed thirty-eight states had ratified the ERA, twenty within three months, many unanimously or by voice vote. By 1977 thirty-five states had approved the amendment, the same number—three states short of what was needed—as time ran out for ratification in 1982, after Con-

A pro-ERA banner takes center stage along with Congresswoman Bella Abzug, shown here speaking at a New York Women's Equality rally in 1974. *Photo by Bettye Lane*

gress voted a two-year extension. The amendment lost by only a few votes several times in Illinois and in Florida and once in Oklahoma. By one calculation, the ERA would have achieved ratification if seven votes had been changed.

The ERA had been defeated by several factors, including savvy opposition that managed to exploit the conflict between feminists and housewives and the underlying tension within the women's movement over the issue of gender equality and the protection of gender differences. Organizations opposed to the women's liberation movement, such as "Women Who Want to Be Women," "Happiness of Womanhood," and "Females Opposed to Equality," declared their satisfaction with the status quo, under perceived attack by the ERA. The most visible and formidable opponent was conservative Phyllis Schlafly, founder of STOP ERA in 1972, who mounted an unrelenting attack to demonize feminists and arouse deep-seated fears that the ERA would destroy the family and women's protected place in society. Schlafly linked the ERA with *Ms.* magazine and women's lib, which she charged with being "anti-family, anti-children, and pro-abortion. It is a series of sharptongued, high-pitched, whining complaints by unmarried women. They view the home as a prison, and the wife and mother as a slave. . . . Women's lib is a total assault on the role of the American woman as wife and mother, and on the family as the basic unit of society."

Schlafly and others opposed to the ERA claimed that the amendment would decriminalize rape, legalize homosexual marriages, integrate public rest rooms, end gender segregation in prisons and schools, mandate women's combat service in the military, and make every wife in the United States legally responsible to provide 50 percent of the financial support of her family, thereby forcing into the workforce women who might prefer to stay home with their children. ERA opponents successfully turned the debate over women's equality into a referendum on the traditional sanctities of motherhood and family, an issue that could not be effectively silenced by a divided women's movement that had never fully made peace or accommodation with the majority of women who willingly defined themselves as homemakers. For homemakers the ERA offered little but the threat of ending the role and identity they embraced.

As in the 1920s, the women's movement in the 1960s and 1970s was also divided over the central notion of whether equality should represent an elimination of gender distinctions or protection for unique gender differences. The movement had helped to make women aware of their important identity as women, and the ERA seemed to threaten that hard-won distinction in a gender-neutral world. In a sense, the struggle over the ERA and its eventual defeat, the culmination and climax of political solutions concerning the status of women, reveals the central ambiguity in the goals of the women's movement. Defined in opposition to traditional concepts of femininity, the movement during the 1970s was insufficiently broad to include both feminists who saw their identity in terms of careers for whom equality meant the elimination of job discrimination promised by the ERA and women who demanded different protection for their unique roles as mothers and caregivers to their families. The failure of the amendment stemmed from the inability of proponents to satisfy the latter group that the ERA was in their best interest as well. The larger implication of the fight for the ERA is whether future gender equality or gender difference can be truly quantified and reconciled.

Since the defeat of the Equal Rights Amendment, progress by women in areas of discrimination on the job and elsewhere has muted somewhat the need for a constitutional guarantee of equality. Most legal scholars agree that the ERA would have relatively little impact in the short run since the Supreme Court has already decided that the Fourteenth Amendment bars most forms of legalized sex discrimination. The longer-term benefit of the ERA would be more symbolic, asserting to judges and legislatures that the nation wants them to promote equality for women. Despite the National Organization for Women's renewed campaign for the ERA, announced in 1987, conditions for ratification have worsened since 1972. Proponents have been unsuccessful in convincing opponents that changes opposed by a majority of Americans, such as women in combat and homosexual marriages, and other issues that remain contentious, like abortion, will not be mandated under the ERA. It is far more likely that the ending of discrimination will continue to be fought for instead in a series of smaller battles, not by the sweeping statement of the ERA, and that the amendment's goals will eventually be accepted as implied in existing constitutional guarantees.

Title IX of the Education Amendments of 1972 Prohibits Discrimination on the Basis of Sex in Federally Funded Education Programs

If you grew up female in America, you heard this: Sports are unfeminine. And this: Girls who play sports are tomboys or lesbians. You got this message: Real women don't spend their free time sliding feet-first into home plate or smacking their fists into soft leather gloves.

So you didn't play or you did play and either way you didn't
quite fit. You didn't fit in your body—didn't learn to live there,
breathe there, feel dynamic and capable. Or maybe you fell madly,
passionately in love with sports but didn't quite fit in society, never
saw yourself—basketball player, cyclist, golfer—reflected in movies,
billboards, magazines. . . .

If you grew up male in America, you heard this: Boys who *don't*
play sports are sissies or faggots. And this: Don't throw like a girl. You
got this message: Sports are a male initiation rite, as fundamental
and natural as shaving and deep voices—a prerequisite, somehow, to
becoming an American man. So you played football or soccer or
baseball and felt competent, strong, and bonded with your male
buddies. Or you didn't play and risked ridicule. . . .

Insidiously, our culture's reverence for men's professional sports
and its silence about women's athletic accomplishments shaped,
defined, and limited how we felt about ourselves as women and men.

> Mariah Burton Nelson, *The Stronger Women Get, the More Men
> Love Football: Sexism and the American Culture of Sports*

For more than a quarter of a century, the provisions of Title IX,
designed to eliminate gender discrimination in education, have dramatically opened up school sports programs to women and challenged the
cultural stereotypes around the issue of athletics that Mariah Burton
Nelson has diagnosed. Its critics have charged that women's athletic success has come at the expense of men's programs and that the full implementation and implication of Title IX will result in a massive quota
system extending far beyond sports into every aspect of the academic
curriculum to achieve numerical equality regardless of gender interest.
Yet the principal legacy of Title IX has been a profound change in
women's participation in sports as well as phenomenal strides in athletic
accomplishments. Evidence, such as the remarkable recent successes of
the Olympic women's basketball, softball, soccer, and hockey teams, the
debut and popularity of the WNBA, and increased media attention and
product endorsements for women athletes, suggests that women are
beginning to rival men in fan interest and sports opportunities and that
an important cultural shift has taken place on the playing fields, marking
a change in women's identity and possibilities both as athletes and
beyond in competitive areas once regarded exclusively as the province of
men. Sports have always been an important indicator of gender assumptions, and Title IX has helped to change the rules of the games.

The history of American women in sports has its roots in the nineteenth century, when conventional notions of a feminine ideal were anti-

thetical to athletic participation by women. Sports require vigor and action, whereas the womanly ideal emphasized delicacy and passivity. Other elements of the ideal—modesty and propriety—were also threatened in the rough-and-tumble world of sports, with the threat of injury contrary to the primary female attributes: the ability to attract a husband and to bear children. Acceptable athletic activities for women—croquet, archery, bowling, tennis, and golf—were opportunities for a respectable social encounter with men, an activity for the upper classes who had the leisure and means to belong to clubs that facilitated play. Clothing restrictions limited movement, and strenuous exercise was decidedly unladylike.

When more women began to attend college in the latter half of the nineteenth century, attitudes changed, and physical exercise and training in sports began to be regarded as essential for women to increase the physical stamina necessary to endure the stress and strain of higher education. As the first president of Smith College remarked in his inaugural address in 1875: "We admit it would be an insuperable objection to the higher education of women, if it seriously endangered her health. . . . We understand that they need special safeguards. . . . With gymnastic training wisely adapted to their peculiar organization, we see no reason why young ladies cannot pursue study as safely as they do their ordinary employments."

Sports began to be implemented into the collegiate physical education curriculum at the end of the nineteenth century to promote health and such social values as teamwork and skills and accomplishments that could be utilized in later years. Archery, fencing, swimming, rowing, cycling, track and field athletics, and bowling were among the sports introduced into the college curriculum during the late nineteenth century to complement gymnastic training. Intercollegiate sports for women were initiated when basketball was introduced at Smith College in 1892, soon after the game was invented. Control of competition by the Amateur Athletic Union (AAU) in the 1920s extended women's participation in sports to the national and international level.

Although sports in the twentieth century increasingly became more acceptable for women's participation, on college campuses the inequality of facilities, support, and participation between men and women was left unaddressed until the passage of Title IX on June 23, 1972. By threatening to remove federal funds to schools that discriminated based on gender in its programs, Title IX forced schools to correct gender bias and produced a massive change in college and high school sports programs for women. In 1970 participation by women in intercollegiate sports programs was about 7.5 percent; by 1978 that percentage had grown to almost 32 percent. Since 1971 the number of women who participate in collegiate varsity sports increased by nearly 250 percent, to more than 110,000. The average number of women's teams per school rose from 5.61 to 7.5. By 1996 39 percent of college athletes were women, and women's sports scholarships are up from $100,000 in 1972 to $180 million. At the high school level, prior to Title IX only one in twenty-seven girls played sports; the ratio is now one in three.

Title IX has had a profound effect on changing opportunities for women athletes despite legislative setbacks and resistance to full compliance. Opponents of Title IX, including the Reagan administration, sought to limit application and enforcement; and the Supreme Court in *Grove City College* v. *Bell* in 1984 ruled that federal funds could be removed only from programs found to be discriminatory. Since athletic programs received no direct federal funds, they were therefore now exempt from Title IX sanctions. The ruling effectively gutted the Title IX program. However, the Civil Rights Restoration Act of March 1988 legislated that if one part of an educational institution received federal funds, the entire institution and all of its programs were responsible for Title IX mandates. To reach compliance, schools scrambled to subtract males and add females to their sports programs, replacing Title IX's original emphasis on avoiding discrimination with a numerical gender balance, sometimes eliminating some male teams, rather than creating

The provisions of Title IX resulted in greater participation among girls and college women in a variety of sports. Here, the women's rugby team at Wesleyan University in Connecticut mix it up during a game. *Photo courtesy of Wesleyan University*

new and expensive women's teams, with Title IX blamed for the eliminations. As Donna Lopiana, executive director of the Women's Sports Foundation, has observed: "We have always said that it is inappropriate for the Title IX solution to bring the level of men's sports down to the women's level." However, the highly publicized elimination of minor and less lucrative men's sports other than football and basketball in the pursuit of Title IX compliance has found an easy target in the quota system that schools have used to redress discriminatory practices. According to Deborah Brake, senior counsel at the National Women's Law Center, "There's been a backlash against a lot of the gains we've won. We're seeing the have-nots versus the haves. Instead of blaming football and basketball, which continue to hog resources, other men's sports like gymnastics and wrestling are blaming women."

Although courts have backed the antidiscrimination standards of Title IX against a number of legal challenges, most publicly the 1991 attempt by Brown University to withdraw funding from its women's gymnastics and volleyball teams, the debate over how equality in school programs can be achieved is expected to continue as a male versus female contention for limited resources rather than an issue of equal opportunity for both genders. As Lopiana summarizes the legacy of Title IX, "It's a half-full, half-empty story. The downside is it's taken twenty-five years, and the treatment of athletes is still uneven. The good news is that we've reached a critical mass of the first generation of mothers and fathers who grew up thinking it was fine for their daughters to play sports."

As important as the enhanced participation of women in sports that Title IX has insured is the changed perception of the female athlete and increased respect for women's accomplishments. Skill levels have improved among women athletes. Between 1967 and 1987, for example, women marathoners have cut nearly an hour off the world record. Along with highly publicized stories of high school women successfully joining men's teams in baseball, football, and wrestling, women athletes have gained notoriety for invading male professional athletic turf. Former college star and 1976 Olympian Nancy Lieberman made headlines in 1986 when she became the first woman to play men's pro basketball for the United States Basketball League, and Lynette Woodard became the first female Harlem Globetrotter the same year. Women sports figures have emerged as celebrities and role models, attracting men as well as women fans, a fact advertisers have seized on by offering more product endorsements to women stars. Through the opportunities afforded by Title IX, the image of the female athlete has emerged as a challenge to previous ideals of women. Studies have shown that women who participate in sports have enhanced self-esteem, discipline, and team orientation that are likely to translate into success in the corporate world beyond the playing field. Title IX has helped insure that the woman athlete is no longer an exception or a freak of nature, but a normal aspect of achievement by women when given the opportunity to compete in areas once viewed as exclusive, male sanctuaries.

The First Rape Crisis Centers Open

A female definition of rape can be contained in a single sentence.
If a woman chooses not to have intercourse with a specific man
and the man chooses to proceed against her will, that is a criminal
act of rape.

Susan Brownmiller, *Against Our Will: Men, Women and Rape*

Sexual violence, which may legally include any form of sexual assault as well as intercourse, has, like battering, been a weapon used for centuries to punish, intimidate, and subjugate women simply because they are women. Sexual violence has been perpetrated on females of every class (although the poor and disenfranchised have been the most frequent victims) and in every stage of life, from infancy, toddlerhood, and girlhood (when in recent years it has carried the appellation "sexual abuse") to old age. In the twentieth century the American civilian and wartime military judicial systems were forced by an increasing socially and politically vigilant citizenry to address the issue of sexual violence as never before.

During the twentieth century, as in centuries past, rape persisted as a common by-product of war. Before the increasing presence of women in the military during the late 1970s and 1980s, war was conceptualized as an event in which only men participated. In writing on the history of rape in war, Susan Brownmiller has observed, "Victory in arms brings group power undreamed of in civilian life. Power for men alone. . . . A certain number of soldiers must prove their newly won superiority— prove it to a woman, to themselves, to other men. In the name of victory and the power of the gun, war provides men with a tacit license to rape. In the act and in the excuse, rape in war reveals the male psyche in its boldest form, without the veneer of 'chivalry' or civilization." It is well-known that sexual violence was committed by German, Japanese, Russian, and Moroccan soldiers during World War II, but American GIs raped women, too. By June 1947 there had been a total of 971 courts-martial for rape; 52 of those convicted were executed. Over two-thirds of the convictions took place during the Allied occupation of conquered countries. During the Korean Conflict there were approximately 23 convictions for rape and 9 convictions for assault with intent to rape. During the Vietnam War, a conflict famous for its steady flow of disinformation, rapes were underreported, and there were fewer convictions than in previous wars.

One incident during the Vietnam War involving rape that made headlines and was forced to a resolution took place in My Lai village in 1968 and is historically referred to as the "My Lai massacre." At My Lai U.S. soldiers went on a rampage, systematically raping and abusing women, who were then killed (a total of 347 women, men, and children were officially reported murdered at My Lai). Several members of Charlie Company, commanded by Lt. William Calley, were charged with rape, but the charges were quietly dropped. The incident remained unknown to the American public until 1969, when a series of letters by a former soldier to government officials forced the army to take action. In 1970 five soldiers were court-martialed on charges of premeditated rape and murder. None of the soldiers or officers charged were executed; Lieutenant Calley was convicted, sentenced to life imprisonment, and released in 1974. After the My Lai incidents, soldiers admitted to reporters that rape was standard operating procedure with U.S. troops.

In civilian life, instances of rape, whether marital, date, or statutory, as well as other forms of sexual assault have been less easy to cover up, although until the 1970s rape victims who brought charges against their attackers were at the mercy of antiquated state legislation that made convictions difficult and of male judges and juries who tended to blame the woman for somehow inciting the act or failing to prevent it (even today there are judges who maintain this unfortunate attitude). In 1906, for example, a Wisconsin court of appeals acquitted an accused rapist despite evidence that the sixteen-year-old victim had screamed, tried to get away from her attacker, and was nearly strangled. The court ruled that because she did not testify that she had used her hands, feet, or pelvic muscles to demonstrate her lack of consent (which fell under the consent provision present in the legal system since 1874) and because she was not bruised and had no torn clothing, any claim that she offered "utmost resistance" was "well nigh incredible." Forty-three years later little had changed: a Texas court acquitted an accused rapist, ruling that the victim's "feigned and passive resistance" did not constitute sufficient grounds for a case of rape.

In 1953 an article in the *Yale Law Journal* suggested that rape victims bore a responsibility for the actions of their attackers because of the "unusual inducement to malicious or psychopathic accusation inherent in the sexual nature of the crime." Model penal codes of the next two decades incorporated this mistaken concept. From today's perspective it is difficult to understand why Ivy League law students and professors, as well as legislators, were incapable of realizing that rape is a crime of violence rather than an expression of sexuality. The resistance issue was raised again, more insidiously, in 1966, when an article on rape in the *Stanford Law Review* stated, "Although a woman may desire sexual intercourse, it is customary for her to say 'no, no, no' (although meaning 'yes, yes, yes') and to expect the male to be the aggressor . . . the problem of determining whether the female really meant yes or no is compounded when, in fact, the female had no clearly determined attitude—that is, her attitude was one of ambivalence." The article went on to define the standard of resistance as high enough "to assure that the resistance is unfeigned and to indicate with some degree of certainty that the woman's attitude was not one of ambivalence or unconscious compliance and that her complaints do not result from moralistic afterthoughts," but it also must be low enough "to make death or serious bodily injury an unlikely outcome of the event."

There was little ambivalence on the part of feminists and other supporters of the revived women's movement to take assertive action regarding the rights of rape victims. In 1971 the first public rape victims' speak-out was held at St. Clement's Episcopal Church in New York City. The following year the Bay Area Women Against Rape (BAWAR) crisis center was opened in Berkeley, California. Other centers were opened in Michigan, Los Angeles, and Washington, D.C. By 1980 there were over four hundred rape crisis centers nationwide. Since their inception, these centers, as well as rape hot lines, have offered free professional counseling and legal and medical information and have resulted in a greater number of sexual assaults reported to law enforcement officers. The efforts of women's groups and dedicated individuals on behalf of rape victims also resulted in an expansion of victims' rights and the introduction of rape prevention programs. In 1975 the Michigan state Legislature enacted comprehensive rape law reforms, specifically eliminating the physical resistance requirement and limiting the circumstances and extent to which a victim's sexual history can be introduced. In the years to come, Michigan's laws concerning rape laws would be considered models for other states and would lead to the introduction of the Privacy Protection for Rape Victims Act in Congress.

The 1980s and 1990s saw legislation addressing the issues of date rape and sexual assault on college campuses. The Student Right to Know and Campus Security Act required colleges and universities to collect data on campus crime and to publish crime statistics on a yearly basis so that prospective students could make informed choices in their selection of schools. The Campus Sexual Assault Victim's Bill of Rights Act of 1991, later known as the Ramstad Amendment to the Higher Education Act, required colleges to develop and publicize a campus sexual assault policy. Many college campuses during the 1990s have sponsored "Take Back the Night" protests against sexual assault.

Despite sexual assault reform legislation, there have been court rulings in recent history that have raised serious concerns about how far state judicial systems have actually evolved since the turn of the century with regard to rape cases. In 1983, for example, in the case of *State* v. *Lester*, a North Carolina appeals court overturned the conviction of a man found guilty of having raped his three daughters. The man had been known to carry a gun, had often battered the girls' mother, and had threatened to kill them all, but the court inexplicably found that the girls had no reason to fear that he would use force and further determined that they did not put up enough resistance. The issue of sexual assault on campus was explored in a provocative 1993 book, *The Morning After: Sex, Fear, and Feminism on Campus*, by Princeton graduate student Katie Roiphe. In the book Roiphe suggests that male sexual assault has been exaggerated and even invented by mass hysteria, thus setting back the cause of women's liberation, "denying female desire," and infantilizing women. The question of what constitutes sexual consent, on and off campus, in charges of sexual assault has contributed to the perception of invention and exaggeration and in some instances has made the establishment of guilt in rape cases difficult, especially when there is no physical evidence of violence, but only one testimony against the other. At the turn of the new millennium, the burden of proof in sexual assault crimes continued to remain with the victim.

1973

Abortion Is Legalized

I save lives. . . . I respect those people who have picketed outside my office for 25 years, in and out of snowstorms. Obviously they believe in what they are doing and are very persistent. At the same time, I have taken care of many of their wives and children and even some of the people on the picket line who suddenly find themselves in a way different situation than they ever thought possible. I know what would happen if they were successful politically—a lot more tragedy, a lot more deaths. I saw what it was like when it was illegal.

> Dr. David Bingham in Jack Hitt, "Who Will Do Abortions Here?"
> *New York Times Magazine*, January 18, 1998

One of the most controversial issues concerning reproductive freedom for women in the United States has been that of abortion. The debate over the legalization and practice of abortion has centered on moral, religious, emotional, and political considerations and has sharply divided self-described "pro-life" and "pro-choice" activists and adherents. Caught in the middle of the debate are the women and adolescents who have made the difficult decision to have an abortion and who have often faced harassment by "right-to-life" picketers outside abortion clinics. Physicians and clinic workers, who may or may not entirely approve of the procedure but recognize its legality and necessity, have faced the threat of physical danger and even death from militant antiabortion groups and individuals.

Abortion in the United States was first criminalized in the 1860s. Before then, performing an abortion before "quickening," when the fetus first moved in the uterus, was not considered a crime; moreover, an abortion after quickening was not much more than a minor offense. Around 1860, however, there was increasing concern on the part of

physicians regarding the upsurge in the number of abortions being performed and about the health consequences of the abortions. The first
state laws restricting abortions were passed to protect women against
septicemia, often a side effect of the procedure. In addition, the American Medical Association was endeavoring to professionalize the practice
of medicine and wanted to rid the medical community of so-called irreg-
ular doctors, who in their view were not "scientifically trained." These
were doctors who were primarily providing abortions. The AMA counted
on the legal restriction of abortion to drive such doctors out of business.
Physicians led the campaign to prohibit abortion and tried to enlist the
support of the clergy. However, most clergymen did not view abortion as
a religious matter and refused to become involved in the crusade to
enact restrictive legislation because of the prevailing religious belief that
the soul did not come to life until after quickening. Women reformers,
who considered abortion as well as contraception a gross violation of
proper womanhood and an invitation to practice sexual immorality, supported the legislation but were content to let physicians campaign for
it. The medical community found its most receptive allies to be state
legislators, who were also concerned with loosening morals and moreover worried that the increasing use of abortion by white, middle-class
Protestant women would change the population balance. State after state
began enacting laws prohibiting abortion unless a continuation of the
pregnancy endangered the life of the mother.

During the early years of the twentieth century, when birth control
advocates such as Emma Goldman and Margaret Sanger disseminated
information on contraception and contraceptives in defiance of the Comstock Law, illegal abortion was the most widely practiced form of birth
control. Even after the Comstock Law was liberalized in 1929 and
repealed in 1936, women continued to have illegal abortions. Before the
advent of the vacuum aspirator, abortions were performed by having a
curette, or sharp instrument, inserted into the uterus and scraping the
fetus from the uterine wall. A woman could bleed to death if the curette
pierced the uterus or suffer a fatal infection if the instrument was not
properly sterilized. Women with money could afford to consult a skilled
abortionist. Poor women attempted to abort themselves using folk remedies, charms, or patent medicines, which were ineffective but harmless.
Other methods that involved the insertion of coat hangers, shoe hooks,
knitting needles, and douches were not only ineffective but often led
to sterility and fatality. During the 1930s many women wanting to terminate pregnancies continued to rely on vaginal douching, often with
deadly solutions of water, Lysol, carbolic soap, iodine, and turpentine.

It has been estimated that one million illegal abortions were performed in the United States during the 1950s and that over a thousand women died as a result of abdominal infections from unskilled or unsanitary procedures. Still others were left sterile or chronically ill and emotionally scarred. In the frightening, secret world of illegal abortion in the 1950s and 1960s, most abortionists were interested only in collecting their fees—usually $1,000 or more in cash—and turned women away if they could not pay the asking price. The majority of abortionists cared little for the physical and psychological well-being of the women who came to them for help. Women were sometimes forced to have sexual relations with male abortionists before they would agree to perform the procedure. Concerned with speed and their own protection, abortionists often refused to use anesthesia because it would take too long for women to recover, thus raising the risk of discovery. Women did not receive explanations of what was happening during the procedure; birth control techniques were not discussed, and few if any adequate precautions were taken to prevent hemorrhage or infection. Poor women and women of color were particularly at risk from abortions; 75 percent of women who died as the result of mostly illegal abortions in 1969 were women of color.

In 1962 abortion made headlines when it was reported that Sherri Finkbine, the pregnant host of a children's television program in Arizona, was planning to travel to Sweden to have her fetus legally aborted. For several months Finkbine had been taking the tranquilizer thalidomide, which her husband, a high school teacher, had obtained in Europe because it was banned in the United States. When the news broke that thalidomide was responsible for terrible birth defects in newborn babies in Europe and the United Kingdom, the thirty-year-old mother of four and her husband decided to seek an abortion. The couple's decision provoked condemnation from the Vatican and thousands of critical and threatening letters. After U.S. medical authorities refused to approve Finkbine's abortion, she flew to Sweden, where the procedure was performed, and doctors verified that her baby would have indeed been deformed. When Finkbine returned to the United States she was fired from her television job. The controversy sparked by Sherri Finkbine's abortion gradually died down, but it had served to remind the public, if only briefly, that women were going to find a way to have abortions if they felt they needed them.

During the 1960s members of the liberal clergy and women's groups set up their own referral services to help women obtain safer illegal abortions. One support group, the Chicago-based Jane Collective, helped over eleven thousand women get safe first- and second-trimester abortions for as little as $50, with the result that many of Chicago's expensive and unsafe abortionists were put out of business. By the end of the decade, as the women's movement was gaining momentum, women's groups held demonstrations and speak-outs at which many women talked about their experiences undergoing illegal abortions. Members of the women's movement, supported by civil liberties groups, marched, rallied, and lobbied for abortion on demand. By the early 1970s some states had liberalized their abortion laws, allowing the procedure in certain cases—for example, when pregnancy was the result of rape or incest or when the woman was under fifteen years of age; other states allowed abortion on demand through the twenty-fourth week from the last menstrual period. Physicians in the 1960s and 1970s argued for the overturning of restrictions after having witnessed the costs of illegal abortions in terms of maternal injuries and death. In 1972 the fledgling feminist publication *Ms.* magazine carried an advertisement headlined "We Have Had Abortions" that was signed by such prominent women as Lillian Hellman, Billie Jean King, Susan Sontag, Gloria Steinem, and Barbara Tuchman.

A number of abortion cases were brought before the U.S. Supreme Court, including one in which a married pregnant woman called "Jane Roe" sued a Florida district attorney who blocked her attempts to obtain an abortion. On January 22, 1973, the Court ruled 7–2 in the case of *Roe v. Wade* that abortion should be a decision between a woman and her physician. The Court stated that the "right of privacy . . . founded in the Fourteenth Amendment's concept of personal liberty . . . is broad enough to encompass a woman's decision whether or not to terminate her pregnancy." Justice Harry A. Blackmun, who wrote the majority opinion, held that through the end of the first trimester of pregnancy, only a woman and her doctor have the legal right to decide on abortion and that the state's interest in a woman's welfare is not "compelling" enough to warrant any interference. For the next trimester a state could "regulate the abortion procedure in ways that are reasonably related to maternal health." For the last trimester, at the time when a fetus was determined to be "viable," or capable of existing outside the womb, a state might "regulate the abortion procedure in ways that are reasonably related to maternal health," including the licensing and regulation of facilities. As a result of the Court's ruling, the number of illegal abortions and the rates of maternal mortality were greatly decreased. It has been estimated that prior to 1973 there were from 200,000 to 1.2 million abortions performed per year; that figure rose to over 1.5 million abortions in 1980 and remained between 1.5 million and 1.6 million annually by 1990.

The landmark Supreme Court decision of 1973 created a firestorm of controversy. The women's movement greeted it as a victory in the struggle for female reproductive rights and echoed Planned Parenthood Fed-

A pro-choice demonstration makes its way across New York's Fifth
Avenue to St. Patrick's Cathedral in 1974.   *Photo by Bettye Lane*

eration Alan F. Gutmacher's assertion that the Court's decision had been
"a wise and courageous stroke for the right to privacy and for the protection of a woman's physical and emotional health." Terence Cardinal
Cook of New York called the Court's action "horrifying." Antiabortion
forces led by the Catholic Church hierarchy, by fundamentalist Christian
groups, and "right-to-life" organizations, such as Operation Rescue,
founded in 1988 by New York used-car salesman Randall Terry, lobbied
to eliminate abortion and used such strategies as the picketing and pad-
locking of abortion clinics in a policy of harassment and intimidation.

The antiabortion faction was handed the first of several victories in
1976 when the Hyde Amendment to the health, education, and welfare
appropriations bill cleared Congress by a vote of 256–114. The amendment, named for its sponsor, Republican Illinois congressman Henry

Armed with slogans and an empty crib, anti-abortion activists mark the sixteenth anniversary of *Roe v. Wade* by picketing the Planned Parenthood office in Schenectady, New York. *UPI/Corbis-Bettmann*

Hyde, barred the use of federal funds for abortions "except where the life of the mother would be endangered if the fetus was brought to term." The previous year some 250,000 to 300,000 women had received Medicaid-funded abortions. Critics labeled the new legislation discriminatory and unconstitutional, while supporters, apparently unaffected by the negative impact the amendment would have on the health and well-being of poor families, as well as the possibility of more children on the welfare rolls, contended that federal tax revenues should not be used to fund an operation that a substantial percentage of Americans considered immoral.

In 1980 the Supreme Court upheld the Hyde Amendment in the case of *Harris* v. *McRae*. In 1989 Congress voted to authorize Medicaid payment for abortions for victims of rape and incest, but President George Bush vetoed the measure and Congress failed to override. The same year, the Court ruled in the case of *Webster* v. *Reproductive Health Services* that states could limit access to abortion. The ruling included a preamble stating that "the life of each human being begins at conception" and a provision allowing states to prohibit "public facilities" and "public employees" from being used to perform or assist in abortions in cases in which a woman's life was not at risk. The Court upheld one of the strictest parental notification laws in the nation in the case of *Hodgson* v. *Minnesota* (1990) and in the case of *Rust* v. *Sullivan* (1991) upheld a gag rule prohibiting counselors and doctors in federally funded family-planning clinics from providing information and referrals about abortion. In 1992, despite reaffirmation of its 1973 *Roe* v. *Wade* decision, the U.S. Supreme Court continued to erode abortion rights in the case of *Planned Parenthood* v. *Casey*, in which it upheld a Pennsylvania law limiting a woman's access to the procedure. In the same year, a Mississippi law requiring a twenty-four-hour waiting period was upheld by the Court.

During the later 1980s and 1990s antiabortion extremists resorted to terrorism in an attempt to achieve their goal of a complete ban on abortions. Clinics were firebombed and sprayed, squirted, or injected with noxious, industrial chemicals, resulting in the injury and deaths of clinic workers, and between 1993 and 1994 physicians were murdered. In 1993 President Bill Clinton marked the twentieth anniversary of *Roe* v. *Wade* by signing memoranda reversing abortion restrictions imposed by the Reagan and Bush administrations. As a result, federally funded clinics became free to provide abortion counseling; military hospitals were allowed to perform abortions; fetal tissue could be used in federally-financed research, and federal aid was allowed to international family-planning programs that included abortion-related activities. In addition, the memoranda called for a review of the policy against the importing of the abortifacient drug RU-486, which is widely used in France. The latest controversy regarding abortion has been over the issue of late-term or partial-birth abortion. In 1996 President Clinton vetoed a bill that would have banned late-term abortions.

Despite the willingness of an increasingly conservative Supreme Court to uphold the 1973 decision guaranteeing women the right to have an abortion, the terrorism and harassment that has taken place since *Roe* v. *Wade* has resulted in fewer physicians willing to perform the procedure, almost no courses on abortion taught in medical schools, and little if any research on the subject. "The medical establishment has been scared off," writes Jack Hitt, "leaving the practical day-to-day work of abortion overwhelmingly to the same doctors who first pioneered it twenty-five years ago. Now these doctors are getting old and there is the prospect of their not being replaced." Caught between medical and political interests are pro-choice women who have witnessed the erosion of abortion rights since 1976 and continue to face legal and constitutional uncertainty regarding this aspect of reproductive freedom. As Supreme Court justice Ruth Bader Ginsburg stated during her 1993 Senate confirmation hearings, "The state controlling a woman would mean denying her full autonomy and full equality."

1976

The First Women Are Admitted
to U.S. Military Academies

The Secretaries of the military departments concerned shall take such action as may be necessary and appropriate to insure that female individuals shall be eligible for appointment and admission to the service academy concerned, beginning with appointment to such academy beginning in the calendar year 1976, and the academic and other relevant standards required for appointment, training, graduation, and commissioning of female individuals, shall be the same as those required for male individuals, except for those minimum essential adjustments in such performance standards required because of physiological differences between male and female individuals.

> From Public Law 94–106, signed by President Gerald R. Ford on October 7, 1975

The debate over whether or not one of the last bastions of higher education—the U.S. service academies—should be opened to women was finally resolved on behalf of coeducation by Congress in 1975, despite opposition by the administrations of West Point, Annapolis, and the U.S. Air Force and Coast Guard academies, alumni, and the command of the armed forces, all of which had been nearly unanimous against admitting women. In April 1974 the Departments of the Army, Navy, and Air Force issued official statements against admission of women to their academies, a position that the Department of Defense supported. Since women were barred from combat, they argued, women had no need for the training the academies offered, and it was essential that the expensive training opportunities be reserved for those who would be asked to serve in leadership roles in combat situations. Women were also seen as a threat to the traditions and the standards of the academies. As Air

Force Academy superintendent Lieutenant General Albert P. Clark explained in an argument that was echoed by academy leaders: "The environment of the Air Force Academy is designed around these stark realities [of combat]. The cadet's day is filled with competition, combative and contact sports, rugged field training, use of weapons, flying and parachuting, strict discipline and demands to perform to the limit of endurance mentally, physically, and emotionally." The implication was clear: Women in the service academies simply could not cut it. Even many women in the military opposed admission. Retired Colonel Jacqueline Citron, who had led women pilots in the Women's Air Service Patrol (WASP) during World War II, argued that since women could not be in combat situations, they should not receive the special training given at the service academies. Captain Robin L. Quigley, the women's director for the navy, agreed that women need not be trained for seagoing and combat specialties in which they were denied service.

Against such opposition and the still controversial issue of women in combat, the push to make the service academies coeducational began in earnest in 1972. Senator Jacob Javits of New York nominated a woman to the Naval Academy, but her admission was denied for gender reasons. Congress then began to consider the issue of integrating the academies with both men and women students. In 1973 a woman who had been denied admission sued the navy, and pressure for Congress to act increased. Supporters argued that women were denied equal opportunities for military advancement since, unlike graduates of officer training and reserve programs, which did admit women, graduates of the service academies received regular, rather than reserve, commissions, and women excluded from the academies were denied the preferment that academy graduates received. To the charge that service academy training was unnecessary for women who were denied combat service, supporters, such as Congresswoman Patricia Schroeder of Colorado, argued that women should be allowed to attend for the same reasons men did—to be trained as good officers and to receive a fine education. She and other supporters pointed out that the academies did not train men solely for combat. In the air force, for example, less than 40 percent of academy graduates between 1964 and 1973 had specialized in combat jobs. Women were now free to pursue all but three of twenty-four career fields in the military, and academy training would help improve their career and leadership aspirations. In 1972 Congress debated a resolution stating that a woman nominated to a service academy should not be denied solely on the basis of her gender. It passed the Senate but was defeated in the House of Representatives.

When the House passed the Stratton Amendment on May 20, 1975, calling for women to be admitted to the service academies on the same basis as men by a vote of 303 in favor to 96 opposed, the military began planning for the inevitable admission of women. Prototype uniforms for the cadets were designed and planning work undertaken for construction changes to academy facilities. After the law opening up the academies to women was passed, the military conducted an extensive study to determine the anticipated physical capabilities and limitations of the incoming women. Sixty high school women volunteers were tested to determine the effect of various physical exercise programs, the physical capabilities of women in comparison with men, and whether the Physical Aptitude Exam (throwing a basketball for distance, performing a standing long jump, doing a shuttle run between two lines for a total of three hundred yards, and performing a minimum of six pull-ups) was a valid predictor of female performance. Other studies were conducted to determine the ability of women cadets to withstand the rigors of military training during the first summer's cadet basic training and to examine the psychological, sociological, and cultural differences between men and women.

In the summer of 1976, 119 women matriculated at the Military Academy, 81 at the Naval Academy, and 157 at the Air Force Academy. Each academy handled the arrival of women differently, which had a major effect on the first class of women and their attrition rate. At West Point few concessions were offered women cadets, who were expected to maintain traditional tough standards administered by many academy supervisors and upperclassmen who remained convinced that the admission of women was a mistake. At Annapolis women midshipmen were expected to blend in as quickly and unobtrusively as possible. At the Air Force Academy, however, a considerable effort was made to celebrate the new woman cadet as worthy and to establish an esprit de corps among female and male cadets. The result was positive. When the first class of women graduated from the Air Force Academy, in 1980, a higher percentage of women who had entered in 1976 graduated than did men, and women experienced fewer academic failures—one in ten compared with men's one in five. At West Point only 62 women of the original 119 graduated, an attrition rate considerably above that for men. The pressure on women cadets was intense and unrelenting. As Carol Barkalow, a member of West Point's first class of women cadets, explains in her account, *In the Men's House:* "Women, in particular, became a target group for special hazing, though certainly men were not exempt. The difference was, men had to prove themselves weak before they became subject to this kind of harassment, women had to prove themselves strong before they were spared it." The difficulties experienced by the first women cadets at the Naval Academy have continued into the 1990s with sexual harassment complaints and hazing scandals making headlines. Marsha Evans, who became the navy's first woman battalion commander in 1986, has stated that even after a decade of attending the academy, women are still being "treated badly." "I couldn't believe the sexism," she has reported, "the lack of respect for me as a woman." Carol Burke, a former history professor at the academy, in an article in 1992 described academy traditions that were demeaning to women, including jokes and marching songs that described graphic violence against women and sexual abuse.

The evidence of a pervasive climate of demeaning behavior toward women and its tolerance by those in command of the navy gained greater public awareness in the light of the navy's 1991 Tailhook scandal, in which navy aviators and top brass cavorted in a Las Vegas hotel, wearing T-shirts reading "Women Are Property." Scantily clad women tended bar while strippers ended up nude and participating in simulated sex acts with drunken members of the audience (including active and retired admirals and lower-ranking officers). At least twenty-five women were made to run the "gauntlet" of as many as seventy groping male officers. Revelations about the Tailhook sex scandals led the U.S. Senate in 1992 to hold up the promotions and transfers of nearly nine thousand navy personnel and marines until they could prove that were not involved. Two admirals were fired, and one was reassigned. A 1993 report by the

Senior midshipmen at the U.S. Naval Academy in Annapolis, Maryland, congratulate each other in 1992 after one of their graduation ceremonies. *U.S. Navy/Defense Visual Information Center*

Pentagon's inspector general found that 49 civilian women, 22 service-women, 6 female government employees, 6 wives, and 6 servicemen were victims of sexual abuse at the Tailhook convention and recommended that at least 140 officers be brought up on disciplinary charges.

Although incidents like that at Tailhook point to much larger issues of behavior and attitudes to women by the military, much of the resentment expressed by students and faculty at the military academies toward women has its origin in the basic notion that women simply do not measure up. As Jeanne Holm has written in her study, *Women in the Military: An Unfinished Revolution*, "Much of this resentment centered not just around preconceived ideas of what a woman is for, but around the perception that women are not fully part of the team and, hence, do not really belong at the academies." Despite women cadets' strong performance in training and physical exercise and evidence that combat readiness and performance are not adversely affected by women soldiers, opposition to women at the service academies has persisted, particularly among alumni who hold important positions in the U.S. military. In 1979 James Webb, a 1968 Annapolis graduate and former secretary of the navy, wrote an article in the *Washingtonian* called "Women Can't Fight" that lamented changes at the Naval Academy and argued that the physical and mental punishment inflicted on cadets, which he saw as being undermined by admitting women, weakened the officer corps and made them less prepared to deal with the horrors of war. The issue of women in the military, particularly in combat, would continue to influence women's status at the service academies as the military has struggled to define itself around the relatively new concept of coeducation.

Evidence suggests that women in the service academies are rapidly closing the gap in the physical difference between men and women. Studies at West Point have shown that although women have less upper-body strength than men, they possess the same abdominal strength. They have, on average, more acute hearing, are better able to withstand cold, and can burn up fat more efficiently for better endurance on long runs. A possible result of Title IX of the Education Act of 1972, which banned public schools from discriminating against girls' sports programs, has been the increasing participation of girls in competitive sports. By the 1990s it was reported that women at the military academies were able to do more push-ups and pull-ups than their predecessors. Overcoming the emotional and institutional barriers to women in the service academies, however, may continue to prove more difficult than conquering physical obstacles.

1980–1989

During the 1980s, often labeled the decade of the young urban professional, or "yuppie," the emphasis was on the importance of dressing for success in the corporate world. This young woman, a success motivator, had the right look.
Marjorie Nichols/The Schlesinger Library, Radcliffe College

1983

Sally Ride Becomes the First U.S. Woman Astronaut in Space

> At first I was worried that NASA might be setting out to choose a token woman. But out of the thirty-five chosen, six were women. That's not tokenism. I believe that one-third of the scientists at NASA are women.
>
> Sally Ride, on her acceptance in 1978 as an astronaut candidate, quoted in Karen O'Connor, *Sally Ride and the New Astronauts: Scientists in Space*

In June 1983, aboard the space shuttle *Challenger*, astronaut Sally Ride spent six days in orbit as a flight engineer, becoming the first American female astronaut in space twenty years after the first woman orbited above the earth. As they had done in the early days of the space program, the Russians had preceded the United States with woman cosmonaut Valentina Tereshkova, who, in June 1963 aboard *Vostok 6*, spent three days in space and circled the Earth forty-eight times, more orbits than the six previous American male astronauts combined. Like other young Soviet men and women after the August 1961 flight of cosmonaut Gherman Titov, Tereshkova had volunteered to join the Russian space program. She was one of four women parachutists accepted for training. Although most cosmonaut memoirs claim that the women were welcomed "like brothers" by the pilots, Tereshkova admitted years later to an American in the *Apollo-Soyuz* project that the other cosmonauts avoided her "because I have invaded their little playground and because I am a woman." In 1982, nineteen years after Valentina Tereshkova's pioneering flight, Svetlana Savitskaya became the second woman to fly in space on *Soyuz T-7* and aboard the *Salyut 7* space station. Despite having sent the first and second woman into space, Soviet officials disbanded the program to recruit and train female cosmonauts out of their concern

The first six women astronaut candidates, 1978 (*left to right*): Shannon Lucid, Rhea Seddon, Kathryn Sullivan, Judith Resnick, Anna Fisher, and Sally Ride   *NASA*

for the effect of cosmonaut training on women and their families. In 1980 cosmonaut chief Vladimir Shatalov insisted that "we just have no moral right to subject the 'better half' of mankind to such [physical] loads."

When NASA was formed in 1958, President Eisenhower had ordered the agency to choose only military test pilots for the program. Because the pilots were in the military, the records of their training and experience were readily available and they already had security clearances. With women not allowed in combat, there were no female military test pilots. The military requirement was dropped for the second group of astronauts, chosen in 1962. Congress, however, ruled that admitting women to the space program at that point would delay the goal of putting a *man* on the moon before the end of the 1960s. However, the 1972 amendment to the Civil Rights Act of 1964 prevented federal agencies, such as NASA, from discriminating on the basis of sex, race, or national origin, and NASA could no longer exclude women from the astronaut program. Additionally, with the inception of the space shuttle program, in which as many as five mission specialists could join the shuttle's pilots, more opportunities for astronaut crews opened up. NASA's call to recruit its eighth astronaut class, in July 1976, urged women and minorities to apply. By June 1977 over 8,000, including 1,251 women, had applied. Of these, 208 were invited to NASA Johnson Space Center for a week of interviews and medical tests. Finally, on January, 16, 1978, 35 new astronaut candidates (15 pilots and 20 mission specialists) were selected. Six were women: two physicians (Dr. Anna Fisher and Dr. Rhea Seddon), a biochemist (Dr. Shannon Lucid), a physicist (Dr. Sally Ride), a geophysicist (Dr. Kathryn Sullivan), and an engineer (Dr. Judith Resnik). *Apollo* veteran Alan Bean, given the responsibility of training the 1978 class, was initially opposed to women in the space program. "At first I imagined they were just individuals trying to do a man's job," Bean admitted. "I was proven wrong. . . . Females intuitively understand astronaut skills. They perform the mental and physical tasks as well as men." The women underwent the same training and testing as the men, and only a few gender accommodations were made. The seats in the shuttle were changed so they could be adjusted to women's shorter legs, for example, and the selection of personal gear that astronauts could take on the shuttle was expanded to include tampons, skin moisturizers, and "hair restraints."

Eventually, Sally Ride was selected for the seventh shuttle flight, *STS-7*, with a qualifying statement issued by NASA: "Since the women are there because of their skills, Dr. Ride's selection for *STS-7* doesn't imply that she is the best of the women astronauts. Her skills were most needed on this particular mission." Reaction to her selection by her fellow women astronauts was envious but supportive. "Any one of us would like to swap places with Sally," Kathryn Sullivan admitted, "yet being first brings with it an added load of responsibility. I don't know that any one of us can ever put all the skeptics to rest, and it's unfair that Sally should have the burden entirely on her shoulders." Mary Cleave, accepted into the space program in 1980, reported, "Sally was selected for this flight as testimony to her ability to perform the job. . . . There will be a bunch of little girls on this planet who will be looking at Sally and saying, 'Hey, if I want to be an astrophysicist, that's okay.' It gives girls of today options we didn't have when we were kids."

Born in Encino, California, in 1951, Sally Ride had dreamed of being an astronaut from childhood, before the manned space program. She was an exceptional student and athlete, a star college tennis player, and a member of the Stanford University women's rugby team. She graduated from Stanford in 1973, earning a BS in physics and a BA in English literature. She remained at Stanford to gain a Ph.D. in astrophysics and was working there as a teaching assistant and researcher when she was selected as an astronaut. After she was named as the first American woman scheduled to fly in the space shuttle, media attention leading up to her flight was intense. Her name, coincidentally the same as a popular 1960s song, prompted a number of headlines urging her to "Ride, Sally Ride." But Ride continually diverted attention from herself to her role as a member of her crew's team and insisted that she considered herself a scientist, not a *female* scientist. During her six-day *STS-7* flight, in which at age thirty-one Ride was also the youngest American to go into orbit, she took part in the deployment of two communications satellites and in the deployment and retrieval of the German-built Shuttle Pallet Satellite (SPAS-01). She returned to space in October 1984 aboard Shuttle Mission 41-G, in which she deployed the Earth Radiation Budget Satellite and took part in scientific observations of planet Earth. It was during this flight that Kathryn Sullivan, her fellow member of the class of 1978, became the first American woman to walk in space. Ride's third mission, aboard *61-M*, was scheduled for the summer of 1986 but was suspended after the *Challenger* disaster, which took the life of Ride's colleague from the class of 1978, Judith Resnik, the second American woman to go into space. Ride served as the astronaut office representative to the presidential commission investigating the *Challenger* explosion. She continued to work for NASA until 1987, serving as assistant to NASA administrator James Fletcher at NASA headquarters in Washington, D.C., before returning to Stanford for an academic post.

In the wake of the *Challenger* disaster and the death of Christa McAuliffe, the New Hampshire schoolteacher who was chosen from 10,463 applicants as the first private citizen to go into space, NASA suspended shuttle flights for nearly three years, halted regular astronaut recruitment, and began to reconsider the selection of passengers outside the ranks of the military. Since its inception in 1959 the American space program has employed 268 astronauts, about 12 percent of whom have been women. Since 1991 about 30 percent of NASA's overall workforce has been female. With little fanfare compared with that which surrounded Sally Ride's initial flight, Air Force Lieutenant Colonel Eileen Collins became the nation's first woman space shuttle pilot on *STS-63* in 1995; she is scheduled to be NASA's first woman commander of *STS-93*, projected for December 1998. During the 1990s, as NASA's missions have grown more routine in the public's mind, all of America's astronauts, male and female, have receded from the celebrity spotlight, concentrating instead on simply doing their jobs during space flights. The initial 1978 group of women astronauts helped to transform the space program into a working environment open to extremely talented but regular professionals, broadening the concept of the "right stuff" to include individuals of diverse backgrounds and capabilities. Women astronauts have also served to inspire girls to consider careers in science and space and to challenge prevalent notions concerning the ability of women to withstand the demands of space exploration. Ride and the other original women astronauts have insured that in the future both genders will be equally represented in the frontiers of space.

1985

EMILY's List Is Founded to Help Fund Women's Political Campaigns

> You go out and look at your budgets. You think about your priorities.
> Do you want that new pair of shoes, or do you want to be
> represented by Carol Moseley-Braun?
>
> > Ellen Malcolm, founder of EMILY's List,
> > speaking at an Illinois fund-raiser during the campaign
> > of Carol Moseley-Braun in 1992

> Having EMILY's List target your race provides a tremendous
> amount of credibility. People know that they don't just endorse
> candidates they think are good, but who are good and who have
> a shot at winning.
>
> > Jeanne Shaheen, elected governor of New Hampshire in 1996

EMILY's List, the political action committee (PAC) founded by political activist Ellen Malcolm in her Washington basement in 1985, has grown to become the largest PAC in the country and has been called "the best new idea in politics." At the time of its inception, "Nobody took women candidates seriously," Malcolm recalls. "They faced a tremendous credibility gap that played itself out in making it difficult to raise money to compete. And because they couldn't raise money, they couldn't put together a winning campaign. So they were caught in a real vicious circle." EMILY's List was conceived as a way of breaking that circle with early financial support on behalf of Democratic pro-choice women candidates. Its name is an acronym for Early Money Is Like Yeast (it raises dough). Since it started, its membership has grown to forty-five thousand, and EMILY's List has played a significant part in electing forty-two House members, six senators, and three governors.

The brainchild of IBM heiress Ellen Malcolm, EMILY's List grew out

Ellen Malcolm, the founder and president of EMILY's List *Shonna Valeska/EMILY's List*

of Malcolm's developing political involvement and her somewhat painful coming to terms with her wealth and activism. Malcolm's parents both worked for IBM, where her father was a salesman and her mother was an assistant in the sales department. Only six months old when her father died, Malcolm became the sole heir of her father's fortune, which he had inherited from his grandfather, A. Ward Ford, a partner in a business machine company that became IBM. When she was growing up, however, Malcolm did not have a sense that she was richer than her friends in Montclair, New Jersey, an upper-middle-class suburb of New York City. "We were not a jet-setter family," she says. "We had a station wagon and two golden retrievers." Malcolm attended Hollins College in Virginia and became close to friends with backgrounds very different from her family's. By 1968 she had signed on to help in Eugene McCarthy's presidential campaign and went home to Montclair to register voters as Democrats, while her mother was running as a Republican committeewoman. In 1970 Malcolm came to Washington and worked for five years at Common Cause, first as a volunteer and then as a paid field coordinator. Undecided what to do next, she began a process of reassessment. "I think when you have enough money that you don't have to work for a living," she has said, "in some kind of backward way, it makes the choices very difficult."

Malcolm bought a house in Washington and in 1977 went to work as the media director of the National Women's Political Caucus (NWPC), where she met Lael Stegal, then NWPC's development director. Stegal was interested in looking for ways to channel money to women's organizations, and Malcolm confessed to her that she had inherited money and was unsure how to handle it. It was one of the few times that Malcolm had revealed the secret of her wealth to anyone outside her family and its financial advisers. By 1980 Malcolm needed for tax reasons to contribute between $200,000 and $300,000 to deductible causes and with Stegal's assistance began to make funding decisions through a foundation named the Windom Fund after the street Malcolm was living on at the time. Determined to remain anonymous, Malcolm invented a donor, Henrietta C. Windom, who would serve as the public benefactor. While channeling donations to a number of women's political causes, Malcolm enrolled in the MBA program at George Washington University to learn how to manage her fortune herself, and she subsequently increased her assets while focusing her political skills and funds into the strategy that created EMILY's List.

After the bitter defeat of Harriett Woods of Missouri in her first Senate bid in 1982, Malcolm, Stegal, and several women they had met at the National Women's Political Caucus formed a group to determine what they would have to do to elect the first Democratic woman to the Senate. All agreed that the principal stumbling block was the catch-22 of female candidates, identified by Joan Mondale, a member of EMILY's List advisory board: "You see, what happens to women is that people say they can't win. So they won't give them money. Then they can't raise money. And then they can't win. It's a vicious cycle." To remedy this, twenty-five women gathered in Malcolm's basement in 1985 and launched a letter-writing campaign, asking their friends to join them, to establish a donor network. The name "Emily," which Malcolm made up and feared was "dumb," proved to be an inspiration. As she explains, "If we had decided to become the Democratic Women's Early Money Fund, we probably would have raised $1.98 by now." Members joined for $100, which supported the office, the newsletter, and mailings on behalf of candidates. Members also committed to give at least $100 every two years to two or three candidates endorsed by the list. Under federal election laws, PACs are limited to a $5,000 contribution per candidate in federal races, and individuals are restricted to $1,000 contributions to any one candidate. However, there is no limit to how many individual contributions can be solicited and "bundled" (sent directly to a candidate) as long as checks are written directly to the candidates and the donor network does not cash them. Members of EMILY's List receive candidate profiles and campaign assessments to help them make their choice and then send their checks to EMILY's List, where they are collected and sent to the candidates. To be endorsed by EMILY's List, a candidate must support the Equal Rights Amendment and a woman's right to choose an abortion. As Malcolm has remarked, "Those two issues really are signals to let us know how these women feel about issues overall." Candidates also must be Democrats and stand a good chance of winning. EMILY's List candidates are required not to support or oppose any particular legislation, but to perform their elected position with integrity and good faith.

By the 1986 elections Malcolm had enlisted 1,200 donors from whom she raised nearly $500,000. EMILY's List endorsed two candidates for the U.S. Senate, and Barbara Mikulski of Maryland was victorious, becoming the first Democratic woman senator. Mikulski has attributed her success to the important backing of EMILY's List and its $150,000 contribution. Ahead in the polls, she still could not get the contributions she needed. As Mikulski observes, "We women used to be bake-sale candidates, but Ellen taps into a constituency of professional women who give more." Malcolm had exploited the financial resources of women like herself who had come of age in the late 1960s and 1970s and created the means by which they could ante up to elect other like-minded women. "I used to say we need to teach women how to put zeroes on their checks," Malcolm says. "By 1986, we found a group who'd learned."

Between 1991 and 1992 membership soared from 3,500 to 24,000 in response to the Anita Hill–Clarence Thomas sexual harassment hearings. As Laura Liswood, director of the Council of Women World Leaders at Harvard, has observed, "Women were getting more money themselves and beginning to have discretionary income, women were in the workforce, there were a lot of open [congressional] seats, and, then, they got a big hit after Anita Hill. They [EMILY's List] became the focal point, which heretofore hadn't existed or existed in only a scattered way, for women to unite their energies." EMILY's List was one of the decisive factors in the unprecedented increased representation by women in the House and the Senate after the 1992 election.

By the 1996 elections, members of EMILY's List had written 62,000 individual checks to female candidates for a total of $6.7 million to 204 state and federal campaigns. EMILY's List and Ellen Malcolm have become power brokers to be reckoned with. As Laura Liswood has observed, "Once you become the eight-hundred-pound canary, you get to sing anywhere." Republican women have imitated EMILY's List by forming the WISH List (Women in the Senate and the House) in 1992 to elect Republican women who support abortion rights, and the Susan B. Anthony List, which endorses women of either party who oppose abortion. Organizations on the state level have also been created, such as May's List in Washington State. All recognize the fundamental fact that EMILY's List understood in 1985: If women are to be successful as political candidates, money must be raised and other women mobilized on behalf of women candidates. Although some members of EMILY's List are well-known celebrities, the average member is a working woman who can give $250 to $500 every two years. EMILY's List has created an organization to enable more women to become active in voicing their preferences to help insure that women candidates can more equally compete with their male counterparts.

1986

The Supreme Court Rules Against
Sexual Harassment

That all the stereotypes about women who experience harassment
were paraded out: from the aggressive, oversexed female, to the
disgruntled employee who couldn't cut it and so had to invent a
story, to the rejected suitor who was being vindictive, to the person
who was mentally deranged. They were all offered as explanations
for the very difficult, heartfelt experiences of women throughout
the world. That angers me. I didn't expect the senators to be
experts on sexual harassment, but I did expect them to educate
themselves and not perpetuate these myths.

> Anita Hill, responding to a question in the *New York Times Magazine* in
> 1997 about what still makes her angry concerning sexual harassment

In the last decades of the twentieth century, with greater numbers of
women in the workforce and workers spending more time on the job
than at home, perhaps no workplace issue became as fraught with so
much complexity and controversy as the question of what constituted
sexual harassment. Sexual harassment laws and policies attempted to
draw sharp lines of appropriate and inappropriate behavior between
women and men, supervisor and employee, but could not always serve
to define what are often vague matters of perception and the heart or
close the gap between free expression of speech and feelings.

In 1976 a groundbreaking survey showed that 90 percent of the nine
thousand women who had responded said they had been sexually
harassed on the job. Up to that time, the only recourse for women who
faced unrelenting sexual pressure at work was to quit. Lawyers and
women's groups increasingly began to feel that Title VII of the Civil
Rights Act of 1964, barring job discrimination on the basis of sex, might
be used against sexual coercion on the job. The courts, however, were

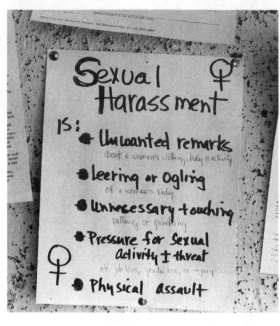

Sexual
Harassment
IS:
• Unwanted remarks
  about a woman's clothing, body or activity
• Leering or Ogling
  of a woman's body
• Unnecessary touching
  patting or pinching
• Pressure for Sexual
  Activity ± threat
  of job loss, grade loss, or injury
• Physical assault

A notice displayed at New York University's Loeb Student Center in 1981 listed the different forms of sexual harassment. *Photo by Bettye Lane*

not sympathetic, ruling that harassment was a private matter, not a legal one. The legal theory that paved the way for a judicial attitude change was supplied by a young Yale University legal scholar, Catherine A. MacKinnon. In her 1979 study, *Sexual Harassment of Working Women*, MacKinnon demonstrated that sexual harassment "wasn't personal, it wasn't biological, it wasn't trivial or interpersonally romantic. What it was was group-based, based on sex—because a person is a woman, a member of a social group." According to MacKinnon, women who became involved with their superiors sexually had little choice, regardless of whether the relationship was consensual. Sexual harassment, therefore, was a form of sex discrimination. MacKinnon's theory tying harassment with discrimination had a powerful influence on legal thinking as the Supreme Court took up its first sexual harassment case in 1986.

The case, *Meritor Savings Bank* v. *Vinson*, involved consensual sex between bank teller Mechele Vinson and her boss. In the 1970s Vinson claimed that her boss began to ask her for dates. At first she declined, but eventually she relented, and she estimated that they had sex forty or fifty times. She claimed that she had been pressured into the relationship and that he had exposed himself, groped her at work, and even raped her several times. Vinson was never fired or demoted when she objected. Vinson lost her court case, but with the support of several women's groups she appealed, with MacKinnon as one of her lawyers, to the Supreme Court. The Court ruled in her favor, arguing that sexual harassment so "severe or pervasive" as to "alter the conditions of employment and create an abusive working environment violated Title VII." William H. Rehnquist, then an associate justice, supported the view that it did not matter whether Vinson consented to the sex. He wrote, "The correct inquiry is whether respondent by her conduct indicated that the alleged sexual advances were unwelcome, not whether her actual participation in sexual intercourse was voluntary."

The Supreme Court's groundbreaking ruling not only justified prosecuting sexual harassment as a form of sex discrimination, but held that speech or conduct in itself can create a "hostile environment," like the one Vinson alleged at Meritor, and that unwelcome verbal or physical behavior, if "severe or pervasive" enough, is discriminatory even when there are no adverse job effects for resisting. The issue of who is liable for a supervisor's harassing actions was left unclear, and the Court's ruling left companies scrambling to institute sexual harassment policies, including total bans on interoffice relationships and such famous overreactions as the dismissal of a Miller Brewing executive for recounting to a co-worker what was perceived to be a sexually provocative episode of the *Seinfeld* TV sitcom.

High-profile cases of sexual harassment spurred a national debate on sex in the workplace and appropriate or inappropriate behavior on the job. The most famous was the 1991 televised Senate Judiciary Committee confirmation hearings on the nomination of Clarence Thomas to the Supreme Court, in which Anita Hill testified that Thomas had sexually harassed her during his tenure as chairman of the Equal Employment Opportunity Commission. The Senate Judiciary Committee at first refused to act on Hill's charges, but when they became public and seven women members of the House of Representatives protested the committee's inappropriate response to Hill's charges, Hill was called to testify. Hill recounted Thomas's offensive behavior and advances that she repeatedly rejected, which finally caused her to resign from the EEOC. Hill was treated with scant civility by the all-male committee, accused of being a "woman scorned," of fabricating her story from the pages of a lurid novel, and of being the pawn of feminist and liberal groups opposed to the Thomas nomination. Thomas denied all of Hill's allegations and charged that he was a victim of an "electronic lynching." The Senate Judiciary Committee voted in favor of Thomas's confirmation, and although polls indicated that most women did not believe that Thomas was in fact guilty of sexual harassment, Anita Hill's treatment by the committee outraged many others, sparking a national debate on what constituted sexual harassment and how workplace relationships should be handled.

The 1994 civil suit brought by Paula Jones against President Bill Clinton in which she accused him of "sexually harassing and assaulting" her at the Excelsior Hotel in Little Rock in 1991 similarly made sexual harassment front-page news. Jones's case was finally dismissed in 1998 by Judge Susan Webber Wright, who ruled that she had not proven her charge that she had suffered job setbacks or psychological damage from the incident. The alleged conduct, though "boorish and offensive" in Wright's opinion, "was brief and isolated; did not result in any physical harm . . . did not result in distress so severe that no reasonable person could be expected to endure it." The later accusation that President Clinton engaged in sexual relationship with a White House intern, Monica Lewinsky, likewise generated intense controversy over what is and is not appropriate behavior between supervisors and employees, between private acts and public responsibility.

In June 1998 the Supreme Court clarified the often confusing and contradictory case laws on sexual harassment in the workplace after its 1986 ruling in decisions that made some lawsuits against employers easier to win while limiting the legal exposure of companies that have effective antiharassment policies in place. The Court affirmed its position that an employee who resists a supervisor's advances need not have suffered a tangible job detriment to pursue a lawsuit against a company, but that if a company has an antiharassment policy with an effective complaint procedure, the employee is expected to use it. The Court's ruling was praised by both management and civil rights groups for bringing coherence to sexual harassment laws and providing incentives for preventing harassment. "It's a win-win for employers and for all women in America," said Kathy Rodgers, executive director of the NOW Legal Defense and Education Fund.

Amid the titillation and controversy over sexual harassment cases, it is important not to overlook the core issue of equal opportunity for women in which sex should not become a means for either advancing or impeding employment prospects. The challenge raised by sexual harassment prevention is how a sexually neutral workplace can be achieved without compensating sacrifices of free speech and natural human expression. To ward off abuses, there has been a chilling side effect in the modern workplace of repression of even the most innocuous remark or gesture for fear it may be misconstrued as harassment. Men have been, unfairly in some cases, cast in the role of sexual predators, while women have been seen as helpless victims who need special protection. The challenge remains to find the balance between the public and the private, between respect for equality and protection of personal freedom, while continuing legal intervention in situations where sexual harassment does take place.

1988

The Supreme Court Prohibits Discrimination Against Women in Private Social Clubs

> It's caused great personal schisms. The feelings run very, very high.
> Guys that used to be friends don't speak to each other anymore. It's
> very unfortunate.
>
> On a couple of occasions I felt I was damn near about to come to
> blows with an older chap, a hard core, anti-woman type. I've never
> gotten so mad at somebody who's not a member of my family.
>
> Comments by two members of New York City's Century Club
over the issue of accepting women members, quoted in
the New York Times, August 22, 1987

Along with military colleges, men's private social clubs, those bastions
of male exclusivity and bonding, were the last remaining organizations
that finally, reluctantly, opened their doors to women members in the
late 1980s. In the face of the anticipated Supreme Court decision supporting a New York City law prohibiting sexual discrimination by social
clubs that finally came down in 1988, a number of Manhattan's oldest
and most exclusive all-male clubs scrambled to redefine their stand on
admitting women. The most contentious battle was waged at New York's
Century Club, located in a stately baroque revival building near Fifth
Avenue. Its 1,900 members were drawn from New York's cultural, professional, and political worlds, and the issue of admitting women had
split its ranks for years.

Opening the club to women would "break down the effortless, uncon-
strained companionship among men and the casual freedom of association," as an internal 1982 club petition asserted. Opponents invoked the
example of Margaret Mead, who, it is alleged, was asked to consider
joining the club around 1970. "She wrote a letter thanking the club for
the honor," remembers artist Sidney Simon. "But she said that from her

New York's stately Century Club. In 1987 members of this exclusive male preserve
fought a contentious battle over whether or not to admit women.   *The Century
Association*

wide experience with civilization, society always had a need for a place
where men can be by themselves and where women can be by themselves, and she declined." Some members resigned over the issue,
including Judge Robert H. Bork, President Reagan's nominee for the
Supreme Court, who quit in 1985. Other men refused nomination to the
club. In 1986 the New York Commission on Human Rights began to
apply pressure on the Century Club when it began to investigate
whether the club was violating Local Law 63, enacted in 1984, which
forbids discrimination against women in business establishments that are
not "distinctly private" and therefore are places of "public accommodation." According to the law, an establishment is not "distinctly private"
if it has a membership of more than four hundred, if it serves regular
meals (at which business will likely be done), if its dues are sometimes
paid by members' employers, and if nonmembers sometimes rent private rooms for parties and meetings. The Century Club met all these
disqualifying conditions. In their defense, many members denied that
business was done in the club. It was, they contended, a club for relaxed
and enlightened discussion of arts and letters. But as Richard Kahn, a
New York real estate developer, has pointed out, "It's a wonderful social

club, but it's not merely that. There's all sorts of bonding and either direct or indirect business going on. It's usually very subtle, but it clearly affects people's careers, and not being there can be detrimental."

Kahn's observation makes it clear why women's groups have fought for admission into such protected male sanctuaries as part of their quest for equal opportunities in business careers. Men's clubs, like the Century, represent an informal network of connections that advances men's careers. As such, women, they argue, are entitled to share in these advantages. After efforts by the Century Club to change club policies to make it "distinctly private" failed, in a straw poll conducted in August 1987 members voted overwhelmingly (70 percent in favor and 28 percent opposed) to admit women if Local Law 63 was upheld by the Supreme Court as constitutional. As Timothy Prentice, a sculptor and club member, said of the poll results, "I'm greatly cheered by this. For a long time, members said, 'Not now, not too soon.' It was like apartheid—apartheid in a teapot. But now it's been aired long enough that people realize it's inevitable."

Around the country private clubs that maintained one-sex-only membership policies faced similar pressure to change. As Aubrey King, a vice president and director of government relations for the National Club Association, which represents one thousand private clubs in the United States, observed in the fall of 1987, "We're facing an inquisition, and it's spreading rapidly around the country." Some clubs, fearing resistance to the new laws would be too costly, bowed to the inevitable. But other clubs put up a costly legal fight. "This law has been bitterly challenged. It's been quite extraordinary," said Carol Ziegler, general counsel for the New York City Commission on Human Rights, which is responsible for making private clubs comply with the law. "It's amazing the amount of money and time some of these clubs have been willing to commit to battle this."

Finally, the issue of the constitutionality of New York's Local Law 63 was argued before the Supreme Court on February 23, 1988, and on June 20, 1988, the Court unanimously decided in favor of the New York City statute. In the wording of the Court's ruling:

> On its face, Local Law 63 does not affect "in any significant way" the ability of individuals to form associations that will advocate public or private viewpoints. . . . It does not require the clubs "to abandon or alter" any activities that are protected by the First Amendment. . . . Instead, the Law merely prevents an association from using race, sex, and other specified characteristics as shorthand measures in place of what the city considers to be more legitimate criteria for determining membership.

With its ruling, the Supreme Court allowed the New York law to stand and supported the contention that social clubs like the Century are private clubs in name only, that in terms of size, services, and financing, such clubs function as places of public accommodation and therefore must not discriminate by race or gender. By accepting this distinction, the Court helped end the barriers that private clubs placed in the career paths of female professionals. Despite dire predictions that admitting women would end private, single-gender clubs in America, clubs with women members have persisted and flourished, proving that ending sexual discrimination in membership was the right thing to do. As Nobel Prize winner in economics and Century Club member Wassily Leontief argued in support of admitting women, "We should help strengthen the position of women in our life in the United States. We are like an eight-cylinder car that only runs on six cylinders, or four cylinders."

1990–1999

The 1990s may be looked back upon as the decade of the family.
Many women of the '90s were working mothers who, with their
husbands, tried to balance the demands of a career with the joys of
family life.

1992

The American Association of University Women Publishes *How Schools Shortchange Girls*

Construction of the glass ceiling begins not in the executive suite but in the classroom. It starts in preschool, when girls get less teacher attention, and lessons focus on the developmental needs of boys. By the time the girls reach high school, they have been systematically tracked toward traditional sex-segregated jobs, away from areas of study that lead to high-paying jobs in science, technology, and engineering. . . . America cannot afford to squander half its talent.

> Alice McKee, president of the American Association of University Women Educational Foundation

In February 1992 the American Association of University Women (AAUW) released "How Schools Shortchange Girls," a report reflecting the most comprehensive research ever conducted to assess the gender gap in American schools. The study presented "compelling evidence that girls are not receiving the same quality, or even the quantity, of education as their brothers," according to AAUW Educational Foundation president Alice McKee, who went on to say in the report's foreword, "This latest report presents the truth behind the myth—that boys and girls receive equal education. The wealth of statistical evidence must convince even the most skeptical that gender bias in our schools is short-changing girls—and compromising our country." The report offered this disturbing conclusion despite considerable gains among women in measures of educational success. In 1970 5 million college students were male, and 3.5 were female. In 1989 7.3 million were female and 6.5 were male. Only 8 percent of medical degrees were awarded to women in 1970; by 1989 33 percent went to women. Even with these quantitative gains, the study suggested there existed a qualitative imbalance in gender performance in schools. "The bias that exists in how girls are taught is no longer blatant," Sharon Schuster, president of the AAUW, explained, "but they experience it on a daily basis." Despite the fact that girls got better grades than boys and were more likely to go on to college, girls, according to the report, had less confidence in their abilities, had higher expectations of failure, and developed more modest career aspirations. The result, the report concluded, was that girls were less likely to reach their potential than boys. "How Schools Shortchange Girls" set out to document this dilemma, explain its causes, and offer solutions.

Researchers at the Wellesley College Center for Research on Women examined more than one thousand publications about girls and education, including hundreds of research studies. They concluded that teachers paid less attention to girls; girls still lagged behind boys in math and science scores, and even those who did well in those subjects tended not to choose math and science careers; sexual harassment of girls by boys was increasing; tests remained biased against girls, hurting their chances of scholarships and college admission; textbooks ignored or stereotyped women; and girls learned almost nothing about such pressing topics they face as sexual abuse, discrimination, and depression. The study suggested that although girls and boys started school roughly equal in skills and confidence, gender bias quickly and negatively affected girls' performance and undermined their self-esteem. Teachers tended to pay more attention to boys in class and to give them more encouragement. If boys called out in class, teachers listened. When girls called out, they were often told to raise their hands if they wanted to speak. Boys ironically did well by being bad. They were the troublemakers who intimidated girls into silence and demanded an inordinate amount of teachers' attention. Research also indicated that educators from the preschool level and beyond tended to choose classroom activities that appeal to boys. Girls tended to learn better in cooperative settings where students work together, while boys learned better in competitive settings that have formed the educational model for most schools. The differences between the sexes was deemed to be greatest in science. Even though girls and boys took about the same number of science courses, several studies suggested that teachers encouraged male students to work with laboratory equipment, especially in the more complex sciences. For example, one study found that 51 percent of boys in third grade had used a microscope, compared with 37 percent of girls. Even those girls who did well in science and mathematics tended not to pursue careers in those fields. Studies of girls who continued to study science after high school showed that encouragement by teachers was crucial in their decision.

By high school, girls were experiencing deep feelings of inadequacy and a lack of academic confidence that was expressed in a number of ways. Girls did not participate in equal proportion to boys in advanced-level courses. In one survey, 7.6 percent of boys chose calculus, compared with 4.7 percent of girls; one-fourth of high school boys took physics, but only 15 percent of girls did. The study also showed that vocational education programs were often geared to males despite the fact that 45 percent of the workforce was female. There existed a gender gap in scores on standardized tests, especially in math and science, which the report blamed partly on lingering bias in both testing and the curriculum. In 1991 boys beat girls on the college-admission SAT test by eight points in the verbal score and forty-four points in math. Lacking self-confidence and encouragement from teachers, girls were also subjected to sexual harassment from their male classmates, behavior that the report asserted was tolerated by teachers. As the report stated, "Students sit in classrooms that, day in, day out, deliver the message that women's lives count for less than men's."

Included among the forty recommendations in the report for changes to correct the gender bias girls experienced in schools were enactment and enforcement of policies against sexual harassment, stricter enforcement of Title IX (the federal law that prohibits discrimination in educational institutions), and the revision of the curriculum to emphasize the experiences of girls and women. Educators were urged to help girls develop a positive self-image, to encourage them to study math and science to enhance career opportunities, to create gender-neutral tests, and to incorporate teaching methods that could lower or eliminate gender gaps in the classroom. Perhaps the greatest significance of the AAUW report was to call attention to the problems faced by girls in schools that had been previously ignored. "A lot of what is going on is unintentional," observed Keith Geiger, president of the National Education Association, whose members were urged to implement many of the report's recommendations, "but the fact is that in our schools, we treat girls differently than we do boys. . . . We need to raise people's consciousness and bring about constructive change." The report supported many of the findings uncovered by psychologist Carol Gilligan, who diagnosed a developmental crisis among adolescent girls that their school experience exacerbates. Eating disorders, high rates of depression and suicide, and low physical and mental esteem were all symptoms of complex problems that the report highlighted. (It should be noted, however, that by the end of the decade the rate of teen suicide was greater among boys than girls.)

Critics argued that the report underplayed the considerable advances women have made academically, pointing out that girls were more likely to finish high school than boys and to attend colleges and universities in greater numbers, and that the gender gap in professional schools was closing. Diane Ravitch, an assistant secretary of education, complained that much of the report was "just special pleading and, frankly, whining." She argued that researchers "picked the wrong target" and that rather than sexism in education, the problem was sexist attitudes encouraged by television, advertising, and the movies. Others charged that by overdramatizing gender bias and downplaying considerable improvements, the AAUW insured front-page publicity but distorted a more complex problem surrounding girls' academic performance. One logical solution to the differences in classroom behavior, ignored by the AAUW report, would be single-sex schools where male behavior would no longer be able to set the tone for female learning. Other solutions, critics argued, such as making sure that an equal number of female and male authors are taught, made a social and cultural point but had dubious educational validity. Others charged that the report's focus on the problems of girls masked much larger problems inherent in American education harmful to both sexes.

Whether gender bias constituted the widespread problem the AAUW report suggested, the heightened awareness of the gender messages students receive and how they are translated into academic performance was raised by the study and remains significant in exposing conscious and unconscious stereotyping that contributes to gender inequality. According to Susan McGee Bailey, director of the Wellesley research center that mounted the study, "I think you can look at any situation and see the progress or see the ways we have to go. But I think it's dangerous to say that because one-third of our medical students are now women the struggle for gender equality is over. There is a great deal more to be done."

✌

An Unprecedented Number of Women
Run for National Office

As recently as the late 1960s, one of the surest means by which a woman could become a member of Congress was to have a husband who was a Congressman die while in office. . . . The difficulty women have had breaking into high elective office on their own is undeniable. The first Republican woman elected to the U.S. Senate

completely on her own merits was Nancy Kassebaum in 1978. The
first Democrat was Barbara Mikulski in 1986. The extremely low
percentage of female candidates who have been elected without the
help of a dead relative is testimony to the social and institutional
road blocks that prevent women from entering into and succeeding
in electoral politics. The "matrimonial connection" no longer offers
the quickest route to Congress for women but many fundamental
questions persist as to whether the congressional election process is
open to female candidates.

Richard Logan Fox, *Gender Dynamics in Congressional Elections*

The unprecedented success of women candidates running for national
office in 1992 set off a media frenzy that loudly proclaimed yet another
"year of the woman" (1974, 1984, and 1990 were also so heralded as
women's years, with only minor electoral gains for female candidates).
With 106 women winning major party nomination for House races, the
number of women in the House almost doubled from 28 to 47 (23 were
reelected incumbents; 24 were newcomers). In 1990 7 percent of the
House membership was female. That percentage increased to 11 percent in 1992 (the same percentage was seen after the 1994 election). In
the Senate, there were 2 women senators in 1990; after 1992 there were
6, with the number increasing to 8 in 1994. Although 1992 undoubtedly
represented a milestone in the history of women seeking and winning
national elective office in the United States, Congress has not come close
to reflecting the gender of the electorate (52 percent of the voting age
population is female). Jeanette Rankin's early call that women representatives should make up "half the House" remains an illusive goal. It is
useful to look closely at the 1992 election to understand the nature of
women's electoral gains and the continuing challenges women politicians
face.

A number of factors came together to cause and make possible the
participation and success of women candidates in 1992. One was the
1991 televised Senate Judiciary Committee's hearings on the nomination of Supreme Court nominee Clarence Thomas. The hearings offered
the powerful and symbolic spectacle of a dignified and plausible law
professor, Anita Hill, who had accused Thomas of sexually harassing her
while she was working for him at the EEOC, being ungraciously and
condescendingly derided by a panel of older white men. Public opinion
widely supported the contention that Hill had been badly treated by the
panel and that the hearing would have been conducted differently if
women were represented on the Senate committee. This served to

Senator Carol Moseley-Braun of Chicago taking a question during a press conference. In 1992 Moseley-Braun became the first African-American woman elected to the U.S. Senate.

mobilize women to action in the 1992 elections as candidates and as vocal and financial supporters of improved political gender representation. The elections also offered opportunities for women candidates on the national level because a large number of women had made a steady climb in local and state politics. In 1970 women held only 4.5 percent of seats in state legislatures; by 1992 that number had risen to 18.4 percent. More women were, therefore, represented in the pool of possible candidates, and the 1992 election offered opportunities for them in greater numbers. In the House of Representatives there were 75 of 435 open seats in which no incumbent was running—more than there had been in over forty years. The recent House banking and postal service scandals also made incumbency a vulnerability.

Equally damaging to incumbents was the widespread public dissatisfaction with the status quo and a demand for change. A CBS News/*New York Times* poll taken in March 1992 indicated that only 18 percent of Americans approved of Congress's job performance, one of the highest levels of voter dissatisfaction recorded since the inception of public opinion polls. Women candidates, able to capitalize on voters' desire for change, were successful in achieving major party nominations for national offices in unprecedented numbers. The resulting media attention in such highly visible races as Carol Moseley-Braun's historical bid to become the first African-American woman senator and the possibility in California that both senators from the nation's most populous state would be women, if Barbara Boxer and Diane Feinstein were elected, helped build momentum during women's campaigns. Political action committees, such as EMILY's List and the Women's Campaign Fund, raised and spent money on behalf of women. EMILY's List alone contributed over $6 million to female candidates, four times greater than their previous record $1.5 million in 1990. Similarly, the Women's Campaign Fund almost doubled its previous record level of contributions.

All these factors helped make the 1992 election one in which women candidates captured media attention, a factor that helped insure the resulting 1992 electoral gains. The successes of 1992 were not repeated in the 1994 elections, however. In 1994, despite record numbers of women candidates in the House (112) and the Senate (9), women gained only one Senate seat and no House seats. By the 1994 race, women candidates had retreated from appeals based on gender and were no longer seen by the media as new and different. In addition, there was no electrifying event such as the Clarence Thomas hearings to mobilize women voters behind women candidates. Without the gender positives from which women candidates profited in 1992, the result of the 1994 election reopens the question of why women have had such difficulty being represented in larger numbers in high elected office.

Women political candidates find themselves in a difficult double bind. As one political consultant has commented about his female client: "You have to be careful in presenting the candidate. She must appear as a likable feminine figure . . . but at the same time she must appear tough and ready to fight political battles. . . . Women have to play two roles as politicians." Responding to voters' still traditional notions about gender traits and roles, women candidates must fulfill expectations as both mother and caretaker of her family and extracompetent public servant, roles that are not always compatible. Women must also be perceived as more socially successful than their male counterparts, maintaining stereotypical feminine qualities, while also showing a toughness and tenacity that proves they can be effective campaigners and legislators, attributes that are contrary to the traditional concept of femininity. Given the heightened scrutiny that candidacy for national office produces, many highly qualified female candidates may not choose to accept the unfair burden or cope with the double messages that women must endure when they enter public life.

Other factors that have adversely affected women politicians are gender discrimination, which promulgates the view that women are not as capable as men, and the socialization that has historically caused women and men to pursue different career paths. The professions from which most politicians are drawn are still dominated by men. In 1980 male lawyers outnumbered female lawyers by six to one; by 1994 the gap had closed to four to one, but the difference remains substantial. In business, only 16 percent of managers and administrators were women in 1970; by 1988 the proportion had risen to 39 percent; and by 1994 the figure was 43 percent, still a significant gap. As a 1994 study conducted by R. Darcy, Susan Welch, and Janet Clark in *Women, Elections, and Representation* concluded: "The fact that women have less education and lower occupational status than do men accounts for a significant part of their underrepresentation in office."

There are, however, signs of changes to come. By the end of the twentieth century women held over 20 percent of the seats in state legislatures, a major base for national candidacy. Political action committees such as EMILY'S List have helped women candidates with important funding to solidify the credibility of women's campaigns. The appointment of such women Cabinet members as Janet Reno and Madeleine Albright also helped change attitudes about women's capacity to hold important national offices. It remains to be seen whether women will continue to be willing to meet the extra challenges faced by female political candidates and whether the playing field can be sufficiently leveled to allow for full and equal representation of women in government.

1993

All Branches of the Military Are Ordered to Examine and Justify Policies That Exclude Women From Combat Duty

> I think women are too valuable to be in combat.
>
> U.S. Secretary of Defense Caspar W. Weinberger to the Defense Advisory Committee, on Women in the Military, 1986

Perhaps no other gender issue surrounding the issue of women's equality has caused as much divisiveness as whether or not women in the military should share combat duty with men. Historically it has been assumed that women would neither want to engage in combat nor be physically or emotionally capable of doing so. War has generally been seen as primarily a male activity from which women have been excluded. Instead women have often been seen not as participants, but as the objects of wars, whose protection has justified combat. Women's role in war has been to inspire and keep the home fires burning as guardians and icons of the ideals of peace and domestic tranquillity, war's opposites. Yet history records numerous examples of women on the battlefield, and increasingly in the twentieth century women have fought to overcome exclusion from war based on their gender, either as an important symbolic sign of full equality with men or as getting over a final barrier to women pursuing leadership careers in the military.

There is evidence of women soldiers on the battlefield disguised as men during the American Revolution, Civil War, and Spanish-American War. From the Revolution to Vietnam, women nurses have served on or close to the battlefield and have been wounded and killed by enemy fire. Yet the military has excluded women from combat duty even as the various military branches have opened up noncombatant service fields to women. The Women's Armed Services Integration Act of 1948 contained provisions that excluded women from combat assignments, including ground combat, air combat, and serving on war vessels in the navy. As women were being integrated into the various branches of service instead of remaining in separate corps, the Combat Exclusion Law remained in effect. The law could be loosely applied to modern warfare, particularly when the boundaries of the modern battlefield are blurred. As Jeanne Holm, author of *Women in the Military: An Unfinished Revolution* and the air force's first brigadier general, has stated, "Modern weapons do not distinguish between combatants and noncombatants." Critics have charged that combat exclusion provisions were being used for purposes of sexual discrimination and to restrict the number of women in the military, and have demanded that more exact distinctions be made between combat and combat support, positions which women could fill despite the exclusionary laws. In 1987 the Department of Defense Task Force on Women in the Military called for clearer standards for evaluating whether certain types of noncombatant positions should be opened to women. The Risk Rule of 1988 was written to provide service branches with a standard for determining how women could serve. Under this rule, noncombatant positions could be closed to women only when they involved "risks of exposure to direct combat, hostile fire, or capture." With this distinction, some thirty thousand additional noncombatant positions were made available to women.

The debate over women in combat intensified during the 1991 Persian Gulf War, during which several women were killed and two army women became prisoners of war. During the war, women served in combat support jobs alongside men, and as Captain Cynthia Mosley, who commanded a combat support company in Iraq, stated, "Nobody cares whether you're male or female. It's just: 'Can you do the job?' " Yet a 1992 poll showed that the American public was about equally divided over the issue of whether or not women should be assigned to combat jobs. Even those who supported the idea did not believe that women should serve in ground troops, only in the air or on combat vessels, and about half of those who favored the idea of lifting the ban on women in combat thought combat participation should be voluntary. On April 23, 1993, Secretary of Defense Les Aspin ordered an end to the ban on women in combat aviation jobs and urged the navy to increase women's assignments to sea duty. He also ordered all branches of the service to examine and justify existing policies that excluded women from combat duty. The subsequent repeal of the combat exclusion provisions gave the branches more options in deciding how women could serve, opened up thousands more jobs for women, and gave women opportunities for promotion within the highest military ranks.

In the air force, when the WAF (Women in the Air Force) was created in 1948, thirteen of the forty-three career fields were deemed "fully suitable" for women—in meteorology, air traffic control, finance, and camera repair. During the 1960s air force women, trained and experienced in intelligence, communications, and logistics, resented not being sent to Vietnam to perform jobs they felt they were highly qualified to do. During the 1980s women served during the invasion of Grenada on the crews of airlifters and tankers. In the raid on Libya women served on planes that refueled F-111s that carried out the raid. In Panama, in 1990, women pilots flew in troops and supplies. During Operation Desert Storm, 12,500 women from the U.S. Air Force served in tanker, transport, and medical evacuation aircraft, as well as in aircraft maintenance and as munitions experts. By 1990 women were eligible for 97 percent of all jobs in the air force, made up the largest percentage (14.7) of those women on active duty in any of the branches of the armed forces, and constituted 19 percent of air force reserve personnel. Between 1989 and 1995 the number of women trained to be air force pilots nearly doubled. By 1995 there were also ten women flying combat aircraft, and 99 percent of all air force jobs were open to women. Only a few positions that involved a high potential for direct ground combat remained closed.

In the army the first women to serve officially were nurses, when the Army Nurse Corps was established in 1901. During World War II the

Fully equipped Marine recruits from the Woman Recruit Training Command march into the field for individual tactics and combat training.   *U.S. Marine Corps/Defense Visual Information Center*

Women's Army Auxiliary Corps (WAAC) was created, and in 1943 the WAAC was reorganized as a regular part of the army as the Women's Army Corps (WAC), offering its members military status and veterans' benefits. Throughout the 1950s and 1960s increasing numbers of jobs were opened to women. During the 1970s women were admitted to the Reserve Officer Training Corps (ROTC), and the creation of an all-volunteer force enabled more women to join the military and take part in the same training programs as men. As of 1991 women in the army served in 52 percent of all positions, making up 12.2 percent of the total on active duty. Still excluded from units that are likely to be involved in direct ground combat, women in the army have been admitted to positions in the military police, military intelligence, support teams, and engineer companies.

In the navy women have served since the formation of the Navy Nurse Corps in 1908. During World War II the Women Accepted for Voluntary Emergency Service corps (WAVES) was established. After the war a ceiling of 2 percent was set on the number of women who could serve in the military and limited women to certain ranks. By the 1970s the navy admitted women to its Reserve Officer Training Corps (ROTC). By 1995 55,548 were on active duty (about 11 percent of the force). Of these, 7,985 were officers. Women served aboard forty combatant vessels, including amphibious assault vessels and aircraft carriers. As of 1995 206 served as pilots and 77 as naval flight officers.

While great strides have undoubtedly been made by women in the military, true equality remains elusive and problematic. Scandals have produced headlines about the issue of sexual harassment. Opinion remains divided over whether military training should remain integrated and the nature of unisex military facilities. But women have won the major battle to overcome exclusion from the majority of military specialties formerly closed by gender and bias. The issue of women in combat remains a controversial one, even among high-ranking women officers. A 1997 study by RAND's National Defense Research Institute has found that only 815 of the 47,544 combat-related military jobs were held by women in 1993 and 1994. Although these jobs have been opened to women, some commanders have been reluctant to allow women to fill them, despite the fact that "gender integration is perceived to have a relatively small effect on readiness, cohesion, and morale," according to one study. Even though other nations have eliminated all barriers to women in combat (Canada, opened all military jobs to women except on submarines in 1989), the American military and the public continue to struggle with the image of the woman warrior.

1996

The Supreme Court Orders the Virginia Military Institute, the Last All-Male, State-Sponsored Military College, to Admit Women

The kicking and screaming stopped once the decision was handed down. We complied in good faith with energy and prepared very carefully.

Josiah Bunting III, superintendent of VMI

The 1996 Supreme Court ruling that publicly supported schools must offer equal opportunity to women or lose state financing opened the door to women cadets for the first time at the Virginia Military Institute (VMI) since its founding in 1839. The High Court voted 7–1 (with Clarence Thomas, father of a VMI student, abstaining) to end the gender discrimination at any public schools. VMI was one of the final holdouts to coeducation among the nine senior military colleges in the country—West Point, the Naval Academy, the Air Force Academy, VMI, the Citadel, Texas A&M, Virginia Tech, North Georgia College and State University, and Norwich University in Northfield, Vermont—and the last public school to refuse to admit women. The Court's decision shook VMI to its core, with alumni and staff initially predicting the end of the school as they knew it as a custodian of cherished values of southern honor and military toughness. The school's board of visitors initially responded to the Supreme Court's ruling by considering turning the school private but voted 9–8 to maintain its public status to keep the $11.4 million annual subsidy from the state of Virginia. As VMI's superintendent and a 1963 graduate of the school, Major General Josiah Bunting III, observed, "I wish we were still a men's college, but we lost in court. Our intent now is to retain every conceivable feature of the place." VMI embarked on a plan to preserve its traditions under the pressure of forced accommodation of women cadets to its ranks.

VMI had the examples of the opening of the military academies in 1976 and the difficult experiences of its principal rival, the Citadel, to guide its transition to coeducation. At none of the military colleges was the process without difficulties, particularly in an atmosphere in which military colleges have drawn increasing negative attention for its cadets' behavior. West Point was the scene of a sexual harassment "groping" scandal in 1994 and a rape trial in 1997. Although the male cadet was acquitted of a charge of raping a female cadet, the trial focused national attention on the heavy off-campus drinking by cadets. The Air Force Academy had a number of sexual harassment complaints in 1993 and 1995, and the Naval Academy has been rocked by charges of sexism, a major cheating incident in 1992, and drug and car-theft incidents in 1995. Perhaps the most telling examples of what should not be done in opening a military school for the first time to women cadets were the experiences at the Citadel in Charleston, South Carolina, the only other all-male public military institution. In 1995 the Citadel opened its doors to women after Shannon Faulkner was admitted under a federal court order. She quit in less than a week under the strain of the school's physical demands and media attention. Two of the four women who followed her in 1996 withdrew after they alleged that they had been hazed by male cadets in abusive ways, with their clothes set on fire and deodorant sprayed in their mouths. One male cadet was dismissed for his role in the incident, and nine others were disciplined. For VMI, the Citadel's unfortunate experience with coeducation was instructive. According to General Bunting, "It's a little bit like having someone cross a minefield a hundred yards ahead of you—you learn what to avoid."

VMI resisted immediate entrance of women before an assimilation plan was drafted following a thirteen-month study period. Produced by faculty, students, alumni, and outside experts, which included visits to fourteen coed colleges to study their programs, the plan included dating policies, building women's bathrooms, lowering mirrors to accommodate shorter female cadets, and hiring its first full-time female recruiter. To prevent the difficulties experienced by the first few women at the Citadel, VMI decided to recruit a larger class of women cadets. As Bunting has explained, "You've got to have a genuine cohort—what used to be called a critical mass—to form a support system for all of its members." Recruiters also worked out an exchange program with Norwich University and the Corps of Cadets at Texas A&M to bring in a number of women in upper-class ranks to serve as mentors. After two female cadets from the Citadel were found to have pelvic stress fractures from trying to keep up with the traditional thirty-inch pace of their longer-legged male peers, VMI decided to assign its female cadets to units com-

A women cadet in training during her first year at VMI, fall, 1997   *Photo courtesy of the Virginia Military Institute*

posed of shorter men to take shorter strides without stress. All this planning and preparation has been cited by Bunting as VMI's good-faith effort to make coeducation work at the school. "I don't care what people think," Bunting has said. "So long as we know we have done our level best in accordance with our conscience, our authority, and the understanding of the law, we can abide by the consequences with something approaching serenity."

VMI's first class of thirty female cadets entered in 1997. Although certain accommodations were made, VMI—unlike the Citadel or even the army—required its women cadets to meet the same physical fitness standards as men: sixty situps within two minutes, five pull-ups, and a 1.5-mile run in twelve minutes or less. First-year cadets, called "rats," still had to endure a year-long initiation rite of verbal abuse and grueling physical tests designed to build character and bond together each first-year class. Reaction by male cadets was resigned, but some feared that the arrival of female cadets would degrade the all-male military environment. As one upper-class cadet remarked, "It's inevitable. I'm not out to get anyone, but at the same time I'm not out to help them, either."

Beth Hogan, the first female cadet to enroll officially, withdrew in January. Six other female cadets left the school before the end of their first year, an attrition rate of 23 percent compared with a 15 percent rate among male first-year cadets. After VMI's first year of coeducation,

Superintendent Bunting was quoted as calling women a "disruptive influence," despite a comparatively smooth transition to coeducation. According to Bunting, "Young people who are thrown together fall in love and have physical relationships, and those things have an effect on the efficiency of a fighting unit." As Bunting has observed, "The particular genius of VMI has been to put together young men in their adolescence when they are particularly susceptible to romantic appeals to testing their manhood through military service or danger or shared adventure alongside other young men. Women have different feelings. I don't think those experiences are available to them."

VMI, like the Citadel and the military academies before it, continues to struggle to find a way to preserve the traditions that students and alumni cherish while reforming male bastions that are resistant to change. It is likely that as more women cadets progress through the ranks, the process will be easier for all involved. At issue is the continuing relevance of traditional military schools whose very identity seems inextricably linked with a past in which women had no part. Women continue to express interest in attending military colleges for the same reasons men cite: a chance to learn self-discipline and leadership and to perform under intense pressure. The question remains whether an egalitarian atmosphere can be achieved without the threat of sexual harassment and gender discrimination. The experiment in accommodation and equality at VMI and the Citadel will determine whether change of such institutions is possible to redefine a code of honor and performance that can accept women as members and equals.

1997

Ellen DeGeneres's Sitcom Character Comes Out

> Yep, I'm gay.
>
> Caption of the April 14, 1997
> *Time* magazine cover of Ellen DeGeneres

In perhaps one of the most highly anticipated and publicized dual coming-outs in history, after a series of carefully placed rumors and coy denials, television actress and comedian Ellen DeGeneres in an April 14, 1997, cover story in *Time* magazine finally admitted that she was gay. Three weeks later Ellen Morgan, the character she played on her ABC sitcom, *Ellen*, realized that she is a lesbian, becoming the first openly gay series lead character in television history. As the show's co–executive producer Vic Kaplan remarked, DeGeneres "is a trailblazer. She's opening up new territory." And the actress herself hoped that *Ellen* will "make some changes in people's attitude." A year later ABC canceled *Ellen* amid charges by DeGeneres that the network had abandoned the program and critics' contention that the show's gay-oriented humor was too controversial for television. Although 36.2 million viewers watched the episode in which Ellen Morgan came out of the closet, the show averaged just 12.4 million viewers during the 1997–1998 season. "We put the show on and truly supported it in the midst of tremendous pressure," explained Stuart Bloomberg, chairman of ABC Entertainment, "because it was funny. But as the show became more politicized and issue oriented, it became less funny, and the audience noticed." DeGeneres countered bitterly, "I was fired basically because I'm gay." According to her, ABC "got pressure from all these groups of people, and they collapsed. They basically sabotaged the show." Whatever the causes for the failure of a program to sustain an audience with a leading lesbian character, played by an openly gay actress, the situation is still remarkable in the history of gays in America and indicative both of changed attitudes as

In a bold and courageous move,
actress and comedian Ellen
DeGeneres came out during a 1997
episode of her sitcom, *Ellen*. By
identifying herself publicly as a
lesbian DeGeneres hoped to change
public attitudes toward gays. *Photo
courtesy of Touchstone Pictures and
Television*

well as the distance lesbians still
have to go for full acceptance.

Lesbians in twentieth-century
America have faced the rejection
of the very concept of emotional
and sexual attraction among
women, have been labeled as
deviants and relegated to the
clandestine bohemian fringe, but
in the 1960s and 1970s they
began to gain gradual although limited acceptance in the mainstream as
lesbian feminists mounted a spirited campaign for recognition and equal
rights. When Kate Millett, author of *Sexual Politics*, who appeared on the
cover of *Time* as a spokesperson of the women's liberation movement in
1970, was "outed" at a lecture by an insistent question about her sexuality, her admission that she was a lesbian caused shock waves through
the feminist movement and resulted in public vilification. More than
twenty-five years later, Ellen DeGeneres's sexual preference is still the
occasion for headlines, but the admission that an openly gay actress can
successfully (albeit temporarily) portray a gay character on national television clearly indicates a shift in attitudes and wider acceptance of lesbians in society and popular culture. No longer invisible on the fringes of
society, lesbians have won increased recognition of their right to express
their sexual preference honestly. The modern lesbian feminist movement shared many of the same goals of the women's movement of the
1960s and 1970s, although feminists were not always pleased to find lesbians among their ranks. When lesbian activist Rita Mae Brown
attempted to confront heterosexism in the women's movement in 1970,
National Organization for Women president Betty Friedan denounced a
supposed "lavender menace" threatening feminist credibility. Brown and
other suspected lesbians were purged from NOW. Later, solidarity
between lesbian and heterosexual feminists was forged, and NOW
embraced lesbian rights as central to the feminist agenda.

By the 1990s lesbians in public life had gained a great deal of media attention, particularly from President Clinton's policy of inclusion of the gay community in his administration, most notably by the 1993 nomination of Roberta Achtenberg for assistant secretary for fair housing at the Department of Housing and Urban Development. The Achtenberg nomination marked the first time a president had appointed an openly gay person to a position that required Senate confirmation. In the contentious three-day debate over her nomination, Senator Claiborne Pell of Rhode Island spoke out in favor of Achtenberg: he revealed that his daughter was a lesbian and that he did not want to see her "barred from a government job because of her orientation." It was believed to be the first time a senator had announced publicly that a member of his family was gay, certainly the first such announcement on the Senate floor. With magazine cover stories in the national media, 1993 began to be called "the Year of the Lesbian." There was so much attention regarding lesbian and homosexual issues that a 1994 cover of *New York* magazine asked, "Is Everybody Gay?" The issue of gay marriage, which the Clinton administration did *not* support, drew media attention as well.

In the entertainment industry, however, women openly coming out has been fraught with peril. For straight actors playing gay roles, the stigma began to fade, helped by William Hurt in *Kiss of the Spider Woman* (1985) and Tom Hanks in *Philadelphia* (1993), both of whom won Oscars for their performances. Public acceptance of and industry attitudes toward openly gay women have been slower to change. Sheila Kuehl, a gay actress, who played the bookish Zelda Gilroy on the 1960s sitcom *The Many Loves of Dobie Gillis*, saw her career ended when a CBS executive described her as "a little too butch." Amanda Bearse, who appeared in the Fox series *Married . . . with Children* and came out in 1993, recalls being told by her manager in the 1980s, "If you're under twelve and a tomboy, you're cute. After that you're nothing but a dyke." Efforts to overcompensate by acting more "feminine," she says, "made my blood boil. I felt they were saying, 'If this is who you are, don't show it.' "

DeGeneres's decision to come out herself and to reveal her character's lesbianism came slowly. When Patrick Bristow, who has been openly gay throughout his career, was hired in 1994 to play a "straight" character on *Ellen*, the actor's bravura performance encouraged the writers to change the character to a homosexual friend of Ellen Morgan. During a taping break in 1996, DeGeneres confessed to Bristow that "I'm thinking of doing what you did." The show was adrift, largely because of DeGeneres's own ambiguity about her public self and her central character. By revealing the gayness of both the actress and the character, DeGeneres could energize and focus on both. She found support when she floated the idea, and by spring 1997 her character made her dramatic revelation of her lesbian identity in a one-hour special that included support from prominent celebrity guest stars Laura Dern, k.d. lang, and Oprah Winfrey. Reverend Jerry Falwell, who had labeled the actress "Ellen DeGenerate," urged a boycott of the show's sponsors, and advertisers, such as Chrysler and Wendy's, pulled their ads from the episode. However, the show was also praised by Vice President Al Gore for its honesty. As Sheila Kuehl remarked about the daring of DeGeneres's decision, "Advertisers, networks, producers, and fans have to haul out their prejudices and say, 'Does this make a difference in how I feel about this woman?' " "The ice has been broken," Amanda Bearse observed. "We are in every job, we're every color. We're not out to take over the world. We just want to live in it."

If Ellen DeGeneres shattered a major barrier, the cancellation of *Ellen* after a year suggested that problems remained for a gay star on television. The show's producers had promised ABC that they would tread lightly around Ellen's homosexuality, but DeGeneres's character landed a girlfriend, and then the series featured a controversial two-second first kiss between the pair and eventually showed them in bed together. The show was also criticized for its relentlessly lesbian themes. "Even gay viewers are saying we're too much in-your-face," observed Tim Doyle, executive producer of *Ellen*. In her defense, DeGeneres claimed that the show's demise stemmed from ABC's lack of promotion and support. She also protested ABC's insistence that a parental warning be broadcast before each episode, an advisory that did not appear on other shows with homosexual characters or strong heterosexual content. According to DeGeneres, the disclaimer sent a message that "gay people don't deserve equal treatment." "People got the message from ABC," Doyle explained, [that] "we're ashamed of this show." Audiences seemed to find the show's entertainment suffering at the expense of its gay message. "After a while people get tired of being educated," remarked Jonathan Stark, a former producer of the show. "I love watching Ellen as a comic, not a spokesperson." Another producer, Tracy Newman, admitted that DeGeneres "got heavy-handed. The very thing that made her the right person to do the coming-out episode was missing—the light touch."

Despite the failure of *Ellen* to sustain a large popular audience with its lesbian themes and gay central character, network executives announced plans to release other television shows with gay characters. Whether Ellen DeGeneres will survive the stereotyping of the industry and the public's mind is difficult to foresee. "If I do it right," DeGeneres has stated, "I'm gonna have a career that will grow, and I'll look back on this as my infancy stage." It may well be that the film and network television industry is also in its infancy in its willingness to portray lesbian themes. The progress made by lesbians to gain acceptance has been waged over a series of battles to change public opinion, and despite the setback of the cancellation of *Ellen*, lesbian identity and culture have succeeded in becoming an accepted part of the history and social development of the twentieth century. As *New York Times* columnist Anna Quindlen wrote in 1994, "The time has come. You can feel it, in a hundred little ways year after year. It is so certain and inevitable, that the next century will be a time in which it is not simply safe, but commonplace, to be openly gay."

APPENDIX

INFLUENTIAL FIRSTS

1900–1909

First Field Hockey Games in the United States

In 1901 Constance Applebee of England organized a series of matches at Bryn Mawr, Mount Holyoke, Radcliffe, Smith, Vassar, and Wellesley Colleges and then formed an Olympic team in Philadelphia. Field hockey has since become a staple of girls' physical education programs in schools across the country. In 1922 the U.S. Field Hockey Association became the first organization to establish standards of play for female hockey players in schools, clubs, and colleges.

First Woman to Become a Popular Songwriter

A child music prodigy, Carrie Jacobs Bond composed the ever-popular wedding song, "I Love You Truly," in 1901. Her 1910 song, "A Perfect Day," sold approximately five million copies in ten years. Bond wrote over 400 songs and had some 170 of them published.

First Army Nursing Corps

In 1901 Dr. Anita Newcomb McGee, who had served as the first woman assistant surgeon of the U.S. Army, drafted the section of the Army Reorganization Act that permanently established the Army Nursing Corps.

First Woman Ambulance Surgeon

Although Emily Dunning graduated second in her class at Cornell University School, she was turned down for work at New York City's Governeur Hospital because she was a woman. She applied again and in 1903 was accepted at the hospital as an ambulance surgeon, despite protests from medical interns throughout the city who had petitioned to block her appointment. In 1905 Dunning became a member of the hospital surgical staff and the first woman to serve as a house surgeon in a New York City hospital.

First Woman Elected President of an International Labor Union

Agnes Nestor, a factory worker from the age of fourteen, helped organize the International Glove Workers Union in 1902 and the same year founded Operators Local #1 of the IGWU. In 1903 a women's local was formed, with Nestor as president. Nestor, who served on the executive board of the National Women's Trade Union League and was president of the Chicago chapter from 1913 until her death in 1948, also helped organize unions in the needle trades and participated in garment workers' strikes, including the Great Uprising of 1909.

First Woman to Become a Bank President

In 1903 Maggie Lena Walker, a member of the Grand United Order of St. Luke, an African American fraternal society, founded and became president of the St. Luke Penny Savings Bank in Richmond, Virginia. When the St. Luke Penny Savings Bank merged with other African American banks in 1929 to become Consolidated Bank and Trust Company, Walker chaired the board of directors. Walker was also the founder, in 1912, of the Richmond Council of Colored Women.

First Woman to Command the Salvation Army in the United States

The daughter of the Salvation Army's cofounders, Evangeline Booth became the organization's leader in 1904, after her brother resigned as director. In 1934 she was named general of the International Salvation Army, a post she held until 1939. The Salvation Army expanded its social services and disaster relief work under Booth's leadership.

First Woman Interior Decorator

In 1905 New York socialite and tastemaker Elsie de Wolfe launched her career as an interior decorator by successfully decorating the Colony Club, New York City's first club for women. The term "interior decorator" was created in 1910 to describe her. De Wolfe, who was known as "the chintz lady" and who started the long-lasting fashion trend of wearing short white gloves, wrote numerous magazine articles on interior design. These articles were compiled in an influential book on interior decoration, entitled *The House in Good Taste*.

First Woman Voted Into Elective Office by an All-Male Electorate

In 1907 Kate Barnard was elected Oklahoma commissioner of charities and corrections, defeating her Republican opponent by over thirty-five thousand votes. She ran again in 1910 and won a second term. A labor activist, Barnard fought for pension benefits for widows, opposed the blacklisting of union members, and was an advocate of Native American rights.

First Woman to Serve as Senator of Phi Beta Kappa

In 1907 Mary Emma Wooley, president of Mount Holyoke College and one of the first two women to graduate from Brown University, became the first woman senator of Phi Beta Kappa, the oldest Greek-letter fraternity in the United States. In 1932 Wooley became the first woman to represent the United States at a major diplomatic conference when she was appointed by President Herbert Hoover to the delegation attending the Geneva Conference on Reduction and Limitation of Armaments.

First Woman Elected to the American Academy of Arts and Letters

In 1908 eighty-nine-year-old poet and biographer Julia Ward Howe, whose best-known work is "The Battle-Hymn of the Republic," became the first woman member of the academy. She remained its only woman member until 1930.

First President of the American Home Economics Association

The association, dedicated to the "improvement of living conditions in the home, the institutional household, and the community," was cofounded in 1908 by Ellen Richards, a chemist, educator, and organizer of the American home economics movement. In 1899 Richards had conducted a series of seminars in Lake Placid, New York, to discuss the impact industrialization and urbanization were having on the lives of homemakers and to design high school and college curricula for a new domestic science seminar attendees named "home economics." Richards served as the association's president until 1910.

1910–1919

First National Nonsectarian Interracial Organization for Girls

The Camp Fire Girls was founded in 1910 by Charlotte and Luther Gulick and Chauncey Laughlin. The first encampment, called WoHeLo (Work, Health, Love) and attended by seventeen girls, was held in Maine. The organization, which now includes boys and girls and is called Camp Fire, promotes activities designed to generate good mental and physical health. In 1997 Camp Fire had a membership of approximately seven hundred thousand.

First Women's Agricultural Training School

In 1911 philanthropist and suffragist Alva Belmont donated two hundred acres of land in Hempstead, Long Island, for the purpose of establishing a training farm and agricultural school for young women aged sixteen and over. There were 630 applicants to the school; 20 were accepted. The students took classes in farming, cooking, and housekeeping and were paid an allowance that was increased in proportion to the income generated by their work on the farm.

First Woman Head of a Major U.S. Government Bureau

Julia Lathrop was appointed director of the newly formed Children's Bureau of the U.S. Department of Labor by President Taft in 1912. During her nine-year directorship Lathrop worked for passage of the

Sheppard-Towner Maternity and Infancy Protection Act, which was enacted in 1921.

First Women Admitted to the American College of Surgeons

In 1914 Alice Gertrude Bryant and Florence West Duckering were among the approximately one thousand candidates admitted to the year-old ACS.

First Women to Win the Pulitzer Prize in Biography

In 1917 Maud Howe Elliott and Laura E. Richards, the daughters of Julia Ward Howe, won the first Pulitzer Prize in biography for their work, *Julia Ward Howe, 1819–1910.*

First Professional Adoption Agency in the United States

The Cradle Society of Evanston, Illinois, opened in 1918. One of the founders was physician and medical researcher Gladys Dick, who with her husband, George, later isolated the streptococcus that causes scarlet fever and introduced the Dick test, a skin test for detecting susceptibility to the disease.

First Woman Head of a Metropolitan Library System

Linda A. Eastman, a cofounder of the Ohio Library Association and its first woman president, was unanimously elected director of the Cleveland Public Library system in 1918. Eastman became president of the American Library Association in 1928.

First Woman to Run for the U.S. Senate

In 1918 Anne Henrietta Martin, a suffragist, pacifist, and legislative chair of the National Woman's Party, ran for office in Nevada after the death of the sitting senator. Martin ran as an independent and was defeated. She ran again in 1920 and was defeated a second time.

First Woman Editor in Chief of a Law Review

Mary H. Donlon, a law student at the Cornell University Law School, edited the *Cornell Law Quarterly* in 1919 and 1920. Donlon graduated in 1921 and was admitted to the bar the same year.

1920–1929

First Woman Assistant Attorney General of the United States

In 1920 Annette Abbott Adams, a U.S. district attorney in San Francisco, was appointed assistant attorney general under Attorney General A. Mitchell Palmer. Adams's job was to prosecute violators of the Volstead Act. She served in the cabinet until Warren G. Harding became U.S. president in 1921.

First Woman Member of the U.S. Civil Service Commission

In 1920 President Woodrow Wilson appointed writer and suffragist Helen Hamilton Gardener to serve on the thirty-seven-year-old commission. The appointment also made her the first woman to serve on any federal commission. Gardener had worked with Elizabeth Cady Stanton on her *Woman's Bible* during the 1890s and in 1917 became vice president of the National American Woman Suffrage Association.

First Internationally Licensed African American Woman Pilot

Refused flying lessons in her native Texas because of her race, Bessie Coleman decided to travel to Europe to learn to fly. In 1918 she went to France with a Red Cross unit attached to a French flying squadron. Taught to fly in ten months by French pilots, Coleman earned her license in 1921. The following year, after returning to the United States, she made three short flights in an exhibition honoring a black infantry group of the New York National Guard. Coleman, who dreamed of opening a flying school for African Americans, was killed in 1926 when she was thrown from the open cockpit of her plane during a flying exhibition in Jacksonville, Florida.

First Woman Awarded the Pulitzer Prize for Drama

In 1921 Zona Gale received the award for the dramatization of her novel, *Miss Lulu Bett.*

First Woman Awarded the Pulitzer Prize for Fiction

Edith Wharton received the prize in 1921 for her novel *The Age of Innocence.*

First Woman Member of the National Academy of Sciences

In 1925 medical researcher Florence Sabin, whose work on tuberculosis led to a dramatic drop in death rates from the disease, received membership in the academy.

First Woman to Swim the English Channel

Of all the first facts regarding women's achievements, this is probably the most famous. In 1926 Gertrude Ederle, an Olympic swimmer who held twenty-nine national and world records between 1921 and 1925, swam a course of thirty-five miles from Cap Gris-Nez, France, to Dover, England. Her time was fourteen hours and thirty-one minutes—one hour and fifty-one minutes faster than any previous male channel swimmer.

First Woman Appointed as a U.S. Federal Judge

Genevieve Cline, a former vice president of the Ohio branch of the National Association of Women Lawyers and a merchandise appraiser at the port of Cleveland during the Harding administration, was appointed to the U.S. Customs Court by President Calvin Coolidge in 1928.

First Nurse-Midwife Association in the United States

In 1928 the American Association of Nurse-Midwives, a group of sixteen nurse-midwives from the Frontier Nursing Service, was established in Kentucky. In 1968 the association merged with the American College of Nurse-Midwives, whose members are nationally accredited registered nurses who provide gynecological services and prenatal care for mothers and babies.

First Woman to Direct Sound Movies

In 1929 Dorothy Arzner, who had directed several silent movies, including the prize-winning 1927 film *Fashions for Women*, was chosen by Paramount to direct the studio's first sound picture, *The Wild Party*. Arzner, the only woman director of the 1930s, directed fourteen movies during the decade, including *Christopher Strong*, with Katharine Hepburn, and *The Bride Wore Red*, starring Joan Crawford. During World War II Arzner made Women's Army Corps training films for the U.S. Army.

1930–1939

First Woman to Win the Nobel Peace Prize

The prize was awarded in 1931 to social worker and Hull House settlement founder Jane Addams, who shared it with educator Nicholas Murray Butler. Addams was also the first woman elected president of the National Council of Charities and Corrections (1909), the first to receive an honorary degree from Yale University (1910), the first head of the National Federation of Settlements (1911), and the first woman to make a nominating speech at a national political convention (1912). In 1920 Addams helped found the American Civil Liberties Union.

First Woman Commercial Airline Pilot

The holder of numerous women's aviation records between 1930 and 1958, Ruth Nichols was hired in 1932 as a pilot for New York and New England Airways. In 1939 she started a flying school for women at Adelphi College in Garden City, New York, and the following year organized Relief Wings, a civilian air ambulance service. The assets of Relief Wings were made available to the U.S. government during World War II and financed the establishment of the Civil Air Patrol, which Nichols directed until 1949.

First Woman Member of the U.S. Cabinet

In 1933 President Franklin Roosevelt appointed New York State Industrial Commissioner Frances Perkins secretary of labor, a post she held until 1945. As labor secretary Perkins was responsible for much of the New Deal legislation drafted during the 1930s.

First Woman on the U.S. Court of Appeals

After ratification of the Nineteenth Amendment in 1920, Ohio attorney and former suffragist Florence Ellinwood Allen ran in a nonpartisan election for common pleas court judge and won against nine male opponents. She became the first woman elected to the Ohio Supreme Court in 1922. She served there until 1934, when President Franklin Roosevelt appointed her to the Sixth Circuit Court of Appeals in Cincinnati.

First American Woman to Win the Nobel Prize for Literature

In 1938 Pearl Sydenstricker Buck, the Pulitzer Prize–winning author of *The Good Earth*, was awarded the Nobel Prize. Born in 1892, Buck had spent the first eight years of her life in China with her missionary parents and returned there with her husband, a farm management specialist, to teach English literature at Nanking, National Southeastern, and Chung-Yang Universities. In 1949 she founded Welcome House, which provided care for the children of Asian women and American soldiers. The Pearl Buck Foundation, to which Buck consigned most of her royalties, provides adoption services for Amerasian children.

1940–1949

First Woman to Be Elected to Serve in Both Houses of Congress

In 1940, after completing the unexpired term of her late husband in the U.S. House of Representatives, Republican Margaret Chase Smith of Maine was elected to a full term in the House. She served three terms and in 1948 was elected to the Senate. She won reelection to the Senate in 1954, 1960, and 1966 but was defeated by Representative William J. Hathaway in the 1972 Senate race.

First Woman Awarded the Purple Heart

Anna Leah Fox, head nurse at Hickam Field in Honolulu, Hawaii, during the Japanese attack on Pearl Harbor on December 7, 1941, received the Purple Heart in 1942 for being wounded in the attack.

First Woman Awarded the Pulitzer Prize for History

In 1942 Margaret Leech received the prize for *Reveille in Washington,* an account of Washington, D.C., during the Civil War years. In 1960 Leech was again awarded the Pulitzer in history, for *In the Days of McKinley.* She was the only woman to win the award twice.

First Woman to Pilot a Jet Plane

In 1944, at Wright Field in Dayton, Ohio, Ann Baumgartner, a pilot with the Women's Auxiliary Ferrying Squadron (WAFS), flew the United States' first experimental jet, the YP-59. Baumgartner reached a speed of 350 miles per hour and an altitude of 35,000 feet.

First Woman Officer for a Major National Political Party

In 1944 Dorothy Bush became secretary of the national Democratic Party. A familiar figure at Democratic conventions for nearly five decades, Bush called the roll of the states at national nominating conventions and kept the vote count for presidential nominees. Bush held the post until 1989.

First Woman to Receive the Bronze Star

First Lieutenant Cordelia E. Cook of the Army Nurse Corps was awarded the Bronze Star for meritorious service in January 1944. Stationed in Italy, Cook had continued to nurse wounded soldiers after her field hospital was bombed in November 1943. Cook was also awarded the Purple Heart in January 1944 after being wounded by artillery fire.

First Woman Scout for a Major League Baseball Team

In 1946 the Philadelphia Phillies hired Edith Houghton as their team scout. Houghton had previously been a star shortstop with the Philadelphia Bobbies, a women's team.

First Woman to Win the Nobel Prize in Physiology or Medicine

In 1947 Gerty Radnitz Cori, a Prague-born naturalized citizen of the United States, shared the prize with her husband, Carl Cori, and Bernard Houssay of Argentina. The Coris, who were pharmacologists and biochemists, won the award for their work in carbohydrate metabolism and enzymes.

First Woman Elected President
of the American Public Health Association

Martha May Eliot, an official of the U.S. Children's Bureau from 1924 to 1956, introduced the use of social workers in public health programs and directed a federal program to provide health care and assistance for the wives and infants of armed forces personnel during World War II. In 1947 Eliot was elected president of the American Public Health Association, a position she held until 1949, when she became assistant director general of the World Health Organization.

First Woman Fellow of the American Institute
of Electrical Engineers

Edith Clarke, one of three women members of the seventeen-thousand-member AIEE and a professor of electrical engineering at the University of Texas, was elected a fellow of the institute in 1948. Clarke was responsible for simplifying and increasing the mathematical computations involving electrical power and transmission lines.

First Woman Appointed to the Federal
Communications Commission

Attorney Frieda B. Hennock was appointed to the FCC in 1948. During her seven-year tenure she persuaded the FCC to reserve approximately 242 television channels for educational and noncommercial programming.

First Woman Ambassador

In 1949 President Harry Truman named Eugenie Moore Anderson, a Truman supporter and member of the Democratic National Committee, ambassador to Denmark. In 1951, while serving as ambassador, Anderson became the first woman to sign a treaty between the United States and another nation when she signed a friendship, commerce, and navigation treaty between Denmark and the United States.

First Woman Treasurer of the United States

Georgia Neese Clark of Richland, Kansas, president of the Richland State Bank and a member of the Democratic National Committee, was appointed U.S. treasurer by President Harry Truman in 1949.

1950–1959

First Woman to Receive the Pulitzer Prize
for International Reporting

Maggie Higgins, a war correspondent, Berlin bureau chief, and Tokyo bureau chief for the *New York Herald Tribune,* had covered the liberation of Dachau concentration camp by the Allies during World War II and the Nuremberg war crimes trial. The only woman war correspondent during the Korean conflict, Hopkins was awarded the prize in 1951 for twenty-three months of reporting from the Korean battlefront.

First Woman Appointed to the First Chair in a Major Orchestra

Doriot Anthony Dwyer, the great-grandniece of Susan B. Anthony and a founder of the National Council for Women, was second flutist with the Los Angeles Philharmonic. In 1952 she joined the Boston Symphony Orchestra as a first-chair flutist.

First Woman Pilot to Break the Sound Barrier

Aviator Jacqueline Cochran, a member of the Women's Auxiliary Ferrying Squadron and director of the Women's Air Service Pilots (WASPs) during World War II, broke the sound barrier in 1953. Cochran flew a Canadian Sabre jet faster than Mach 1 (the speed of sound) three times in six hours and broke three men's records. In 1960 she became the first woman pilot to fly at Mach 2 and in 1962 the first to pilot a jet in a transatlantic flight.

First Woman Secretary of the U.S. Department
of Health, Education, and Welfare

Oveta Culp Hobby, the first director of the Women's Army Auxiliary
Corps (later the WAC) and the first woman to receive the U.S. Army
Distinguished Service Medal for her service during World War II, was
named director of the Federal Security Administration (FSA) by President Eisenhower in January 1953. In April of that year the FSA was elevated to cabinet status as the Department of Health, Education, and
Welfare and Hobby became its first secretary. She was the second
woman cabinet member in U.S. history—the first was Labor Secretary
Frances Perkins in 1933.

First Woman Elected President of the American
Psychoanalytic Association

In 1958 Marion E. Kenworthy, known as the "mother of psychiatric
social work," was elected president of the forty-seven-year-old APA,
established to set standards for the training and practice of psychoana-
lysts. In 1930 Kenworthy was the first woman to achieve the rank of professor of psychiatry at the Columbia University School of Social Work.

1960–1969

First Woman to Qualify as an Astronaut

In February 1960 military pilot Jerrie Cobb passed the seventy-five qual-
ification tests administered to male astronaut candidates. Three years
later she was one of three women recommended for astronaut service.
However, NASA was not yet ready to accept women astronauts.

First U.S. Woman to Win the Nobel Prize in Physics

Maria Goeppert-Mayer shared the 1963 award with American and
German physicists Eugene Wigner and J. H. D. Jensen. They received
the prize for their work on the structure of the atomic nucleus.

First Girl to Play Organized Baseball With Boys

In 1963 nine-year-old Nancy Lotsey was admitted to the New Jersey
Small-Fry League. In her first game she hit a home run and was the
winning pitcher. Her team won the league championship with a 10–1
win–loss record.

First Woman to Serve on the Interstate Commerce Commission

West Virginia attorney Virginia Mae Brown was appointed to the eleven-
member ICC by President Lyndon Johnson in 1964. Brown headed the
commission from 1969 to 1970.

First Woman to Fly Solo Around the World

In 1964 thirty-eight-year-old Jerrie Mock, piloting a Cessna 180, completed the 22,858.8-mile flight in twenty-nine days, eleven hours, and fifty-nine minutes, with twenty-one stopovers.

First Woman to Head a Job Corps Program for Women

In 1964 President Lyndon Johnson asked educator Bennetta Washington to launch and direct the Job Corps program for women, which organized job training centers throughout the United States. Washington remained with the Job Corps until 1980.

First Woman Ordained a U.S. Presbyterian Minister

Rachel Henderlite became minister of the All Souls Presbyterian Church in Richmond, Virginia, in 1965 after unanimous approval by the 125 commissioners in the Richmond presbytery. In 1976 Reverend Henderlite also became the first woman president of the Presbyterial Council of Church Union.

First Woman to Complete a Solo Sail Across the Pacific Ocean

In 1969 Sharon Sites Adams sailed a thirty-one-foot ketch from Yokohama, Japan, to San Diego, California, a distance of approximately 6,620 miles. She made the trip in seventy-four days, seventeen hours, and fifteen minutes.

1970–1979

First Woman to Be Ordained a Minister in the American Lutheran Church

Barbara Andrews, a paraplegic, was ordained in 1970. She began her ministry in Minneapolis, Minnesota, and also served as acting pastor of the Resurrection Lutheran Church in Detroit, Michigan.

First Woman Jockey to Ride in the Kentucky Derby

In 1970 Diane Crump rode Fathom in the race at Churchill Downs. The horse finished fifteenth in a field of seventeen. Crump had been the first woman to ride in a parimutuel race in North America, when she rode at Hialeah Park in 1969. Jockey Patricia Cooksey was the second woman to ride in the Derby and the first to ride in the Preakness.

First Person Awarded the Pulitzer Prize for Criticism

Ada Louise Huxtable, architecture critic for *The New York Times* and one of the founders of the Landmarks Preservation Commission for New York City, received the prize in 1970, in recognition of her efforts to promote and preserve quality in architecture.

First Woman Vice President of the United Mine Workers

Olga Madar, who had joined the UAW staff in 1944 while an employee at the Willow Run, Michigan, bomber plant, was elected member-at-large of the labor union's national board in 1966. In 1970 she became the UAW's first woman vice president.

First Woman Director of the American Association of Advertising Agencies

Mary Andrews Ayres, executive vice president at Sullivan, Stauffer, Colwell & Bayes, Inc., and one of only three women board members in the top twenty U.S. advertising agencies, was elected director of the fifty-four-year-old American Association of Advertising Agencies in 1971.

First Women Secret Service Agents

In 1970 the Treasury Department, responding to a general directive issued by President Nixon concerning the appointment of more women in responsible government positions, recruited the first women secret service agents.

First Woman Awarded the Pulitzer Prize for National Reporting

In 1971 freelance writer Lucinda Franks shared the prize with journalist Thomas Powers for *The Making of a Terrorist*, five articles written for United Press International on a Weather Underground activist killed in a Greenwich Village town-house-turned-bomb-factory in 1970.

First Woman Head of Daytime Programming at a Major Television Network

In 1972 Lin Bolen was promoted from her job in the prime-time programming department of NBC in Los Angeles to head of daytime programming at the network's headquarters in New York. The promotion made her the highest-ranking woman at any major U.S. network. During her tenure at NBC Bolen expanded soap operas from thirty minutes to one hour and backed the production of game shows.

First Woman U.S. Navy Admiral

In 1972 Captain Alene B. Duerk, chief of nursing services at Great Lakes Naval Hospital and director of the Navy Nurse Corps, was promoted to rear admiral.

First U.S. Woman Rabbi

In 1972 twenty-six-year-old Sally Priesand was ordained as a full-time rabbi at the Monmouth Reform Temple in Tinton Falls, New Jersey. By 1981 there were 35 women rabbis out of 1,325, and roughly one-third of all Reform rabbinical students were women. In 1985 Amy Eilberg was ordained the first woman rabbi in Conservative Judaism.

First Women FBI Agents

J. Edgar Hoover, director of the Federal Bureau of Investigation since 1924, had forbidden the training and hiring of female agents. When Hoover died in 1972, Acting Director L. Patrick Gray III changed the policy. The first two women to successfully complete the FBI training course, at Quantico, Virginia, were thirty-one-year-old Joanne Pierce, a former nun from Niagara Falls, New York, and twenty-five-year-old Susan Lynn Roley, a former U.S. Marine lieutenant.

First National Basketball League for Girls

In 1974 the All-American Girls' Basketball Conference, Inc., was formed in East Greenwich, Rhode Island. The conference featured a senior division (ages fourteen and fifteen) and junior division (ages twelve and thirteen).

First Elected Governor Who Did Not Follow Her Husband Into Office

In 1975 Congresswoman Ella Grasso of Connecticut, a Democrat, was elected the state's governor in a landslide victory. She was reelected in 1978 with more than 75 percent of the state's town votes.

First Woman Cantor in Reform Judaism

In 1975 Barbara Herman became a cantor at Beth Sholom Temple of Clifton-Passaic, New Jersey. The number of women cantors in Conservative and Reconstructionist Judaism rose slowly but steadily after Herman's achievement.

First Woman Secretary of the U.S. Department of Housing and Urban Development

In 1975 President Gerald Ford named Carla Hills secretary of HUD, a post she held until 1977. Hills went on to serve as a director of several U.S. corporations, including IBM.

First Woman President of the Screen Actors Guild

Although the nominating committee favored a man as SAG president in the 1975 election, actress Kathleen Nolan won the presidency of the forty-two-year-old organization with a two-to-one victory margin out of the eight thousand votes cast. Nolan's best-known roles have included Wendy in the Broadway production of *Peter Pan*, starring Mary Martin, and Kate on the TV series *The Real McCoys*.

First Woman Assistant Secretary of the U.S. Air Force

In 1976 President Gerald Ford named Juanita Ashcroft assistant secretary for manpower and reserve affairs, the highest civilian post ever given to a woman in the U.S. Air Force.

First Woman Chief of Protocol for the President of the United States

Former child and teenage movie star Shirley Temple Black was appointed chief of protocol in 1976 by President Gerald Ford.

First Woman Veterinarian at a U.S. National Zoo

In 1976 Suzanne Kennedy was hired as veterinarian at the National Zoological Park in Washington, D.C.

First Woman Coanchor of a Daily Evening News Program

In 1976 Barbara Walters, a former cohost of NBC's *Today* show, was teamed with Harry Reasoner as a newscaster on the ABC Evening News. The arrangement lasted until 1978. Walters went on to host a series of celebrity interview programs and to cohost the ABC-TV newsmagazine *20/20*.

First Woman to Win an Award From the Directors Guild of America

Filmmaker Perry Miller Adato won the award for her television documentary *Georgia O'Keeffe*, shown on public television in 1977. In 1982 and 1986 Adato won a second and third Directors Guild award for her documentaries on Carl Sandburg and Eugene O'Neill.

First Woman to Be Appointed Undersecretary of the U.S. Treasury

In 1977 President Jimmy Carter appointed Bette B. Anderson, vice president of the credit administration department of the Citizens and Southern Bank in Savannah, Georgia, and president of the National Association of Bank Women, to serve as undersecretary of the treasury.

First Woman Driver in the Indianapolis 500

The first woman ever to enter the Indianapolis 500, Janet Guthrie, a physicist and aerospace engineer, qualified for the 1977 race but was forced to quit after twenty-six laps because her car developed a leaky valve. The following year she became the first woman to complete the event. She drove with a broken wrist and finished eighth.

First Woman Secretary of the U.S. Department of Commerce

President Jimmy Carter named economist Juanita Morris Kreps to the cabinet post in 1977. In 1972 Kreps had been the first woman director of the New York Stock Exchange Board of Directors.

First Woman Rector of an Episcopal Church

Women had been ordained priests of the church since 1974, but it was not until 1977 that the first woman attained the position of rector—the person in charge of the parish and one with considerable influence in selecting clergy—when Beverly Messenger-Harris was appointed rector of Gethsemane Episcopal Church in Sherrill, New York.

First Woman Chair of the Equal Employment Opportunities Commission

In 1977 President Jimmy Carter appointed attorney Eleanor Homes Norton chair of the EEOC. Norton had previously worked as assistant legal director of the American Civil Liberties Union and was chair of the New York City Commission on Human Rights. One of the first to advocate the use of Ms. rather than Miss or Mrs., Norton cofounded the Black Feminist Organization in 1973. She served at the EEOC until 1981. In 1990 Norton was elected as a nonvoting delegate from Washington, D.C., to the U.S. House of Representatives.

First Women Rhodes Scholars

When business magnate and colonialist Cecil Rhodes established the Oxford scholarships in his will, he intended them for male college graduates from the British colonies. In 1976 the Rhodes trustees modified the will under the British Sex Discrimination Act. The following year twenty-four of the seventy-two Rhodes scholars were women, including thirteen from the United States.

First Woman Major General of the U.S. Army

Mary Clarke, the last commander of the Woman's Army Corps, became part of the regular army when the WAC was dissolved in 1978. That same year she was promoted to major general and reassigned as commander of the U.S. Army Police and Chemical School at Fort McClellan, Alabama. She also received a Ph.D. in military science from Norwich University in Northfield, Vermont.

First U.S. Secretary of Education

In 1979 President Jimmy Carter named Shirley Hufstedler secretary of the newly created Cabinet Department. Hufstedler, who had been serving on the Ninth U.S. Circuit Court of Appeals and was the senior woman judge in the nation, was picked by over nine hundred constitutional lawyers polled by the *National Law Review* as their choice for the next Supreme Court vacancy.

First Woman to Command a U.S. Coast Guard Vessel at Sea

From 1979 to 1981 Beverly Kelley commanded the ninety-five-foot Coast Guard patrol boat *Cape Newagen*. Kelley and her crew received a Coast Guard citation for their rescue work during a Hawaiian storm in 1980.

1980–1989

First Woman Elected to the AFL-CIO Executive Council

Joyce D. Miller, a leading spokesperson for women labor unionists and an advocate for working women, was elected to the council in 1980. At the time, Miller was vice president of the Amalgamated Clothing and Textile Workers; she had previously been president of the twelve thousand-member Coalition of Labor Union Women. Miller's election to the council was made possible by the waiver of a rule limiting membership to one representative from each union. The waiver was designed as a means toward including a greater representation of women and minorities within the AFL-CIO leadership.

First Woman Justice of the U.S. Supreme Court

In 1981 President Ronald Reagan chose Arizona judge Sandra Day O'Connor as the first woman to sit on the Supreme Court.

First Foundation Dedicated to the Support of Breast Cancer Research

Nancy Brinker of Dallas, Texas, founded the Susan G. Komen Foundation in 1982, in memory of her sister, who died of breast cancer in 1980. By the end of 1985 the foundation had received over $1 million in donations.

First Woman Dean of a Major Graduate Business School

In 1983 economist Elizabeth Bailey was named dean of the Graduate School of Industrial Administration at Carnegie Mellon University. In 1977 Bailey had become the first woman to serve on the Civil Aeronautics Board. She filled an unexpired term at the CAB, then served a full term of six years.

First Winner of the Olympic Women's Marathon

The women's marathon was held for the first time at the 1984 Olympics in Los Angeles. The winner, Joan Benoit, ran the 26-mile, 385-yard race in two hours, twenty-four minutes, and fifty-two seconds.

First Woman to Head the Business and Legal Departments of a Major Movie Studio

In 1984 attorney Helene Hahn, a senior vice president at Paramount Pictures, was hired by Walt Disney Pictures as senior vice president of business and legal affairs.

First Woman Executive Director of the American Bar Association

In 1987 the 360,000-member ABA, long known as a bastion of male conservatism, hired attorney Jill Wine-Banks as its executive director. Wine-

Banks had earlier served as an assistant Watergate special prosecutor and general counsel to the U.S. Army. She resigned as executive director of the ABA in 1990, insisting that she had realized all the major goals she had set for the job.

First Woman to Manage a Major Presidential Campaign

Harvard Law School professor Susan Estrich managed Democrat Michael Dukakis's 1988 campaign for the presidency. As a law student at Harvard, Estrich also became the first woman president of the *Harvard Law Review*.

First Woman to Play on a Men's Varsity Baseball Team

In 1989 eighteen-year-old Julie Croteau played first base for St. Mary's College in St. Mary's, Maryland, an NCAA Division III team. While a high school student in Manassas, Virginia, Croteau had played three years of junior varsity baseball but was rejected by the senior varsity team. She filed a lawsuit against the school and lost. The summer after graduating from high school, she played first base for the Fredericksburg, Virginia, Giants, a semiprofessional team.

1990–1999

First Woman Surgeon General of the United States

In 1990 pediatrician and public health advocate Antonia C. Novello was sworn into office as surgeon general by Sandra Day O'Connor, the first woman Supreme Court justice.

First Woman President of the American Civil Liberties Union

Attorney Nadine Strossen was general counsel to the ACLU from 1986 to 1991, when she became the seventy-one-year-old organization's first woman president. Strossen has also served on the boards of the Human Rights Watch and the National Coalition Against Censorship.

First U.S. Woman Poet Laureate

Mona Van Duyn was appointed U.S. poet laureate by the Library of Congress in 1992. The following year Rita Dove became the first African American and the first black woman poet laureate.

First Woman to Serve as U.S. Secretary of State

In 1997 President Bill Clinton named Madeleine Albright, U.S. ambassador to the United Nations and an authority on European affairs, to the cabinet post. After she was confirmed as secretary of state by the Senate, Albright became the highest-ranking woman government official in U.S. history.

BIBLIOGRAPHY

Adam, Barry D. *The Rise of a Gay and Lesbian Movement*. New York: Twayne, 1995.

Addams, Jane. *Peace and Bread in Time of War*. New York: Macmillan, 1922.

Aresty, Esther B. *The Best Behavior: The Course of Good Manners—From Antiquity to the Present—As Seen Through Courtesy and Etiquette Books*. New York: Simon & Schuster, 1970.

Asbell, Bernard. *The Pill: A Biography of the Drug that Changed the World*. New York: Random House, 1995.

Banner, Lois W. *American Beauty*. New York: Alfred A. Knopf, 1983.

Barkalow, Carol. *In the Men's House: An Inside Account of Life in the Army by One of West Point's First Female Graduates*. New York: Poseidon Press, 1990.

Barry, Kathleen. *Susan B. Anthony: A Biography of a Singular Feminist*. New York: New York University Press, 1988.

Blum, Daniel. *A Pictorial History of the Silent Screen*. London: Spring Books, 1953.

Boston Women's Health Collective. *The New Our Bodies Ourselves*. New York: Simon & Schuster, 1992.

Brownmiller, Susan. *Against Our Will: Men, Women and Rape*. New York: Simon & Schuster, 1975.

_____. *Shirley Chisholm*. Garden City, New York: Doubleday, 1970.

Brumberg, Joan. *The Body Project: An Intimate History of American Girls*. New York: Random House, 1997.

Burrell, Barbara C. *A Women's Place Is in the House: Campaigning for Congress in the Feminist Era*. Ann Arbor: University of Michigan Press, 1994.

Butler, Susan. *East to the Dawn: The Life of Amelia Earhart*. Reading, Mass.: Addison-Wesley, 1997.

Cahn, Susan K. *Coming on Strong: Gender and Sexuality in Twentieth-Century Women's Sports*. New York: The Free Press, 1994.

Campbell, D'Ann. *Women at War with America: Private Lives in a Patriotic Era*. Cambridge, Mass.: Harvard University Press, 1984.

Carter, Pam. *Feminism, Breasts and Breastfeeding*. New York: St. Martin's Press, 1995.

Cassidy, Robert. *Margaret Mead: A Voice for the Century*. New York: Universe Books, 1982.

Chase, Edna Woolman and Ilka Chase. *Always in Vogue*. New York: Doubleday & Company, 1954.

Cohen, Marcia. *The Sisterhood*. New York: Simon & Schuster, 1988.

de Beauvoir, Simone. *The Second Sex*. New York: Modern Library, 1968.

Degan, Marie Louise. *The History of the Woman's Peace Party*. New York: Garland, 1972.

Erens, Patricia, ed. *Sexual Strategies: The World of Women in Film.* New York: Horizon, 1979.

Evans, Mary. *Simone de Beauvoir.* New York: Tavistock, 1985.

Evans, Sara M. *Born for Liberty: A History of Women in America.* New York: The Free Press, 1989.

Faludi, Susan. *Backlash: The Undeclared War Against American Women.* New York: Crown Publishers, 1991.

Fitzgerald, Tracey A. *The National Council of Negro Women and the Feminist Movement, 1935–1975.* Washington, D.C.: Georgetown University Press, 1985.

Flammang, Janet. *Women's Political Voice: How Women Are Transforming the Practice and Study of Politics,* Philadelphia: Temple University Press, 1997.

Flexner, Eleanor. *Century of Struggle: The Woman's Rights Movement in the United States.* Cambridge, Mass.: Harvard University Press, 1959.

Foner, Philip S. *Women and the American Labor Movement: From Colonial Times to the Eve of World War I.* New York: The Free Press, 1979.

_____. *Women and the American Labor Movement: From World War I to the Present.* New York: The Free Press, 1980.

Fox, Mary Virginia. *Women Astronauts.* New York: Julian Messner, 1984.

Fox, Richard Logan. *Gender Dynamics in Congressional Elections.* Thousand Oaks, Calif.: Sage Publications, 1997.

Frank, Brady. *Hefner.* New York: Macmillan, 1974.

Freedman, Rita Jackaway. *Beauty Bound.* New York: Lexington Books, 1986.

Friedan, Betty. *The Feminine Mystique.* New York: W. W. Norton, 1963.

Goldstein, Leslie Friedman. *Contemporary Cases in Women's Rights.* Madison, Wisc.: University of Wisconsin Press, 1994.

Gordon, Linda. *Woman's Body, Woman's Rights: A Social History of Birth Control in America.* New York: Penguin Books, 1976.

Graham, Hugh Davis. *The Civil Rights Era.* New York: Oxford University Press, 1990.

Halberstam, David. *The Fifties.* New York: Villard Books, 1993.

Hall, Rob. *Rape in America: A Reference Handbook.* Santa Barbara, Calif.: ABC-Clio, 1995.

Hanson, Elizabeth I. *Margaret Mitchell.* Boston: G. K. Hall, 1991.

Haskell, Molly. *From Reverence to Rape: The Treatment of Women in the Movies.* New York: Penguin Books, 1974.

Heilbrun, Carolyn G. *The Education of a Woman: The Life of Gloria Steinem.* New York: Dial Press, 1995.

Holt, Rackham. *Mary McLeod Bethune, A Biography.* New York: Doubleday, 1964.

Honey, Maureen. *Creating Rosie the Riveter: Class, Gender, and Propaganda During World War II.* Amherst, Mass.: University of Massachusetts Press, 1984.

Howard, Jane. *Margaret Mead, a Life.* New York: Simon & Schuster, 1984.

How Schools Shortchange Girls—The AAUW Report: A Study of Major Findings on Girls and Education. New York: Marlowe & Company, 1992.

Hymowitz, Carol, and Michaela Weissman. *A History of Women in America.* New York: Bantam Books, 1978.

Jacobs, William Jay. *Women in American History.* Beverly Hills, Calif.: Benziger Bruce & Glencoe, 1976.

Josephson, Hannah. *Jeanette Rankin: First Lady in Congress.* New York: Bobbs-Merrill Co., 1974.

Katz, Ephraim. *The Film Encyclopedia.* New York: HarperCollins, 1994.

Kennedy, Susan E. *If All We Did Was to Weep at Home.* Bloomington: Indiana University Press, 1979.

Kessler-Harris, Alice. *Out to Work: A History of Wage-Earning Women in the United States.* New York: Oxford University Press, 1982.

Kinsey, Alfred C., et al. *Sexual Behavior in the Human Female.* Philadelphia: Saunders, 1966.

Lenskyj, Helen. *Out of Bounds: Women, Sports, and Sexuality.* Toronto: Women's Press, 1986.

Lerner, Gerda, ed. *Black Women in White America: A Documentary History.* New York: Vintage Books, 1972.

Levin, Martin, ed. *Hollywood and the Great Fan Magazines.* New York: Arbor House, 1990.

Lord, M. G. *Forever Barbie: The Unauthorized Biography of a Real Doll.* New York: Morrow, 1994.

Lunardini, Christine. *What Every American Should Know About Women's History: 200 Events that Shaped Our Destiny.* Holbrook, Mass.: Bob Adams, 1994.

Matteo, Sherri. *American Women in the Nineties: Today's Critical Issues.* Boston: Northeastern University Press, 1993.

Mead, Margaret. *Blackberry Winter: My Early Years.* New York: Morrow, 1972.

Mills, D. Quinn. *Not Like Our Parents: How the Baby Boom Generation is Changing America.* New York: William Morrow and Company, Inc., 1987.

Mirabella, Grace. *In and Out of Vogue.* New York: Doubleday, 1995.

Minnich, Elizabeth, Jean O'Barr, and Rachel Rosenfeld, eds. *Restructuring the Academy: Women's Education and Women's Studies.* Chicago: University of Chicago Press, 1988.

Mitford, Jessica. *The American Way of Birth.* New York: Dutton, 1992.

Orenstein, Peggy. *SchoolGirls.* New York: Doubleday, 1994.

Paris, Bernard J. *Karen Horney: A Psychologist's Search for Self-Understanding.* New Haven: Yale University Press, 1994.

Pottker, Jan, and Bob Speziale. *Dear Ann, Dear Abby: The Unauthorized Biography of Ann Landers and Abigail Van Buren.* New York: Dodd, Mead, 1987.

Robinson, David. *The History of World Cinema.* New York: Stein and Day, 1973.

Robinson, Paul. *The Modernization of Sex.* Ithaca, N.Y.: Cornell University Press, 1976.

Rosen, Marjorie. *Popcorn Venus: Women, Movies & the American Dream.* New York: Coward, McCann & Geoghegan, 1973.

Rosen, Ruth. *The Lost Sisterhood: Prostitution in America, 1900–1918.* Baltimore: Johns Hopkins University Press, 1982.

Rothman, Sheila. *Woman's Proper Place: A History of Changing Ideals and Practices, 1870 to the Present.* New York: Basic Books, 1978.

Rupp, Leila J., and Verta Taylor. *Survival in the Doldrums: The American Women's Rights Movement, 1945 to the 1960s.* New York: Oxford University Press, 1987.

Salter, David F. *Cracking the Old Boys' Network: The Tragedies and Triumphs of Girls and Women in Sports.* Westport, Conn.: Praeger, 1996.

Scott, Anne Firor. *Natural Allies: Women's Associations in American History*. Urbana, Ill.: University of Illinois Press, 1991.

Searles, Patricia, and Ronald J. Berger, eds. *Rape and Society*. Boulder, Colo.: Westview Press, 1995.

Sherrow, Victoria. *Encyclopedia of Women and Sports*. Santa Barbara, Calif.: ABC-Clio, 1996.

_____. *Women in the Military: An Encyclopedia*. Santa Barbara, Calif.: ABC-Clio, 1996.

Taylor, Robert Lewis. *Vessel of Wrath: The Life and Times of Carry Nation*. New York: New American Library, 1966.

Trager, James. *The Women's Chronology: A Year-by-Year Record, from Prehistory to the Present*. New York: Henry Holt, 1994.

Trent, Paul. *The Image Makers: Sixty Years of Hollywood Glamour*. New York: Crescent Books, 1972.

Walker, Nancy. *Women's Magazines, 1940–1960: Gender Roles and the Popular Press*. Boston: Bedford, 1998.

Ware, Susan. *Holding Their Own: American Women in the 1930s*. Boston: Twayne, 1982.

_____. *Still Missing: Amelia Earhart and the Search for Modern Feminism*. New York: W. W. Norton, 1993.

Wertz, Richard W., and Dorothy Wertz. *Lying-In: A History of Childbirth in America*. New York: The Free Press, 1977.

Westkott, Marcia. *The Feminist Legacy of Karen Horney*. New Haven: Yale University Press, 1986.

Weyr, Thomas. *Reaching for Paradise: The Playboy Vision of America*. New York: Times Books, 1978.

Winship, Janice. *Inside Women's Magazines*. New York: Pandora Press, 1987.

INDEX